A SHORT HISTORY OF
FILM

A SHORT HISTORY OF FILM

SECOND EDITION

WHEELER WINSTON DIXON & GWENDOLYN AUDREY FOSTER

RUTGERS UNIVERSITY PRESS
NEW BRUNSWICK, NEW JERSEY

Second paperback printing, 2015

Library of Congress Cataloging-in-Publication Data

Dixon, Wheeler W., 1950–

A short history of film / Wheeler Winston Dixon and Gwendolyn Audrey Foster.

p. cm.

Includes bibliographical references and index.

ISBN 978–0-8135–6055–7 (pbk. : alk. paper)—ISBN 978-0-8135-6057-1 (e-book)

1. Motion pictures—History.   2. Motion picture industry—History.

I. Foster, Gwendolyn Audrey.   II. Title.

PN1993.5.A1D53 2008

791.43′7—dc22

2007022097

Visit our website: http://rutgerspress.rutgers.edu

Manufactured in the United States of America

To the filmmakers,
historians,
and critics
of the twenty-first century

CONTENTS

ACKNOWLEDGMENTS

Our first thanks go to Leslie Mitchner of Rutgers University Press for commissioning this volume and believing in it from the outset. We also give our deepest thanks to Dana Miller for a superb typing job; to Jerry Ohlinger for the many stills that grace this volume; to Michael Andersen for his assistance with the bibliography; to Dennis Coleman for help in research; to Virginia Clark for tirelessly checking facts and copyediting the first draft; to Eric Schramm for an excellent job of copyediting subsequent drafts; and to David Sterritt for a thorough and meticulous reading of the final text.

We would also like to thank our many colleagues in the Department of English at the University of Nebraska, Lincoln, and our chair, Joy Ritchie, for help and support in creating this work. For their many invaluable insights, we would like to thank our friends and companions over the years, too numerous to mention here, who first saw these films with us; the discussions we have had with our colleagues in film studies at other universities are surely reflected in this text as well. Finally, we thank the University of Nebraska Research Council for a Maude Hammond Fling Research Fellowship that aided us considerably in the completion of this book.

We wish to note that the material incorporated in this text on Dorothy Arzner, Jean Cocteau, Danièle Huillet, Jean Renoir, and Jean-Marie Straub, written by Wheeler Winston Dixon, originally appeared in *The Encyclopedia of Film*, edited by James Monaco and James Pallot (New York: Perigee/Putnam, 1991), provided by Baseline StudioSystems. The material on Chantal Akerman, Dorothy Arzner, Jacqueline Audry, Joy Batchelor, Kathryn Bigelow, Muriel Box, Vera Chytilová, Julie Dash, and Doris Dörrie, written by Gwendolyn Audrey Foster, from *Women Film Directors: An International Bio-Critical Dictionary,* is reproduced with permission of Greenwood Publishing Group, Westport, Connecticut. This material has been significantly revised for its inclusion here.

TIMELINE

1832   The Phenakistoscope, a spinning wheel with an image at its center that seems to move, is invented by Joseph Plateau in Belgium.

1834   William Horner refines Plateau's Phenakistoscope into the Zoetrope.

1872   Edweard Muybridge shoots his famous series of still images of a horse in motion to settle a bet; when viewed in sequence, the stills form a primitive movie.

1873   Alice Guy, the first woman film director, is born in France.

1880   China and the United States sign a trade and immigration treaty.

1881   U.S. President James Garfield is assassinated.

Fyodor Dostoevsky dies.

Czar Alexander II of Russia is assassinated.

1882   Étienne-Jules Marey invents his "shotgun" camera.

Britain invades Egypt.

Birth of director Lois Weber.

1883   The French Impressionist painter Edouard Manet dies.

The Brooklyn Bridge opens.

The birth of the U.S. Navy, with the construction of three battleships.

1884   Belgium opens the Congo to free trade, under the colonial rule of King Leopold.

Birth of African American filmmaker Oscar Micheaux.

1885   Germany colonizes Tanzania and Togoland.

1886   British film pioneer William Friese-Greene begins work on a motion picture camera and projector.

1887   War breaks out between Ethiopia and Italy.

President Grover Cleveland signs the Interstate Commerce Act, regulating railroads.

Celluloid nitrate film is invented.

1888   Inventor Louis Aimé Augustin Le Prince shoots a short film of traffic on a bridge in Leeds, England; the film is probably the first movie ever shot and then shown to the public.

George Eastman produces the first lightweight camera and trademarks the Kodak name.

Anita Loos, American screenwriter, is born.

1889   The Oklahoma Land Rush.

The Johnstown Flood in Pennsylvania kills 2,000 people when a dam bursts.

George Eastman manufactures celluloid roll film.

1890   William Kennedy Laurie Dickson builds the first modern movie camera, the Kinetograph, under instructions from Thomas Alva Edison.

1893   Mary Pickford, silent screen star, is born.

1894   Thomas Edison shoots *Fred Ott's Sneeze* in his Black Maria.

The first Kinetoscope parlor opens in New York.

1895   Auguste and Louis Lumière hold the first public screening of their films.

1896   Alice Guy directs her first film, *The Cabbage Patch Fairy*.

Thomas Edison shoots *The Kiss,* the first kiss in screen history.

1898   Alice Guy shoots primitive sound films in France using the Chronophone process.

The first films are shot in Japan.

1900   Max Planck formulates quantum theory.

Kodak introduces the Brownie camera.

The Boxer Rebellion in China.

Sigmund Freud publishes *The Interpretation of Dreams*.

The hamburger is invented.

1901 Queen Victoria dies.

The first transatlantic radio signal.

Walt Disney is born.

The first Nobel Prizes are awarded.

U.S. President William McKinley is assassinated; Theodore Roosevelt becomes president.

1902 Director William Wyler is born.

Mount Pelée erupts in Martinique.

The Boer War ends.

The teddy bear is introduced, in homage to Theodore Roosevelt.

Georges Méliès has a hit with his special effects extravaganza *A Trip to the Moon*.

1903 The Wright brothers make their first airplane flight at Kitty Hawk, North Carolina.

The ice cream cone is patented.

Plague strikes India.

The first World Series is played.

The Great Train Robbery is filmed by director Edwin S. Porter. U.S. film production is centered in New York and New Jersey.

1904 The Russo-Japanese War begins.

The milkshake mixer is invented.

Construction starts on the Panama Canal.

The Trans-Siberian Railway is completed.

The New York City subway opens.

1905 Actress Greta Garbo is born.

First U.S. pizza parlor opens.

Einstein proposes the Special Theory of Relativity.

"Bloody Sunday" in the Russian Revolution of 1905.

Cecil Hepworth produces and directs *Rescued by Rover* in England.

1906 Upton Sinclair writes *The Jungle,* exposing conditions in meatpacking plants.

San Francisco earthquake occurs.

The Biograph Film Studio opens in New York.

Edwin S. Porter directs the trick fantasy film *Dream of a Rarebit Fiend.*

Elvira Notari, Italy's first woman director, begins making films.

1907 Pablo Picasso introduces Cubism.

First electric washing machine.

Rules of war established at the Second Hague Peace Conference.

Edwin S. Porter directs *Rescued from an Eagle's Nest,* starring future director D. W. Griffith.

1908 There are more than 8,000 nickelodeon movie theaters nationwide in the United States.

Ford introduces the Model-T automobile, in "any color you want, so long as it's black."

Earthquake in Italy kills 150,000.

Thomas Edison forms "The Trust" to monopolize motion pictures.

D. W. Griffith directs his first one-reel film, *The Adventures of Dollie.*

1909 The NAACP is founded.

Japan's Prince Ito is assassinated.

Plastic is invented.

There are 9,000 movie theaters in the United States.

35 mm becomes the internationally recognized theatrical film gauge.

1910 The Boy Scouts are established in the United States.

Thomas Edison presents his own sound film process, the Kineto-phone.

Florence Lawrence becomes the first real movie star for IMP as a result of Carl Laemmle's publicity campaign.

D. W. Griffith shoots *In Old California* in Hollywood; the move west has begun.

Alice Guy founds Solax, her production company, after moving to the United States.

The first African American film production company, William Foster's Foster Photoplay Company, opens its doors in Chicago.

1911   The Chinese Revolution.

Standard Oil Company is broken up.

Roald Amundsen reaches the South Pole.

The Incan City of Machu Picchu is discovered.

Ernest Rutherford discovers the structure of an atom.

1912   The *Titanic* sinks.

SOS is accepted as the universal distress signal.

The birth of *Photoplay*, the first movie "fan" magazine.

Carl Laemmle forms Universal Pictures Company out of his IMP company and other, smaller companies in a merger.

Mack Sennett sets up shop as the Keystone Film Company and begins making slapstick comedies.

1913   The zipper is invented.

Henry Ford creates the assembly line.

Personal income tax is introduced in the United States.

First crossword puzzle is published.

The Los Angeles Owens Valley Aqueduct is opened.

1914   Archduke Ferdinand is assassinated; World War I begins.

The Panama Canal officially opens.

Cecil B. DeMille's *The Squaw Man* is the first Hollywood feature film.

Charlie Chaplin's tramp character first appears in *Kid Auto Races at Venice*.

Lois Weber's feature-length parable *The Hypocrites* opens.

1915   D. W. Griffith's *The Birth of a Nation* is released.

Germans use poison gas as a weapon.

Theda Bara, one of the movies' first "vamps," stars in *A Fool There Was.*

Louis Feuillade directs the epic French crime serial *The Vampires.*

The Technicolor Corporation opens for business.

1916   Easter Rising in Ireland.

Battle of Verdun.

Battle of the Somme.

The first self-service grocery store opens in the United States.

Lois Weber's film on abortion, *Where Are My Children?* opens to great controversy.

1917   Russian Revolution.

The United States enters World War I.

The Lincoln Motion Picture Company, a pioneering African American film studio, is founded.

John Ford directs his first film, *The Tornado.*

UFA, the giant German film studio, opens its doors.

1918   Influenza epidemic.

Daylight Savings Time is introduced.

Russian Czar Nicholas II and his family are killed.

The U.S. Supreme Court orders the Edison "Trust" to dissolve.

1919   Prohibition begins in the United States.

Treaty of Versailles ends World War I.

Walt Disney and Ub Iwerks join forces as an animation team to make cartoons.

Robert Wiene directs the classic horror film *The Cabinet of Dr. Caligari* in Germany.

Oscar Micheaux directs his feature-length *Within Our Gates.*

1920   The Harlem Renaissance begins.

The first commercial radio broadcast is aired.

Women are granted the right to vote in the United States.

Charlie Chaplin, Douglas Fairbanks, D. W. Griffith, and Mary Pickford form United Artists.

Alice Guy directs her 248th and final film, the feature length *Tarnished Reputations.*

1921   The Irish free state is proclaimed.

Rudolph Valentino stars in the steamy romantic melodrama *The Sheik.*

Comedian Roscoe "Fatty" Arbuckle is arrested for rape and murder; he is later acquitted, but the scandal rocks Hollywood.

Lois Weber's *The Blot,* a plea for social tolerance, opens.

1922   Kemal Atatürk founds modern Turkey.

Reader's Digest begins publication.

Robert Flaherty completes the pioneering documentary *Nanook of the North.*

F. W. Murnau directs the classic vampire film *Nosferatu* in Germany.

Rin Tin Tin becomes an animal star, predating Lassie by several decades.

1923   *Time* magazine is founded.

The Charleston becomes popular on American dance floors.

Lee de Forest demonstrates Phonofilm, his sound-on-film process, which will eventually become the industry standard.

Cecil B. DeMille directs his first version of *The Ten Commandments.*

Kenji Mizoguchi directs his first film, *Resurrection of Love,* in Japan.

1924   The first Olympic winter games.

J. Edgar Hoover is appointed as FBI director.

The Leopold and Loeb murder case.

Erich von Stroheim completes his epic film *Greed,* released in a brutally cut version.

Sam Goldwyn, Louis B. Mayer, and the Metro Pictures Corporation create MGM.

1925   Adolf Hitler publishes *Mein Kampf.*

The Scopes monkey trial puts the theory of evolution in the public eye.

Universal releases *Phantom of the Opera* with Lon Chaney Sr., "The Man of 1,000 Faces."

Sergei Eisenstein directs *Battleship Potemkin* in Russia.

Charles Chaplin writes, stars in, directs, and produces the classic comedy *The Gold Rush*.

1926 A. A. Milne publishes *Winnie-the-Pooh*.

Magician Harry Houdini dies.

Robert Goddard fires his first liquid-fuel rocket.

Warner Bros. debuts the film *Don Juan* with synchronized sound effects and music.

Death of screen romantic idol Rudolph Valentino.

1927 Charles Lindbergh flies solo across the Atlantic.

The British Broadcasting Company (BBC) is founded.

The Jazz Singer is the first widely screened feature film with talking sequences interspersed into an otherwise silent film.

Abel Gance completes his first version of his epic film *Napoleon*.

The Academy of Motion Picture Arts and Sciences is founded.

1928 The first *Oxford English Dictionary* is published.

Bubble gum is invented.

Mickey Mouse makes his screen debut in the short cartoon film *Plane Crazy*.

The Lights of New York is the first all-talking film, and the first Warner Bros. gangster film.

Germaine Dulac directs the Surrealist classic *The Seashell and the Clergyman*.

1929 The stock market crashes; the Great Depression begins.

Car radios are introduced.

The first Academy Awards ceremony is held.

Dziga Vertov's *Man with a Movie Camera* is an early example of hyper-edited Soviet cinema.

Dorothy Arzner directs *The Wild Party,* about "Jazz Age" youth.

1930   Sliced bread is first available.

Josef Stalin begins collective farming in the Soviet Union.

Pluto is discovered and designated a planet.

Silent star Greta Garbo successfully graduates to "talkies" in *Anna Christie*.

René Clair's *Under the Roofs of Paris* is an early musical hit.

1931   Al Capone is imprisoned for income tax evasion.

The Empire State Building is completed.

The Scottsboro Boys are accused of rape.

Fritz Lang directs the suspense thriller *M*, starring Peter Lorre.

Bela Lugosi stars in the horror film *Dracula*.

1932   Franklin Delano Roosevelt is elected president of the United States.

Air conditioning is invented.

The Lindberghs' baby is kidnapped.

Walt Disney shoots *Flowers and Trees* in the new three-strip Technicolor process.

Jean Renoir directs *Boudu Saved from Drowning*.

1933   Adolf Hitler becomes chancellor of Germany.

Prohibition ends in the United States.

Fred Astaire and Ginger Rogers are teamed for the first time in *Flying Down to Rio*.

Jean Vigo directs *Zero for Conduct*, about rebellion at a French boys' school.

The British Film Institute, now one of the world's largest film archives, opens.

1934   The Dust Bowl.

The outlaws Bonnie and Clyde are killed in an ambush.

The first cheeseburger is created.

Mao Tse-tung begins the Long March.

Leni Riefenstahl directs the Nazi propaganda film *Triumph of the Will*.

1935   Germany issues the anti-Jewish Nuremberg laws.

Social Security is enacted in the United States.

Alcoholics Anonymous is founded.

Rouben Mamoulian's *Becky Sharp* is the first feature film shot in three-strip Technicolor.

The Museum of Modern Art Film Library opens.

1936   Hoover Dam is completed.

King Edward VIII abdicates the British throne for "the woman I love," American Wallis Warfield Simpson.

The Spanish Civil War begins.

The Cinémathèque Française, one of the world's great film archives, is founded.

Dorothy Arzner directs *Craig's Wife*.

1937   The Golden Gate Bridge opens.

Japan invades China.

Amelia Earhart vanishes during a flight.

The Trail of the Lonesome Pine becomes the first Technicolor film shot entirely on location.

Disney creates the first feature-length animated cartoon, *Snow White and the Seven Dwarfs*.

1938   Nazi Germany takes over Austria without firing a shot.

British prime minister Neville Chamberlain announces "peace in our time."

Georges Méliès dies.

"The Night of Broken Glass" (*Kristallnacht*) in Germany.

Sergei Eisenstein directs the epic *Alexander Nevsky*.

1939   World War II begins in Europe.

The first commercial flight over the Atlantic.

The German-Soviet non-aggression pact is signed.

Gone with the Wind, The Wizard of Oz, Ninotchka, Mr. Smith Goes to Washington, Stagecoach, and *Dark Victory* are all released in one of Hollywood's peak years.

Jean Renoir directs his masterpiece comedy of manners, *Rules of the Game.*

1940   Leon Trotsky is assassinated in Mexico by agents of Stalin.

Nylons are introduced.

The Battle of Britain.

John Ford directs *The Grapes of Wrath,* based on John Steinbeck's novel.

Animator Joy Batchelor founds Halas and Batchelor, Britain's biggest animation house, with her husband John Halas.

1941   The Manhattan Project commences work on an atomic bomb.

The Japanese attack Pearl Harbor; United States enters World War II.

Mount Rushmore is completed.

John Huston directs his first film, the crime classic *The Maltese Falcon.*

Humphrey Jennings directs the wartime documentary *Listen to Britain.*

1942   The Battle of Stalingrad.

The T-shirt is introduced.

Japanese Americans are held in internment camps in the United States.

The Battle of Midway.

Actress Carole Lombard is killed in a plane crash.

1943   French Resistance leader Jean Moulin is killed.

The Warsaw Ghetto uprising.

Sergei Eisenstein publishes *Film Sense,* one of the first key books of film theory.

Dorothy Arzner directs her last film, *First Comes Courage.*

Maya Deren co-directs the classic American experimental film *Meshes of the Afternoon* with Alexander Hammid.

1944   D-Day; the Allies invade German-occupied France.

Ballpoint pens go on sale.

First German V1 and V2 rockets are fired.

The De Havilland decision marks the end of the "endless" seven-year contract, in which studios tack on "suspension" periods to the length of a contract.

Otto Preminger directs the murder mystery *Laura*.

1945   Hitler commits suicide; Germany surrenders.

The United States drops atomic bombs on Japan; World War II ends.

The microwave oven is invented.

Roberto Rossellini releases *Open City* in Italy, generally regarded as the first Neorealist film.

Marcel Carné's French Resistance masterpiece *The Children of Paradise*.

1946   The Nuremberg war crimes trials.

Dr. Benjamin Spock publishes *The Common Book of Baby and Child Care*.

The Cannes Film Festival debuts.

William Wyler directs the classic "coming home" film, *The Best Years of Our Lives*.

Jean Cocteau directs *Beauty and the Beast* in newly liberated France.

1947   The Dead Sea Scrolls are discovered.

The Polaroid camera is invented.

Jewish refugees aboard the *Exodus* are turned away by England.

Jackie Robinson breaks Major League Baseball's color ban, signing with the Brooklyn Dodgers.

The House Un-American Activities Committee subpoenas its first wave of witnesses in an investigation of Communist infiltration in Hollywood.

1948   Mahatma Gandhi is assassinated.

The State of Israel is founded.

The big bang theory is formulated.

The Paramount decree requires the major movie studios to sell off their theater chains.

Vittorio De Sica's *The Bicycle Thief* is another key Neorealist film.

1949   George Orwell publishes *Nineteen Eighty-four*.

The seven-inch 45 rpm single record is introduced.

The Soviet Union gets the atomic bomb.

China becomes a Communist nation.

The Road Runner and Wile E. Coyote make their screen debuts in *Fast and Furry-ous*.

1950   The Korean War begins.

Joseph McCarthy conducts investigations into Communist influence in the U.S. government.

The first *Peanuts* cartoon strip is published.

Screenwriters John Howard Lawson and Dalton Trumbo are sent to jail for contempt of Congress.

Robert Rossen's *All the King's Men* chronicles the life of a politician with dictatorial ambitions, from Robert Penn Warren's novel, modeled after Louisiana's Huey P. Long.

1951   South Africans are required to carry cards identifying their race.

Color television is introduced.

Winston Churchill is reelected prime minister of Great Britain after several years out of office.

Jackson Pollock's "drip" paintings are shown.

André Bazin establishes the journal *Cahiers du Cinéma* in France, and the auteur theory is born.

1952   The polio vaccine is created.

Car seat belts are introduced.

Princess Elizabeth becomes queen of England at age twenty-five.

Bwana Devil, the first 3-D film, is released; the 3-D film craze begins.

The first Cinerama film is shown to the public.

1953   DNA is discovered.

Julius and Ethel Rosenberg are executed in the United States for espionage.

Henri-Georges Clouzot directs the suspense thriller *The Wages of Fear*.

Ida Lupino directs the drama *The Hitch-Hiker,* her most successful film as director.

Yasujiro Ozu directs his masterly film of modern Japanese life, *Tokyo Story*.

1954   The first hydrogen bomb is detonated.

Roger Bannister breaks the four-minute mile.

The landmark U.S. Supreme Court decision, *Brown vs. Board of Education,* on segregated schools.

Federico Fellini directs the classic Italian film *La Strada*.

Godzilla makes his screen debut.

Agnès Varda directs *La Pointe Courte*.

1955   James Dean is killed in a car crash.

Disneyland opens.

Rosa Parks refuses to give up her seat on a bus in Montgomery, Alabama.

The Warsaw Pact is signed.

Blackboard Jungle uses Bill Haley's "Rock Around the Clock" over the credits, the first use of rock 'n' roll in a Hollywood film.

1956   Elvis Presley appears on "The Ed Sullivan Show."

Grace Kelly marries Prince Rainier III of Monaco.

The Hungarian Revolution.

The Suez Crisis.

Videotape becomes a staple of television production.

1957   Dr. Seuss publishes *The Cat in the Hat*.

The Soviet satellite *Sputnik* is launched.

The U.S. surgeon general reports a link between smoking and lung cancer.

Roger Vadim's *And God Created Woman* brings a new level of sexuality to the screen.

Ingmar Bergman directs his allegorical film about life and death, *The Seventh Seal*.

1958   Hula hoops become popular.

Chinese leader Mao Tse-tung launches the "Great Leap Forward."

Orson Welles's *Touch of Evil* and Alfred Hitchcock's *Vertigo* open within a month of each other.

Andrzej Wajda's thriller *Ashes and Diamonds* electrifies Polish youth.

Satyajit Ray directs *Pather Panchali,* an uncompromising look at poverty in India.

1959   Fidel Castro becomes dictator of Cuba.

Alaska and Hawaii become the forty-ninth and fiftieth states.

An international treaty makes Antarctica a scientific preserve.

The "kitchen debate" between Vice President Richard Nixon and Soviet Premier Nikita Khrushchev.

The French New Wave bursts onto the screen with François Truffaut's *The 400 Blows* and Jean-Luc Godard's *Breathless*.

1960   The first televised U.S. presidential debates, between Richard Nixon and John F. Kennedy.

Alfred Hitchcock's *Psycho* is released.

Dalton Trumbo receives screen credit for writing the script to Otto Preminger's *Exodus,* signaling the end of the HUAC blacklist.

Federico Fellini directs his epic film about modern decadence in Rome, *La Dolce vita*.

Roger Corman directs the original *Little Shop of Horrors,* featuring a young Jack Nicholson.

1961   First U.S. troops are sent to Vietnam.

The Soviets launch the first man into space.

The Bay of Pigs invasion.

The Berlin Wall goes up.

Alain Resnais directs *Last Year at Marienbad,* a hallucinatory film about time and memory.

1962   The Cuban missile crisis.

Andy Warhol exhibits his first Campbell's soup can paintings.

Telstar, the first communications satellite in orbit, is launched, relaying television pictures from the United States to France and England.

Dr. No is the first James Bond movie.

More than 700 foreign films are released in U.S. theaters.

1963   Federal legislation mandates equal pay for women.

President John F. Kennedy is assassinated; Vice President Lyndon Johnson is sworn in.

Betty Friedan publishes *The Feminine Mystique.*

Martin Luther King Jr. delivers his "I Have a Dream" speech in Washington, D.C.

Shirley Clarke directs her drama of African American life, *The Cool World,* in Harlem.

1964   Nelson Mandela is sentenced to life in prison in South Africa.

The Beatles come to the United States.

Martin Luther King receives the Nobel Peace Prize.

Sidney Poitier becomes the first African American to win the Academy Award for Best Actor.

Stanley Kubrick's nightmare comedy, *Dr. Strangelove or: How I Learned to Stop Worrying and Love the Bomb.*

1965   The first space walk, on the *Gemini 4* mission.

The New York City blackout.

The United States sends 3,500 troops to Vietnam.

Japan's bullet train opens.

Malcolm X is assassinated in New York.

1966   Mao Tse-tung launches the Cultural Revolution.

The Black Panther Party is established.

"Star Trek" television series premieres.

The Motion Picture Production Code considerably relaxes as the result of such films as Mike Nichols's *Who's Afraid of Virginia Woolf?* and Michelangelo Antonioni's *Blow-Up.*

Ousmane Sembène directs *Black Girl,* the first indigenous African feature film.

1967   The United States and Soviet Union sign a space demilitarization treaty.

The Six Day War in the Middle East.

Sony introduces a low-cost black-and-white home video recorder, The PortaPak.

Jean-Luc Godard releases his apocalyptic vision of modern society in collapse, *Weekend*.

Roger Corman's *The Trip* is the first Hollywood film to deal with psychedelic drugs.

1968   The death of the pioneering woman film director, Alice Guy, goes unnoticed by the general press.

The Tet Offensive; the death toll of U.S. soldiers killed in the Vietnam War passes 30,000.

Martin Luther King Jr. and Robert F. Kennedy are assassinated roughly a month apart.

Russian tanks put down the "Prague Spring" in Czechoslovakia.

The Motion Picture Association of America develops a new rating system.

1969   Charles Manson is arrested for the murder of actress Sharon Tate, the wife of director Roman Polanski, and four others in Los Angeles.

The concert at Woodstock draws 400,000 people for three days of music.

Neil Armstrong becomes the first man on the moon.

Sony introduces the videocassette recorder for home use.

Sam Peckinpah's *The Wild Bunch* brings a new level of violence to the screen.

1970   Computer floppy disks are introduced.

Singer Janis Joplin and rock guitarist Jimi Hendrix die.

Earth Day is observed for the first time.

The Beatles break up.

Four students protesting the Vietnam War are killed by National Guard troops at Kent State.

1971   "All in the Family" debuts on television.

Video cassette recorders are introduced.

The Pentagon Papers are published in the *New York Times*.

The United Kingdom changes to the decimal system for currency.

Computer Space is the first video arcade game.

1972   *Ms.* magazine debuts.

Break-in at the Democratic National Committee headquarters in the Watergate office complex.

"Blaxploitation" films such as *Hit Man* and *Blacula* become popular.

Deep Throat brings X-rated pornography to regular movie houses.

Magnavox introduces Odyssey, the first home video game system; Atari is founded.

1973   *Skylab* is launched.

Abortion is legalized in the United States.

Sears Tower, the tallest building in the world, is built in Chicago.

Fritz the Cat is the first X-rated feature-length animated cartoon.

George Lucas directs *American Graffiti*.

1974   Dancer Mikhail Baryshnikov defects from the Soviet Union.

Haile Selassie, emperor of Ethiopia, is deposed.

President Richard Nixon resigns due to the Watergate scandal.

Patty Hearst is kidnapped.

Roman Polanski's *Chinatown* is released.

1975   Pol Pot becomes the Communist dictator of Cambodia.

Civil War in Lebanon.

Jaws premieres and becomes the model for the modern movie blockbuster.

Robert Altman directs the quirky, multi-character film *Nashville*.

Sony introduces Betamax video recorders for home use.

1976   North and South Vietnam join to form the Socialist Republic of Vietnam.

VHS home video recording is introduced; it will soon eclipse the Betamax format.

Premiere of Barbara Kopple's documentary *Harlan County U.S.A.,* about a strike at a Kentucky coal mine.

Director Bernardo Bertolucci's *1900,* a tale of political turmoil, is released.

1977   The mini-series "Roots" airs on television.

South African anti-apartheid leader Steve Biko is tortured to death.

George Lucas's *Star Wars* is released.

John Badham's *Saturday Night Fever* is a huge hit, signaling the dominance of disco music.

Steven Spielberg releases *Close Encounters of the Third Kind.*

1978   "Mork and Mindy" debuts on television, making an instant star of Robin Williams.

The world's first test-tube baby is born in England.

Jim Jones and more than 900 followers commit mass suicide at "Jonestown" in Guyana.

Karol Józef Wojtyla, from Poland, becomes Pope John Paul II.

John Carpenter's *Halloween* starts a horror movie franchise.

1979   Sony introduces the Walkman.

Ayatollah Khomeini becomes leader of Iran; revolutionaries take American hostages in Tehran.

Mother Teresa is awarded the Nobel Peace Prize.

The China Syndrome, about the dangers of nuclear reactors, opens just before the Three Mile Island accident in Pennsylvania.

The Australian cinema comes roaring back to prominence with *Mad Max,* starring Mel Gibson.

1980   U.S. rescue attempt to save hostages in Tehran fails.

The Rubik's Cube craze.

Ted Turner establishes CNN, a 24-hour news network.

Pacman video game is released in Japan.

Director Rainer Werner Fassbinder's epic fifteen-and-a-half-hour *Berlin Alexanderplatz* is serialized on television.

1981 Sandra Day O'Connor becomes the first woman to serve on the U.S. Supreme Court.

Assassination attempts on Pope John Paul II and President Ronald Reagan.

IBM introduces personal computers.

The AIDS virus is identified.

MTV debuts as a 24/7 video music network.

1982 Argentina invades the Falkland Islands.

Tylenol is pulled from shelves after seven deaths due to cyanide tampering.

Michael Jackson releases his album *Thriller*.

Walt Disney Studios' *Tron* is an early example of computer animation.

Steven Spielberg releases *E. T.: The Extra Terrestrial*.

1983 The Soviets shoot down a South Korean airliner.

The U.S. Embassy in Beirut is bombed, killing sixty-three.

Cabbage Patch Kids become a fad.

Sally Ride becomes the first American woman in space.

Ronald Reagan announces the "Star Wars" defense plan.

1984 The PG-13 movie rating is created.

Kathryn Sullivan becomes the first woman to walk in space.

"The Cosby Show" debuts on television.

The Vietnam War Memorial opens in Washington, D.C.

India's Prime Minister Indira Gandhi is assassinated by two bodyguards.

1985 Mikhail Gorbachev calls for *glasnost* (openness) in the Soviet Union.

The first Live Aid concert.

The first Blockbuster video store opens.

Rock Hudson dies of AIDS.

Akira Kurosawa's late samurai epic *Ran*.

1986   The space shuttle *Challenger* explodes after liftoff, killing all seven crewmembers.

Spike Lee's *She's Gotta Have It* is released.

Chernobyl nuclear accident.

President Ferdinand Marcos flees the Philippines.

Ted Turner buys MGM and sells off most of the studio, but keeps the film library for his cable television stations.

1987   DNA is first used as evidence in criminal trial.

Colonel Oliver North testifies before Congress in the unfolding Iran-Contra scandal.

The New York Stock Exchange suffers a 500-point drop on "Black Monday."

Ousmane Sembène and Thierno Faty Sow direct the epic Senegalese film *Camp de Thiaroye*.

1988   Fifty-two percent of U.S. homes have cable television.

Thirty-five thousand Americans have died of AIDS.

Commercial e-mail is launched.

Pan Am flight 103 blows up over Lockerbie, Scotland.

The Film Preservation Act takes effect, preserving five films a year for future generations.

1989   The Berlin Wall falls in Germany; revolutions across Soviet-dominated Eastern Europe.

Students are massacred in China's Tiananmen Square by government troops.

The *Exxon Valdez* spills millions of gallons of oil off the coast of Alaska.

James Cameron's *The Abyss* makes extensive use of computer-generated imagery.

Tim Burton directs *Batman*.

1990   The Hubble telescope is launched into space.

Nelson Mandela is freed from prison.

Lech Walesa becomes the first president of Poland.

Philip Kaufman's *Henry and June* is the first NC-17 rated film.

Matsushita, a Japanese electronics firm, buys MCA Universal.

1991 The Soviet Union collapses.

South Africa repeals apartheid laws.

U.S.-led Operation Desert Storm liberates Kuwait following Iraqi invasion.

Disney and Pixar join forces to create computer-generated feature films.

James Cameron's *Terminator 2: Judgment Day* is a huge leap forward in computer-generated effects.

1992 Riots break out in Los Angeles after the verdict in the Rodney King beating trial.

The Cold War officially ends.

"Barney and Friends" and "Baywatch" dominate television.

The bungee jumping craze peaks.

Seventy-six percent of all U.S. homes have VCRs.

1993 The World Trade Center is bombed by terrorists; six are killed and a thousand are wounded.

Cult headquarters in Waco, Texas, are raided by federal troops; more than seventy die.

Steven Spielberg's *Jurassic Park* takes computer-generated imagery to a new level of realism.

The Doom video game is released.

America Online launches large-scale network e-mail; use of the Internet surges.

1994 Nelson Mandela is elected president of South Africa.

O. J. Simpson is arrested for double murder.

The Rwandan genocide begins.

Steven Spielberg, David Geffen, and Jeffrey Katzenberg found Dream-Works Studios.

Robert Zemeckis's *Forrest Gump* seamlessly inserts new footage with archival material.

1995   The Ebola virus spreads in Zaire.

Gas attack in Tokyo subway.

The Oklahoma City bombing.

Israeli prime minister Yitzhak Rabin is assassinated.

Dogme 95, a movement by Danish directors Thomas Vinterberg and Lars von Trier to make simple, low-cost, non-genre films, is founded.

1996   Mad cow disease hits England.

JonBenet Ramsey is murdered.

The Coen brothers direct the quirky murder mystery *Fargo*.

Theodore Kaczynski, the "Unabomber," is arrested.

France agrees to end nuclear testing.

1997   Hong Kong is annexed by China.

Princess Diana dies in a car crash in France.

The tallest buildings in the world are built in Kuala Lumpur, Malaysia.

James Cameron directs *Titanic,* the costliest and most successful film in history.

Wong Kar-Wai's coming-of-age drama *Happy Together* is released.

1998   President Bill Clinton is impeached but remains in office following the Lewinsky scandal.

India and Pakistan test nuclear weapons.

Viagra is introduced.

Google goes online.

HDTV broadcasts begin.

1999   Columbine High School massacre in Colorado.

The euro becomes the new European currency.

The Blair Witch Project, produced for less than $30,000, becomes a surprise hit.

TiVO is introduced.

Roberto Benigni releases his comedy/drama about the Holocaust, *Life Is Beautiful*.

2000   The film industry is now controlled by six major companies: Disney, NBC Universal, Time Warner, Sony, Fox, and Viacom.

North and South Korea sign a peace accord.

Vicente Fox is elected president of Mexico.

The U.S. Supreme Court ends the election recount in Florida, making George W. Bush president.

America Online buys Time Warner.

2001   Hironobu Sakaguchi's *Final Fantasy: The Spirits Within* is the first fully computer-generated feature film that aims for pictorial realism; it fails at the box office.

Ariel Sharon is elected prime minister of Israel.

The World Trade Center is destroyed and the Pentagon is damaged in terrorist attacks.

Oklahoma City bomber Timothy McVeigh is executed.

Kyoto protocol on global warming is enacted, without the United States.

2002   Halle Berry wins Best Actress and Denzel Washington wins Best Actor at the Academy Awards.

Former Yugoslavian president Slobodan Milosevic goes on trial for war crimes.

North Korea begins nuclear rearmament.

The United Nations passes a resolution asking Iraq to disarm.

"The Osbournes" debuts on MTV, creating a model for "reality TV."

2003   Disney abandons traditional animation in favor of computer-generated feature cartoons.

Baghdad falls to U.S. troops in the early stages of the Iraq War.

Liberian president Charles Taylor flees the country.

Saddam Hussein is captured by U.S. troops.

Libya admits responsibility for the 1988 Lockerbie bombing.

2004   Michael Moore directs the guerrilla documentary *Fahrenheit 911*.

NATO admits seven new countries from Eastern Europe.

Palestinian leader Yasser Arafat dies in France.

Gay marriage is legalized in Massachusetts.

Martha Stewart goes to prison for obstruction of justice.

2005   Paramount buys DreamWorks.

Pope John Paul II dies.

George Clooney directs *Good Night, and Good Luck,* about the Mc-Carthy era.

London is hit by terrorist bombings.

Israel evacuates from the Gaza Strip.

2006   Paul Greengrass directs *United 93,* the first Hollywood film centering on the events of 9/11.

The Walt Disney Company purchases Pixar.

Ang Lee directs *Brokeback Mountain,* the first gay-themed mainstream western.

Iran resumes nuclear research; North Korea fires test missiles.

YouTube explodes on the Web.

2007   Former Communist countries Bulgaria and Romania are admitted into the European Union.

Senegalese director Ousmane Sembène dies at the age of eighty-four.

Tony Blair steps down as prime minister of England.

Iran announces plans to go nuclear.

Ingmar Bergman and Michelangelo Antonioni die.

2008   Stock markets around the world plunge.

Charlton Heston and Paul Newman die.

Barack Obama becomes President of the United States.

No Country for Old Men wins an Academy Award for Best Picture.

Population of the United States passes 300 million.

2009   Israeli troops cross the border into Gaza.

Unemployment in the United States reaches 8.1 percent; worst since 1983.

Bernard Madoff pleads guilty to a Ponzi scheme.

James Cameron's *Avatar* opens in theaters.

Michael Jackson dies.

2010   A 7.0-magnitude earthquake devastates Port-au-Prince, Haiti.

Winter Olympics are held in Vancouver, Canada.

Christopher Nolan's *Inception* opens in theaters.

U.S. Senate votes to repeal "Don't Ask, Don't Tell" restrictions on gays and lesbians serving in the military.

Russia wins bid to host the 2018 World Soccer Cup.

2011   The Arab Spring movement begins in Tunisia.

Muammar Gaddafi, Osama bin Laden, and Kim Jong-Il die.

Kate Middleton marries Prince William at Westminster Abbey.

News of the World phone hacking scandal erupts.

Amy Winehouse dies.

2012   Greek debt crisis erupts.

Whitney Houston dies.

The Hunger Games opens in theaters.

Facebook has more than 900 million users.

Summer Olympics are held in London.

A SHORT HISTORY OF

ONE

THE INVENTION OF THE MOVIES

BEGINNINGS

Motion pictures don't really move. The illusion of movement on the cinema screen is the result of "persistence of vision," in which the human eye sees twenty-four images per second, each projected for 1/60th of a second, and merges those images together into fluid motion. But it took thousands of years to put this simple principle into practice, and the motion picture camera as we know it today is the result of experimentation and effort by many different inventors and artists, working in different countries throughout the world. The principle of persistence of vision was known as far back as ancient Egypt, but despite numerous experiments by Athanasius Kircher (whose 1646 text *Ars Magna Lucis et Umbrae* described the use and construction of what we now know as the "magic lantern"), as well as contributions by the Chevalier Patrice D'Arcy and Sir Isaac Newton regarding the mechanics of the human eye, it was not until 1824 that Peter Mark Roget explained what the process entailed.

Roget believed that persistence of vision was caused by the retina's ability to "remember" an image for a fraction of a second after it has been removed from the screen; later research demonstrated, however, that it was the brain's inability to separate the rapidly changing individual images from each other that caused the phenomenon. Simply put, persistence of vision works because the brain is receiving too much information too rapidly to process accurately, and instead melds these discrete images into the illusion of motion.

The theory of stringing together still images to create this illusion of movement can also be seen in the early work of Claudius Ptolemy in 150 C.E. Al Hassan Ibn Al Haitham, a famous Muslim scientist and inventor who died in 1038, was one of the first to describe the workings of the camera obscura, in which an image from the world outside is captured through a peephole and "projected" on the wall of a darkened room (albeit upside down) as a real-life "motion picture." There are also references in Lucretius to "moving pictures" circa 98–55 B.C.E., and one can find another early expression of the desire to create movement from still images in primitive cave paintings, Egyptian hieroglyphics, and friezes decorating the walls of the Parthenon in ancient Greece. But at this early stage in the development of "moving pictures," a practical device for creating the illusion of movement from a series of still images had yet to be developed.`

As the centuries rolled on, "magic lantern" displays and shadow "puppet plays" in China, Java, France, and other nations of the world became popular entertainment. The puppet plays depended upon crude marionettes casting shadows on a translucent screen before the audience; "image lantern" presentations were essentially elaborate slide shows, in which a variety of glass plates were illuminated by candles and mirrors to cast images onto a projection screen. Dominique Séraphin's famous Parisian Shadow plays entranced audiences from 1784 until 1870; and the Phenakistoscope, a moving wheel with mirrors and slits that allowed viewers to peek inside and see figures "move," was renamed the Zoetrope and marketed as a novelty for the home viewer in the 1860s. During the same period, Philippe-Jacques de Loutherbourg created the Eidophusikon, a special effects extravaganza that used miniatures illuminated by candlelight and oil lamps.

In addition, Ottomar Anschutz created the Electrical

A Zoetrope in action; the figures inside seemed to move when the disc was rotated.

[LEFT]: A sequence of action stills by Eadweard Muybridge; the beginnings of the modern motion picture.

[RIGHT]: Étienne-Jules Marey's "shotgun" camera, first devised in 1882, and adapted for paper film in 1888.

Tachyscope, which used a flickering light to illuminate a series of still photographs placed along the circumference of a rotating disk, much like the Zoetrope. He later developed this device into the Projecting Electrotachyscope, which projected these moving images on a screen. "Phantom trains" were also popular during this period, in which "passengers" would "travel" the world through the illusion of projected backdrops, while primitive hydraulic devices created the sensation of movement, much like today's amusement rides at Universal Studios and Disneyland. As a sort of precursor to the big-budget cinema spectacles of the 1950s, Robert Barker's Panorama, which played in Edinburgh in 1787, presented to audiences views of huge paintings that re-created famous historical tableaux. Such early "magic lantern" devices as the Chromatrope, Eidotrope, and Pieter van Musschenbroeck's magic lantern used mechanical apparatus to shift the images in front of the audience's eyes, creating the illusion of movement.

Yet all these early gestures toward what would become the motion picture remained merely tantalizing hints of what might be accomplished until the late nineteenth century, when a series of inventions by a number of technicians and artists throughout the world brought the idea of moving pictures to primitive fruition. Perhaps the most famous progenitor of the cinema was Eadweard Muybridge, who created "motion studies" of cats, birds, horses, and the human figure in 1872, using a series of up to forty still cameras whose shutters were released by trip wires activated by Muybridge's subjects.

3

THE FIRST "MOVIES"

Working in Palo Alto, California, Muybridge's most celebrated experiment took place near the beginning of his career, when he was hired by Leland Stanford, then governor of California, to settle a bet as to whether or not a horse had all four legs in the air during a race or relied upon one leg on the ground at all times to keep balanced. In 1878, Muybridge used his trip-wire technique to produce a series of images of a galloping horse at a Palo Alto racetrack, decisively demonstrating that a horse did indeed have all four legs off the ground when running at a fast clip. By 1879, Muybridge was using his Zoöpraxiscope to project these brief segments of motion onto a screen for audiences; the average clip ran only a few seconds. This is the beginning of projected motion pictures, arising from a series of stills taken by a number of different cameras, run together rapidly to create the illusion of motion. Another cinematic pioneer, Étienne-Jules Marey, invented what might be considered the first truly portable moving picture camera in 1882, a "machine-gun"-styled affair that photographed twelve plates in rapid succession on one disc. In 1888, Marey

An early study of the human form by Eadweard Muybridge.

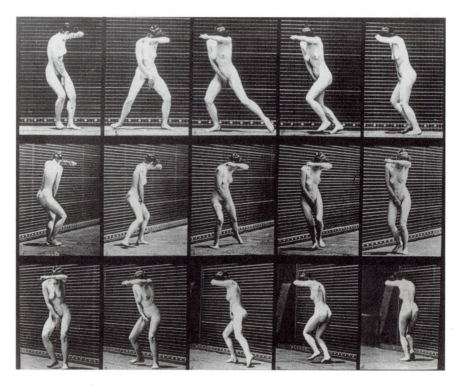

switched to Eastman paper film instead of glass plates and was able to record forty images in one burst, using only one camera.

Perhaps the most mysterious figure of the era is Louis Aimé Augustin Le Prince, whose experiments in cinematography were revolutionary and remain controversial to this day. In Paris in 1887, Le Prince built a sixteen-lens camera, capable of photographing sixteen images in rapid succession of a single scene. By March or April of 1888, working in Leeds, England, Le Prince successfully created a single-lens camera that used a series of photographic plates to record motion, later replacing the plates with perforated paper film from the George Eastman company, as Marey had, for greater ease of projection. In October 1888, Le Prince photographed his brother Adolphe playing the "melodeon" (a primitive accordion) in the garden behind his laboratory.

In the same month, he photographed members of his family in the same garden at Oakwood Grange, strolling through the grass. In the summer of 1889 (although some historians say 1888), Le Prince photographed what would become his most famous sequence: a shot of pedestrians and traffic crossing Leeds Bridge. Twenty frames of this historic film survive today.

Le Prince was also working on a projection device for his images, and by the winter of 1889 he had perfected a projection device using the "Maltese cross movement," a gear that pulled down the perforated film images one at a time for successive projection to create the smooth illusion of movement. In the first months of 1890, Le Prince photographed short films in Paris and screened them for the governing body of the Paris Opera. With his single-lens camera, his projection device, the use of the Maltese cross movement (still used in most film projectors and cameras to this day), and his groundbreaking public projection of his work, Le Prince seemed poised on the brink of success.

But then the inexplicable happened. After visiting his brother in Dijon in September 1890, Le Prince boarded a train bound for Paris intent on presenting his invention to the world. He never arrived at his destination. In one of cinema's great mysteries, Le Prince seemingly vanished from the train before it arrived in Paris, along with his invention. Although a full-scale investigation was launched into Le Prince's disappearance, no trace of the inventor or his devices was ever found. To this day, the riddle of what happened to Le Prince's camera and projector remains a tantalizing enigma, and one can only speculate as to what history might have recorded of his accomplishments had he not disappeared without a trace.

Other inventors, certainly, were working along similar lines. William

Friese-Greene, an Englishman, was also involved in creating an early version of the motion picture camera and projector, and is claimed by the British as the inventor of motion pictures. In that same country, Birt Acres produced and screened his films on a device he dubbed the Kineopticon, which was patented in May 1895 and publicly demonstrated in early 1896. Robert W. Paul was another early British film pioneer. In Germany, Max and Emil Skladanowsky invented their own cinema camera and projection system, the Bioscope, and in France, Henri Joly created the competing Photozoötrope.

In America, Woodville Latham and his sons, Gray and Otway, created the

Four frames from the Lumière brothers' brief comedy *L'Arroseur arrosé (Tables Turned on the Gardener,* 1895).

Panoptikon, yet another projection device, and introduced the "Latham Loop," a device that allowed the film running through a projector a brief respite before being pulled down for projection, thus preventing the film from being ripped by the "pull-down" motion of the Maltese cross device. Thomas Armat and C. Francis Jenkins created the Phantoscope, which was then bought up by the inventor and entrepreneur Thomas Alva Edison, who renamed it the Vitascope, and later, with refinements, the Kinetoscope.

Thus, working at roughly the same time, William Friese-Greene, Louis Aimé Augustin Le Prince, Gray and Otway Latham, Max and Emil Skladanowsky, and many other film pioneers all made significant contributions to the emerging medium. But despite all their work, two individuals, through a combination of skill and luck, stand out as the "inventors" of the cinema, although they were really just the most aggressive commercial popularizers of the new medium.

THE LUMIÈRE BROTHERS

The brothers Louis and Auguste Lumière are generally credited with making the first commercial breakthrough in combining the photographic and projection device into one machine in early 1895. Their camera/projector, the Cinematographe, was patented on 13 February 1895, and the first Lumière projections took place shortly thereafter, on 28 December 1895, in the Salon Indien of the Grand Café in Paris. The brothers presented, in such landmark films as *La Sortie des usines Lumière* (*Workers Leaving the Lumière Factory*), *L'Arroseur arrosé* (*Tables Turned on the Gardener*, in which a gardener is watered with his own hose by a young prankster), and *Repas de bébé* (*Feeding the Baby*), a world that was at once realistic and tranquil, gently whimsical, and deeply privileged. In many respects, the Lumière brothers were the world's first documentary filmmakers, and their short films (about one minute in length) remain invaluable as a slice of upper-middle-class French society at the turn of the century that would otherwise have been forgotten. One of the Lumières' most famous early films was *L'Arrivée d'un train à La Ciotat* (*Arrival of a Train at La Ciotat*, 1895), in which a train pulls into a railroad station. Early patrons were so amazed that some are said to have fled the theater in fright, certain that the train would run them over. The Lumières made literally hundreds of these one-shot, one-scene films, and for several years continued to present them to an enthusiastic public captivated by the simple fact that the images moved. It was the first successful commercial exploitation of the medium.

Frames from the Lumière brothers' *L'Arrivée d'un train à La Ciotat* (*Arrival of a Train at La Ciotat*, 1896).

THOMAS EDISON

Of all the early film pioneers, it was Edison and his associates who most clearly saw the profit potential of the new medium. For the Lumière brothers, the cinema was but a curiosity; Louis had famously declared that the Cinematographe was "an invention without a future." Edison, however, saw the chance to make real money. Even his early pieces, such as *Blacksmith Scene* (1893), *Horse Shoeing* (1893), and *Edison Kinetoscopic Record of a Sneeze* (better known as *Fred Ott's Sneeze*, 1894), were deliberately staged rather than films of real events. In *The Barber Shop* and *Sandow* (both 1894), Edison designed hermetically sealed spaces to contain the human body and to draw the viewer's attention to it. *Sandow* fea-

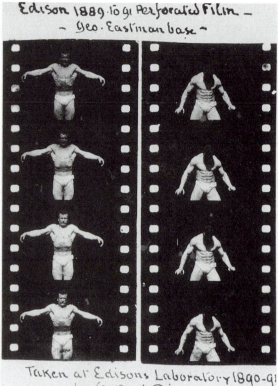

Edison 1889. to 91 Perforated Film -
- Geo. Eastman base -

Taken at Edisons Laboratory 1890-91
by WKLaurieDickson -
Part of the 1889 same Exhibit -

A filmstrip from Thomas A. Edison's
Sandow (1894).

tured muscleman Eugen Sandow flexing his muscles for the gaze of Edison's camera. *Carmencita* (1894) was a brief documentary of a Spanish dancer performing her sexually charged routine for the presumably male audience. *Annabelle the Dancer* (1895), featuring Annabelle Whitford Moore performing an energetic dance in a long flowing gown, was shown in the first public display of Edison's Kinetoscopic films using Thomas Armat's Vitascope projector. The film was hand-tinted in various colors and shown at Koster & Bial's Music Hall in New York City on 23 April 1896. Edison had intended his films to be peep-show entertainments, but he soon changed his mind as he saw the commercial potential of projected motion pictures. Now, with the Vitascope apparatus, he recycled his earlier films for public projection.

In the earliest Edison films, there is no attempt to disguise the artificiality of the spectacle being created for and recorded by the camera. In all of Edison's films, it is the body—at work, at play, or preening for the camera—that is the center of our attention, in contrast to the films of Auguste and Louis Lumière, which photographed life in a direct and unadorned fashion, with minimal staging. As late as 1898, Edison's technicians were still using bare or simple black backgrounds to film *Serpentine Dance* and *Sun Dance* (both 1897, starring the dancer Annabelle), as well as *Ella Lola, a la Trilby* and *Turkish Dance, Ella Lola* (both 1898). This last film became a celebrated censorship case when Ella Lola's suggestive body display was obscured, in some versions, by the insertion of an optically superimposed grid, which covered the offending portions of her anatomy.

Other early Edison films, including *Newark Athlete, Men Boxing* (both 1891), *Man on Parallel Bars, Fencers* (both 1892), *Wrestling Match, Athlete with Wand,* and *Unsuccessful Somersault* (all 1894), continued his film factory's fascination with the human body. As the novelty of captured motion

An Edison Kinetoscope parlor, circa 1894.

wore off, Edison was pushed by economic need to create more bizarre entertainments, notably *Boxing Cats* (1898), in which two cats duke it out in a
miniature boxing ring in a parody of his "fight" films *Leonard-Cushing Fight*
and *Boxing Match* (both 1894). Even in works that were devoid of violence,
like *Highland Dance* (1894), Edison was constructing a gallery of films that
involved exaggerated masculinity (the boxing films) and stylized sensuality
(the Ella Lola and Carmencita films). In addition, Edison's film *The Kiss*
(1896) created a sensation, and led to some of the earliest examples of censorship in the cinema. In subsequent films, he continued to pursue his interest in the bizarre and unusual, for he knew that by appealing to the basest
appetites of his viewers he was simultaneously pursuing the surest avenue to
commercial success. Thus he produced *Rat Killing* (1894), in which a dog
leaps upon a group of large rats and kills them, followed by no fewer than
three sequels, *Rats and Terrier No. 2, Rats and Terrier No. 3,* and *Rats and
Weasel;* all four films were shot on the same day in 1894. In this, Edison was
foreshadowing the now prevalent practice of shooting several sequels to a
successful film simultaneously once a proven market has been established.
Ever the master exploitationist, Edison knew what the public would pay to
view, even adding the grotesque "novelty" of a weasel to replace the terrier in
the last of the series. Seeking additional ways to exploit his new invention,
Edison was also responsible for the first filmed advertisement, *Dewar's Scotch
Whiskey,* shot in 1897, which introduced the slogan "Dewar's: It's Scotch."

Edison's *The Kiss* (1896).

Not surprisingly, Edison specialized in such highly commercial films as *Buffalo Bill* (a record of rifle shooting by the famed western "fighter"), as well as *Sioux Ghost Dance, Indian War Council,* and *Buffalo Dance.* All these were shot on the same day in the fall of 1894. The exoticization inherent in these manufactured spectacles continued in such films as *Pedro Esquirel and Dionecio Gonzales* (*Mexican Knife Duel*), *Vincente One Passo* (*Lasso Thrower*), and *Sheik Hadji Taviar*, all shot on 6 October 1894 at Edison's Black Maria. Indeed, as can be seen from this hectic production pace, Edison was already anticipating the studio system of supply and demand, churning out new and highly commercial product on an assembly-line basis.

Edison set down the basic precepts upon which commercial Hollywood movie production, distribution, and exhibition are still based: give the audience spectacle, sex, and violence, yet simultaneously pay lip service to the dominant social order. Early cinema audiences were often an unruly bunch, drawn to nickelodeons and Kinetoscope parlors through the lure of sensation alone. By 1907, roughly two million viewers attended the nickelodeons daily, and by 1908, there were more than 8,000 nickelodeons in existence in the United States. Admission was a nickel, and accompaniment was usually from an upright piano at the front of the hall. Early nickelodeons had a gen-

Thomas Edison's Black Maria, one of the world's first film production studios.

erally rough reputation and often a fly-by-night quality, inasmuch as most were converted storefronts or livery stables and could fold up and move on at a moment's notice. Edison's ultra-commercial films fit right in, presenting a world of idealized romantic couples, racist stereotypes, and relentless exoticism, leavened with a healthy dose of sadism and voyeurism to titillate the public. In short, Edison knew what the public wanted.

GEORGES MÉLIÈS'S WORLD OF FANTASY

While Edison, along with Étienne-Jules Marey, Louis Aimé Augustin Le Prince, and the Lumière brothers, was inventing the foundation of the modern motion picture, other early practitioners of the cinematic art were creating worlds of their own. Georges Méliès was a former magician who became involved in film as a way to further his obsession with illusion. His trademark brand of phantasmagorical wizardry made him the godfather of special effects cinema in the hundreds of films he created in his Paris studio, including *Le Spectre* (*Murder Will Out*, 1899) and *Le Rêve de Noël* (*The*

11

George Méliès's *Le Voyage dans le lune* (*A Trip to the Moon*, 1902) made science fiction a "reality" for early cinema audiences.

Christmas Dream, 1900). In *Escamotage d'une dame chez Robert-Houdin* (*The Conjuring of a Woman at the House of Robert Houdin*, 1896), Méliès makes a woman vanish before our eyes. In *L'Hallucination de l'alchemiste* (*The Hallucinating Alchemist*, 1897), he presents the viewer with a gigantic star sporting five female heads. *Les Aventures de baron de Munchhausen* (*Baron Munchhausen's Dream*, 1911) features a woman/spider construct that anticipates the Scorpion King in a much later film, Stephen Sommers's *The Mummy Returns* (2001). In *Le Chaudron infernal* (*The Infernal Boiling Pot*, 1903), three young women are boiled alive in a gigantic cauldron.

Méliès's most famous film, *Le Voyage dans la lune* (1902), distributed in the United States and England as *A Trip to the Moon*, ranks as one of the cinema's first (if not the first) science fiction films, combining spectacle, sensation, and technical wizardry to create a cosmic fantasy that was an international sensation. The film also created many of the basic generic situations that are still used in science fiction films today. A visionary scientist proposes a trip to the moon and is met with derision. Defying the scientific establishment, he pushes on with the construction of his rocket, aided by a few close associates. After much preparation, the rocket is successfully launched and, in one of the most famous shots in the history of cinema, hits the "man in the moon" in the eye, landing in a triumphant close-up of the moon's face. On the moon, the scientists are captured and taken to the moon's ruler, who proposes to put the scientists on trial for daring to enter his domain. But the leader of the scientists breaks free, makes a mad rush for the ruler's throne, and destroys him by hurling him to the ground where he vanishes in a puff of smoke. The group escapes and races back to their rocket ship, which is now conveniently located on the edge of the moon. Beating off their pursuers, the scientists manage to tip the rocket off the moon so that it falls back to Earth, controlled solely by gravity. Fortunately for the scientists, the rocket lands in the ocean, immediately floats to the surface, and is triumphantly towed into safe harbor by a steamboat.

About fourteen minutes long, *A Trip to the Moon* was an enormous critical and commercial hit.

Méliès's films, like those of Edison and the Lumière brothers, relied on a fixed camera position, but within this limitation he created a basic library of special effects that would dominate the cinema until the advent of the digital era in the late twentieth century: double exposures, dissolves (one image "melts" into another), mattes (in which one portion of the image is "masked off" and then rephotographed to create spatial, or spectacular, illusions), reverse motion, cutting in the camera (to make objects appear and/or disappear), and numerous other cinematic techniques.

For all his showmanship, Méliès was an unsuccessful businessperson, and his films were often bootlegged in foreign countries. Near the end of his career he went bankrupt, partially because of the extensive pirating of his work, but also as a result of overspending on increasingly lavish spectacles. The negatives for Méliès's films were melted down by a creditor for their silver content. Many of his films survive today only through the illegal copies that helped to bankrupt him.

ALICE GUY

Although many film histories ignore her importance in cinema history, the Frenchwoman Alice Guy is one of the inventors of the narrative film. Few of her films survive today, however, due to the twin exigencies of neglect and cellulose nitrate decay (all films made before 1950 were photographed on nitrate film, which produced a superior image but was highly flammable and chemically unstable). Indeed, her remarkable body of work went almost unnoticed until the late 1970s, when feminist historians began to reintegrate her life work into film history and scholarship.

Guy was born in Paris in 1873. She was raised by a middle-class family, the youngest of four daughters of a bookseller. Educated at a convent in Switzerland, she was hired as a secretary by Léon Gaumont. Not very long afterward, she began to take on more duties at the studio. In fact, Guy helped her employer build the first Gaumont studio in France.

Gaumont experimented with moving cameras and projectors, eventually building a 35 mm (standard theatrical gauge) camera combined with a projector. Then he designed and built an inexpensive machine for projection only, which was to be marketed to other distributors in the industry. Guy worked closely with him on these projects. Her first stabs at direction were

A portrait of Alice Guy in 1896.

instructional films, newsreels, and other short subjects, meant for advertising, promotion, and demonstration purposes. Gaumont was interested only in technique. Guy was the artistic side of the partnership.

In 1896, she directed *La Fée aux Choux* (*The Cabbage Patch Fairy*), one of the world's first films with a plot. Described as a picture postcard that springs to life, the film tells the story of a woman who grows children in a cabbage patch. Guy shot the film with the help of Yvonne Mugnier-Serand in the garden of Gaumont's house, with a few backdrops for sets and some friends as actors. The film displayed the French style of light humor and an appreciation for magic and the fantastic, similar to that of Méliès and other early French film directors.

After her first narrative film, Guy began to make films with well-known French stage performers. She would tackle many different genres: fairy tales, fantasy films, horror films, comedies, and trick films, making dozens of films for Gaumont, such as *La Première Cigarette* (*The First Cigarette*, 1904). In her 1903 film *Faust et Méphistophélès* she was already using close-ups to heighten dramatic effects. Guy also included shots of actors reacting to one another. In another short film, *Le Crime de la Rue du Temple* (*The Crime in Temple Street*, 1904), she used innovative cinematic devices such as masking and double exposure.

Guy was fond of literary classics such as Victor Hugo's *Notre-Dame de Paris,* which she adapted for the screen as *La Esmeralda* (1905). One of the most famous works she directed during her early years was *La Vie du Christ* (or *La Naissance, la vie, et la mort*

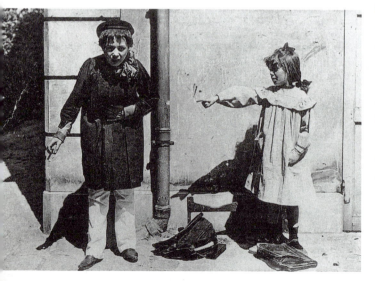

A scene from *La Première Cigarette* (*The First Cigarette*), directed by Alice Guy for Gaumont in 1904.

A scene from Alice Guy's Gaumont production *La Vie du Christ* (*The Life of Christ,* 1906).

de Notre-Seigneur Jésus-Christ, 1906, and released in the United States as *The Birth, the Life, and the Death of Christ*). Made specifically to compete with the Pathé release of the same name, it was an ambitious production that had a lavish budget, large crew, and hundreds of extras, in settings designed and executed by Henri Ménessier. Guy managed to skillfully incorporate the use of numerous extras to give added depth to her work, the same way that the American director D. W. Griffith did many years later in *The Birth of a Nation* (1915) and *Intolerance* (1916), with one subtle but telling difference: most of the onlookers in this version of the Christ tale are women and children. In addition, Guy used lap dissolves to show angels hovering over Christ at his birth and employed deep photographic space to suggest a sense of visual depth and detail that is missing in many early silent films. Under Gaumont's supervision, Guy also went on to direct many of the earliest sound films. Gaumont invented a device that recorded sound on wax cylinders, called the Chronophone. It worked by recording sound synchronously with the camera's recording of the visuals. Starting in the late 1890s, Guy directed at least a hundred of these new "talking pictures."

Around this time Guy started to hire more directors to keep up with the output at Gaumont studios. She hired Ferdinand Zecca, who later became a well-known French director, as her assistant. When she could no longer handle the entire production end of Gaumont single-handedly, Guy signed on Ménessier as permanent set designer, Victorin-Hippolyte Jasset as production manager, and, later, Louis Feuillade as scriptwriter. Many film historians would subsequently forget Guy's contributions but remember everyone she hired, and even misattribute her films to them.

On an expedition to film a bullfight sequence in Nîmes, France, Guy met Herbert Blaché, an English cameraman. They were married on Christmas Day in 1906 and then moved to New York to run Gaumont's American production

Alice Guy directing an early film in the
Solax Studios in the early 1900s.

office. After taking two years off to have children, Guy formed her own company, Solax, in 1910, supervising more than three hundred releases over the next five years. With Blaché in charge of Gaumont's New York office, Guy was able to make full use of that studio's technical facilities, as well as gain access to Gaumont's American clients, who would distribute her films. Located first in Flushing, New York, Solax eventually moved to Fort Lee, New Jersey, where a number of fledgling film companies were setting up production facilities at the dawn of the studio era.

Perhaps one of the reasons Guy's films have been lost to history is her distinct style of direction. Her films are highly theatrical, and film critics have traditionally despised theatricality. Her use of deep-focus photography, lush, expensive sets, and theatrical subjects may also have been ahead of its time. In addition, for many years it appeared that only a few of Guy's films had survived. But due to renewed interest in her work, many rare prints of her films have been recovered throughout the world, preserved in archives, and in some cases distributed.

EDWIN S. PORTER

While Alice Guy was blazing new cinematic advances in France and later in the United States, Edison was moving ahead with the development of the motion picture with the aid of Edwin S. Porter, whose films *The Life of an American Fireman* and particularly *The Great Train Robbery* revolutionized the cinema. *The Life of an American Fireman* (1903) is a brief film of six minutes, in which a fireman, dozing at his station, dreams of his wife and child at home. Suddenly, the alarm sounds, and the fireman is off to put out yet another blaze—but this time, it is at his own home. The fire brigade pulls up, and in a neat mixture of actual "newsreel" footage (Porter and his crew waited at a firehouse until a call came in, and then documented the crew in action) and staged footage, the fireman's wife and child are rescued from the blazing house.

Interestingly, the rescue is shown twice, once from the inside of the house, as the firemen break in through the window, and again from the outside, as the firemen ascend the ladder to the woman's bedroom and then descend with the wife and her child. Intercutting for suspense is limited to the opening sequence of the dreaming fireman at the station, juxtaposed with his dream image of his wife and child at their home, but at this early date, Porter felt compelled to use the interior and exterior angles as separate units, rather than intercutting them to create the illusion of one continuous act. In addition, the film was shot on paper film, rather than cellulose nitrate film, and so has a rather flat and misty look to it. Nevertheless, the technical innovations in the film are many: a close-up of the fire alarm being activated, the use of both medium and wide shots, the intercutting of actual footage with staged sequences, and the use of dissolves as transitions between scenes to suggest the passage of time.

Even more daring is Porter's *The Great Train Robbery* (1903), which, as with Méliès's *A Trip to the Moon*, presents in microcosm the basic generic conventions of the western in a violent, one-reel short film. The plot is simple: a train is hijacked by bandits intent on stealing the mail, and they successfully carry out their nefarious plans, killing the train's engineer and the mailroom attendant in the process. They force the train's passengers to disembark, line up, and hand over their valuables. When one man tries to make a break for it, the robbers shoot and kill him in cold blood. Escaping with their loot, the robbers are followed by a posse in hot pursuit, who shoot them down in the woods of Fort Lee, New Jersey (where the film was actually shot), and recover the stolen goods. In the film's famous final shot, one of the actors aims his gun directly at the audience and fires twice, in a stark and completely disconnected close-up.

Running only twelve minutes and containing just fourteen shots, *The Great Train Robbery* nevertheless represented a significant step forward in cinematic grammar. The film used intercutting for suspense (a telegraph operator knocked out at the beginning of the film is revived by a young girl who discovers him by accident; will he be able to spread the alarm in time?); parallel editing (the robbery takes place as the telegraph operator is being revived, and the robbery concludes as the posse is being formed to pursue the

Edwin S. Porter's *The Great Train Robbery* (1903) established the conventions of the western genre.

bandits); and camera angles that view the action from a variety of vantage points, usually to the left or right of the actors, rather than placing the actors directly in front of the camera.

In addition, *The Great Train Robbery* served as the training ground for one Gilbert M. "Broncho Billy" Anderson, who played several roles in the film (the man who tries to escape and is shot; a tenderfoot whom the posse forces to dance with gunfire at a square dance) and later became the movies' first cowboy hero. As effective as the film was, Anderson realized that it lacked one key element: a central protagonist for the viewer to identify with. As "Broncho Billy," he pioneered the "aw, shucks" cowboy hero, later personified by Gene Autry, Hopalong Cassidy, and Roy Rogers, in a string of silent westerns starting with *The Bandit Makes Good* (1908). Anderson's concept was so successful that he ultimately cranked out four hundred films in the "Broncho [later Bronco] Billy" series from 1907 to 1914, establishing him as one of the screen's first bona fide film stars. Porter, however, would experience his greatest success with *The Great Train Robbery,* and although he made many other films, he was unable to adapt to changing times and ultimately retired in 1915.

WINSOR MCCAY

Newspaper cartoonist Winsor McCay, who created the famous "Little Nemo in Slumberland" comic strip in the early 1900s, broke into animated films with his 1911 short *Little Nemo* and then went on to animate *Gertie the Dinosaur* (1914), a short film in which the brontosaurus Gertie frolics through a series of prehistoric adventures. The film's novelty was so great that McCay often appeared in person with the film, seemingly instructing Gertie to perform various tricks or talking back to her when she misbehaved. Both films used literally thousands of drawings, each photographed one frame at a time, to create the illusion of movement. In 1918 McCay created his most ambitious film, the realistic *The Sinking of the Lusitania*, which documented the famous naval disaster. By the early 1920s, however, he dropped out of the animated cartoon business and returned to his comic strips, leaving the field wide open for other animated cartoon pioneers, such as Walt Disney and Ub Iwerks.

A frame from Winsor McCay's pioneering animation film *Gertie the Dinosaur* (1914).

19

EARLY WORLD CINEMA

At the same time that *The Great Train Robbery* was making its mark in cinema history, many other cineastes around the world were also advancing cinema both as a commercial medium and an art form. Cecil M. Hepworth, working in England, began his career as an actor in director James Williamson's *Fire* (1903) before making his famous narrative film *Rescued by Rover* (1905), which Hepworth produced, wrote, directed, and starred in, along with his wife and child. *Rescued by Rover* is often cited as the first film that used paid actors, in the person of Hepworth's immediate family; it is also the forerunner of the Rin Tin Tin and Lassie films, in that an omniscient dog, the Hepworths' own Rover, is really the star of the film.

The plot of *Rescued by Rover* is simple and straightforward: a vengeful Gypsy who has been rebuffed while panhandling kidnaps the Hepworths' infant child. The Gypsy absconds with the child to an attic garret, and then proceeds to drink herself into a blind stupor. When they discover the abduction the Hepworths are at a loss, but Rover seizes the moment and is soon hot on the baby's trail. Finding the infant in the Gypsy's squalid lair, Rover returns to his master, convinces Hepworth to follow him, and together man and dog rescue the child. The smooth cutting of the film's chase sequences was unparalleled at the time, and the naturalism of the film (shot for the most part on location, with only a few sets) was a further revelation. In addition, the film ends with a freeze-frame of the happy family reunited, a device that has become a cliché but was then strikingly original.

In Germany, the producer, inventor, and impresario Oskar Messter supervised the creation of more than three hundred films from 1896 through 1924, becoming the father of the German film industry. In France, screen comedian Max Linder, for many observers the forerunner of Charles Chaplin, was already honing his comic craft in films like Albert Capellani and Lucien Nonguet's *La Vie de Polichinelle* (*The Legend of Polichinelle,* 1907), an elaborately staged farce, while in Italy, Arturo Ambrosio and Luigi Maggi created the first of many versions of *Gli Ultimi giorni di Pompeii* (*The Last Days of Pompeii,* 1908), beginning a long tradition of Italian spectacle that was followed by such epics as Enrico Guazzoni's *Quo Vadis?* (1912) and numerous other "sword and sandal" films.

At the same time, the first legal battles over the use of the cinematographic apparatus were being fought, as Thomas Edison sought to suppress his rivals with a series of lawsuits. Edison had first begun asserting his position as the inventor of the motion picture projector and camera (which he was not) as early as 1897, in a suit against cameraman and inventor William K. L. Dickson and Edwin S. Porter, two of Edison's most gifted film technicians, who had (briefly) dared to break away from their mentor. But other, more intense battles for supremacy in the new medium lay ahead, as Edison formed the Motion Picture Patents Company in 1908 and attempted to monopolize the cinema trade.

From a technical standpoint, even in the late 1890s and early 1900s, the cinema had already begun to experiment with synchronized sound (in the films of Alice Guy for Gaumont's Chronophone, as well as other related processes, which date from the late 1890s) and the use of hand-tinted, or machine-applied, color. In Australia, the pioneering director Charles Tait brought to life the violent career of a legendary outlaw in *The Story of the Kelly Gang* (a k a *Ned Kelly and His Gang,* 1906), one of the first narrative films to run a respectable seventy minutes, or the standard feature length we have grown accustomed to today. "Newsreels" of sporting events, most notably the Jim Jeffries–Thomas Sharkey fight of 3 November 1899, photographed by Biograph using multiple cameras in its brutal entirety, became popular with audiences and led to early attempts at film censorship.

*   *   *

The infant medium was growing up rapidly, creating documentaries, exploitation films, brief narratives, and films of ever-increasing length and ambition. Impresarios around the world were copying, pirating, and importing motion picture cameras to create a bewildering series of actualities, staged dramas, comedies, and phantasmagorical spectacles, copying, for the most part, the leading pioneers. But as yet, film still had not acquired a detailed grammar of shots and editorial practices; while much had been accomplished, much remained to be done. D. W. Griffith, Thomas Ince, Lois Weber, and other key filmmakers of the silent era would transform the innovations of the end of the nineteenth century into an international industry, starting with the use of the studio system, and with it, the foundations of genre filmmaking, the star system, and the industrialization of the cinema.

TWO

THE BIRTH OF AN AMERICAN INDUSTRY

Edison was perhaps the most ambitious and ruthless of the early film moguls; though film production was just a sideline for him, he rapidly sought to make the cinema an industry operating in an assembly-line manner. In the wake of his vision of film as commerce, other pioneers rapidly crowded into the new medium. But it was a relative Johnny-come-lately, D. W. Griffith (born David Llewelyn Wark Griffith), who through shrewd self-promotion and sheer industry rose to the greatest prominence.

D. W. GRIFFITH

Initially hostile to the fledgling medium, the theatrically trained Griffith made his screen acting debut (as Lawrence Griffith) in *Rescued from an Eagle's Nest* (1908; directed by J. Searle Dawley, with Edwin S. Porter as cinematographer), simply because he was low on funds. Gradually, Griffith saw the potential of film as a narrative form, and, borrowing techniques from Porter, Guy, Méliès, and other early cineastes, he directed his first one-reel short, *The Adventures of Dollie*. Once launched as a director, Griffith found that he liked the speed and immediacy of film. Between 1908 and 1913, he directed roughly 450 short films, mining not only cinema's technical and narrative past but also Victorian literature and drama to create a style that owed much to his literary predecessors yet was deeply popular with the public. In addition, Griffith was not shy about touting his accomplishments, creating a public image as the sole narrative innovator in the industry and the inventor of cinematic grammar, which he manifestly was not. What Griffith brought to his films was a sense of speed, pacing, and an amalgamation of existing techniques to create a deeper use of close-ups, cross-cutting for suspense, the use of fade-outs to express the passage of time, and other refinements that gave his films a style all their own, along with his use of a recognizable stock company of players.

While his early films used intercutting of simultaneous events to create suspense—and *The Lonely Villa* (1909), for example, used a then-unprecedented number of camera setups to enhance the speed of the narrative—Griffith was most at home with the conventions of Victorian melodrama. Working with his favorite cameraman, G. W. "Billy" Bitzer, Griffith nevertheless enlarged the technical grammar of the cinema, and, like Alice Guy before him, insisted on rehearsals and on reducing actors' movements to make his scenarios seem more natural. At the same time, like Guy, Griffith cut across film genres, creating gangster films (*The Musketeers of Pig Alley,* 1912); "message" pictures that critiqued social ills (*A Corner in Wheat,* 1909); and a raft of westerns, romances, and comedies. However, by 1913 he was aware of the fact that European filmmakers were having commercial and critical success with longer films, such as Henri Desfontaines and Louis Mercanton's *Queen Elizabeth* (*Les Amours de la reine Élisabeth,* 1912), part of the *film d'art* movement, starring the great stage actress Sarah Bernhardt.

Billy Bitzer at the camera (left) and director D. W. Griffith (right) on the set of one of Griffith's films.

Even more influential for Griffith were Enrico Guazzoni's *Quo Vadis?* a nine-reel (roughly 120 minutes at silent speed) Italian film produced in 1912, which was released internationally to considerable acclaim, and Giovanni Pastrone's *Cabiria* (1914), another Italian epic that demonstrated that audiences were begging for both spectacle and lengthier narrative structures. Griffith had experimented with longer-format films as early as 1911's *Enoch Arden,* a two-reeler that was finally released in two parts, much to Griffith's displeasure. He therefore embarked upon the production of the four-reel *Judith of Bethulia* (1914), working in secret, with a budget of

A scene from *Queen Elizabeth* (1912), Henri Desfontaine and Louis Mercanton's *film d'art* starring Sarah Bernhardt (standing, right).

$18,000. The biblical melodrama was a success, allowing him to press ahead with the film for which he is best known, *The Birth of a Nation*.

This film reflects Griffith's stubborn prejudices, for which he is also well remembered. He was a deeply patriarchal director who viewed women as either icons of virtue or maidens in distress, and he was also a thoroughgoing racist. Like most of his films, *The Birth of a Nation* reflects a narrow worldview based on the director's limited social experience. A sweeping epic of the South during the Civil War, the film used meticulous period reconstructions, a large cast, and a then-unheard-of budget of $110,000. *The Birth of a Nation* opened at the Liberty Theater in New York on 3 March 1915, with a running time of nearly two and a half hours and an unprecedented admission price of two dollars. As commercial entertainment it was an immediate box office success. After viewing the film at the White House, President Woodrow Wilson said that "it is like writing history with lightning, and my one regret is that it is all so terribly true."

The film's final sequence, in which the Ku Klux Klan rescues Lillian Gish and Miriam Cooper from attempted rape by a band of marauding blacks, is one of the most astonishing and repellent sequences in motion picture history. Blacks protested in Boston even before the film opened, decrying the project's unrelenting racism, but Griffith, who had seen his family's fortunes brought low in the aftermath of the Civil War, felt that his portrayal of the conflict and its social ramifications was fair and evenhanded. The director was bewildered by the reaction of African American church leaders and organizations, insisting that the film was simply the truth and that he "loved the Negro." Both he and Thomas F. Dixon Jr., the author of the

24

books (*The Clansman* and *The Leopard's Spots*) upon which the film was based, reveled in the storm of controversy. Neither man admitted to the depth of the film's unrelenting racial hatred or to the damage that it caused to American race relations—including a revival of activities by the Klan, who used the film as a recruiting tool.

Technical sophistication notwithstanding, *The Birth of a Nation* remains at the center of debate and controversy. But it is important to note that the African American community responded to the release of the film with urgency, consistency, and organization. One African American filmmaker, Oscar Micheaux, made a film entitled *Within Our Gates* (1919) as a direct response to Griffith, alluding to white-on-black rapes and lynchings to counter the false and backward representations of black-on-white rape obsessions in *The Birth of a Nation*.

Griffith's ultimate response to his critics was to create the massive epic *Intolerance* (1916), intercutting four different narratives of social and political intolerance from history—war in Belshazzar's Babylon, the persecution of the Huguenots in Renaissance France, the story of a

A panoramic shot from D. W. Griffith's *Birth of a Nation* (1915).

young man wrongly accused in the then-contemporary slums of America, and the crucifixion of Jesus—to prove his point that revolutionary ideas have always been persecuted. As the shooting of *Intolerance* progressed, Griffith constructed massive sets to depict the bygone glories of Babylon and plowed nearly $1.9 million of his own money into the project, buying out his backers when they balked at both the length and expense of the picture. Before he was through filming, he had shot more than four hundred reels of film for the production, or about sixty-five hours of raw footage, and pro-

The famed Babylon set from D. W. Griffith's *Intolerance* (1916).

duced a final cut three and a half hours in length. The public reception, unfortunately, was disastrous. Audiences seemed confused by the interlocking quartet of narratives, linked only by the image of Lillian Gish rocking the "cradle of civilization," as the past and present collided in an overwhelming avalanche of images. Griffith soon realized that the film was both too ambitious and too abstract for commercial audiences and eventually withdrew it from circulation, leaving the Babylonian and modern sections of the film as two separate features in an attempt to recoup *Intolerance*'s staggering cost. But it was to no avail: the film was dead at the box office, and he would spend the next several years paying off the debts of his failed epic.

Griffith never recovered commercially; he retreated into more conventional Victorian melodramas such as *Orphans of the Storm* (1921) to pay the bills. When sound came, he was resolutely unable to adapt, and his final feature, *The Struggle* (1931), an earnest tract about the perils of alcoholism, was so dated that distributors changed the title to *Ten Nights in a Bar Room* and attempted to sell it as a comedy to increase revenue. Griffith reluctantly retired from the industry, except for rare public appearances at social events, and died, all but forgotten, in 1948.

LOIS WEBER

While Griffith labored on his epic films, other figures, both in the United States and abroad, were making their mark in the industry. Lois Weber, in particular, deserves attention. Born in 1881 in Allegheny, Pennsylvania, Weber was a child prodigy, touring as a concert pianist until the age of seventeen. Before she became an actress and director, she worked as a social activist. She began writing for early motion pictures at Gaumont, where she was known by her married name, Mrs. Phillips Smalley. After writing screenplays,

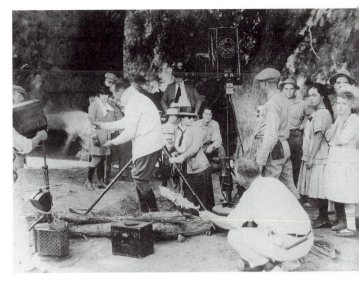

Lois Weber on the set (in hat, center), directing one of her many films.

she began acting in films with her husband at Gaumont, starring in a number of films directed by Herbert Blaché (husband of Alice Guy). Weber also directed many films, including early sound-on-disc shorts produced at Gaumont. She rapidly became one of the highest-paid directors in the industry and was associated with Edwin S. Porter, Carl Laemmle, and Hobart Bosworth in her business dealings. She was one of the first American women directors to head her own production unit, Lois Weber Productions, in 1917. In her own time, she was as well known as D. W. Griffith and Cecil B. De-Mille, but she was subsequently consigned to an insignificant footnote by film historians seeking to create masculine heroics in the industry's narrative history.

Her many films as director include *The Troubadour's Triumph* (1912), *The Jew's Christmas* (co-director, Phillips Smalley, 1913), *Hypocrites* (1915), *The Hand That Rocks the Cradle* (co-director, Phillips Smalley, 1917), *The Blot* (1921), and *What Do Men Want?* (1921). Although the bulk of her work was done in the silent era, she continued directing until 1934, helming the talkie *White Heat* (not to be confused with the 1949 Raoul Walsh film with James Cagney). In all her films, Weber dealt with social issues that she felt were of great importance—for example, birth control in *Where Are My Children?* (1916) and the plight of the poor academic class in *The Blot*. Weber's use of the camera shows great attention to little details, like the worn sofa in an in-

Lois Weber's social-problem drama *The Blot* (1921), with Claire Windsor and Louis Calhern.

digent professor's living room, or a meager snack of weak tea and crackers served to impress a guest; her search for realism extended to her use of natural-source lighting for exterior sequences and the use of actual locations, instead of sets, for establishing shots. Weber's characters are fully developed personalities rather than stock, instantly readable figures. In her early Universal/Jewel productions, she also experimented with color, using expressive blue, green, red, or yellow tints to enhance pictorial values.

THOMAS INCE

Another major figure during this formative era was Thomas Ince, who perhaps more than any other producer, except for Edison, put the motion picture industry on the map as a business. Ince got his start working for Carl Laemmle, perhaps the most industrious of the independent producers, one who would challenge Edison's domination of the motion picture business. As a director, Ince made a number of interesting and influential films, most notably *Civilization* (1916), a pacifist religious parable, but his lasting influence can best be felt as a producer in his introduction of the assembly-line system of studio production. Working with storyboards and using tight control over his directors, he decreed that the films he produced would be shot to order—that is, exactly as he planned. In this manner, he was able to oversee the production of numerous features simultaneously and worked with a number of major filmmak-

Thomas Ince, who created the prototype for the assembly-line studio system of mass production.

ers-to-be, including Henry King. But his cookie-cutter method reduced his directors to the status of glorified traffic cops, and thus the films he produced, while commercially successful, were creatively unadventurous.

Once Edison began cranking out his highly exploitative shorts, he attempted to monopolize the industry and created the Motion Picture Patents Company (also known as the Trust) in 1908, combining his own Edison operation with six other production companies—Essanay, Kalem, Lubin, Vitagraph, Biograph, and Selig—to create a massive company designed to dominate film production and distribution. To further consolidate his hold on the industry, he struck a deal with George Eastman, founder of Eastman Kodak, whereby Eastman would supply perforated celluloid film only to members of the Trust. Shortly afterward, the French companies Pathé, Méliès, and Gaumont joined the group, so that ten companies now controlled the bulk of motion picture production not only in the United States, but in Europe as well. Together, the members of the Trust cleared—through their wholly owned distribution arm, the General Film Company—$1.25 million per year.

CARL LAEMMLE AND THE TRUST

Carl Laemmle was the first to fight back. The future founder of Universal Pictures, Laemmle created the Laemmle Film Service, later known as the Independent Moving Pictures Company (IMP), and began a bedrock campaign to shake nickelodeon owners out of their torpor and challenge the Edison Trust. One of the claims that the Trust made was that their ownership of the film industry was based on the fact that each of the ten companies possessed patents that were essential in the production of motion pictures. In truth, the patents were all based on the same basic principles that had been set down by the Lumière brothers, Le Prince, and others years before, but rather than sue each other—which was the situation before Edison created the Trust—the nine companies decided to agree that, among them, they jointly held the requisite patents. Key among these patents was the Latham Loop, initially devised by

Carl Laemmle, the founder of IMP, and later Universal Pictures.

Woodville Latham, which kept projected motion pictures from jamming in the projection gate. Edison had acquired the patent from Latham in 1897 and launched suits against all his competitors at that time; in addition, Edison had also acquired a similar apparatus from inventor Thomas Armat in 1896.

The flurry of lawsuits that followed was designed to keep timid producers in a perpetual state of fear and obligation; to add insult to injury, in addition to forcing exhibitors to screen only films made by the Motion Picture Patents Company and distributed by the General Film Company, the same exhibitors also had to pay a $2.50 per week licensing fee simply for adhering to the Trust's dictates. This was in addition to the Trust's licensing fee of ten cents a foot for each film screened by any exhibitor.

Laemmle declared open war on the Trust, aided in a competitive way by William Fox, whose Fox Film Corporation more or less ignored the Trust's dictates. Laemmle went much further, ridiculing the Trust with satirical cartoons in trade newspapers and exhorting nickelodeon owners to "come out of it" and book films from Laemmle's rival exchange at a fraction of the cost. Edison responded, as he often did, with lawsuits, coercive action, and, when all else failed, violence, hiring gangs of armed thugs to smash the production and exhibition equipment of those rival producers, distributors, and exhibitors who defied him.

Laemmle's film exchange was a place where nickelodeon owners could rent, rather than buy, films for exhibition. When Edison tried to block exhibitors from screening Laemmle's existing supply of Edison Trust films, Laemmle began making shorts of his own for rental and used the industrious Thomas Ince as one of his key house directors—in time, Ince would direct some two hundred short attractions for Laemmle. In addition, a group of small companies—such as Majestic, Rex, Powers, and others—combined to form the Motion Picture Distributing and Sales Company, which directly confronted the Trust as a monopoly in court.

Finally, Carl Laemmle struck a decisive blow against the Trust in 1908 by luring actress Florence Lawrence, known as "The Biograph Girl," away from Biograph and signing her for his IMP Company, where she promptly became known as "the Imp Girl." Laemmle did this in part because he was willing to give her name billing, something that Biograph, as part of the Edison Trust, was loath to do. Edison felt that if the public didn't know the names of his actors, they wouldn't be able to increase their salary demands because of burgeoning popularity. Yet he failed to realize that a star's popularity could potentially sell a film to audiences on name value alone. Thus,

Laemmle created the star system as we know it today. To celebrate Lawrence's signing, he also staged an elaborate publicity campaign in which he claimed to debunk "the blackest and at the same time the silliest lie" that Lawrence had been accidentally killed by a streetcar in St. Louis. What Laemmle neglected to mention in the splashy series of ads—all with the banner headline "We Nail a Lie"—was that he himself had started the rumors in order to generate publicity for Lawrence's signing. Nevertheless, the ruse worked, and Florence Lawrence went on to become one of IMP's major early stars.

All this was too much for Edison and his Trust compatriots, and soon the Motion Picture Patents Company was tied up in a seemingly endless round of litigation. In 1915, the courts ruled that the Trust was, in fact, a monopoly, and Edison's scheme collapsed. The independents had won and such producers as Laemmle, Adolph Zukor, Jesse Lasky, Samuel Goldwyn, Louis B. Mayer, and others rushed in to fill the need for product, creating a dynamic and highly competitive studio system that survives to the present day, in such companies as Twentieth Century Fox, MGM, Paramount, Universal, and what became other major Hollywood studios.

THE ROAD WEST

This was another major change from the days of Edison—film production was now firmly anchored on the West Coast, and by the time D. W. Griffith produced *Intolerance* in Los Angeles in 1916, 60 percent or more of the industry was located there. New York, however, remained a powerful force in the financing and distribution of motion pictures, and all the major studios maintained East Coast branches to keep abreast of new developments in the theatrical world (then as now centered on Broadway, with vaudeville—live song and dance theaters—added to the mix). The weather in Los Angeles was also more reliable, so that film production could continue uninterrupted.

What brought the film companies to Hollywood was, in truth, a range of reasons. The constant sunshine was one factor, as well as the greater variety of filming locations. Another reason was the distance from Edison's Trust. In addition, the West Coast provided producers the opportunity to juggle checks from banks all the way across the country. Some of the smaller companies in Los Angeles would draw a check on a New York bank, rush into production with a short film, and then quickly release the film to exhibitors.

By the time the box office takings were in, they could cover the New York bank draft—or, if necessary, another check drawn on a Los Angeles bank could temporarily cover the overdraft. Thus, some of the nervier independents obtained free bank loans for their films, although the practice was discontinued as soon as a more sound financial footing was achieved.

By this time, Hollywood received a second shot in the arm, in the unlikely form of World War I. From 1914 to 1918, while the rest of the world concentrated on fighting the innumerable battles of the war, America kept cranking out a steady stream of film productions for international distribution. With their native studios on virtual hiatus, the rest of the world gobbled up Hollywood product, which was easy to export, particularly given the fact that since all films were silent, all that was needed for foreign audiences was a new set of intertitles.

CHARLES CHAPLIN

Other key American filmmakers of the period included producer/director Mack Sennett, whose Keystone Film Company's slapstick comedies emphasized action and fast-paced, pie-in-the-face comedy over narrative subtlety. Sennett's most famous discovery was undoubtedly Charles Chaplin, whom he found working with an English music hall troupe. In his second film for Sennett, *Kid Auto Races at Venice*

The Keystone Kops in action.

(1914), Chaplin created for the first time the basic structure of his famous Little Tramp character, in a brief and completely plotless film that was typical of Sennett's output. To save money, Sennett would often build his short films around real-life events, and in this case he sent Chaplin and a two-man crew to film a soapbox derby race in Venice, California. The film's entire running gag consisted of Chaplin trying to get into the newsreel footage of the race and being repeatedly thrown out by irate officials in the process.

Sennett also invented the famous Keystone Kops troupe, a group of slap-

32

stick performers who pretended to be policemen, and whose exploits invariably included wild chases, car crashes, pie fights, and spectacular stunts. But Chaplin was easily Keystone's biggest star, and his rise was meteoric. Sennett hired him in 1913 at $150 a week for Keystone; by 1918, he had signed a $1 million deal for eight films a year with First National Studios, after moving rapidly through Keystone, Essanay Studios, and Mutual Pictures on his way to international superstardom. The silent film was the perfect medium for Chaplin's Little Tramp character and his delicate pantomime. Over time, however, Chaplin's portrayals grew more expressive and less frenetic as he began to exert more control over his work, serving as producer, writer, director, and star on his best short films.

Chaplin, too, was one of the first stars to take over the day-to-day operation of his own business affairs, founding United Artists Studios with Griffith, action star Douglas Fairbanks Sr., and silent ingénue Mary Pickford in 1919. His first feature, *The Kid* (1921), was an international success, and he soon moved on to make the masterful comedy *The Gold Rush* (1925), which many consider his finest film. The deeply felt romance *City Lights* (1931), a silent with musical accompaniment (scored by Chaplin himself), was also a hit with critics and audiences. Chaplin was one of the last American holdouts against sound, convinced that the introduction of spoken dialogue would rob the Little Tramp of much of his pathos, humor, and universal humanity.

THE RISE OF THE STUDIO SYSTEM

It was during the teens in Hollywood, too, that the major studios as we know them today began to take shape. Carl Laemmle folded his IMP Company into a group of smaller companies to create Universal Pictures in 1912; the aforementioned William Fox, Laemmle's ally in the war against the Edison Trust, created the Fox Film Corporation in 1915; it would later merge with Twentieth Century Pictures in 1935, under impresario Darryl F. Zanuck. Metro Goldwyn Mayer (MGM), with its famous lion logo at the start of each film and the motto "Ars Gratia Artis" (Art for Art's Sake) boldly emblazoned across the screen, followed in 1924, rising out the combined talents of Samuel Goldwyn, Marcus Loew, Louis B. Mayer, and financial wizard Nicholas Schenck. Goldwyn would soon leave the group to form the eponymous Goldwyn Pictures, and Louis B. Mayer would become undisputed chief of production for decades, although he, too, had to answer to Schenck, whose offices were in New York, on all major financial matters. Adolph Zukor's Famous Players merged with Jesse Lasky's Feature Play Company to form Paramount Pictures (also known as Paramount Publix), using the Paramount distribution exchange to market their pictures to a series of wholly owned theaters across the United States; by the mid-1930s, Paramount would effectively have a monopoly on film production and distribution through Zukor's strategy of "vertical integration," in which studio-owned theaters could play only Paramount product, thus ensuring a steady market for the studio's films.

Jack, Sam, Albert, and Harry Warner formed Warner Bros. in 1923; soon, Jack L. Warner emerged as the head of production in Hollywood though he also had to answer to a higher power—in his case his brother Harry—on matters of finance. United Artists was moving along at a solid clip, buoyed by the success of Mary Pickford's star vehicles and Douglas Fairbanks Sr.'s swashbucklers. Columbia Pictures was founded by Jack and Harry Cohn in 1924, with Jack emerging as the financial czar and Harry as perhaps the most ruthless studio boss in Hollywood, eventually nicknamed "White Fang" by writer Ben Hecht and later "King Cohn" for his brutal manner of doing business. But although Harry Cohn may have been the most abrasive of the studio bosses, all these men were exceptionally tough businessmen in a business that was rapidly consolidating its hold on the American public.

In addition to the majors, a number of minor studios would eventually join the Hollywood roster. These included Herbert J. Yates's Republic Pictures, which specialized in westerns and children's serials and absorbed the smaller Mascot Pictures corporation of Nat Levine, which also dealt primarily in action fare; Monogram, which would come to its greatest prominence in the 1940s as the home of an interminable series of Bela Lugosi horror movies and Bowery Boys comedies; and Producers' Releasing Corporation (PRC), reputedly the cheapest studio in Hollywood history, where two-day westerns were cranked out with alarming regularity in the 1940s, along with five-day film noirs dealing with the darker side of human existence. RKO Radio Pictures joined this group of minor studios in the early 1930s, and thus the players in the American film industry for the greater part of the twentieth century was set in a matter of a few years. In the 1950s, such independents as American International Pictures would come along to challenge the system, but from the 1910s through 1955, the majors reigned supreme. There were, of course, exceptions. Although he released his films through United Artists, Chaplin remained a true independent, with his own studio facility in Los Angeles (now the home of A & M Records).

EARLY MOVIE STARS

While Chaplin was one of the greatest of the early cinema stars, he had considerable competition from a number of newcomers, many of whom, like Chaplin, hailed from vaudeville or the music hall stage. John Bunny, a rotund comic, became the screen's first lovable fat man until his death in 1915; Francis X. Bushman and Beverly Bayne were one of the screen's first romantic teams—married in real life, they were forced to keep their nuptials a secret to appease their fans. Alla Nazimova became the screen's first sophisticated European leading lady in such films as *Billions* (1920), while Mary Pickford, whose salary demands rivaled those of Chaplin, was dubbed "America's sweetheart" for a succession of films in which she portrayed a poor young woman adrift in an often hostile world, such as Paul Powell's *Pollyanna* (1920). Pickford's later films used oversized props and children's clothing to continue the deception that she was still the ageless young waif of her earlier films. When sound came, Pickford failed to adapt and shortly thereafter retired from the screen.

"Instant read" typecasting also became popular, with a readily recognizable hero and heroine as the center of the plot, attended to or menaced by a gallery of iconic maternal and paternal figures, swarthy villains, or seductive women, better known as vamps. Theda Bara (real name Theodosia Goodman) became the screen's first *femme fatale* in her groundbreaking vehicle *A Fool There Was* (1915), starting a craze for decadent romances that lasted throughout the 1910s and revived in a slightly less theatrical manner in the 1940s.

Mary Pickford (center, seated) in Paul Powell's *Pollyanna* (1920).

Mabel Normand, a Mack Sennett protégée, was perhaps the screen's greatest silent comedienne, and also tried her hand at directing. Outrageous comics like Ben Turpin (famous for his trademark crossed eyes); Roscoe "Fatty" Arbuckle, an amply proportioned slapstick comedy master; and Larry Semon, an expert in pie fights and thrill chase comedies, all took their place on the

Buster Keaton in *The General* (1927), co-directed by Keaton and comedy specialist Clyde Bruckman.

screen. Along with Chaplin, the most important comics of the era were undoubtedly Buster Keaton and Harold Lloyd, both masters of the sight gag, but in a very different fashion.

Keaton entered the cinematic arena in 1917 and worked mostly with Fatty Arbuckle in his initial efforts. But by 1919, following Chaplin's example, Keaton opened his own production company and created some of his finest short films, such as *Cops* (1922) and *The Balloonatic* (1923), both co-directed by the gifted Edward F. Cline. By 1924, with *Sherlock Jr.,* he had entered feature filmmaking with a decisive impact, and he followed it up with *The General* (1927, co-directed with Clyde Bruckman), often acknowledged to be his finest film. *The General*'s plot is classic Keaton: as Johnny, a would-be soldier for the South during the Civil War, Keaton is turned down for service because he is more useful to the Confederacy as a railroad engineer. Johnny must overcome the scorn of his comrades and the indifference of his girlfriend, Annabelle, by using his beloved locomotive, nicknamed the General, to assist the South in a crucial battle against the Union forces. The slap-stick sequences, involving pratfalls, misfiring cannons, and a collapsing railroad bridge, are expertly woven together in a semi-serious narrative depicting the brutality of the Civil War, all orchestrated to brilliant effect.

Keaton's humor derived from his lack of expression or emotion, no matter how perilous the situation in which he might find himself. Nicknamed

Harold Lloyd in Fred Newmeyer and Sam Taylor's *Safety Last* (1923).

"the Great Stoneface," he remained seemingly impassive in the face of perpetual comic disaster and enjoyed his greatest success during the silent era. With the coming of sound, his roles diminished, and he was often teamed—much to his detriment—with the fast-talking verbal comedian Jimmy Durante.

Harold Lloyd had much the same career trajectory; a specialist in "thrill" comedy, Lloyd would climb buildings and seemingly risk his life in such classic shorts as Fred C. Newmeyer and Sam Taylor's *Safety Last* (1923), in which his fresh-faced persona seemed at odds with the danger his character incessantly courted on the screen. Lloyd did many of his own stunts, though he "cheated" distance and perspective in some of his most ambitious thrill comedies to heighten the effect. Born in Nebraska in 1893, he began his career working for Edison and later moved over to Mack Sennett's Keystone Studios, but the two comic geniuses didn't click. It was at Hal Roach's studio that Roach and Lloyd came up with the basic character for Lloyd's most successful screen comedies: a mild-mannered, bespectacled man, unwittingly caught in situations of dire peril. By the 1920s, such films as Newmeyer and Taylor's *The Freshman* (1925) and Ted Wilde's *Speedy* (1928) had cemented Lloyd's reputation as the king of comedy thrills. Sound, however, did little to

37

enhance his career, and he made his last film in 1947, Preston Sturges's *The Sin of Harold Diddlebock* (a k a *Mad Wednesday*).

Early film serials, such as Charles Brabin's *What Happened to Mary?* (1912), Louis J. Gasnier and Donald MacKenzie's *The Perils of Pauline* (1914), and Howard Hansel's *The Million Dollar Mystery* (1914), introduced audiences to the self-reliant heroine, in stories that ran as long as twenty chapters or more. Each new installment played weekly, leaving the protagonist in impossible danger in a cliffhanger ending, only to find a way to safety in the next installment. In the wake of "Broncho Billy" Anderson, whose cowboy films were by his own admission fanciful romances, former Shakespearean actor William S. Hart brought a new realism to the screen, directing and appearing in such westerns as *The Gun Fighter* (1917). Hart's films galvanized the public with a new vision of the West as a hostile, unforgiving terrain. In contrast to Broncho Billy's films, many of Hart's westerns have tragic endings. He typically portrayed women as vamps or seductresses, bent on his own character's destruction. Using spare sets, harsh lighting, minimal makeup, and scenarios that highlighted suffering and pathos, his vision of the West is closest to films of Clint Eastwood, such as *Unforgiven* (1992), in their uncompromising depiction of the desolate American frontier.

Other stars of the period included Pola Negri, a seductive vamp of the period who also excelled in straight dramatic roles, such as in Ernst Lubitsch's *Forbidden Paradise* (1924), and Clara Bow, known as the "It" girl for her numerous portrayals of flaming youth run wild in the early 1920s (the name derived from her vivacious appearance, with plenty of sex appeal, in Clarence G. Badger's 1927 film *It*). Rudolph Valentino was the personification of the Latin lover, in a series of ornate costume dramas such as Joseph Henabery's *A Sainted Devil* (1924), Rex Ingram's *The Four Horsemen of the Apocalypse* (1921), and his signature role in George

Rudolph Valentino in George Melford's *The Sheik* (1921), an icon of 1920s romance.

Stan Laurel and Oliver Hardy play their own children with the aid of oversized sets and props in James Parrott's comedy short *Brats* (1930).

Melford's *The Sheik* (1921). Rin Tin Tin became one of the first animal stars, as the "wonder dog" who could do anything—a precursor of Lassie. Horror films boosted the great Lon Chaney Sr., better known as "the Man of a Thousand Faces," who dominated the genre in the 1920s with such films as Wallace Worsley's *The Hunchback of Notre Dame* (1923) and Rupert Julian's *The Phantom of the Opera* (1925). Though in his early years he also worked as a writer and director, Chaney, an expert at makeup, created all the fantastic faces for which he became known as an actor, appearing in over 150 films before his death in 1930, shortly after the release of his only talking film, Jack Conway's *The Unholy Three*, a remake of his 1925 hit film (directed by Tod Browning) of the same name.

Two comics who easily made the transition from silent film to sound were Stan Laurel and Oliver Hardy, who first teamed together in Fred Guiol's *Slipping Wives* (1927) and quickly became one of the most popular and influential teams in cinema history, with such films as James Parrott's *Brats* (1930), Ray McCarey's *Scram!* (1932), and their only film to win an Academy Award as Best Short Subject, Parrott's *The Music Box* (1932). The original "dumb and dumber" comedy team, Laurel and Hardy (Laurel, thin and perpetually bewildered; Hardy, stout and aggressive, yet equally confused) soon became cult figures whose popularity survives to the present day. Specialists in physical comedy, they made even the simplest task (such as moving a piano into a house in *The Music Box*) outrageously difficult and habitually left destruction and chaos in their wake.

SHOWMANSHIP, SCANDAL, AND SPECTACLE

The era also saw the rise of the movie palace, as marble nickelodeons became splendid pleasure domes dedicated to public entertainment, such as Radio City Music Hall in New York and the Roxy in Los Angeles. Paramount began an aggressive policy of theater ownership to make sure that their films would find an appreciative audience, and instituted the policies of block booking (in which a theater owner had to take an entire slate of films from a studio, including lesser ones, in order to get the hit films) and blind bidding (in which theater owners were forced to bid on a hot film sight unseen, and play it no matter what it eventually turned out to be). Although block booking and blind bidding were eventually outlawed, the practice continues today in a subterranean fashion; theater chains that don't regularly play a studio's minor films are sometimes denied a shot at more lucrative titles.

And yet, in the midst of all this production and prosperity, a storm was brewing. It would not fully come to a boil until 1934, the early sound era, but the 1920s saw the beginning of a phenomenon that the studios both feared and ultimately capitulated to: organized censorship. A series of scandals erupted, including the murder of director William Desmond Taylor in 1922, who left behind love letters naming the popular stars Mabel Normand and Mary Miles Minter as two of his better-known paramours. Also in 1922, Fatty Arbuckle was indicted in the death of young star Virginia Rappe; it was said that Arbuckle had raped her at a party that had turned into an orgy, although Arbuckle was eventually acquitted of the charge. Arbuckle, Minter, and Normand were all forced to leave the screen as a result of the ensuing bad publicity; pathetically, Arbuckle tried to make a comeback several years later under the name Will B. Good, but to no avail. At the same time, one of the silent era's most popular stars, Wallace Reid, died in 1923 as a result of morphine addiction and alcoholism at the age of thirty-one, and mainstream America demanded that the motion picture industry clean house.

In late 1922, the motion picture studios chose Will H. Hays, then the postmaster general in the Harding administration, to head the newly formed Motion Picture Producers and Distributors of America, or the

Director Dorothy Davenport Reid (left) and scenarist Adela Rogers St. Johns, who wrote many screenplays during her long career as a writer, and often worked with Reid, seen here in the early 1920s.

MPPDA. Soon known informally as the Hays Office, the MPPDA set about to police the private lives of the stars, inserting morality clauses in the contracts of all studio personnel that subjected them to immediate dismissal if they failed to live up to a stringent code of personal conduct. Not coincidentally, Wallace Reid's wife, actress Dorothy Davenport Reid, became a director in 1923 with her production of *Human Wreckage* (in which she also starred), about the evils of narcotics—made with the approval and assistance of the Hays Office.

CECIL B. DEMILLE

The chief benefactor of the new code was director Cecil B. DeMille, an energetic showman who soon set about making a series of transparently moralistic features such as *Old Wives for New* (1918), *Don't Change Your Husband* (1919), and *The Ten Commandments* (1923). Each offered spectacles of sin and destruction, but with a difference: the last reel of each DeMille film showed miscreants being firmly punished. So long as such behavior was not condoned, DeMille was able to get away with a great deal of sex and violence

41

on the screen. *The Ten Commandments* (which DeMille would remake in 1956) featured the familiar biblical story intercut with a modern tragedy of greed, sin, and decadence in which a young married man, intent on making quick money, falls in with a scheming adventuress and eventually contracts leprosy as a result of their relationship. In a blind rage, he murders her. Needless to say, the young man pays dearly for his transgressions, killed in an accident as he seeks to escape from the punishment he so obviously deserves. Thus was established the typical DeMille formula; sin, sex, and titillation—but in the end, adherence to an absolute moral code.

ROBERT FLAHERTY

At the same time, Robert J. Flaherty was busy creating a new form: the popular documentary. Flaherty's *Nanook of the North* (1922) was the first straight documentary film that was also a commercial success, detailing the daily life and hardships of the Eskimo Nanook and his family, who lived, hunted, and built igloos in Hudson Bay, Canada. *Nanook* was actually Flaherty's second stab at the film; in 1913, he shot 35,000 feet of 35 mm film in the same area, documenting Eskimo life, but the cellulose nitrate film was destroyed in the cutting room when Flaherty accidentally dropped a lit cigarette on the master negative, and the entire film went up in flames. In 1920, he again set out for the frozen north, this time with $50,000 in backing from Revillon Frères, the fur merchants. His equipment included a portable developing lab, so that he could process his film on location and view the rushes to see if he was satisfied. This time, Flaherty was more careful in the editing process, and the finished film (much of it staged for the cameras, despite its documentary feel) was distributed internationally to critical acclaim and excellent returns. The drama of the film arose from Nanook's ceaseless struggle against the elements, simply trying to survive from one day to the next; ironically, Nanook himself died of starvation not long after the film was completed.

Robert Flaherty's pioneering documentary *Nanook of the North* (1922).

Flaherty's second feature, *Moana* (1926), was a poetic tale of the South Seas and more specifically life in Samoa, but it failed to ignite the same degree of public interest. The director was then asked by MGM to collaborate with W. S. Van Dyke on the 1928 melodrama *White Shadows in the South Seas,* but the workmanlike Van Dyke (who would later rise to fame as the director of the *Thin Man* series of detective mysteries, starting in 1934) soon clashed with Flaherty, and Flaherty was taken off the film. In 1929, he teamed with German director F. W. Murnau to create *Tabu;* again, he clashed with his co-director, and Murnau took over the completion of the film, released in 1931, which emerged as a dark, melodramatic project. Subsequent films by Flaherty include *Man of Aran* (1934), about fishermen working off the coast of Ireland, which is perhaps the purest of his later films, along with two sponsored films, *The Land* (1942), created for the U.S. Department of Agriculture, and *Louisiana Story* (1948), which was financed by the oil company that became Exxon. Flaherty's independence and uncompromising spirit kept him out of cinema's mainstream, and he never re-created the impact of *Nanook of the North.*

Recent scholarship has uncovered the fact that Flaherty staged many sequences in *Nanook* and his other ethnographic films for the convenience of the cameraman and/or greater dramatic effect. Nevertheless, by shooting on location and using non-actors as his protagonists, Flaherty's partially staged documentaries created a new film genre.

THE MAN YOU LOVE TO HATE

Another major figure of the late silent era, and a tragic one, was Erich von Stroheim, who sought to make films of extreme naturalism and went to what some viewed as excessive lengths to achieve his ambition. Von Stroheim viewed society as inherently decadent and cast himself in the lead of many of his films, notably *Foolish Wives* (1922), in which he plays a vile seducer who preys upon innocent women, a role that he relished. Billed as "the Man You Love to Hate," von Stroheim's intense desire for realism drove him to spend more than a million dollars to create *Foolish Wives,* a record at the time.

Von Stroheim's jaundiced view of society reached its pinnacle in *Greed,* completed in 1924 after nearly two years of shooting for Metro-Goldwyn Pictures Corporation. Based on Frank Norris's novel *McTeague,* the film is a bleak story of human frailty and despair. But what happened to the film itself is even more dispiriting. Von Stroheim's final cut ran forty-two reels, at a

Erich von Stroheim and Mae Busch in
von Stroheim's *Foolish Wives* (1922).

time when a standard feature might run ten to fourteen reels. He suggested that half the film could be shown in the afternoon, and then, after a break for dinner, the second half. Goldwyn would have none of this and forced the director to cut the film to a mere twenty-four reels, then ruled that even this was too long for theatrical release. Eventually von Stroheim's friend, the director Rex Ingram, cut the film to eighteen reels. But even this cut was deemed too long by Irving Thalberg, the newly appointed head of production at what had by this time become MGM, who ordered the film cut to ten reels, no matter the damage. Further, Thalberg saw to it that all the trimmed scenes and outtakes were destroyed, melted down for their silver nitrate content, so that von Stroheim's original cut could never be reconstituted. Those who had seen the forty-two-reel version, or even Ingram's eighteen-reel version, wept when they saw the drastically cut result on the screen. Jumbled, choppy, and often incoherent, the final ten-reel version of *Greed* still displayed undeniable touches of cinematic brilliance, but von Stroheim's reputation had been destroyed.

Labeled hard to work with, von Stroheim soon left MGM after one more film, *The Merry Widow* (1925). Moving to Paramount, he fared little better, creating *The Wedding March* (1928), another exceedingly long opus that went over budget. On *Queen Kelly* (1929), an independent production, he was backed by financier Joseph P. Kennedy, with Gloria Swanson, one of the silent era's greatest stars, in the leading role. But Swanson detested von Stroheim and fired him before shooting was complete; Swanson then finished the film with another director, and von Stroheim predictably disowned the film. Finally landing at Fox, he began his only talkie as a director, *Hello, Sister* (a k a *Walking Down Broadway*, 1933), but again the film was taken away from him and extensively reshot and reedited by others (Alfred L. Werker, Alan Crosland, Raoul Walsh). From 1933, von Stroheim had to support himself as an actor and be content with the international acclaim he had received for his silent efforts. He never directed a film again.

EARLY AFRICAN AMERICAN FILMMAKERS

The first African American director was William Foster, whose Foster Photoplay Company opened its doors in Chicago in 1910. Lacking any camera equipment, he borrowed a portable 35 mm camera from a local photography shop and taught himself how to use it. Foster, who used his full-time job as stage manager for the Pekin Theatre to recruit actors, wrote, produced, photographed, and directed eighteen short films in 1910 and 1911. His early films included *The Birth Mark* (1910), *The Butler* (1910), and *The Railroad Porter* (1911), all with financing from white backers. But lacking any real distribution set-up beyond the Midwest, his company was forced to dissolve due to lack of funds. Nevertheless, he remained convinced that African Americans should make films for themselves, and his groundbreaking productions served as a model for better-known black directors who followed.

In the early 1910s, "race" films began to make their appearance throughout the United States, with all-black casts and production crews, and screened in rented halls, churches, and segregated theaters that formed an underground circuit of movie venues that catered specifically to African American audiences. A few theaters on the racially segregated TOBA (Theatre Owners Booking Agency), which specialized in live vaudeville or music hall presentations, would also occasionally run a film as part of their program. These race films, made on impoverished budgets, flourished through the late 1940s, long after the medium had converted to sound, giving blacks entertainment they could directly identify with, rather than the all-white films that Hollywood and other production centers worldwide produced. It was only as mainstream cinema began to belatedly recognize the importance of African American culture in the early 1950s to the present day that the race film market collapsed and with it, the segregated theaters in which the films were presented.

The race film was pioneered by actor Noble Johnson's Lincoln Motion Picture Company, which he founded on 24 May 1916 with his brother George to produce films of moral uplift for African American audiences. The company's first film, *The Realization of a Negro's Ambition* (1916), was an "up from the bootstraps" film, in which a young man leaves home to find success in the world. This was followed by the wartime drama *A Trooper of Cavalry K* (1917), *The Sage-Brush League* (1919), and Lincoln's final film as a production company, *By Right of Birth* (1921). However, though these films were produced by and starred African Americans, they were all directed by

Harry A. Gant, a white director who continued making all-black films into the sound era, with such productions as the musical *Georgia Rose* (1930). The Lincoln Motion Picture Company worked hard to gain distribution for its films, but in the end the company was forced to close its doors in 1921, and Noble Johnson went back to work as an actor in mainstream Hollywood films, appearing in numerous films in supporting roles, such as Irving Pichel's *The Most Dangerous Game* (1932), in which Johnson played a Russian Cossack.

The most prolific and important African American filmmaker in the United States during this period was Oscar Micheaux. Born on a small farm outside of Metropolis, Illinois, Micheaux started his creative career as a writer. Although his novels, such as *The Conquest: The Story of a Negro Pioneer* (1913) and *The Homesteader* (1917) were self-published with little or no publicity, he managed to make a living for a time selling copies of them from door to door. But when the Lincoln Motion Picture Company tried to buy the rights to *The Homesteader* for a movie, partly in response to the release of *The Birth of a Nation,* he held out to direct. The company refused to accept his conditions, so he raised the money and directed the film himself in 1919. Micheaux followed this up with his searing tale of racial prejudice in modern America, *Within Our Gates* (1920), which he wrote and directed. With a violent story line involving rape and lynching, the film was controversial from the start, but the director kept on making films, often self-financed, and distributed them on a "state's rights" basis, moving from town to town across the country until he had made enough money for his next production.

Micheaux made many silent films—more than twenty in all—writing the scripts, casting for actors in music halls and cabarets, completing his features in short periods on painfully low budgets, sometimes as low as $5,000. In 1925, he scored a coup with the casting of African American singer-activist Paul Robeson in the silent film *Body and Soul,* and then produced the first sound film directed by an African American, *The Exile,* in 1931. Although Micheaux's films moved away from the then-current stereotypes of blacks as servants and comic buffoons, they failed to acknowledge the existence of black poverty in America and existed in an artificially created world in which all blacks were well off and well educated and lived in a separate-but-equal world of their own. Because of this, they were often criticized by the African American press of the era.

Micheaux's later sound films, such as *The Girl from Chicago* (1932), are similarly low-budget affairs, but as time went on his work became increasingly controversial. *God's Step Children* (1938) was picketed by pro-Communist groups protesting its theme of "passing for white," something that Micheaux explored in many of his films. Having actually acquired a mainstream distributor, RKO, Micheaux was heartbroken when the company was forced to cease distribution. The director fell back into obscurity for a number of years afterward, but reemerged in 1948 with his final production, *The Betrayal*, which was extensively reviewed in both the black and the white press. With the rediscovery of several of Micheaux's "lost" films—among them the revolutionary exposé *The Symbol of the Unconquered* (*A Story of the Ku Klux Klan*), made in 1920—a complete reassessment of his work is now an ongoing project for many film historians. Micheaux is undoubtedly one of the most complex and underappreciated filmmakers, and also one of the most culturally important, in American film history. Though there are many production flaws in his low-budget films, it is a miracle they were made at all in view of the unremitting racism of the period, and they stand as a testament to Micheaux's unwavering determination as an artist and social critic.

In the wake of Micheaux's work, several other African American filmmakers also began to enter the field, the most important of which was Spencer Williams. An actor who financed his productions through white backers, Williams broke into the race film market with the religious parable *The Blood of Jesus* (1941), in which he also starred, and then continued with a wide variety of genre films including *Dirty Gertie from Harlem U.S.A.* (1946), an uncredited version of Somerset Maugham's short story "Rain," and *Jivin' in Be-Bop* (1946, co-directed with Leonard Anderson), which served as a showcase for jazz greats Dizzy Gillespie, Milt Jackson, and Ray Brown.

After his final film as a director, *Rhapsody of Negro Life* (1949), Williams returned to acting full-time, ironically cast as Andy in the television series "Amos 'n' Andy," based on the long-running, deeply racist radio show that was a national hit in the 1930s and 1940s. Williams directed eleven feature films in all, running the gamut from moral fables to escapist musicals, and was a more commercial director than Micheaux, who as the writer, director, and producer of his forty-one films had a more direct social message in his work. But these pioneers, until recently forgotten by many, paved the way for such artists as Spike Lee in the 1980s, when a number of African American directors were at last restored to the director's chair.

SILENT MOVIE MASTERS

Despite the fact that the studio system often stifled individual creativity, a number of gifted filmmakers managed to strike a balance between art and

The chariot race from Fred Niblo's *Ben-Hur* (1925).

commerce and adapted to the studio system, making personal films that were also commercially successful. Allan Dwan, Rupert Julian, Henry King, and Fred Niblo all made expert genre films ranging from melodramas to action spectacles, and Dwan and King went on to long and distinguished careers in the sound era. Niblo's *Ben-Hur* (1925), with a chariot race supervised by action director B. Reeves "Breezy" Eason, was a huge commercial success, while John Ford

began his long love affair with the western directing *The Iron Horse* (1924). Harry O. Hoyt's *The Lost World* (1925) was an early version of Sir Arthur Conan Doyle's classic story about a scientific expedition that encounters prehistoric monsters during a jungle trek; the film's special effects were deftly handled by Willis H. O'Brien, who would later work his magic in the classic *King Kong* in 1933, directed by Merian C. Cooper and Ernest B. Schoedsack. King Vidor's *The Crowd* (1928) depicted the dehumanizing world of big business with brutal accuracy, while Josef von Sternberg's *The Salvation Hunters* (1925)

Greta Garbo, one of the most enigmatic stars of 1930s Hollywood.

consisted of a series of motionless tableaux depicting the drabness of everyday life.

Clarence Brown, a director of silent films known for his romantic lyricism, began directing in 1920. After spending time as an assistant to director Maurice Tourneur, Brown established himself as a director with *The Eagle* (1925), starring screen heartthrob Rudolph Valentino. Above all, Brown was widely respected as Greta Garbo's most accomplished director, guiding the star through the silent films *Flesh and the Devil* (1927) and *A Woman of Affairs* (1928) and directing five of her most successful sound films, including her debut talkie *Anna Christie* (1930), *Anna Karenina* (1935), and *Conquest* (1937). With his late film *Intruder in the Dust* (1950), Brown used his considerable storytelling abilities to create a social message film that is a striking plea for racial tolerance.

Swedish director Mauritz Stiller was imported to the United States by MGM,

Michael Curtiz (far right in suit, seated on ladder) directs a crane shot for his film *20,000 Years in Sing Sing* (1932).

bringing with him a young Greta Garbo as his protégé. While Stiller failed to click as a director in Hollywood, Garbo's first film, Monta Bell's *Torrent* (1926), electrified both critics and audiences, and a new star was born in the celluloid firmament. Other European directors who were lured to Hollywood in the final days of the silent era included Ernst Lubitsch, whose sophisticated sex comedies such as *The Marriage Circle* (1924) and *So This Is Paris* (1926) marked the beginning of a long career that would stretch into the 1940s in Hollywood, and the Hungarian Michael Curtiz, who began with silents and would later become one of Warner Bros.' most prolific directors. One of Curtiz's key early works was *20,000 Years in Sing Sing* (1932), in which tough con Tom Connors (Spencer Tracy) battles his way through prison life in brutally fatalistic fashion.

49

THE MOVE TO SOUND

But behind the scenes in the late 1920s, a revolution was brewing. Lee de Forest, the pioneer inventor who created the vacuum tube, the television picture tube, and the modern optical sound track system that was used in talking pictures for most of the twentieth century, was busily working in his small laboratory to bring synchronized sound to film. By 1923, de Forest had already licked the basic problems of recording sound on film; but while de Forest used his sound process in a number of short novelty films, it was up to Warner Bros., perhaps the most thinly capitalized of the major studios, to make the first feature film with talking sequences in 1927's *The Jazz Singer*, directed by Alan Crosland. Calling their rival process Vitaphone, Warner Bros. lured Al Jolson away from Broadway to play the title role in the film, about the son of a Jewish cantor who refuses to follow in his father's footsteps, preferring to sing jazz music.

Warners was alone in embracing sound; at the time, all the other major studios considered talking films a fad, and Warners only went ahead with Vitaphone because without some kind of gamble the studio faced almost certain bankruptcy. Sound was seen as a gimmick, not something for everyday use, a fad of

Al Jolson sings in Alan Crosland's *The Jazz Singer* (1927), the first widely distributed part-talking feature film.

which the public would soon grow tired. After all, Vitaphone short sound films had been around since 6 August 1926, when chief censor Will Hays, speaking on film, presented a series of Vitaphone shorts that combined, in Hays's words, "pictures and music" to create a convincing illusion of reality. The Vitaphone shorts had gone over well with audiences—but a feature? In fact, most of *The Jazz Singer* is silent, with music and sound effects added later, but in the few, brief sound segments of the film (recorded on separate discs, and then played back in electronic synchronization with the film image, rather than being photographed on the side of the film as striations of light and dark in the de Forest "variable density" optical sound method), Al Jolson captivated audiences with his ad-libs, including the famous line, "Wait a minute—wait a minute, I tell you! You ain't heard nothin' yet!" Almost overnight, silent films

A location scene from King Vidor's early sound film *Hallelujah!* (1929), which used a largely African American cast.

were nothing more than a memory. The major studios climbed reluctantly on board and adopted the sound-on-film method as more reliable than the Vitaphone disc process.

As a result, intertitles quickly vanished from films, as Broadway actors and writers were imported to Hollywood by the trainload to create "canned drama," or "teacup drama," in which the camera, immobile and positioned inside a soundproof, asbestos-lined booth, simply recorded the action and dialogue in one take. The inventiveness of the silent cinema was instantaneously jettisoned in favor of the "all-talking" film, the first completely sound film being Warners' *Lights of New York* (1928), a gangster melodrama indifferently directed by Bryan Foy. But quality, for the moment, didn't matter. The actors spoke, the dialogue was clearly recorded, and audiences were thrilled. For the moment, it was enough. King Vidor's first sound film was a musical drama set in the South, *Hallelujah!* (1929), unusual for the time as the first Hollywood studio film with an all-black cast. Future developments would refine the art of sound recording so that by the mid-1930s, it was flawlessly integrated with the picture, and the camera was liberated once

51

more to smoothly glide across the set as required by the more adventurous among the Hollywood directors. But in embracing the new technology, they could also employ the rich heritage of European cinematographic techniques that were the result of ceaseless experimentation by continental directors from the dawn of cinema onward.

*   *   *

We next look at how the film medium progressed in Europe and the rest of the world during the golden era of the silent films, and how the European lessons of the primacy of the image were eventually employed in Hollywood, even if, for the present, it was simultaneously in thrall to and visually shackled by the new technique of sound. This period of awkward transition from silents to sound in Hollywood would not last long, however, due in large part to the visual vitality of films made throughout the rest of the world, films that fully exploited a free and plastic use of the cinema.

THREE

WORLD CINEMA: THE SILENT ERA

EARLY FRENCH CINEMA

While film in America was rapidly transforming itself into an industry, in the rest of the world the cinema was more interested in personal expression and issues of national identity almost from its inception. The assembly-line model embraced by Hollywood was fine for turning out "product," but throughout Europe, Asia, and the Middle East, the film medium was also seen as a potential art form, albeit with strong commercial overtones. Not that the financial aspect of filmmaking was being ignored—far from it. The serials of Louis Feuillade, such as *Fantômas—À l'ombre de la guillotine* (*Fantômas*, 1913), *Judex* (1916), and most notably *Les Vampires* (*The Vampires*, 1915), were shot entirely on location, featured thrilling crime narratives that captivated audiences, and were rousing box office successes in France and throughout the world.

At the same time, on the other end of the cultural spectrum, the *film d'art* was rapidly rising in prominence, using stage productions with theatrical actors to present classic plays on the screen. But the *film d'art* actually represented a drastic step backward in the evolution of the motion picture as an art form, for all its cultural pretensions. Audiences and directors alike came to realize that these canned stage plays represented an artistic dead end. Compared to the vitality and kinetic energy of Feuillade's serials, the *film d'art,* shot entirely on transparently artificial sets, seemed flat and uninviting, with camera movement nonexistent and cutting reduced to scene shifts from one static tableau to the next.

The major French companies, Pathé, Gaumont, and Éclair, were all hit hard by the effects of World War I and forced to cut back on production, as well as re-release earlier films to satisfy the demands of the box office. The comedian Max Linder, the French Chaplin, became a resounding success with local audiences, as a slick man-about-town inevitably involved in a series of comic misadventures. Other French films of note during this period include Albert Capellani's *Notre Dame de Paris* (*The Hunchback of Notre Dame,* 1911), an adaptation of Victor Hugo's novel, as well as the first French newsreels, Pathé-Journal and Éclair-Journal, inaugurated in 1911 and 1912, respectively.

Abel Gance

Abel Gance began directing in 1912 with a series of short, almost experimental films using colored tints and exaggerated camera angles to create a dynamic visual sensibility all his own. By 1917, with *La Zone de la mort* (*The Zone of Death*), Gance had become a major force in French cinema, a commercial filmmaker who was also a filmic visionary. Gance's major work, one that would revolutionize the cinema, was undoubtedly *Napoléon* (1927, reedited 1934 and 1971), a sweeping epic on the life and times of the great French leader. The first version, a silent with an original orchestral score by Arthur Honegger, was conceived as a three-screen film, gesturing toward the multiscreen experiments of the 1960s, an indication of how far ahead of his time Gance really was. The three separate screens were positioned together to create one gigantic canvas, using three projectors to create either three individual images, or one giant panorama, or two framing shots on the left and right with another image in between, or any combination of these possibilities. Gance also used color tints and a highly mobile camera—handheld in many in-

A scene from the first version of Abel Gance's epic film *Napoléon* (1927).

54

stances—to achieve an intensity that had yet to be seen in the commercial cinema.

Although *Napoléon* was undoubtedly a work of personal passion for Gance, it was also a project that realized sufficient profits at the box office to justify its huge production cost. He called this three-screen interlocking process Polyvision, and it was, in many respects, the forerunner of the Cinerama process that was created in the early 1950s to lure television viewers away from their sets and back into movie houses. Gance's enormously ambitious project used thousands of extras and gigantic sets; it ran twenty-eight reels in length at its initial release. The first version was undoubtedly the most effective of the many permutations that the film would go through in subsequent years; the 1934 recut version included newly photographed sync-sound sequences with the original cast members intercut with the silent 1927 footage; the 1971 version used hastily staged, flatly photographed material with new actors, intercut with both the 1927 and 1934 material, to the great detriment of the original film. In 1979, film archivist and historian Kevin Brownlow supervised the definitive version of the film in its original silent form with a running time of roughly five hours and a new musical score by Carl Davis (for a 1980 London screening), and later a score by Carmine Coppola for a series of screenings in 1981 starting at New York's Radio City Music Hall. The reception was rapturous and a fitting tribute to Gance, who lived to see the reconstruction of the film before dying shortly afterward at the age of ninety-two.

Early French Experimental Filmmakers

Other influential French filmmakers of the period included the theorist and filmmaker Louis Delluc, whose early death in 1924 deprived cinema of one of its most important and perceptive critics and champions. In such deeply experimental films as *Fièvre* (*Fever,* 1921) and *L'Inondation* (*The Flood,* 1924), Delluc challenged audience expectations as to what a film should be and expanded the boundaries of narrative cinema. Germaine Dulac, a pioneering female avant-garde filmmaker of this period, also made substantial contributions of her own to the experimental cinema. Born Charlotte Elisabeth Germaine Saisset-Schneider in Amiens, France, in 1882 to an educated, upper-middle-class family, Dulac began a career as a socialist journalist in Paris for *La Française,* one of France's first feminist publications. She also wrote for *La Fronde,* a radical lesbian journal, and studied photography, music, philosophy, and art. As a promoter of the first *ciné* clubs, or film

A scene from Germaine Dulac's *La Coquille et le clergyman* (*The Seashell and the Clergyman,* 1928).

clubs, devoted to watching and discussing non-mainstream films, Dulac became actively involved with a group of intellectuals dedicated to redefining the art of cinema. The group included Louis Delluc, Marcel L'Herbier, and Marie Epstein, another important woman director.

Dulac's best-known films are *La Souriante Madame Beudet* (*The Smiling Madame Beudet,* 1922) and *La Coquille et le clergyman* (*The Seashell and the Clergyman,* 1928), but Dulac also made a six-episode serial, *Âmes de fous* (a k a *Âmes d'hommes fous,* 1918), unique because it combines the structural elements of the cliffhanger with the surrealistic and impressionistic techniques of experimental filmmaking. *Âmes de fous* includes atmospheric effects that serve to express an interior psychological state of female duality. *Gossette* (1923) is another little-known serial she directed. In the film, a young female heroine is kidnapped and drugged. Dulac used a wide-angle lens, repeated images, and distorting devices to render the subjective point of view of the central female heroine.

Dulac's film career was diverse; she could work in the area of pure Impressionism, as in the case of *The Seashell and the Clergyman,* or in pure documentary, with the newsreels she produced at Gaumont, or in a sort of hybrid form between narrative and Impressionist filmmaking, as in *The Smiling Madame Beudet* and the serials she directed. Dulac was dedicated to freeing the cinematic art form from links to literature, theater, and standard narrative expressions. Like Maya Deren, a key experimental filmmaker in the 1940s in the United States, she lectured and wrote a personal manifesto of the cinema—a cinema based on dream, desire, and the language of form over content. *The Smiling Madame Beudet* is an exemplary manifestation of Dulac's theory and perspective. It depicts a housewife's psychological escape from a boorish husband. Here Dulac used technical devices of film that are the equivalent of poetic metonyms in language or experiments in texture and form in painting, such as double exposures, superimpositions, masks, distorting lenses, and uses of gauzes. These techniques display a filmmaker playing with form itself, not content with film's subject-object relationship between viewer and screen. With *The Seashell and the Clergyman,* Dulac overhauls narrativity entirely and presents us with pure feminine desire, intercut against masculine desires of a priest. Above all, Dulac is responsible for "writing" a new cinematic language that expressed transgressive female desires in a poetic manner.

Among Dulac's aforementioned colleagues, Marcel L'Herbier directed *Eldorado* (a k a *El Dorado,* 1921) and *L'Inhumaine* (*The Inhuman Woman,* a k a *The New Enchantment,* 1924), which betrayed a certain conventionality in their cinematic structure before he scored with *L'Argent* (*Money,* 1928), a highly original adaptation of a novel by Émile Zola. Marie Epstein, a director in the French avant-garde, has been marginalized in most cinema histories, often mentioned only in passing in film encyclopedias under the entry for her brother, Jean Epstein, and her other collaborator, Jean Benoît-Lévy. In their productions she served as co-director, though she was credited as writer. She was also an actress and, later, a film archivist at the Cinémathèque Française.

Marie Epstein's scenarios and films combine social issues—particularly the plight of poor children and disadvantaged women—with poetic imagery and advanced cinematic techniques. The best-known collaboration between Epstein and Benoît-Lévy is *La Maternelle* (*Children of Montmartre,* 1933). Several other Benoît-Lévy/Epstein films are also worth noting for their avant-garde techniques, feminine modes of subjectivity, and female-centered subject matter. *Altitude 3,200* (*Youth in Revolt,* 1938) depicts life and love in a utopian community, while *Hélène* (1936) is a film told from the perspective of a single mother. *La Mort du cygne* (*Ballerina,* 1938, directed by Benoît-Lévy alone) is told from the point of view of a young female ballet dancer who has such a desire to succeed that she causes her rival to have an accident. The film won the Grand Prix du Film Française at the 1937 Exposition. *Peau de pêche* (*Peach Skin,* 1929), *Maternité* (*Maternity,* 1929), and *Coeur de Paris* (*Heart of Paris,* 1931) treat the subject of children with great sensitivity and frequently rely upon a child's subjective point of view. Epstein employs repetitive poetic motifs throughout these films.

Madeleine Renaud (right) comforts the young child Paulette Élambert (left) in Jean Benoît-Lévy and Marie Epstein's *La Maternelle* (*Children of Montmartre,* 1933). Courtesy Metropolis Pictures/Photofest.

René Clair and the Surrealists

René Clair was another silent innovator, whose Surrealist film *Entr'acte* (*Intermission,* 1924) is a classic of its kind. Composed of a sequence of utterly unrelated scenes, the film ends with a funeral procession that gradually speeds up until all the participants are running after the hearse; to further complicate matters, at its climax the scene is intercut with a point-of-view shot of the world sweeping by at great speed, taken from the first car on an amusement park roller coaster. The Surrealists believed passionately in the chance encounter of persons and objects to create art, and they willfully defied logic and reason, as well as specific symbolic systems, in their search for a vision of the world in which the absurd reigned supreme. Clair went on to more conventional filmmaking with his silent comedy *Un Chapeau de paille d'Italie* (*An Italian Straw Hat,* 1928), and then to a feature-film career that included three groundbreaking sound films. *Sous les toits de Paris* (*Under the Roofs of Paris,* 1930) is a romantic musical about Parisian street life; *Le Million* (*The Million,* 1931), a fantasy/musical detailing the search for a missing lottery ticket in the working-class sections of Paris; and, perhaps most famous, *À Nous la liberté* (*Liberty for Us,* 1931), the tale of two convicts, one of whom escapes prison and starts an enormously successful factory before the other is released and looks him up on the outside. These films, using tightly syn-

58

A bizarre game of chess in René Clair's comic short Dada film *Entr'acte* (*Intermission*, 1924).

The lively poster for René Clair's sound masterpiece *À Nous la liberté* (*Liberty for Us*, 1931).

Convict Louis (Raymond Cordy) escapes from prison and opens a factory in René Clair's *À Nous la liberté* (*Liberty for Us*, 1931), but finds he can't escape his past.

René Clair's *Paris qui dort* (*The Crazy Ray*, 1925); the last "living" people in Paris, atop the Eiffel Tower.

chronized music and images to create a fairytale world of light and sound, were internationally popular because they needed few subtitles to put their ideas across to the audience. Clair's delightful musicals put the French sound film on the map throughout the world. Although he had been initially suspicious of sound, he soon became one of the most inventive and fluid of the early sound auteurs.

Before he abandoned Surrealism, Clair made one last fantasy film, the silent featurette *Paris qui dort* (literally *Paris Asleep*, a k a *The Crazy Ray*, 1925), in which a disparate group of Parisians awake in a city that has been depopulated overnight—everyone seems to have disappeared. While at first they take advantage of this state of affairs to dine in the finest restaurants, help themselves to free samples at the bank, and generally live like kings and queens, eventually they realize they are bored and lonely. At length the group discovers that Paris has been put to sleep by the experimental ray of a mad professor, and after a series of comic misadventures they restore the city to life. While the forty-five-minute film is on one level a straightforward narrative, Clair's use of camera tricks and editing techniques gives the project an appropriately dreamlike air, and the result is one of the glories of the early French cinema.

Luis Buñuel and Salvador Dali

Other important French film artists of the era also embraced Surrealism, perhaps none more scandalously than Luis Buñuel, whose *Un Chien andalou* (*An Andalusian Dog*, 1929) consisted of a series of shocking sequences designed to challenge any audience. A hand opens to reveal a wound from which a group

Luis Buñuel in the late 1920s.

of ants emerge; a young man drags two grand pianos across a room, laden with a pair of dead donkeys and two nonplussed priests, in a vain attempt to win the affection of a woman he openly lusts after. These are just two of the more outrageous sequences in the film; perhaps the most famous scene occurs near the beginning, when Buñuel himself is seen stropping a razor on a balcony and then ritualistically slitting the eyeball of a young woman who sits passively in a chair a moment later. Co-directed and co-written by Buñuel and the Surrealist painter Salvador Dalí, *Un*

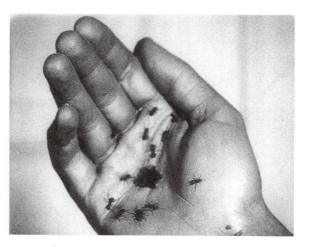

A disembodied, decaying hand in close-up, with live ants spilling out from its center, in Salvador Dalí and Luis Buñuel's *Un Chien andalou* (*An Andalusian Dog*, 1928).

Lya Lys as the tormented lover in Salvador Dalí and Luis Buñuel's scandalous *L'Âge d'or* (*The Age of Gold,* 1930).

Chien Andalou's sixteen-minute running time was sufficient to cause riots when it was first screened.

Buñuel and Dalí would collaborate on one more film together, the very early sound picture *L'Âge d'or* (*The Age of Gold,* 1930), but the two artists fell out on the first day of shooting, with Buñuel chasing Dalí from the set with a hammer. *L'Âge d'or* was savagely anticlerical, and the initial screening caused such a riot that the film was banned for many years before finally appearing in a restored version on DVD. *L'Âge d'or* loosely follows two lovers whose passion defies society's conventions; the film begins with a documentary on the mating habits of scorpions and ends with an off-screen orgy in a monastery. Buñuel, when asked to describe *L'Âge d'or*, said that it was nothing less than "a desperate and passionate call to murder."

Man Ray and the Avant-Garde

Man Ray, yet another follower of the Surrealist movement, was more famous as a still photographer and painter, but almost as an aside to his other work he created the very short (three-minute) film *Le Retour à la raison* (*Return to Reason,* 1923), an absurdist collage made up of random photographed footage and images Ray created in his darkroom by sprinkling thumbtacks, salt, and various other items directly onto the film, then exposing it briefly to light. *Emak-Bakia* (1926) and *L'Étoile de mer* (*Star of the Sea,* 1928) followed; of the two films, *Emak-Bakia* is slightly more ambitious, or perhaps more unusual: it recycles images from *Return to Reason,* intercut with footage of a nude Kiki, Ray's mistress, and one sequence in which Ray throws the camera into the air and lets it crash to the ground, thus recording the sensation of weightlessness and then an abrupt return to earth.

Other avant-garde filmmakers of the period include Dimitri Kirsanoff, Jean Painlevé, and Jean Vigo. Kirsanoff made the superbly evocative film *Ménilmontant* (1926), a thirty-eight-minute silent film about two young sisters struggling through a life of hardship and prostitution in one of the poorer districts of Paris. Painlevé, a specialist in scientific photography, cre-

ated a series of Surrealist films such as his sound short *L'Hippocampe* (*The Seahorse,* 1934). Vigo made the silent Surrealist documentary *À propos de Nice* (a k a *Nizza,* 1930), followed by a bizarre sound aquatic short, *Taris, roi de l'eau* (*Jean Taris, Swimming Champion,* 1931), documenting the prowess of a French swimming champion, who appeared to literally walk on water in the last shot. Vigo is best remembered, however, for two sound films, *Zéro de conduite* (*Zero for Conduct,* 1933) and *L'Atalante* (1934), discussed in Chapter 5.

Carl Th. Dreyer's Silent Masterpiece

One of the greatest silent films emanating from France in the late 1920s was not the work of a French director at all, but rather of the Danish filmmaker Carl Theodor Dreyer. Dreyer's film *La Passion de Jeanne d'Arc* (*The Passion of Joan of Arc,* 1928) follows the youthful Joan (Renée Falconetti) through her final days on earth, as she is judged by the English in a kangaroo court where the only certain verdict is death at the stake. Falconetti's dazzling performance conveys the simple faith, deep compassion, and surprising inner strength of the young woman, and Dreyer, working with the superb cameraman Rudolph Maté (later a director in his own right), frames Joan against a series of flat, hostile backgrounds as she is mercilessly interrogated by the judges at her tribunal. Composed almost entirely of extreme close-ups intercut with rigorously designed tracking shots of the judges plotting Joan's inevitable martyrdom, *The Passion of Joan of Arc* is perhaps the finest film of

Reneé Falconetti as Joan in Carl Theodor Dreyer's *La Passion de Jeanne d'Arc* (*The Passion of Joan of Arc*, 1928).

Dreyer's long and illustrious career and a brilliant example of the perfect fusion among director, actor, and cameraman to create a film that remains a wrenching and riveting work of art. Dreyer's work in the sound era continued with *Vampyr* (1932), an atmospheric horror film; then, working in Denmark, he directed *Vredens dag* (*Day of Wrath*, 1943), an allegorical drama centering on medieval witch hunts, the religious drama *Ordet* (*The Word*, 1955), and finally the tale of lost love *Gertrud* (1964). Uncompromising, spare, and visually stunning, Dreyer's few movies are a major contribution to the history of film.

Jean Renoir

Jean Renoir is arguably the greatest artist the cinema has ever known, simply because he was able to work effectively in virtually all genres without sacrificing his individuality or bowing to public or commercial conventions. Although he was the son of the famed Impressionist painter Auguste Renoir, his visual sensibility was entirely his own, and the technical facility that marks his films is the result of long and assiduous study. Renoir's first serious interest in cinema developed while he recuperated from a wound suffered in the Alpine infantry in 1915. His first active involvement came in 1924, when money from the sale of his father's paintings allowed him to begin production on *Une Vie sans joie* (*Catherine*). Renoir wrote the scenario and co-directed with Albert Dieudonné; Renoir's young wife, Andrée Madeleine Heuschling Hessling, a former model of his father's, was the star, billed as Catherine Hessling.

Renoir's first film as solo director was *La Fille de l'eau* (*Whirlpool of Fate*, 1925), in which he also served as producer and art director, with Hessling again starring. Anticipating Jean Vigo's *L'Atalante* of 1934, the film's plot centers on a young woman who lives and works on a riverboat. Its modest success led Renoir to plunge, somewhat impulsively, into directing *Nana* (1926), an adaptation of the Zola novel, which now looks uncharacteristically stagebound. Nearly bankrupt, Renoir had to take out a loan to finance his next film, *Sur un air de Charleston* (*Charleston*, 1927), a seventeen-minute fantasy that featured Hessling teaching the popular title dance in costumes that were as brief as possible. After the film attained only limited success, Renoir accepted a straight commercial directing job on *Marquitta* (1927), now lost. His next significant film was *Tire-au-flanc* (*The Sad Sack,* 1928), a military comedy that François Truffaut would call a visual tour de force, and that marked the director's first collaboration with actor Michel Simon. The working relationship between Renoir and Hessling, meanwhile, had taken its toll; the couple separated in 1930.

To prove that he understood the new medium of the sound film, Renoir directed a down-and-dirty comedy based on a farce by Georges Feydeau, *On purge bébé* (1931). The film was shot on a very brief schedule, with Renoir apparently letting the camera run for as long as possible during each take, in order to work around the clumsy sound-on-disc recording apparatus. He also inserted a number of instances of mild "blue humor" (such as the sound of a toilet flushing off-screen). Perhaps because he had aimed so resolutely for commercial success, Renoir's first talkie was a huge hit, allowing him to rush into production on his first major sound film, *La Chienne* (*The Bitch,* 1931). This was also his first film edited by Marguerite Renoir, with whom Renoir became romantically involved and who would take on his name, though they never married. It was on this film, too, that Renoir developed his early strategy of sound shooting. In the face of objections—from his producers down to his sound technicians—he insisted on using only natural sync-sound,

Michel Simon and Janie Marèse in Jean Renoir's tragic drama of sexual obsession, *La Chienne* (*The Bitch,* 1931).

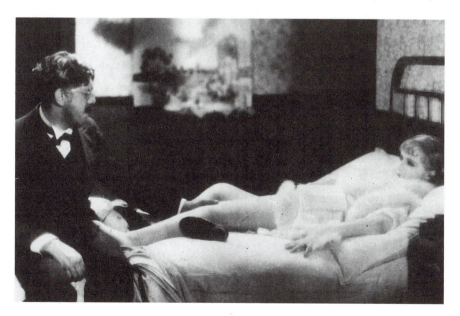

recorded for the most part in actual locations. He also made extensive use of a moving camera, particularly in one sequence where the camera waltzes around the dance floor, keeping perfect time with the actors.

Renoir next directed his brother Pierre in *La Nuit du carrefour* (*Night at the Crossroads*, 1932), a brilliant but little-seen detective film based on one of Georges Simenon's Inspector Maigret novels. He followed it with the delightful *Boudu sauvé des eaux* (*Boudu Saved from Drowning*, 1932), using his by now polished on-location sync-sound shooting technique to tell the tale of Boudu (Michel Simon), a hobo who is fished out of the Seine after a suicide attempt by a well-meaning bourgeois bookseller, Édouard Lestingois (Charles Granval). Taken into the Lestingois household, Boudu wreaks havoc until he escapes during a boating accident, free to wander again. The charm and invention of this beautiful film make it one of the outstanding works of the early sound cinema (it was remade in 1986 by Paul Mazursky as *Down and Out in Beverly Hills*). Though he made a name for himself in this period, Renoir's best work still lay ahead.

SILENT FILMS IN ITALY

In Italy, the spectacle reigned supreme, as producers vied to outdo each other in presenting historical re-creations on a vast scale. In 1910, Mario Caserini's *Lucrezia Borgia* and Enrico Guazzoni's *Brutus* offered the public thrills and decadent delights, with lavish costumes and sets that made up in excess what they lacked in historical accuracy. Giovanni Pastrone's *Cabiria* (1914), at a length of 123 minutes, was an even more ambitious spectacle and influenced D. W. Griffith's *Intolerance* two years later with its impressive sets and epic scale.

Elvira Notari

The Italian cinema also gave the world one of film's true pioneers, director Elvira Notari. Notari is the unheralded inventor of Neorealist cinema. Between 1906 and 1930, she directed over sixty feature films and hundreds of documentaries and shorts for her own production company, Dora Film. In addition, she usually served as writer and co-producer, working with her husband, Nicola, a cameraman, and her son, Eduardo, an actor. The rediscovery of Notari's work throws into question a number of traditional notions of Italian cinema. Her early films were almost completely oppositional to the slick super-spectacles of the North. Dora films were shot on location, using the lower-to-middle-class streets of Naples, often with nonprofessional actors. Notari loved to show the crude living conditions of real people and the politics of the underclass.

Notari's films were noteworthy for being hand-colored in a rainbow of hues frame by frame or colored in dye-tinting machines that gave a uniform color to the images (deep blue, perhaps, for scenes of melancholy; red tints for anger) and synchronized with live singing and music. The results are exceptionally erotic, visceral, and often violent. Her work focuses on the plight of the underprivileged, especially women who refuse to conform to societal codes of behavior. *È Piccerella* (1922) is a melodrama about a woman named Margaretella who is courted by two men; she is attracted to the sinister Carluccio instead of the "good" Tore and meets her demise in the end. *À Santanotte* (*On Christmas Eve*, 1922) is similarly downbeat, violent, and highly effective.

Italian Spectacles and Romantic Dramas

Just as the silent Italian cinema truly began to flourish, the twin exigencies of World War I and changing audience taste brought about a rapid shift in the country's filmmaking. The war caused producers to create more patriotic films that supported the propaganda efforts of the government. Such transparently jingoistic productions as André Deed's *La Paura degli aeromobili nemici* (*Fear of Enemy Flying Machines*, 1915) and Segundo de Chomón's animated children's film *La Guerra e il sogno di Momi* (*The War and Momi's Dream*, 1917) contributed to the war effort, but with the end of the conflict, a new genre that might be called "Diva" cinema came into prominence.

The figure of the actress as diva had been introduced before the war, in such films as Mario Caserini's *Ma l'amor mio mon muore* (*Love Everlasting*, 1913), but after the war a whole group of players, including Pina Menichelli, Lyda Borelli, and Soava Gallone, flooded the screens with tales of decadent romance in which men were invariably lured to their doom through the machinations of sexual enticement and the promise of forbidden love. Nino Oxilia's *Rapsodia Satanica* (*Satanic Rhapsody*, 1915), Pastrone's *Il Fuoco* (*The Flame*, 1916), and Lucio D'Ambra's *La tragedia su tre carte* (*Tragedy on Three Cards*, 1922) are emblematic of this cycle. But the demand for spectacles and "vamp" romances eventually collapsed under the strain of ceaseless repetition, and the Italian cinema began to cannibalize itself, remaking a number of films several times over, including a new version of *Quo Vadis?* in 1925

67

(directed by Gabriellino D'Annunzio and Georg Jacoby) and of *Gli Ultimi giorni di Pompeii* in 1926 (*The Last Days of Pompeii*, directed by Carmine Gallone and Amleto Palermi).

In the final days of the Italian silent cinema, a series of "muscle man" films came into play, revolving around the character of Maciste, a slave possessed of seemingly superhuman strength. First seen in Luigi Romano Borgnetto and Vincenzo Denizot's *Maciste* (1915), this strongman character was quickly recycled in an endless series of sequels from *Maciste alpino* (*Maciste in the Alpine Regiment*, a k a *The Warrior*, 1916) to Guido Brignone's *Maciste all' inferno* (*Maciste in Hell*, 1925). What is perhaps most interesting about this initial period of Italian cinema is that it rapidly codified the two central genres that would define it throughout the twentieth century: the historical spectacle of Roman decadence, and the Maciste, or Hercules, films, which would become staples of the industry in the late 1950s and throughout the 1960s in newer remakes, in color and CinemaScope (and other wide-screen processes). Until this later cycle again exhausted itself through ceaseless recapitulation, the Italian cinema consisted largely of huge costume-bin historical pageants, endless strongman films, and, in the 1960s, a new genre, the horror film, which had not been a major genre in the silent Italian era.

SILENT FILMMAKING IN ENGLAND

In England, the key film genres rapidly codified themselves into the colonial romance, parody films, melodramas, and domestic comedies. Following Cecil M. Hepworth's success with *Rescued by Rover* (1905), the English film industry rapidly sought to emulate the American production-line method, with generally unsatisfactory results. Quantity was not the problem; originality, and even basic quality in production values, was. English producers rapidly realized that in order to create a significant quantity of films, a "series" formula was essential. Thus the *Lieutenant Daring* series was extremely popular from 1911 on, detailing the exploits of a dashing military officer in service to the empire, as exemplified by *Lieutenant Daring and the Dancing Girl* (1913) and *Lieutenant Daring and the Plans for the Mine Fields* (1912). As films became longer and more ambitious, such directors as Graham Cutts created convincing melodramas, including *Woman to Woman* (1923), starring Clive Brook (who would later go on to a solid career in American sound films) and Betty Compson, as well as *The Rat* (1925), with matinee idol Ivor Novello. Maurice Elvey, director of *Nelson* (1918), was more typical of the English silent cinema, however, creating a film that was slow moving, poorly acted, and unconvincingly staged. Such productions were no match for American competition, and it was not until the late 1920s and the ascent of Alfred Hitchcock that the English film would truly begin to establish a national identity.

Hitchcock, known to audiences throughout the world as the master of suspense, began his career in 1919, when he got a job creating title cards for Paramount's London branch. By 1922 he was an assistant director, and he finally got his chance to advance to full director on *The Pleasure Garden* (1925), a German film shot in Munich with English financing. Working in Germany, Hitchcock picked up touches of the visual style known as Expressionism, a dark and moody approach to lighting and camera placement that he soon utilized in his first true suspense film, *The Lodger* (1927), the screen's most accomplished Jack the Ripper story, with Ivor Novello in the title role. Rapidly adapting to sound films with *Blackmail* in 1929, Hitchcock actually shot most of the film twice: once as a silent and then the key sequences again with dialogue, just as silent films were vanishing from the screen. Such early sound features as *Murder!* (1930) and *The Man Who Knew Too Much* (1934) established Hitchcock as a clever director who used bold visual tricks to embellish his works. Hitchcock's considerable influence continued to manifest itself in England and America.

THE CINEMA IN SCANDINAVIA

In the Scandinavian countries, Holger-Madsen's Danish film *Morfinisten* (*The Morphine Takers*, 1911) was a controversial hit of the period, but the Danish film industry collapsed with the onset of war in 1914 and never really recovered. In Norway, such films as G. A. Olsen's *Kaksen på Øverland* (*The Braggarts of Overland*) and Rasmus Breistein's *Fante-Anne* (*The Lady Tramp*), both 1920, were domestically successful but failed to achieve sufficient production value for exportation. Later productions, such as Walter Fyrst's *Troll-Elgen* (*The Magic Leap*, 1927), had more polish and professionalism, but on the whole the Norwegian cinema in the silent era was a modest affair.

Sweden, of all the Scandinavian countries, probably had the greatest worldwide impact, with such films as the Danish director Benjamin Christensen's *Häxan* (*Witchcraft Through the Ages*, 1922), which was shot in Sweden, and Victor Sjöström's *Körkarlen* (*The Phantom Carriage*, 1921). Sjöström's long career would take him to the United States as well, where he directed an adaptation of Nathaniel Hawthorne's *The Scarlet Letter* with Lillian Gish in 1926, *The Divine Woman* with Greta Garbo in 1928, and his masterpiece *The Wind,* also in 1928 and with Lillian Gish. This last film, though a silent classic, was ultimately screened with synchronized music and effects and an alternate ending, much to Sjöström's displeasure. (Even the director's name had to be Americanized into "Seastrom" to please his Hollywood bosses.) Unhappy in California, Sjöström returned to Sweden, working as an actor and advisor for the giant national film company Svensk Filmindustri. He later appeared in Ingmar Bergman's *Smultronstället* (*Wild Strawberries,* 1957) as an aging professor who returns to his alma mater to receive an award for his academic career and is beset by memories of his youth along the way. Mauritz Stiller was another major Swedish director, whose sophisticated comedies, including *Den Moderna suffragetten* (*The Modern Suffragette,* 1913) and *Kärlek och journalistik* (*Love and Journalism,* 1916), demonstrated a subtle, Continental style that allowed him to blend comedy and melodrama in a deft mixture of slick entertainment.

RUSSIA

Following a period in which domestic filmmaking was noted for its commercial blandness, Russian cinema underwent an explosive series of developments due to the Bolshevik Revolution. Under the czar, escapist entertainment was the order of the day, with such films as Vasili Goncharov and Yakov Protazanov's *Smert Ioanna Groznogo* (*The Death of Ivan the Terrible,* 1909), Goncharov and Kai Hansen's *Pyotr Velikiy* (*Peter the Great,* 1910), Goncharov's *Zhizn i smert A. S. Pushkina* (*The Life and Death of Pushkin,* 1910), Pyotr Chardynin's *Kreitzerova sonata* (*The Kreutzer Sonata,* 1911), and Protazanov's *Pikovaya dama* (*The Queen of Spades,* 1916).

Many of these filmmakers would continue to work after the fall of Czar Nikolai II, but others would flee to Germany, France, and the United States when Vladimir Lenin seized power in October 1917. Quickly sensing the power of the cinema to mold the populace, Lenin pressed ahead with the production of films that frankly espoused the Bolshevik cause.

By 1918, the new regime had launched a series of "*agit-prop*" trains, packed with cinematographic equipment, theater groups, performers, and entertainers, all of which were charged with the task of bringing the revolution to the masses across the country. On the first *agit-prop* train was Eduard Tisse, later the cameraman to the great Soviet director Sergei M. Eisenstein,

A typically kinetic scene from Dziga Vertov's *Chelovek s kino-apparatom* (*The Man with a Movie Camera,* 1929), a visual celebration of Soviet progress.

and future director and *montage* (editing) theorist Dziga Vertov (born Denis Abramovich Kaufman). Vertov served as the editor for the films shot on the train, which were sent back to Moscow for processing and post-production and then dispatched on the next *agit-prop* train as fresh programming in support of the Revolution.

In the following years, Soviet cinema moved ahead stylistically by leaps and bounds, despite the scarcity of new stock and an embargo on films and new photographic materials from the West. In 1919, the industry itself was nationalized, and Dziga Vertov launched his series of *Kino-Pravda* (Cinema Truth) newsreels in 1922, essentially using the *agit-prop* format, but expanding it to dizzying heights through the use of rapid-fire editing, multiple cameras, bizarre camera angles, and the plastic manipulation of space and time through newly devised theories of editing technique. Vertov's most famous film is undoubtedly the silent classic *Chelovek s kino-apparatom* (*The Man with a Movie Camera,*

Dziga Vertov (bottom, center) shooting *Chelovek s kino-apparatom* (*The Man with a Movie Camera,* 1929).

1929), which employs every stylistic trick imaginable to give the viewer an impressionistic look at one day in the life of the fledgling state.

Lev Kuleshov's Editorial Experiments

Lev Kuleshov was the innovator behind many of Vertov's techniques and worked with his students to reedit existing films, such as Griffith's *Intolerance,* to create new effects from stock footage due to the shortage of raw film stock. Kuleshov isolated, among other editing principles, the "Kuleshov effect," in which the face of the actor/director Ivan Mozzhukhin, taken as one continuous close-up and purposefully devoid of expression, was intercut with a body lying in a coffin, a young child with a toy, and a bowl of hot soup. Though the juxtaposition of Mozzhukhin's face with these images was accomplished entirely in the cutting room, viewers immediately discerned in his face sorrow, happiness, and hunger, simply because of the relationship between the actor's face and the other images. In an even more influential experiment, Kuleshov introduced the "creative geography" effect, in which a man and a woman meet, the man points to a building, we see a brief shot of the building, and the couple ascend a staircase to reach the structure. However, all the shots were taken in different places at different times, and some of the images were pirated out of stock footage from existing newsreels. Kuleshov's highly influential theories were soon part and parcel of the Revolution's visual arsenal, but it remained for Sergei Eisenstein to put Kuleshov's discoveries to their best use.

Sergei Eisenstein

Eisenstein's apprenticeship in the cinema came naturally; as a precocious child and the son of a well-off architect, he excelled in drawing and languages and was soon proficient in English, French, and German by the time he entered his teens. After his parents divorced when he was eight, he spent most of his formative years with his father, who enrolled him in the Petrograd Institute of Civil Engineering. While Eisenstein was fairly diligent in his studies, he soon became enamored of the theater, attending plays and dreaming of a career in the arts. When the Revolution overtook the Institute in 1917, he was instantly radicalized and by 1920 was directing theatrical *agit-prop* productions to support it. Meetings with actor Maxim Strauch, a childhood companion, and the theatrical director Vsevolod Meyerhold led Eisenstein to embrace the theater more fully, and by 1923 he had staged his

72

first real production, *The Wise Man,* which included his first short film, *Dnevnik Glumova* (*Glumov's Diary,* 1923), a five-minute narrative that was used as part of the production's multimedia approach.

In 1924 Eisenstein followed this with the theatrical piece *Gas Masks,* which he famously staged in a real gas factory, asking his audience to sit in improvised seats on the shop floor. The theatrical productions were resounding successes, but he wanted to work in film, which he felt was the ideal medium for the expression of his revolutionary (in every sense of the word) ideas concerning shot structure, editing, montage, camera placement, and the power of the iconic image. After a brief apprenticeship with Lev Kuleshov and Esfir Shub, a brilliant editor who showed him the plasticity of the film medium in the cutting room, Eisenstein tackled his first feature as director, *Stachka* (*Strike,* 1925). Using a "montage of attractions," in which various themes are drawn together through the use of intercutting, as well as a "montage of shocks," in which brutal and violent images assault the viewer at key points in the film's narrative, he created a dazzling mosaic of labor unrest and capitalist indifference that galvanized the masses and impressed his superiors.

Eisenstein developed intricate theories of montage that he would later explicate in his writings, such as rhythmic montage, which gradually increased or decreased shot length to build suspense and convey excitement; tonal montage, to convey emotional feeling through the intercutting of associative material; collisionary montage, in which images are "smashed together" to create a dynamic, violent affect; and collusionary montage, in which a series of images are edited together to create a cumulative effect, with a number of simultaneous actions happening at the same time. *Strike* tells of a factory worker's job action that is eventually crushed by management through violence alone, and the final sequence, in which the workers are mowed down with fire hoses and machine-gun fire, intercut with actual scenes from a slaughterhouse, is one of the most brutal in the history of the cinema.

In the same year, Eisenstein also completed *Bronenosets Potyomkin* (*Battleship Potemkin,* 1925), his first undoubted masterpiece, recounting the mutiny of sailors who were sick of the corrupt rule of the czar's minions. Eisenstein's fascination with the editorial process reached its zenith in *Battleship Potemkin,* which was shot on location in Odessa in ten weeks and then edited completely in two blazing weeks to create an eighty-six-minute film with 1,346 shots, at a time when the average Hollywood film comprised fewer than half that number. Working with his cameraman Eduard Tisse, he crafted a typically kinetic piece of political cinema that reached its visual

The Odessa Steps sequence from Sergei Eisenstein's masterpiece *Bronenosets Potyomkin* (*Battleship Potemkin,* 1925); the mother approaches the soldiers with her injured child in her arms.

apotheosis in the famed Odessa Steps sequence, a roughly ten-minute section that graphically depicts the townspeople of Odessa being ritually shot down by the czar's soldiers, as the citizens rush down the enormous outdoor staircase to escape the advancing riflemen, and the soldiers, in turn, march mechanically and mercilessly down the stairs, killing men, women, and children with vicious abandon.

This one sequence took a full week to film and comprises hundreds of individual shots; the average shot length in the sequence is about two seconds, and the camera cuts from point-of-view shots that drag the spectator into the unfolding tragedy, with wide shots of the massacre, to individual close-ups of the participants as they watch the horror unfold. Linking all these images together are brief shots of a baby carriage, with a child inside, careening down the huge stone steps after the death of the child's mother. The soldiers' faces are seen only briefly, especially near the end of the sequence, when one czarist rifleman bayonets the baby in its carriage—an image of such savagery and violence that it shocks audiences even today. This famous scene has been copied by a number of other filmmakers, most notably in Brian De Palma's *The Untouchables* (1987) in which a baby carriage is caught in the middle of a violent shootout, as a direct homage to Eisenstein's editorial techniques.

But the effect of *Battleship Potemkin* inside the Soviet Union, oddly, was muted; it was considered too formalist and avant-garde by Eisenstein's party masters. Abroad, however, the film achieved significant success. Whether or not they agreed with the film's unabashed propaganda, foreign critics and audiences alike were dazzled by the director's inventive, explosive editorial style. His subsequent films *Oktyabr* (*October,* a k a *Ten Days That Shook the World,* 1927, co-directed with Grigori Aleksandrov) and *Staroye i novoye* (*The General Line,* a k a *Old and New,* 1929, co-directed with Grigori Aleksandrov), found even less favor with his superiors, although these works were unabashedly Marxist/Leninist in their political motivation. Joseph Stalin, in particular, was unhappy with the increasingly experimental nature of Eisenstein's films. He personally supervised the recutting of *October* and *The General Line,* in part to satisfy the changing political "realities" of the revolution—in particular, Leon Trotsky's expulsion from the Communist Party—but also to tone down Eisenstein's increasingly radical editorial style. For Eisenstein, the montage of the film becomes a central character in the work's construction, introducing contradictory ideas and opposing social forces in a series of rapidly intercut shots that often stunned his audiences.

Stung by criticisms from a regime he had wholeheartedly supported, Eisenstein was struck by the paradoxical situation in which he found himself. At home, Stalin and his stooges criticized his work mercilessly, charging that he had deserted the ideals of the revolution, but around the world he was being hailed as a cinematic genius whose editorial concepts had irrevocably changed the structure of the motion picture. Feeling that he had little to lose, he embarked on an extensive tour of Europe, where he was lionized by critics and film societies but hounded by the local authorities as a subversive alien. This exodus eventually led to a brief period in 1930 when Eisenstein was put under contract to Paramount Pictures and came to America, ostensibly to direct for the studio. Paramount, however, had not reckoned with the public's increasing antipathy toward the Soviet Union and the Communist Revolution. Although the director created a superb scenario based on Theodore Dreiser's novel *An American Tragedy* (which was later adapted by director Josef von Sternberg and filmed in 1931 at Paramount, and later remade as *A Place in the Sun* by director George Stevens in 1951), he was summarily fired by Paramount in the fall of 1930, after less than a year's employment.

From this point on, Eisenstein embarked on a series of ill-fated projects that would cause him severe personal and financial distress, the most tragic being the production and subsequent destruction of *¡Que viva Mexico!* (a k a *Thunder Over Mexico* in a later version, not edited by Eisenstein). The film, co-directed by Grigori Aleksandrov, was begun in 1930 in Mexico as a trib-

The battle on the ice in Sergei Eisenstein's epic *Aleksandr Nevskiy (Alexander Nevsky,* 1938).

ute to the Mexican people and the painter Diego Rivera, but it was never really finished. Privately financed by novelist Upton Sinclair, the film took two years in planning and production but ended when Sinclair pulled the plug just before Eisenstein was to shoot the film's final sequence. Despite promises, Eisenstein was never allowed to edit the completed footage, and eventually Sinclair sold it to producer Sol Lesser, who created a feature and two shorts from it, entirely ignoring Eisenstein's projected scenario.

When Eisenstein finally returned to the Soviet Union after several years, he was subjected to vicious attacks in the state press. His films were rejected as abstract, and party apparatchiks demanded that he adhere to the tenets of Socialist Realism, structuring his work in a more conventional manner and eschewing the editorial style that had informed the creation of his greatest output. After a show trial in 1935, during which he was forced to repudiate his own works, Eisenstein was allowed to direct only a few more films, most notably *Aleksandr Nevskiy* (*Alexander Nevsky,* 1938; co-director, Dmitri Vasilyev), an epic film about a thirteenth-century Russian prince who successfully fought back a German invasion with a small band of enthusiastic followers. With a superb musical score by Sergei Prokofiev, *Alexander Nevsky* was a substantial hit with the public and his party bosses and played neatly into the government's anti-Nazi campaign as a run-up to World War II.

No matter how powerful the film was, however, there was no getting around the fact that it represented a decisive break from Eisenstein's earlier, hyperedited style, and while it is a masterful work, a great deal of the kinetic energy that suffused his earlier films is absent from the production. Nevertheless, Eisenstein was now back in political favor, and he began work on a trilogy entitled *Ivan Groznyy* (*Ivan the Terrible*) in early 1940, spending two years preparing for the project before shooting began in April 1943. He completed two of the proposed three features in the series, in 1944 and 1946 (co-director, M. Filimonova), the last third of which was shot in color (the director's first use of the process). However, Eisenstein's cinematic approach to his material had altered drastically, and the more traditional editorial structure of *Alexander Nevsky* was now replaced with even longer takes, often lasting several minutes, making extensive use of deep-focus shots in which both the extreme foreground and the extreme background are equally in focus, completely eliminating rapid editorial structures from his visual vocabulary. Neither film found favor with audiences, at home or abroad. In September 1946, he began shooting *Part III* of *Ivan the Terrible,* but production was halted by the director's increasingly poor health. Of roughly twenty minutes shot, only a fragment of film remains; the rest was destroyed under Stalin's orders. Worn down by years of ceaseless struggle, as well as interference from the regime whose cause he had so enthusiastically supported, Eisenstein died of a heart attack in 1948 at the age of fifty.

Eisenstein's colleagues during the silent period in the Soviet Union include Vsevolod Pudovkin, whose most famous film is the political drama *Mat* (*Mother,* 1926), and Aleksandr Dovzhenko, whose film *Zemlya* (*Earth,* 1930) was the antithesis of Eisenstein's work in terms of style and content. Dovzhenko favored long takes and detailed character development rather than the fast cuts and near caricatures favored by Eisenstein. Though Pudovkin and Dovzhenko were clearly overshadowed by Eisenstein's personal flamboyance and directorial brilliance, they managed to create a sizable body of work under Stalin's regime in part because they were not as lionized by the critical establishment abroad. This was also true of Yakov Protazanov, who created the bizarre science fiction film *Aelita: Queen of Mars* in 1924 (known in the USSR simply as *Aelita*), and Abram Room, whose *Tretya meshchanskaya* (*Bed and Sofa,* 1927) offered trenchant social commentary to Soviet audiences. Esfir Shub, always most at home in the editing room and the woman who had first introduced Eisenstein to the concept of kinetic editing in 1923, continued to work on films such as *Padenie dinastii Romanovykh* (*The Fall of the Romanov Dynasty,* 1927), which mixed newsreel footage with staged sequences from existing features to create a film com-

A scene from Yakov Protazanov's early Soviet science fiction film *Aelita: Queen of Mars* (1924).

posed wholly of footage shot by others, not unlike her earliest experiment as part of Dziga Vertov's group.

By 1927, Stalin had become the supreme ruler of the Soviet Union and with his hand-picked assistant, Boris Shumyatskiy, clamped down on all experimentation in the cinema. "Social Realism," the more blatant form of propaganda, became the order of the day; it left little to the imagination of the viewer and required even less from the director. Thus Eisenstein, Vertov, Shub, and their compatriots had presided over a brief shining moment in which the plastic qualities of film were pushed to the limits, from 1924 to 1930. After that, Stalin's totalitarian dictatorship and indifference to artistic endeavor, coupled with Shumyatskiy's myopic lack of vision, ensured that the Soviet cinema would never again rise to the level of international prominence to which Eisenstein had brought it. Not until the 1970s and later the beginnings of *glasnost* would Soviet film rise again to any level of artistic ambition.

EARLY GERMAN FILM

In Germany, a similar period of experimentation was taking place, albeit under radically different circumstances. The prewar German cinema was composed for the most part of "actualities," short films in the manner of the Lumière brothers and later short dramas with child protagonists, such as *Carlchen und Carlo* (1902); "mountain films," a peculiarly German genre set against the backdrop of the country's characteristic terrain, as in *Der Alpenjäger* (*The Alpine Hunter*, 1910); and domestic melodramas, exemplified by the film *Zweimal gelebt* (*Two Lives*, 1912) by Max Mack. By 1913, however, multi-reel films running thirty to fifty minutes were the norm, and action serials rose in popularity with the public, as in France. The French *film d'art* also caused a considerable stir in Germany, leading to the introduction of the *Autorenfilm*, literally "the author's film," which, as in

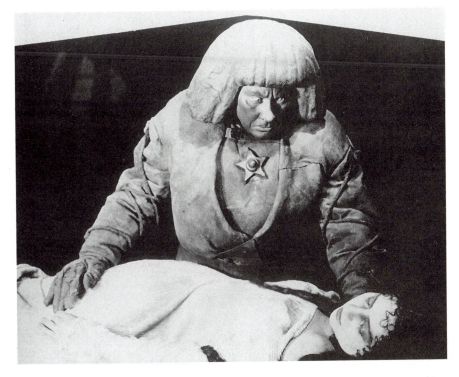

Paul Wegener in his 1920 version of *The Golem,* known as *Der Golem, wie er in die Welt kam,* which Wegener starred in, co-directed, and co-scripted.

France, sought to adapt the works of popular German authors to the screen in stagebound, static productions. Stellan Rye and Paul Wegener made *Der Student von Prag* (*The Student of Prague*) in 1913, and, as World War I began, such films as Franz Hofer's domestic melodrama *Heimgekehrt,* a k a *Weihnachtsglocken* (*Christmas Bells,* 1914) commanded audience attention. Paul Leni's *Das Tagebuch des Dr. Hart* (*The Diary of Dr. Hart,* 1916) is more directly concerned with the war, taking a surprisingly pacifist stand and featuring detailed battle scenes that leave little to the imagination.

While German film production actually increased during this period, as audience demand for Hollywood films plummeted, the films of wartime Germany were not widely exported, so that their influence outside the country was limited. But one director, Paul Wegener, was moving in a new direction that would prove immensely popular worldwide after the war—his almost single-handed creation of the Gothic horror fantasy. In 1915, Wegener co-directed (with Henrik Galeen) and starred in the first version of *Der Golem* (*The Golem*), one of the screen's first true monster films, and followed this success with *Der Rattenfänger von Hameln* (*The Pied Piper of*

Cesare the Somnambulist (Conrad Veidt) awakes from his coffin, as Dr. Caligari (Werner Krauss) looks on intently in Robert Wiene's *Das Cabinet des Dr. Caligari* (*The Cabinet of Dr. Caligari,* 1920).

Hamelin, 1918), which he also directed and starred in, as well as another film based on the Golem character, a gigantic, semi-benevolent monster derived from Jewish folklore, *Der Golem, wie er in die Welt kam,* co-directed with Carl Boese in 1920.

Wegener's early predilection for films of the fantastic and the macabre struck a responsive chord with audiences and led to the production of the first true international German box office success, Robert Wiene's *Das Cabinet des Dr. Caligari* (*The Cabinet of Dr. Caligari,* 1920). Wiene's film, with its bizarre sets and foreshortened perspective to tell the story of a serial killer loose in a modern metropolis, electrified audiences and made a star of Conrad Veidt, playing the role of the murderer Cesare the Somnambulist. The film used flashbacks and Expressionistic lighting, with a shock twist ending that still holds a jolt for the uninitiated, while also containing a surprising amount of graphic violence. Structured as a nightmarish vision of dreamlike insanity, *Caligari* afforded the viewer a glimpse into the soul of a man in torment and created a hermetically sealed world in which gloom, despair, and decay are the dominant emotions. The impact of the film's aggressively warped visual style was debated by audiences and critics alike, but it found overwhelming favor with the public. It is not too much to say that *Caligari* is the forerunner of the modern horror film, although Wiene's subsequent work as a director never approached a comparable level.

At the same time, all the various companies in the German film industry had been consolidated into one gigantic, state-subsidized entity, Universum Film Aktiengesellschaft (UFA). The merger took place in December 1917, and the government, in a state of collapse following Germany's defeat, ceded their financial interest in UFA the next year. Under the artistic direction of

producer Erich Pommer, the company embarked upon the creation of a series of films that would compose the Golden Age of German silent cinema,
among them *Caligari.*

Fritz Lang

The most important UFA director was undoubtedly Fritz Lang, one of the
key personages in cinema history. Whereas Jean Renoir was the supreme
humanist of the cinema, Lang was the eternal pessimist, most comfortable
with scenarios of doom and destruction that reflected his own bleak view
of life. Beginning as a scenarist for director Joe May, Lang was dissatisfied
with the manner in which May translated Lang's vision to the screen and
thus became a director himself. His first film, *Halbblut* (*The Half-Breed,*
1919), a revenge/romance drama, has been lost due to neglect and nitrate
decomposition, as was his next film, *Der Herr der Liebe* (*Master of Love,*
1919). But *Die Spinnen* (*The Spiders*), a two-part crime drama (*Der Gold-
ene See* [*The Golden Lake*] in 1919 and *Das Brillantenschiff* [*The Diamond
Ship*] in 1920), was enormously popular, firmly launched him on his new
career, and tagged him as an action director with a personal stake in his
films.

In fact, Lang was to have directed *Caligari,* but when the project was
turned over to Robert Wiene, Lang added the framing story that provides
the film's twist ending and then moved on to other projects. It was in 1920
that Lang met and began working with scenarist Thea von Harbou, who
would script his most influential German films; the couple married in 1922.
One success followed another, as Lang directed *Der Müde Tod* (*Destiny,*
1921), in which Death intervenes in the destiny of two lovers; *Dr. Mabuse,
der Spieler—Ein Bild der Zeit* (*Dr. Mabuse: The Gambler,* 1922), a two-part
serial-like epic that first introduced the notorious master criminal Dr.
Mabuse to the public; and *Die Nibelungen,* again in two parts (*Siegfrieds Tod*
[*Siegfried's Death*] and *Kriemhilds Rache* [*Kriemhild's Revenge*], both produced in 1924), which used the same source material as Richard Wagner's
Ring cycle, that of the thirteenth-century warrior Siegfried. Each film was
more successful than the last, and Lang refined his kinetic ability as a director, creating films of eye-pleasing spectacle that also contained great depth
as well as the psychological exploration of human frailties.

While the *Dr. Mabuse* films put decadence at the center of the narrative
and viewed the economic hyperinflation of the day as a terminally corrupt
construct, ready to collapse at any moment, the *Nibelungen* films offered the

The futuristic cityscape of Fritz Lang's *Metropolis* (1927).

public pageantry and mythological splendor, as Lang sought to recapture the grandeur of Germany's ancient history. Germany at the end of the First World War was a society in chaos, with inflation reaching catastrophic heights. A wheelbarrow full of bank notes was necessary to purchase a loaf of bread, and the currency was further devalued by the hour. Germany had lost the war, and now it was losing the country itself, together with the hope of a stable, middle-class life. Lang looked around him and saw German society in ruins.

Lang's most impressive achievement during this period is undoubtedly *Metropolis* (begun in 1925, completed in 1927), a massively scaled science fiction saga of a future civilization in which the very poor are condemned to a life of near-slavery to satisfy the needs of the rich. *Metropolis* used thousands of extras, enormous sets, and lavish special effects to dazzle audiences with a Dystopian fable of society gone awry, a world in which justice does not exist. With its vision of a hypercapitalist, consumer-driven world of the future, not unlike postwar Germany, *Metropolis* anticipated, and deeply influenced, most science fiction films of the twentieth century, in particular Ridley Scott's *Blade Runner* (1982) and George Lucas's *Star Wars* films (the first in 1977).

While some have dismissed *Metropolis* as a simplistic allegory, Lang's nightmarish vision of social inequality, bolstered by razor-sharp editing, expressive camera work, and remarkably prescient futuristic props (such as two-way television used as a communication device, monorails, and other technological advances), was an international success. The cost of the film, however, was enormous, and nearly bankrupted UFA during its lengthy production schedule. Lang went on to produce several more features in Germany during the silent era, including *Spione* (*Spies*, 1928) and *Frau im Mond*

(*Woman in the Moon*, 1929), an unusual and lavish science fiction film with a female protagonist.

For his first sound film, Lang directed Peter Lorre in *M* (1931), the story of a psychopathic child murderer who cannot stop himself from committing his horrible crimes. In the film's conclusion, Berlin's underworld crime bosses gather together to stop Lorre's character, repelled by his bestiality and fearful that a police crackdown will hamper their own illicit activities. In response to the Nazis' rise to power in 1933, Lang created *Das Testament des Dr. Mabuse* (*The Testament of Dr. Mabuse,* 1933), a courageous act of social criticism in which he put Nazi slogans and text from Hitler's manifesto *Mein Kampf* into the mouths of Mabuse and his utterly degenerate henchmen.

Dr. Joseph Goebbels, the head of the Reich's Ministry of Propaganda, banned the film but then called Lang in for a meeting; in a surprise move he offered him a key post at the now-Nazified UFA, working on films that would aid the Reich's aims of world domination. Lang knew who had tipped Goebbels off to the subversive content of his latest *Dr. Mabuse* film: it was none other than his own wife and key scenarist, Thea von Harbou, who was drifting into the Nazi orbit and would soon become a reliable screenwriter, and later a director, in service to Hitler's Germany. Von Harbou had collaborated with Lang on the script of *The Testament of Dr. Mabuse* and, alarmed at the direction the film was taking, immediately alerted the authorities to what she viewed as Lang's "disloyalty." In addition, Lang's mother was partly of Jewish ancestry, but Goebbels indicated he was willing to overlook this "crime" if Lang went along with the Nazis' plans.

Lang saw that he was trapped. Pretending to accept Goebbels's offer, Lang almost immediately fled the country, abandoning the negatives of all his films, his personal fortune, and his wife—who promptly divorced him. His act of moral courage in this situation is difficult to overestimate; had he stayed and lent his considerable skill and international reputation to the Nazi movement, he would have been a formidable propagandist for the Reich. But despite his innate pessimism and fatalistic outlook, Lang acted quickly and decisively, removing himself from harm and depriving Hitler of Germany's most popular film director at the height of his early fame.

After his flight from Germany, Lang made one film in France, the fantasy *Liliom* (1934), before coming to the United States, where he began his second career as a director at MGM. Soon, other talented German expatriates fleeing the Third Reich would join him; many of these artists eventually wound up working as filmmakers in the fight against Fascism.

Max Schreck as the vampire in
F. W. Murnau's *Nosferatu* (1922).

F. W. Murnau, Pabst, and the Silent German Movie Masters

Before leaving Germany at this precipitous moment, we should consider some of the other filmmakers who made significant contributions to the cinema in the 1920s. F. W. Murnau directed the classic vampire tale *Nosferatu* in 1922, with a heavily made-up Max Schreck in the title role of a Dracula-like vampire; indeed, Murnau had simply lifted the entire plot line of Bram Stoker's novel *Dracula*, then still under copyright, to create the scenario for his film. Although Stoker himself was dead, his wife was not; she sued Murnau, demanding that the negative and all prints of *Nosferatu* be summarily destroyed. The case dragged on for years, but fortunately several prints of the film survived, and today we can see *Nosferatu* intact as one of the most effective and chilling renditions of the Dracula legend. Murnau went on to create *Der Letzte Mann* (*The Last Man*, a k a *The Last Laugh* 1924), the story of a proud doorman at a plush hotel who is stripped of his uniform and position and forced to work as a janitor in the men's toilets. The film used numerous technical tricks, such as first-person camera work, multiple superimpositions within the frame, and Expressionistic lighting to convey the tragedy and pathos of the doorman's plight, coupled with Emil Jannings's superb performance in the role. As a twist, in the last few minutes of the film, Jannings's character suddenly comes into a fortune, and when we last see him he is comfortably ensconced in the hotel's dining room.

Other important German directors include Georg Wilhelm Pabst, better known as G. W. Pabst, who created the melodrama *Die Freudlose Gasse* (*The Joyless Street*, 1925) and then went on to direct the silent classics *Die Büchse der Pandora* (*Pandora's Box*, 1929) and *Das Tagebuch einer Verlorenen* (*Diary of a Lost Girl*, 1929), two equally downbeat films in which American-born Louise Brooks portrays a woman of easy virtue and few moral scruples. Walter Ruttman created a dazzling documentary, akin to Vertov's 1929 *The Man with a Movie Camera*, with his *Berlin: Die Sinfonie der Großstadt* (*Berlin: Symphony of a Great City*, 1927), using footage shot by Karl Freund, the great cinematographer who had pho-

Emil Jannings reduced to a men's room attendant in F. W. Murnau's *Der Letzte Mann* (*The Last Laugh*, 1924).

tographed Lang's *Metropolis* and who would go on to a long career in America as a cinematographer and director (his last job was, astoundingly, as director of photography on the television show "I Love Lucy" in the 1950s). Curt Siodmak, his brother Robert Siodmak, Edgar G. Ulmer, Billy Wilder, and Fred Zinnemann, all of whom would go on to major careers as directors in American cinema, collaborated on the sexually charged melodrama *Menschen am Sonntag* (*People on Sunday*, 1930), which has recently been restored by the Nederlands Film Archive in Amsterdam after nearly three-quarters of a century as a "phantom film" that was accessible only to a few.

EARLY JAPANESE FILMMAKING

Elsewhere in the world, the cinema was also coming to maturity, especially in Japan, where director Yasujiro Ozu was creating films in his own idiosyncratic style, at the beginning of a long career that would stretch from the late 1920s to the early 1960s, covering not only the transition from silent films to sound, but from black-and-white to color. Sound came late to Japan, in large part because of the *benshi*, narrators who performed during screenings of silent films, commenting on the film's narrative as well as advancing the plots. The *benshi* correctly sensed that the sound film would spell an end to their profession, and they sometimes resorted to violence to press their case, with the result that the first Japanese sound film, Heinosuke Gosho's *Madamu to nyobo* (*The Neighbor's Wife and Mine*) was not released until 1931. Even after this, silent films continued to be produced in large quantity in Japan, not ceasing production completely until 1936. Thus, Ozu's finest silent films include his masterful *I Was Born, But . . .* (*Otona no miru ehon—Umarete wa mita keredo*), a charming coming-of-age comedy, which was completed in 1932, when most of the world was already firmly in the sound era.

Often called the most Japanese of directors, Ozu went on to create films notable for their restrained editorial pace and meditational camera work, which consisted almost exclusively of shots taken by a stationary camera from a low angle, usually about three feet from the ground, mimicking the eye-level of the characters in his films, who habitually sat on cushions or *tatami* mats rather than chairs, in accordance with Japanese social custom. Then, too, Ozu's visual style was almost entirely devoid of such devices as fade-outs or fade-ins, usually used to suggest the passage of time, or any sort of camera movement within the shot. Thus, his camera observes the world with a gaze of serene detachment, and yet this quiet, careful approach to mise-en-scène makes his films deeply compelling.

During the silent era, Japan's film production was remarkably high, almost reaching that of Hollywood, with roughly four hundred films produced in 1931 alone. In large part, this was due to Japan's cultural and social isolation, a situation that would come to an abrupt end with World War II. But despite its insularity, or perhaps because of it, the Japanese silent film achieved a certain purity of aesthetic ambition, and by the 1920s two major genres of cinema had emerged in the furious pace of production: the *gendai-geki,* contemporary drama about family life and social conditions (Ozu's specialty), and *jidai-geki,* films that re-created Japan's feudal, often violent past. A third genre also emerged in the wake of the massive earthquake of September 1923, which devastated Tokyo and Yokohama, and caused an abrupt though temporary cessation of film production, due to the fact that many film production facilities had been destroyed. The *shomin-geki,* or film dealing with the struggle for existence among Japan's blue-collar social classes, was a direct result of this natural disaster.

Important directors during this period in Japanese cinema include Minoru Murata, Kenji Mizoguchi (who created period dramas and contemporary narratives with equal assurance), Heinosuke Gosho, and Teinosuke

Kinugasa, whose film *Jujiro* (*Shadows of the Yoshiwara*, 1928) was the first film to receive general distribution outside Japan. Mizoguchi, Gosho, and of course Ozu would become major directors during the sound era of Japanese cinema, with careers lasting into the 1950s and 1960s. Despite Japan's seemingly closed society, Hollywood films were quite popular in Japan during the silent era, particularly after the 1923 earthquake, and many of the *gendai-geki* films especially were influenced by technical and aesthetic strategies favored by Western cinema.

One of the most unusual films to come out of Japan during this period was Teinosuke Kinugasa's highly experimental *Kurutta Ippeji* (*A Page of Madness*, 1926), which, like *The Cabinet of Dr. Caligari*, used exaggerated sets and heightened theatricality to tell the tale of a mother imprisoned in an insane asylum after the attempted murder of her son. The film's narrative structure is chaotic, proceeding in dreamlike fashion, and Kinugasa is clearly more interested in revealing his characters' inner conflicts than in any sense of traditional plot progression. One of the most individual films of the Japanese silent cinema, *A Page of Madness* was thought to be lost for nearly half a century until Kinugasa discovered a copy of the film in his tool shed in 1971. He had a new print of the film made, added a contemporary musical score, and subsequently re-released the film internationally to great acclaim.

*   *   *

While much of the world found a distinctive national voice during the silent era, many other countries remained in thrall to Hollywood's commercial vision, existing as colonialized outposts of the Western cinematic empire. In England, the Hollywood film rose to such cultural dominance that the government enacted the Protectionist Cinematographic Films Act of 1927, mandating that a percentage of all films screened in England had to have been produced within the country. Hollywood got around this by setting up facilities in England (such as Paramount British, Warners British, and MGM British) to create program pictures, running little more than an hour and produced for £5,000 or less, which became derisively known as "quota quickies." Although the resulting films were shoddy and lacking in artistic innovation, they were, technically, English made. As a result, Hollywood studios could induce local theaters to screen these pictures through block booking, in order for exhibitors to receive the American movies their audiences truly wanted. The effect was to co-opt the nascent British national cinema, which, with the exception of but a few truly indigenous productions, remained moribund.

Elsewhere, the various nations of Africa were still colonized, with France, England, Belgium, and other nations controlling social and imagistic commerce, relying on Hollywood films and the occasional European import to provide programming for the few theaters that regularly screened films for the public. Brazil in the early silent period relied mostly on Hollywood for its films, and the Mexican film industry was similarly dormant. China's film industry was largely subsidized by the West, producing forgettable romances and melodramas, while India was still a part of the British Empire, with local filmmaking confined to carefully censored newsreels and self-congratulatory travelogues. Egypt also relied on American imports for much of its early silent programming, and what little production there was bore the stamp of Hollywood production techniques.

For much of the world, then, the cinema was something that was imported from America rather than created locally, a situation that in many ways persists to the present day. But as we have seen, many countries throughout the world successfully resisted the generic lure of the Hollywood formula, producing films that spoke to issues of national identity and local cultural heritage. Nevertheless, as sound was introduced throughout the globe—emanating, as we have seen, from Hollywood—the major American studios rapidly consolidated their hold on the international film market, by producing, in the 1930s and 1940s, a torrent of star-driven, escapist spectacles, backed by an efficient and far-reaching distribution network. For better or worse, the coming of sound created a period of Hollywood hegemony, in which the American commercial film dominated the world's box office. We will examine the films, directors, and stars that defined what many consider to be Hollywood's most influential and important era.

FOUR

THE HOLLYWOOD STUDIO SYSTEM IN THE 1930S AND 1940S

Sound films had been around since before the turn of the century when Alice Guy shot more than one hundred brief films using Gaumont's Chronophone system, which employed synchronized wax cylinders to record sound using a "Morning Glory" horn, a large acoustical "hearing aid," to capture the voices of the performers. But the Chronophone and similar processes prior to the de Forest sound-on-film process lacked the obvious benefits of electronic amplification, which de Forest's newly perfected vacuum tube made possible. Lee de Forest, in fact, was drawing on a series of experiments that dated back to the nineteenth-century work of the American inventor Joseph T. Tykociner, as well as work done by Eugene Lauste, who also conducted early experiments in sound-on-film. In addition, in 1919, three German scientists, Joseph Massole, Josef Engl, and Hans Vogt, created the Tri-Ergon system, which employed a primitive photographic sensor to transform sound into striations of light and dark, creating the prototype for de Forest's optical sound-track process.

THE COMING OF SOUND

To publicize his new invention, de Forest created roughly one thousand short films featuring comics, musicians, and vaudeville stars of the era. His invention, which he called Phonofilm, was a modest financial success, but without the backing of a major studio sound-on-film remained a novelty. From 1923 to 1927, the studios all resisted the coming of sound, realizing that it would create profound economic and technological changes. As with the advent of color film and later television, Hollywood was resistant to any changes in the status quo, and for all intents and purposes sound was suppressed by the industry until Warner Bros., in dire financial straits, risked nearly everything they owned on *The Jazz Singer* in 1927. When that film clicked resoundingly with the public, a new era was born.

The major battle in the competing sound processes was between de Forest's sound-on-film and Vitaphone's sound-on-disc. Warners opted for sound-on-disc for *The Jazz Singer* and its subsequent talkies, and at first the other studios followed suit. But by 1930, sound-on-film was being used as well, and the need for a standardized system became apparent. Acting with rare unanimity, the studios voted for a sound-on-film process then being touted by Vitaphone, which was largely based on de Forest's work. Theaters, meanwhile, were still scrambling to make the changeover; by 1931, nearly all the nation's theaters were wired for sound. The motion picture industry would benefit from the new technology after the Wall Street crash of 1929 and the onset of the Great Depression, as audiences flocked to theaters to escape the real desperation of their own increasingly uncertain lives.

ESCAPISM

By 1930, ninety million Americans were going to the movies at least once a week, and many families, especially in the larger cities, virtually lived at the movies, watching the same film over and over again in second-run "grind" houses to avoid the cold or to escape the confines of their homes. In the wake of the Crash, many were homeless and jobless, and theaters provided an inexpensive and entertaining way to pass the time indoors. While first-run theaters charged top prices and ran a single feature a few times a day, neighborhood theaters would run two films as a double bill, along with cartoons, travelogues, newsreels, and coming attractions, to create a program running nearly four hours in length, repeated continuously from noon to midnight, or sometimes even twenty-four hours a day. For a populace deprived of the real American dream, the escapist fantasies of the Hollywood dream factory offered some relief from the drudgery of daily existence.

THE STUDIO SYSTEM

The studio system was in essence an assembly line that cranked out roughly a feature film per week for each of the major studios, regimented into "A" pictures, with top casts and directors and luxurious shooting schedules, and "B" pictures, which were shot in one or two weeks on existing sets, using second-string players under contract to the studio for maximum economy. There were also short subjects, cartoons, serials, and even "C" pictures (mostly program westerns) shot on microscopic budgets in as little as two or three days from the barest of scripts. All studios maintained a roster of directors, writers, actors, and technicians under contract, to be used on any project at the whim of their bosses. Literary properties (novels, short stories, plays) for "A" and "B" pictures were purchased and then turned into shooting scripts. Cast, directors, and crew were assigned to shoot the films, while an army of decorators, costume designers, and prop men completed the sets. With shooting finished, the films would be edited into rough cuts and screened for studio executives, who would suggest revisions and retakes, while staff composers would create a suitable musical score. After sneak previews for selected audiences, the films would go out into general release across the country, often in the theaters owned by the studio, thus guaranteeing a regular market for their product. The films would sometimes be re-released later as either a second feature with a new "A" film or alone. The demand for product was intense, and the studios had to maintain a clockwork schedule to satisfy it.

Bela Lugosi as the bloodthirsty count in Tod Browning's *Dracula* (1931).

Almost immediately, each major studio established a generic identity, which differentiated it from its competitors. Warner Bros. specialized in hard-boiled gangster films, social melodramas, and Busby Berkeley's outrageously over-the-top musicals, while Universal rapidly became known as the home of the horror film, with such productions as Tod Browning's *Dracula* (1931), with Bela Lugosi, James Whale's *Frankenstein* (1931), with Boris Karloff, and many other such works. Paramount was home to the madcap antics of the Marx Brothers at their most anarchic, in addition to the sizzling double-entendres of reigning sex goddess Mae West and the droll misanthropy of comedian W. C. Fields. Paramount was also the studio that pushed the envelope of public morality with the greatest insistence, which, as we shall see, had major consequences for the entire industry. Columbia was considered a Poverty Row studio until Harry Cohn

Boris Karloff in the role that made him an instant star, the monster in James Whale's *Frankenstein* (1931).

lured director Frank Capra into his employ. Then, with Clark Gable on loan from MGM as "punishment" for refusing to toe the line for MGM boss Louis B. Mayer, Capra created *It Happened One Night* (1934), which swept the Academy Awards, made Gable a major star overnight, and put Columbia on the map.

MGM was widely considered the Tiffany of all the studios, making all-star vehicles such as Edmund Goulding's *Grand Hotel* (1932) and George Cukor's *Dinner at Eight* (1933), featuring John Barrymore, Greta Garbo, Joan Crawford, Wallace Beery, Jean Harlow, Marie Dressler, and other luminaries from their glittering roster of contract players. According to studio publicity, MGM had "more stars than there are in heaven." Their more modest films still retained a high production gloss, such as the long-running Andy Hardy series, chronicling the small-town life and misadventures of an idealized American family, with a young Mickey Rooney starring as the family's irrepressible teenage son. Twentieth Century Fox came into its own with Henry King's *Lloyd's of London* (1936), starring Tyrone Power. Though Fox was always rather thin in star power, the studio created a vision of America as a great cultural melting pot, relying heavily on non-copyrighted songs of the late nineteenth century. Meanwhile, RKO Radio Pictures' *King Kong* (1933), directed by Merian C. Cooper and Ernest B. Schoedsack and with special effects by Willis H. O'Brien and his assistant, Marcel Delgado, made a

fortune for the studio when it needed it most. In addition, RKO had a string of hits with the dance team of Fred Astaire and Ginger Rogers, beginning with Thornton Freeland's *Flying Down to Rio* (1933), which served as a tonic to the lavish effulgence of Busby Berkeley's anonymous, kaleidoscopic musical production numbers at Warners in such films as Mervyn LeRoy's *Gold Diggers of 1933*.

Performers were typically under contract for seven years, during which a studio would use its considerable resources to build a career, guiding players through a series of minor roles in modest films, along with singing, dancing, and acting classes, grooming them for their big breakthrough. For some, Hollywood stardom never came. The seven-year contracts were entirely one-sided; the studio had a six-month option clause and could terminate an actor's employment on the merest whim, or put someone on suspension for refusing to accept an inferior role, with the suspension period tacked onto the end of the seven-year term.

But for "A" list stars, such as Spencer Tracy, Bette Davis, James Cagney, Greta Garbo, and Joan Crawford, life was very good indeed. The studios mi-

A typically lavish Busby Berkeley production number ("We're in the Money") from Mervyn LeRoy's Depression-era musical *Gold Diggers of 1933* (1933).

cromanaged the stars' personal lives as well as their professional ones: dates were arranged between stars to publicize upcoming pictures, studios arranged low- or no-interest loans to purchase sprawling estates for the actors to reside in, and meals were served in the studio dining room to satisfy individual tastes.

At the same time, a morals clause in each star's contract, prohibiting wild parties, extramarital affairs, and the like, kept actors in line. In addition, directors, cameramen, composers, screenwriters, set designers, costumers, and other key personnel were under long-term contracts so that their services could easily be arranged for several pictures a year. The Hollywood studio system at its zenith was a true factory; in the 1930s and 1940s, a freelance director or star was a rarity. The studio's identity was defined by the stars it had under contract, the kinds of films it made, and the visual look of its product, the result of an army of designers and technicians behind the scenes.

PROBLEMS WITH EARLY SOUND

Technological advances during this period were numerous. The first microphones for recording sound were clumsy and bulky and produced poor sound quality. Technicians insisted that the performers stand next to the microphones for optimal sound quality; this meant that both the camera and the actors stopped moving, resulting in static films that fans and critics alike derisively labeled "teacup drama." Most actors in early sound films were recruited from Broadway; for those who did not have a good speaking voice, the parade was over. John Gilbert, one of the most famous stars of silent films, saw his career crumble because his high tenor voice didn't mesh with the public perception of him as a dashing romantic hero (although rumors persist that his decline was the result of a feud with Louis B. Mayer). In the early days of sound, dubbing and mixing were all but impossible, so that many films were shot with multiple stationary cameras, each in a soundproof booth, while an orchestra played off screen so that all sound could be recorded simultaneously.

Tod Browning (sitting on rafter, left) directs John Gilbert in *The Show* (1927).

Not surprisingly, directors soon balked at these limitations, and audiences grew tired of films in which dialogue was the sole attraction. The early musicals of Ernst Lubitsch, such as *The Love Parade* (1929) and *Monte Carlo* (1930), used extensive post-synchronization to lay in music tracks after the film had been shot silently, allowing the camera to return to its state of mobility. Rouben Mamoulian, one of early sound film's most audacious pioneers, was a proponent of the moving camera in such films as *Applause* (1929), *City Streets* (1931), and his masterpiece, *Dr. Jekyll and Mr. Hyde* (1931), still the most visually stimulating of the many versions of the classic tale. Soon cameras were mounted inside "blimps," which soundproofed the noise of their running electric motors, and microphones were mounted on "booms," long poles that were extended over the actors within a scene to allow mobility for the performers. Editing systems also improved, along with the introduction of separate sound and picture tracks that allowed cutters to freely manipulate the image and audio components of a film, as well as improvements in postproduction sound mixing and dubbing.

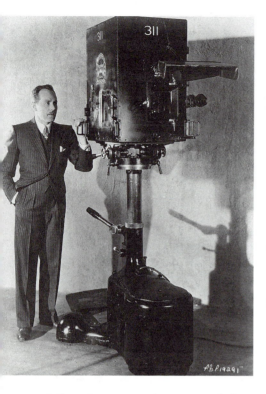

In the early 1930s, sound cameras were bulky and cumbersome.

GLORIOUS TECHNICOLOR

In 1935, Hollywood produced its first three-strip Technicolor feature film, Mamoulian's *Becky Sharp*. Three-strip Technicolor was a color additive process that exposed three separate strands of film in one gigantic camera, and then printed these three strands on top of one another to produce a full color effect. It was a vast improvement over the red and green pallor of "two-strip" Technicolor and the various stencil and dye processes that had been used since the medium's inception, in which film was run through a fixing bath and dyed one "color" for dramatic effect, or hand-colored frame by frame. Created by Herbert T. Kalmus, Technicolor soon became the dominant force in color films, and his company jealously guarded both its process and the equipment used to shoot Technicolor films. In fact, if a producer wanted to use Technicolor, he had to sign an agreement with the company to use Technicolor's camera and Technicolor's own house cameramen, and to employ Natalie Kalmus, Herbert's wife, as "color coordinator." Her taste ran to bold reds, vivid greens, and equally pronounced hues of all the other colors in the spectrum; pastels and shading were out.

If a producer or director argued about the use of color, Natalie Kalmus was quite willing to pull the plug on the whole project. Her sole function was to make sure that Technicolor showed itself to best advantage no matter what the subject matter, which accounts for the vibrancy of color in such classics of the period as *Gone with the Wind* and *The Wizard of Oz* (both 1939). At the same time, by the 1940s black-and-white cinematography had developed into a highly sophisticated art, with the introduction of more sensitive film and the adventurous lighting patterns pioneered by such brilliant cameramen as James Wong Howe, John Alton, Lee Garmes, Gregg Toland, and Nicholas Musuraca. Hollywood in the 1930s and 1940s was, on the whole, a rigidly defined genre factory, in which individual talents were tolerated and encouraged only as long as they added to the hegemony of the studio's hold on the public imagination.

JOHN FORD

Despite the fact that the studio moguls ran their empires like medieval kingdoms, using equal measures of fear, flattery, blandishments, and threats, some of the greatest directors in the history of cinema flourished under the Hollywood studio system. John Ford rapidly established himself as one of the industry's leading lights, specializing in westerns but working across a wide variety of genres. After many years in silent films beginning with *The Tornado* (1917), he scored his first sound success with a brilliant adaptation of Sinclair Lewis's novel *Arrowsmith* in 1931, about an idealistic doctor whose work leads him to question conventional medical ethics. In 1935, Ford directed the classic story of the IRA, *The Informer*, with Victor McLaglen, which again won him numerous plaudits. And yet Ford could direct a Shirley Temple feature such as *Wee Willie Winkie* (1937) with equal assurance, as well as the routine action picture *Submarine Patrol* (1938). In 1939, he directed the classic western *Stagecoach*, which made a star out of John Wayne. Wayne had been kicking around in films since the late 1920s; he and Ford struck up a friendship, and Ford subsequently recommended him for the leading role in Raoul Walsh's *The Big Trail* (1930), but the film failed to click at the box office. Wayne was then too inexperienced to command the au-

John Wayne (foreground) as the Ringo Kid in John Ford's classic western *Stagecoach* (1939).

dience's attention, and for the next nine years he struggled to make a living in a series of forgettable low-budget westerns, at one point even being pressed into service as a singing cowboy in the mold of Gene Autry and Roy Rogers, as "Singin' Sandy Saunders." Ford recognized that with a solid property and skillful direction, Wayne, older and wiser in 1939, would be ideal for the role of the Ringo Kid in *Stagecoach*, and the gamble paid off. As Wayne famously observed, Ford taught him not "how to act, but to react" to the other performers, to keep his gestures to a minimum, and to use his words sparingly.

Ford then went on to what many consider his finest film, *The Grapes of Wrath* (1940), based on John Steinbeck's novel about migrant farmers during the Depression. Henry Fonda, another of Ford's favorite actors, gives an

Henry Fonda as Tom Joad in John Ford's *The Grapes of Wrath* (1940), one of the greatest films ever made about the effects of the Depression on American society.

understated and convincing portrayal of Tom Joad, forced with his family to search for a new beginning in a hostile landscape. When World War II came, Ford created several documentaries for the U.S. Navy before returning to civilian life with a string of classic westerns: *My Darling Clementine* (1946), *Fort Apache* (1948), *She Wore a Yellow Ribbon* (1949), and the masterful work *The Searchers* (1956), often cited, despite its often inherently racist depiction of Native Americans, as the perfect film.

Ford was one of the consummate studio directors, infusing simple material with his core values of duty, honor, and service to one's country. As a visual stylist, he preferred a rigidly stationary camera, known as the "information booth" style of direction, in which the actors enter a scene, play it out, and then exit, all in one take. His coverage of a scene is often simple, but his compositions are striking in their use of depth, light and shadow, and strategic camera placement. For many years, he shot most of his westerns in Monument Valley, Utah, using al-

John Wayne, John Ford, and Ben Johnson on the set of Ford's elegiac western *She Wore a Yellow Ribbon* (1949).

John Wayne and Jeffrey Hunter in John Ford's masterly western *The Searchers* (1956).

most the same location, so that a Ford western is instantly recognizable; fellow directors stayed away from Monument Valley as a sign of respect to him.

HOWARD HAWKS: THE GRAY FOX

Howard Hawks embraced a similar code of professionalism and moral conduct in his films, but Hawks was unique in the 1930s and 1940s because he refused to be tied down to one studio and worked in nearly every genre imaginable, from westerns to musicals, always with remarkable success. As producer of most of the films he directed, he kept a tight rein on the shooting process to ensure that everything was completed on time and under budget. Known as "the Gray Fox" because of his prematurely gray hair, as well as his skills as producer and director, Hawks often said that the key to a good film was simply "three good scenes, and no bad ones." After a brief apprenticeship in the silent cinema, he broke out in 1930 with *The Dawn Patrol*, one of the great wartime aviation dramas. In 1930, working for independent producer Howard Hughes from a screenplay by former newspaperman Ben Hecht, Hawks directed *Scarface* (though it was not released until 1932), one of the most brutal gangster films of the early 1930s, loosely based on the life of Al Capone.

In 1934, Hawks created the quintessential screwball comedy *Twentieth Century,* starring John Barrymore and Carole Lombard, with Barrymore in

Cary Grant, "Baby" (the leopard), and Katharine Hepburn in Howard Hawks's screwball classic *Bringing Up Baby* (1938).

top form as the egomaniacal theatrical producer Oscar Jaffe. *Bringing Up Baby* (1938) was another screwball classic and is considered one of Cary Grant and Katharine Hepburn's finest films; "Baby" is Hepburn's pet leopard, which gets both Grant and Hepburn in and out of a series of absurdist escapades. *His Girl Friday* (1940), a remake of Lewis Milestone's comedy *The Front Page* (1931), teams Cary Grant and Rosalind Russell in a hard-boiled newspaper romance, notable for its cynicism and breakneck pace, as the players breathlessly rattle off their dialogue in record time.

After directing one of the great World War II dramas, *Air Force,* in 1943, Hawks, with the help of his wife, "discovered" Lauren Bacall and cast her opposite Humphrey Bogart in *To Have and Have Not* (1944). The chemistry between Bogart and Bacall was electric and carried over into real life; by 1946's *The Big Sleep,* perhaps the finest hard-boiled detective film ever made, Bogart and Bacall were in the midst of a serious romance, much to Hawks's displeasure (Bogart was married at the time, and Hawks, who had given Bacall the same nickname he used for his own wife, "Slim," also had designs on the young actress). The intricate twists and double crosses in *The Big Sleep,* based on Raymond Chandler's famous Philip Marlowe novel, were so complex that the screenwriters (novelist William Faulkner, Jules Furthman, and Leigh Brackett) sent a telegram to Chandler, asking for clarification on a particular murder in the film. Chandler replied that he had "no idea" who

Humphrey Bogart as Philip Marlowe (right) gets the drop on a stick-up man while Lauren Bacall, as Vivian Sternwood, looks on with admiration in Howard Hawks's complex murder mystery, *The Big Sleep* (1946).

had committed the crime, and the resulting film is a bewildering cross-hatch of murders, swindles, con games, and doubletalk that both mystifies and enthralls the viewer.

As the war ended, Hawks embarked upon one of his most ambitious projects, *Red River* (1948), an epic western starring John Wayne and Montgomery Clift. The movie raised the western to a new level of sophistication, and Wayne's brutal portrayal of a psychotic trail boss who will do anything to get his cattle to market surprised even John Ford, who saw the film and then told Hawks, "I didn't know the s.o.b. could *act.*" Hawks's films are all shot through with a sense of grace under pressure, a certain fatalism in human interactions, and the idea that "a man has to know his limitations." In addition, Hawks pioneered the pre-feminist concept of the "Hawksian Woman," a strong female protagonist who refuses to buckle under to men, is perfectly capable of taking care of herself, and operates smoothly in what Hawks clearly views as a man's world.

HITCHCOCK IN HOLLYWOOD

Meanwhile, Alfred Hitchcock continued his string of suspense classics in England with *The 39 Steps* (1935), *Secret Agent* (1936), *Sabotage* (1936), and

Robert Donat and Madeleine Carroll in Alfred Hitchcock's breakthrough thriller, *The 39 Steps* (1935).

The Lady Vanishes (1938) before accepting an offer from producer David O. Selznick to come to Hollywood and direct *Rebecca* (1940), based on Daphne du Maurier's novel. The film was an immediate box office and critical success, and Hitchcock's American career was launched. Describing the facilities at American studios as "incomparably better" than those he had used in England, Hitchcock began a long string of deeply personal films superficially masquerading as thrillers.

Shadow of a Doubt (1943), with a superb performance from Joseph Cotten as a compulsive murderer of wealthy widows, was followed by *Lifeboat* (1944), a stylistic tour de force in which the surviving passengers of a sunken ship struggle against the elements and each other's jealousies and fears. *Spellbound* (1945) is a psychological murder mystery with a dream sequence choreographed by Salvador Dalí. *Rope* (1948) is the chilling story of two young men who strangle one of their friends and then host a party in which food is served on the trunk containing the dead body. What makes *Rope* so intriguing is that it consists exclusively of lengthy tracking shots, often up to ten minutes long, in which Hitchcock's camera dollies smoothly around the killers' New York penthouse, allowing the tragic narrative to play out in real time with only a handful of edit points in the entire film.

Hitchcock was one of the first directors to have his name above the title as a key selling point, and he is among the few directors whose films almost constitute a genre unto themselves, the suspense-filled "Hitchcock thriller" (similarly, a "Ford western"). A meticulous planner, he storyboarded each of his films from first shot to last before a single foot of film was exposed; he liked to say that this was his favorite part of making a film, because the actual shooting was often boring and laborious.

Hitchcock's most frequent leading men were Cary Grant and James Stewart, actors who could fend for themselves in front of the camera and who traded largely on their own screen personae to bring a role to life. Taciturn

A motley group of survivors faces the perils of the ocean in Alfred Hitchcock's *Lifeboat* (1944), a parable about the need for personal responsibility in wartime.

on the set, Hitchcock drove some of his actors to distraction with his aloof, distanced approach; during the remake of *The Man Who Knew Too Much* (1956), Doris Day almost quit because the director refused to provide any feedback on the set. Finally confronted about his seeming indifference, Hitchcock looked deeply surprised and told Day that no comment from him was necessary, as she was giving "just what I wanted" in her performance. This detachment from the shooting process allowed him to design his films as intricate puzzles that hook the audience with clever and exciting touches.

FRITZ LANG IN AMERICA

Fritz Lang picked up his career in America after his rapid departure from Nazi Germany with *Fury* (1936), an anti-lynching melodrama starring Spencer Tracy. Lang originally wanted the protagonist, the intended victim of the film, to be African American, in order to expose the vicious racism he had observed in the American South. Although he fought with his studio bosses at MGM "like a Trojan," in his own words, he was simply ahead of his time. The film is still a ringing indictment of small-town narrow-mindedness and prejudice. Lang found it difficult initially to work on a Hollywood set—he saw no reason to stop for lunch or dinner if a scene was going well, and rapidly alienated his star, and much of his crew, with his dictatorial attitude—but he soon adjusted to the studio system and became one of Hollywood's most personal, if pessimistic, stylists. After *You Only Live Once* (1937), a superb drama in which Henry Fonda, as an ex-convict, tries to go straight but finds that the deck is stacked against him, Lang was assigned to two Technicolor westerns at Twentieth Century Fox, *The Return of Frank James* (1940) and the epic *Western Union* (1941). When Fox's studio chief questioned whether or not Lang could persuasively handle the material, the director replied that the western was America's great mythic saga, as *Die Niebelungen* was Germany's, and that he felt entirely at home with the epic sweep of the material.

Lang directed the anti-Nazi action drama *Hangmen Also Die* (1943) and went on to make three of his most suspenseful and unremittingly fatalistic films in a two-year blaze of creativity: *Ministry of Fear* (1944), *The Woman in the Window* (1945), and *Scarlet Street* (1945). Ray Milland stars in *Ministry of Fear* as a mental patient caught in a web of espionage, but given his unbalanced state no one will believe him when he tries to go to the authorities. *The Woman in the Window* and *Scarlet Street* have identical casts, and nearly the same plot: 1940s tough-guy Dan Duryea, seductress Joan Bennett, and Edward G. Robinson, cast against type as a mild-mannered victim of Duryea and Bennett's machinations. All three films represent high points in the genre of film noir, a moody, pessimistic style of filming with downbeat plots, unscrupulous protagonists, and dark, atmospheric cinematography that reflected the social malaise and unease of postwar American society. In all these films, Lang developed his view of humanity as essentially flawed, foredoomed, and inherently corruptible.

CHAPLIN IN THE 1930S

As late as 1936, with *Modern Times,* Charles Chaplin was still making silent films with musical accompaniment and sound effects, although that film borrows perhaps too freely from René Clair's early sound masterpiece *À Nous la liberté* (1931); both are satires on the dehumanization of the factory assembly line, though Clair's vision is more romantic and whimsical. Working at his own studio, Chaplin created *The Great Dictator* (1940), the first film in which the Little Tramp character was given a voice. A courageous satire of Hitler, the film initially failed to find favor with the public, perhaps in part because it appeared before the United States entered World War II. Chaplin's final films—*Monsieur Verdoux* (1947), a dark comedy about a serial killer

[LEFT]: Charles Chaplin starred in his own satire on mechanized society, *Modern Times* (1936). [RIGHT]: Charles Chaplin as Adenoid Hynkel, the power-mad dictator of Tomania, in Chaplin's spoof of Hitler, *The Great Dictator* (1940).

with Chaplin in the title role; *Limelight* (1952), a backstage melodrama; *A King in New York* (1957), a mild political satire reflecting Chaplin's disenchantment with the Cold War; and *A Countess from Hong Kong* (1967), a gently amusing farce shot in England and teaming Marlon Brando and Sophia Loren—form a quiet coda to Chaplin's great work as an auteur.

THE LUBITSCH TOUCH

Ernst Lubitsch, as we have seen, began with a series of sophisticated sex comedies in Germany, but unlike Lang he left long before the Nazis came to power. By 1924, he was directing *The Marriage Circle* for Warner Bros. and then moved over to Paramount, where he created his most enduring masterpieces in the 1930s: *The Love Parade* (1929), *The Smiling Lieutenant* (1931), *One Hour with You* (1932, which was begun by director George Cukor), and the sublime *Trouble in Paradise* (1932), all romantic comedies with a bite. Lubitsch used the French music hall star Maurice Chevalier in many of his early films, perhaps most memorably in *One Hour with You* as a doctor caught in a romantic triangle with his wife and her best friend. Lubitsch's style is incom-

Kay Francis, Miriam Hopkins, and Herbert Marshall in Ernst Lubitsch's classic sound comedy *Trouble in Paradise* (1932).

parably light and graceful, and he found ways to suggest sex that smoothly avoided censorship, such as having the shadows of two lovers' heads appear on the pillowcase of their bed to suggest conjugal bliss; such visual tropes, coupled with the director's playful approach to relationships between men and women, gave the director's films what many called "the Lubitsch Touch." In *Trouble in Paradise,* jewel thieves plan to fleece a rich woman out of her wealth, but a romantic triangle disrupts their plans; the film ends with the intended robbery thwarted and the thieves reunited in love and larceny. The essence of Lubitsch is to make the potentially tragic seem as effervescent as a glass of champagne; although perils and heartbreak confront his characters, their elegance and style see them through the most potentially compromising situations.

As World War II approached, Lubitsch directed Greta Garbo in *Ninotchka* (1939), a sophisticated comedy of manners in which Garbo plays a humorless Soviet emissary who falls in love with both capitalism and Melvyn Douglas. *The Shop Around the Corner* (1940), a romantic comedy drama about two workers in a Budapest shop who unwittingly fall in love via the mail, although they detest each other in everyday life, is a typically charming Lubitsch film of mistaken identity, remade by Nora Ephron as *You've Got Mail* (1998).

One of Lubitsch's finest works was *To Be or Not to Be* (1942), a satire of the Nazis with Jack Benny hilariously cast as "that great, great Polish actor, Joseph Tura," involved in a plot to save the Polish underground while his wife fools around with a young lieutenant on the side. As a Shakespearean actor within the film, Benny makes an utterly unlikely Hamlet, and Lubitsch keeps the pace moving crisply in this trenchant piece of social commentary. Surprisingly, it was a commercial failure when first released. In the midst of war, it seems, Hitler was too serious a foe to lampoon for general audiences; in hindsight, *To Be or Not to Be* is one of Lubitsch's most accomplished farces and the highlight of Jack Benny's screen career. In 1943, Lubitsch directed his first color production, the romantic comedy *Heaven Can Wait,* in which an aging roué thinks back over his life of romantic alliances as he is cross-examined by Satan to see whether he belongs in Hell. In all, Lubitsch's carefree attitude toward life, romance, and the battle of the sexes made him an anomaly in Hollywood; although he was an efficient businessman (and for a time the head of production at Paramount), he remained at heart a Continental sophisticate, most at home in a world of gentle romance and light-hearted sexual comedy.

MAX OPHÜLS

If Lubitsch saw the relationship between men and women as a playful battle of wits and whims, Max Ophüls was perhaps the supreme romanticist of the movies, both in his early work in Germany and his later work in the United States. Ophüls did not make a great many films, but his work is marked by a deeply suffused sense of Old World romance and lost splendor. His most famous American film is *Letter from an Unknown Woman* (1948), starring Joan Fontaine and Louis Jourdan in the tale of a young woman who is seduced and abandoned by a brilliant young concert pianist and finds herself alone and pregnant. The story, like most of Ophüls's work, takes place in the nineteenth century, in a zone of memory and nostalgia that renders the viewer spellbound. Ophüls is most noted for his luxurious camera movement, maintaining constant motion throughout often lengthy and complex shots. James Mason, who starred in Ophüls's 1949 melodrama *Caught,* was deeply amused by the director's ceaselessly roving camera setups, and composed a poem in Ophüls's honor, which read in part:

A shot that does not call for tracks
Is agony for poor, dear Max
Once, when they took away his crane
I thought he'd never smile again.

Adventuress Lola Montès (Martine Carol) becomes part of a circus sideshow as Peter Ustinov (lower left) looks on in Max Ophüls's final film, *Lola Montès* (1955).

Ophüls himself noted that "life for me is movement," and a sense of fluid restlessness pervades all his best work. His crowning achievement is undoubtedly *Lola Montès* (1955), a French/West German co-production that recounts the affair of a famous adventuress with King Ludwig I of Bavaria. Shot in dazzling CinemaScope and riotous color, the film cost a then-staggering $3.5 million and was initially, like so many films ahead of their time, a failure at the box office. Much to Ophüls's dismay, the film was then ruthlessly recut and released in the United States under the sensationalistic title *The Sins of Lola Montès,* in a cheap black-and-white version that ruined his masterly color design. Seen today in its original version, the film is an overwhelming experience, a romance of such lavish and epic proportions that it literally confounds the senses.

ORSON WELLES IN HOLLYWOOD

Orson Welles began in the theater as a "boy wonder," then drifted into radio dramas in New York in the 1930s by playing "The Shadow" and other popular characters. It was then that he founded the Mercury Theatre Company, which produced plays on Broadway and on the radio with scandalous success. His 30 October 1938 radio adaptation of H. G. Wells's *War of the Worlds* was his ticket to international fame, or infamy; designed as a breaking news story, Welles's production convinced millions of listeners that Martians were invading the earth, landing en masse in Grover's Mill, New Jersey. There was immediate, widespread panic: churches were jammed with terrified citizens as people prayed for deliverance from the alien onslaught. The second half of the hour-long broadcast made it clear that the entire story was, indeed, fiction, but Welles's brilliant use of the medium had so unnerved the nation that he was summarily forced to apologize for the riots he had caused.

Sensing that he would do just as well in the cinema as he had on stage and in radio, RKO Pictures signed Welles to direct in 1939. Once in Hollywood, Welles locked himself in a screening room for months, taking a self-imposed crash course in cinematic technique, aided by the brilliant cinematographer Gregg Toland. After considering and then abandoning a film adaptation of Joseph Conrad's *Heart of Darkness* (which would have used first-person camera work to force the audience to identity with the protagonist), he settled on a thinly fictionalized life of the notorious yellow journalist William Randolph Hearst. Hearst was an immensely rich and powerful man who controlled much of the nation's media, with a string of newspapers, radio stations, and even a film production company that existed primarily to provide star vehicles for Hearst's longtime mistress, Marion Davies. Welles saw Hearst's career as a tragic example of overreaching, and *Citizen Kane* (1941) is thus the story of a man who has greatness and wealth thrust upon him and then destroys himself and all those around him—friends, wives, business associates—with his greed, thirst for power, and egomania.

Citizen Kane is justifiably one of the most famous works in cinema history. As a debut film (Welles was just twenty-five years old when he began shooting) *Kane* is all the more extraordinary. Welles served as co-writer (with Herman Mankiewicz) and director and also played the Hearst character, Charles Foster Kane, in what would be the greatest performance of his long career. In addition, he kept the production on a tight schedule, contrary to persistent rumors at the time. He even used screen-test footage from the famous breakfast table sequence with Ruth Warrick in the final print, and in the end brought the entire film in for well under a million dollars.

But in his youth and brashness, Welles had not reckoned with Hearst's considerable power and influence. After seeing the film, Hearst used his papers' top gossip columnist, Louella Parsons, to threaten the entire Holly-

[LEFT] Orson Welles (left, pointing) and cameraman Gregg Toland (seated, legs crossed) on the set of Welles's *Citizen Kane* (1941). [RIGHT] A heroic angle shot from Orson Welles's *Citizen Kane* (1941).

wood studio system with a series of embarrassing revelations about the private lives of its top stars unless the negative and all prints of *Kane* were destroyed. A consortium of studio heads offered Welles and RKO a million dollars to destroy the movie, but to their eternal credit RKO refused to negotiate and released the film, uncut, to rave reviews. The film, tracing Kane's life from an unhappy childhood to old age and death through a series of complicated flashbacks, was a masterpiece of set design, camera placement, deep-focus composition, lighting, and editing. Indeed, critical acclaim for *Kane* was overwhelming, especially in Europe and the rest of the world, yet the movie did poorly at the box office. In addition, the film predictably brought down the wrath of the Hearst organization on RKO, which now found itself banned from all Hearst newspapers, both in reviews and advertising. As a result, RKO became invisible to millions of Hearst readers, and Welles acquired a reputation for being a brilliant but difficult and potentially dangerous filmmaker. He would never again have the freedom he had enjoyed on *Citizen Kane*.

Welles's second feature, *The Magnificent Ambersons* (1942), about the decline and fall of a prosperous midwestern family, featured many of the members of the Mercury Theatre unit. Welles's original cut ran 148 minutes, but the studio was no longer willing to accommodate the young director as they had in the past. The film was taken out of his hands and savagely recut to eighty-eight minutes by the film's editor, Robert Wise (later a solid director in his own right), and a happy ending was hastily shot and tacked on to satisfy audiences, who had reacted negatively to the original version in previews. Demonstrating their new attitude toward Welles, RKO released the mutilated version of *Ambersons* on the bottom half of a double bill with Leslie Goodwins's program comedy *Mexican Spitfire Sees a Ghost* (1942).

Welles's career never really recovered, although he displayed flashes of brilliance in his subsequent films and went on to a long career as an actor, voiceover artist, and commercial pitchman. His 1943 production of *Journey into Fear* for RKO was also taken out of his hands, and the film was completed by a former Welles collaborator. Though but a scant sixty-eight minutes, *Journey into Fear* is still talky and tedious, almost entirely devoid of Welles's signature bravura style.

Only two years after his spectacular debut as an auteur, Welles saw his directing career slipping away. It was not until 1946 that he was allowed to direct again, when independent producer Sam Spiegel (then known as S. P. Eagle) agreed to finance the shooting of the modest suspense melodrama *The Stranger*. Welles also stars in the picture as an ex-Nazi in hiding after the war, teaching at a small college in Connecticut. The film went off smoothly during production, but Welles hated the result, calling it "the worst of my films."

Nevertheless, it was a solid commercial success, and at Columbia Pictures Harry Cohn decided to give Welles a shot at directing, starring in, and co-writing *The Lady from Shanghai* (1947), an overheated suspense thriller starring Welles's wife, the glamorous Rita Hayworth. Shooting dragged on for months, as the director supervised location shooting in Mexico and New York City to bring his fevered vision to the screen. When he delivered his final cut, Cohn and the Columbia brass found it incoherent and bizarre (as it is), but they missed the film's originality and quirky brilliance. Substantially recut, the film was shuffled into theaters with a minimum of fanfare, where it failed miserably.

The only studio in Hollywood that would hire Welles now, after long negotiations, turned out to be Republic Pictures, best known for its westerns and Saturday morning serials. Welles then turned out his version of *Macbeth* (1948), a bold attempt to visualize the play in long takes on stark, minimalist sets, but his insistence that the actors perform with thick Scottish accents rendered much of the sound track incomprehensible. His last American film was also one of his best, the dark *Touch of Evil* (1958), which the studio (Universal in this case) again took out of his hands and reedited over Welles's objections. (The film has been restored to the director's original cut and is available on DVD.)

Hollywood was now finished with Welles, but he continued making a series of increasingly marginalized films on shoestring budgets in Europe. His brief Hollywood career, as incandescent as it was, had lasted only seven years, from 1941 to 1948. Still, despite the few films he produced during this period and the continued studio interference he faced, his films display a coherent vision of a world in which absolute power corrupts absolutely; as a visual stylist, his pyrotechnical use of the camera and editing are matched only by Eisenstein.

FRANK CAPRA'S SMALL-TOWN AMERICA

Frank Capra followed up the success of 1934's *It Happened One Night* with a string of sentimental films about small-town American values, which the director himself dubbed "Capra corn." *Lost Horizon* (1937), an atypical trip to exotica for the director, was a critical and financial disappointment, but in such films as *You Can't Take It with You* (1938), *Mr. Smith Goes to Washington* (1939), *Meet John Doe* (1941), and his now classic *It's a Wonderful Life* (1946), Capra extolled the virtues of the common man over the machinations of bankers and corporate interests, creating a comforting world of

The idealistic senator (James Stewart) breaks down in the climax of Frank Capra's *Mr. Smith Goes to Washington* (1939).

working-class, populist values that audiences readily identified with. For most observers, Capra's early films remain his finest work.

In addition to his feature films, during World War II Capra produced and directed the *Why We Fight* series of documentary/propaganda films at the behest of President Franklin Roosevelt to explain to the public the reasons for the U.S. entry into the conflict. The first of these, *Prelude to War* (1943), created the pattern that the rest of the series would follow: a mix of documentary footage, animation, and staged sequences shot in Hollywood to create a compelling blend of images that bolstered the wartime home-front morale.

But as the 1940s rolled on, Capra seemed out of step with the rest of the nation, which had been socially transformed by the war. *It's a Wonderful Life* wasn't a box office hit when first released, as audiences flocked instead to such films as William Wyler's *The Best Years of Our Lives* (1946) for a more realistic vision of life in postwar America. Indeed, the failure of *It's a Wonderful Life* put an end to Capra's independent film company, and his subsequent career was marginal.

GEORGE CUKOR

George Cukor was known in the trade as a "woman's director" because of his skill in directing such stars as Katharine Hepburn, but his credits range over a wide variety of genres. *A Bill of Divorcement* (1932) was Hepburn's screen debut, as the daughter of a man who has been committed to an insane asylum for many years and then returns home to find that his wife has left him for another man. *Dinner at Eight* (1933) is, along with Edmund Goulding's *Grand Hotel* (1932), the definitive all-star film, a shrewd combination of comedy and drama centering on the lives of a group of ambitious Manhattan socialites. *David Copperfield* (1935) is a faithful adaptation of Dickens's classic novel and offered W. C. Fields his only serious role as the perennially bankrupt Mr. Micawber. *Gaslight* (1944), one of the screen's great melodramas, stars Charles Boyer as a husband who contrives to drive his wife (Ingrid Bergman) mad so that he can have her declared insane and gain control of her fortune. Cukor also directed the classic comedy of the sexes *The Philadelphia Story* (1940), with Hepburn, James Stewart, and Cary Grant, and teamed Hepburn and Spencer Tracy in *Adam's Rib* (1949) and *Pat and Mike* (1952). The show business drama *A Star Is Born* (1954), with Judy Garland and James Mason, suffered massive cuts when first released, yet is now recognized as a classic examination of the mechanics of the star system, the Hollywood studio system, and the evanescent nature of celebrity. In all, Cukor's career spanned over five decades; his later works are highlighted in Chapter 8.

"ONE-TAKE" WOODY

W. S. Van Dyke often filmed rehearsals and printed them for inclusion in the final film, allowing him to complete shooting in as little as twelve days. One such film was *The Thin Man* (1934), the first in a series of sparkling comedies starring William Powell and Myrna Loy as Nick and Nora Charles, sophisticated, wealthy Manhattanites who solve murder cases as a hobby. Van Dyke also directed the first major studio film shot on location in Africa, *Trader Horn* (1931); a series of Tarzan films based on Edgar Rice Burroughs's novels, beginning with *Tarzan the Ape Man* (1932), starring Johnny Weissmuller; the epic film on the 1906 earthquake, *San Francisco* (1936); and the lavish costume spectacle *Marie Antoinette* (1938). A jack-of-all-trades, Van Dyke was one of MGM's most dependable house directors, and his early death in 1943 cut short a career that was really just getting started.

Myrna Loy and William Powell as Nick and Nora Charles in W. S. Van Dyke's surprise mystery/comedy hit, *The Thin Man* (1934).

[LEFT] Myrna Loy (extreme left) watches as William Powell toasts director W. S. Van Dyke on the set of *The Thin Man* (1934). [RIGHT] Johnny Weissmuller in the title role of W. S. Van Dyke's *Tarzan the Ape Man* (1932).

SPECTACLE: DEMILLE AND VON STERNBERG

Cecil B. DeMille remained the screen's foremost purveyor of spectacle. His early sound films, such as *Sign of the Cross* (1932), with Charles Laughton as Nero idly plucking his harp while Rome burns, and *Cleopatra* (1934), starring Claudette Colbert, are both sumptuous and licentious; as usual, DeMille missed no opportunity for pageantry and stylized debauchery on his way to the inevitable moralistic ending. As the 1930s progressed, DeMille could be counted on to produce eye-filling, big-budget crowd pleasers such as *The Crusades* (1934), *The Buccaneer* (1938), *Union Pacific* (1939), and *Samson and Delilah* (1949). Many critics have remarked that the true star of all DeMille's films was the director himself, who subordinated the narrative concerns of his works to an almost manic compulsion to pile excess upon excess, until the frames of his films fairly explode with action, spectacle, and armies of anonymous extras.

Josef von Sternberg's calculated exoticism made an overnight Depression-era star out of Marlene Dietrich, beginning with their first collaboration, *Der Blaue Engel* (*The Blue Angel*, 1930), which cast Dietrich as a glamorous seductress who brings about the ruin of a pathetic schoolmaster. Using an intoxicating mixture of light and shadow, von Sternberg's camera

115

Clive Brook and Marlene Dietrich in Josef von Sternberg's exotic *Shanghai Express* (1932).

lingers on Dietrich in such films as *Dishonored* (1931), *Shanghai Express* (1932), *Blonde Venus* (1932), and *The Scarlet Empress* (1934), caressing her body with a simmering bath of incandescent illumination and exotic costumes. Plot and incident are secondary in these films, which really exist to glorify Dietrich's alluring presence, even as they acknowledge her androgynous sexuality (Dietrich kisses a woman on the mouth in *Morocco* [1930]). Dreamlike, ornate, and meticulous down to the last detail, von Sternberg's best films are ultimately a meditation on the power of the constructed image of sexual temptation.

PRESTON STURGES

Preston Sturges emerged as the foremost social satirist of the period. He began his career in 1930, writing dialogue for Paramount. After a stint as a Broadway playwright, he convinced the studio to let him direct *The Great McGinty* (1940). The film's critical and commercial success allowed Sturges to carve out a unique career as both director and writer. Films such as *Sulli-*

van's Travels (1941) and *The Miracle of Morgan's Creek* (1944) effectively punctured the manners and social conventions of the era, using a madcap array of characters stuck in a series of improbable situations to convey the cheerful chaos of everyday existence. *Hail the Conquering Hero* (1944), in typical Sturges fashion, is edgier than standard wartime comedies, satirizing the cult of heroism in its story of a marine reject who is mistaken for a war hero in his hometown. Other Sturges films allowed space for the creativity of his leading ladies to shine. *Palm Beach Story* (1942) stars Claudette Colbert as a loving wife who leaves her impecunious husband and then gets mixed up with a wacky and wealthy family in Florida. Similarly, *The Lady Eve* (1941) features Barbara Stanwyck as a con artist who attempts to scam a wealthy but simple Henry Fonda, only to fall in love, break up, and ultimately exact her revenge. Widely praised as the most brilliant satires in Hollywood, Sturges's movies were compared to those of Capra and Lubitsch. No one since has duplicated his sophisticated screwball style.

THE HOLLYWOOD PROFESSIONALS

Besides these major directors, a veritable army of skilled journeymen were trained to handle everyday directorial assignments. The studios supervised the careers of not only their actors, but also their directors, cinematographers, and other key creative personnel, acting as a sort of finishing school for talent in support of the system. Directors often advanced to their positions from the cutting room, where they learned how to put a film together from the "coverage," or footage that had been shot for each film they were assigned to edit. Such directors included William A. Wellman, known as "Wild Bill" for his rough manner and habit of carrying a gun on the sets to emphasize his authority; he created hard-hitting gangster films such as *The Public Enemy* (1931), which made a star of James Cagney. Indeed, for one of the key sequences in the film, Wellman insisted that real machine-gun bullets be used to blast away a section of a brick wall, just moments after Cagney had ducked behind it. Wellman also directed a variety of other films, including *A Star Is Born*, examining the vagaries of Hollywood, and the biting comedy *Nothing Sacred* (both 1937).

Frank Borzage, one of the most underrated directors of the 1930s and 1940s, scored his first big hit with the silent melodrama *Humoresque* (1920). His style is often dismissed as deeply sentimental, but he won an Academy Award for *Seventh Heaven* (1927) and went on to create, among many other

James Cagney offers Mae Clarke some grapefruit in William A. Wellman's *The Public Enemy* (1931).

works, the Hemingway adaptation *A Farewell to Arms* (1932), *Little Man What Now?* (1934), about the rise of Fascism in Germany, the charming musical *Flirtation Walk* (1934), the religious drama *The Green Light* (1937), and the lavish biblical spectacle *The Big Fisherman* (1959). Borzage emerges as a conscientious craftsman who always brought to his material an extra measure of dignity, coupled with a fluid visual style that extracted the most from his performers.

Mervyn LeRoy, another deeply underrated auteur, specialized in hardboiled films, such as *Little Caesar* (1931), which catapulted Edward G. Robinson to stardom. LeRoy directed an astonishing six films in 1932, including *I Am a Fugitive from a Chain Gang,* an exposé of prison gang conditions in the southern United States; *Three on a Match,* a sordid tale of adultery, kidnapping, drug abuse, and alcoholism; and *Two Seconds,* in which a convict sees his entire life flash before his eyes in the time it takes to execute him.

William Witney became the foremost action specialist in Hollywood, and his rise to the director's chair is typical of the era. Witney began in films as a messenger boy, and after years of work he found a position at Republic as a script supervisor. In 1937, after much lobbying with the front office, Witney began to direct serials, often paired with director John English. Their partnership became the best directorial team in sound action serials, creating chapter-plays such as *The Adventures of Captain Marvel* and *Dick Tracy vs. Crime, Inc.* (both 1941). The serials were shot quickly and economically, costing $200,000 to $300,000 apiece, with shooting schedules of thirty to forty days. Witney was also the person who created modern choreographed fight scenes; he learned how to plan and block a movie fight by watching how Busby Berkeley constructed his dance numbers on the sets of his 1930s musicals. Serials were made by a group of talented professionals working at a furious pace, doing at least fifty to sixty setups in a typical day. In terms of stunt choreography, miniature work, camera work, and narrative pacing, Witney and English have influenced a whole new generation of action film-makers, especially Steven Spielberg and George Lucas, who would pioneer the big-screen blockbuster "comic book" film in the mid-1970s.

Allan Dwan began as a filmmaker in 1911, directing hundreds of pictures for a variety of studios during the silent era. When sound came in, Dwan made the transition effortlessly. He directed the very successful Dumas adaptation *The Three Musketeers* (1939) and the very funny sex comedy *Getting Gertie's Garter* (1945), way ahead of its time in its realistic view of marriage and infidelity. Other notable Dwan films include *Sands of Iwo Jima* (1949), one of the finest movies produced at Republic, and *The Woman They Almost Lynched* (1953), in which Joan Leslie learns to defend herself in a violent frontier town, only to be set upon by the traditional male hierarchy for overstepping a woman's role. Dwan is important because he managed to immerse himself completely in his projects and never allowed his style to impose itself on his material. At the same time, the quiet assurance of Dwan's mise-en-scène is evident in all his work, which is remarkable for its modesty as well as its self-assurance.

Edward Dmytryk came to prominence in the late 1940s as one of the key architects of the postwar genre of film noir (literally "black film"), offering a cynical view of humankind. Dmytryk's breakthrough effort was the Boris Karloff horror film *The Devil Commands* (1941), an interesting and offbeat entry in which Karloff attempts to contact the spirit of his dead wife who has been killed in an automobile accident. The micro-budgeted *Hitler's Children* (1943), a lurid tale of the Hitler Youth, featuring forced sterilizations and the requisite amount of goose-stepping, was one of the top-grossing films of that year. By the mid-1940s, Dmytryk had moved on to "A" pictures such as the detective thrillers *Murder My Sweet* (1944) and *Cornered* (1945), as well as the war film *Back to Bataan* (1945) and the wartime romance *Till the End of Time* (1946). During this period, he also developed his signature lighting technique of simply splashing one light on the wall of a set and letting the shadows dominate the frame. This dark, evocative method perfectly suited the subject matter of Dmytryk's darker films, and, as he noted, it also saved time.

Raoul Walsh chronicled the rise and inevitable fall of gangster James Cagney in *The Roaring Twenties* (1939), and the last days of the tragic bank robber Roy Earle (Humphrey Bogart) in *High Sierra* (1941). Walsh was equally at home with war films, as he proved in *Objective, Burma!* (1945), and comedy/fantasy outings, as in the underrated *The Horn Blows at Midnight* (1945), featuring Jack Benny as the angel Gabriel, dispatched to earth

119

Gangster Cody Jarrett (James Cagney) goes out with guns blazing in the ferocious conclusion of Raoul Walsh's brutal crime drama *White Heat* (1949).

to sound the trumpet announcing the end of the world. Walsh's most enduring achievement, however, is the brutal gangster melodrama *White Heat* (1949), in which psychopathic gangster Cody Jarrett (Cagney) relies upon his mother to keep his gang in line, as he blasts his way from one violent stickup to the next without a shred of conscience.

Jacques Tourneur, working for producer Val Lewton's horror unit at RKO, turned out some of the era's most inventive and atmospheric horror films, far removed from the Universal Studios formula of the Wolfman, Frankenstein's monster, and Dracula. The groundbreaking thriller *Cat People* (1942) tells the tale of a young woman who turns into a leopard when she is sexually aroused. Tourneur makes the film's preposterous premise both believable and ominous; among the many memorable set pieces is an attack on a woman in a deserted swimming pool at night, photographed almost entirely in darkness. Tourneur followed this effort with his Gothic masterpiece *I Walked with a Zombie* (1943), another Lewton production, which transported *Jane Eyre* to the West Indies, and Tourneur's masterpiece, the noir classic *Out of the Past* (1947), a convoluted tale of greed, murder, and betrayal.

After fleeing Nazi Germany, genre stylist Robert Siodmak landed a contract at Universal starting at $150 a week and directed one of the best wartime horror films, *Son of Dracula* (1943), starring Lon Chaney Jr. By the end of the war, however, the classic Universal monsters had reached the end of their collective tether, with the production of Erle C. Kenton's films *House of Frankenstein* (1944) and *House of Dracula* (1945), which teamed up Dracula, the Wolfman, and the Frankenstein monster in a vain attempt to revive flagging audience interest. By 1948, the monsters were being used as comedy foils in *Abbott and Costello Meet Frankenstein*, and it would be a decade before the next great cycle of horror films would emerge, this time in Britain, at Hammer Studios.

At PRC, the smallest studio in Hollywood, *maudit* director Edgar G. Ulmer, whom we last saw working with Fred Zinnemann, Billy Wilder, and Robert Siodmak on *People on Sunday* in Germany in 1930, directed films at a furious pace to create the noir classics *Girls in Chains* (1943), *Bluebeard* (about the famous serial killer of women, 1944), *Strange Illusion* (a modern-day version of *Hamlet*, 1945), and *Detour* (1945), considered by many to be the ultimate noir. Pianist Al Roberts (Tom Neal) hitchhikes to Los Angeles from New York to be with his erstwhile fiancée, Sue (Claudia Drake), who has abandoned him to pursue dreams of stardom in the film capital. On the way to Hollywood, Roberts hitches a ride with a fast-talking hymnal salesman, Charles Haskell (Edmund MacDonald), who abruptly dies. Roberts assumes Haskell's identity, but then picks up Vera (Ann Savage), who had thumbed a ride with Haskell earlier and realizes that Roberts is a fraud. From here, things rapidly become more and more complicated, as Vera blackmails Roberts, threatening to go to the police and implicate Roberts as Haskell's murderer if he fails to obey her slightest whim. Shot in five days on a few spare sets and an astoundingly low $30,000, *Detour* has become an American classic, effectively portraying the hopelessness and despair of a rootless existence on the road.

John Huston, who would go on to greater triumphs as a director in the 1950s and 1960s, made an auspicious debut with the classic crime thriller *The Maltese Falcon* (1941), starring Humphrey Bogart, Peter Lorre, Sydney Greenstreet, and Mary Astor. His later films in the 1940s included *Across the Pacific* (1942), a wartime thriller that reteamed Bogart, Astor, and Greenstreet; the World War II documentary *The Battle of San Pietro* (1945), which showed frontline combat with a realism hitherto unapproached by the cinema; *The Treasure of the Sierra Madre* (1948), a rousing adventure film, starring Walter Huston (John's father) and Bogart in a tale of gold and greed in the Mexican mountains; and *Key Largo* (1948), one of the last great gangster films from Hollywood's Golden Age, again with Bogart, teamed with Bacall (now his wife) and co-starring Edward G. Robinson as aging crime boss Johnny Rocco. With just these few films, Huston established an individual style that favored the actors over camera movement and evinced a strong instinct for narrative drama.

William Wyler, known as "Forty-take Willie" for his tendency to shoot scenes over and over until his actors were forced, often through sheer ex-

Coming home after the war isn't too pleasant for (left to right) Homer Parrish (Harold Russell), Fred Derry (Dana Andrews), and Al Stephenson (Fredric March), three veterans trying to adjust to postwar life in William Wyler's *The Best Years of Our Lives* (1946).

haustion, to drop all their mannerisms and deliver a natural, unaffected performance, guided the volcanic Bette Davis through one of her best roles in *Jezebel* (1938), the story of a headstrong young woman in the antebellum South who insists upon wearing a shocking red dress to a formal ball in defiance of accepted convention. In his other major films of the era, *Wuthering Heights* (1939), the Bette Davis vehicle *The Letter* (1940), and the epic drama of soldiers returning home after World War II, *The Best Years of Our Lives* (1946), Wyler created a delicately nuanced personal universe, in which men and women struggle against their inner natures and society's constraints to fulfill their desires, dreams, and ambitions, often at great cost. Wyler is one of the supreme technicians of the sound era, and his meticulous attention to the mechanics of performance results in some of the most deeply considered and carefully constructed films of the classical cinema.

DOROTHY ARZNER

In an industry that was deeply influenced by a group of women artists from the 1890s onward, only one woman survived the conglomeration of the industry in the late 1920s to direct during the sound era: Dorothy Arzner. Before Arzner, many women had been active as directors in early Hollywood, but nearly all had been pushed out of the industry with the advent of sound. Arzner's entry into the movie business was like that of many male directors. She attended the University of Southern California with plans to become a doctor but dropped out to pursue a career in motion pictures. Her first job was typing scripts. Later she moved up to an editing position as a cutter for Realart Studio, a subsidiary of Paramount. She edited fifty-two films there as chief editor, including the Rudolph Valentino vehicle *Blood and Sand* (1922).

In addition, Arzner directed some of the grueling second-unit scenes for *Blood and Sand,* depicting the bullfights. She bargained with Paramount for her first opportunity as director, *Fashions for Women* (1927). She then directed a handful of other films before hitting her stride with *The Wild Party* (1929), starring Clara Bow. Of all the films she directed for Paramount, *The Wild Party* displays the most overtly expressed lesbian consciousness. Set at an all-female college, the film is ostensibly a heterosexual romance, but Arzner allows same-sex sexuality to develop between peripheral women characters. *The Wild Party* was also hailed for its technical achievements. It was the first sound picture made at Paramount, in which Arzner reportedly suggested the use of a fishing pole as a microphone extension, thus inventing the industry's first boom mike.

Working Girls (1931) continued Arzner's penchant for the creation of all-women environments set against the backdrop of patriarchal societal convention. Many of the themes of *Working Girls,* which revolved around the difficulties women face in the male-defined work environment and the manner in which women are so often pitted against one another in society, are revisited in her famous later movie *Dance, Girl, Dance* (1940).

Arzner's female characters were often career oriented. *Christopher Strong* (1933), starring Katharine Hepburn as a world-famous aviator fashioned after Amelia Earhart, is a classic female narrative woven around the choice between family and career. In *Craig's Wife* (1936), Rosalind Russell stars as a manipulative woman so driven to become the embodiment of the perfect housewife that she destroys everyone around her, including herself. The film is a scathing attack on societal restrictions of women at a time when women were being moved back into the domestic sphere. Arzner's last film, *First Comes Courage* (1943), starred Merle Oberon as a woman who sacrifices love for the safety and independence of her country. Halfway through shooting the picture, however, Arzner became seriously ill with pneumonia and took time off to recuperate, but rather than wait for her return, the studio had the film completed as quickly as possible (with Charles Vidor directing,

Katharine Hepburn and Colin Clive in Dorothy Arzner's feminist aviation drama, *Christopher Strong* (1933).

though only Arzner received screen credit). Bitterly disappointed with having the film yanked from her, Arzner realized that she was too independent-minded to fit into the Hollywood system. Shortly after leaving Columbia, she became a pioneer in directing television commercials (for Pepsi-Cola), and developed one of the first filmmaking courses in the United States, at the Pasadena Playhouse in California. Later, she taught filmmaking at UCLA, where one of her early students was future director Francis Ford Coppola. In 1974, Arzner was finally honored for her work by the Directors Guild of America.

Between 1943 and 1949, no women directed films at any major Hollywood studio. It was not until 1949, when actress Ida Lupino co-produced, scripted, and directed *Not Wanted*, a drama involving teenage pregnancy, that women again became a force behind the camera. Lupino went on to direct a compelling series of dramas and suspense films in the 1950s.

WOMEN'S PICTURES IN THE 1930S AND 1940S

During the thirties and forties, women made up a large proportion of movie audiences. To take advantage, studios developed a genre that came to be known as women's pictures. These movies varied widely, from serious drama to romance to musical to biopic, with one common feature: they all told stories about women for women. A popular theme in the genre was the changing role of women, involving the proprieties of sexuality, women in the workplace, and the choice between love, career, and home. Though sometimes derided by (often male) critics as overly melodramatic, sentimental, and dependent on preposterous turns of plot, the genre was also wildly popular, with movies starring the likes of Bette Davis, Barbara Stanwyck, Joan Crawford, and Kay Francis. Indeed, many women's pictures were once hailed as masterpieces.

Kay Francis often played a woman who worked in a predominantly male field, such as the title role in *Mary Stevens, M.D.* (1933). Mary experiences sexism firsthand when she is snubbed by female patients because she is a woman. When she sets her sights on a male doctor, a friend tells her that she has no chance with men: because Mary works in a male field, "you have no sex appeal." Like many such films, *Mary Stevens, M.D.* sends a conflicting message. On the one hand, Francis's character is a strong female role model. Confident in her medical skills, Mary saves a baby from choking by using one of her own hairpins. But romance only ruins this strong female doctor. She becomes pregnant out of wedlock and is forced to give birth aboard a ship as she flees to Europe in order to have her baby secretly. Her child dies, and feeling at fault Mary decides to give up her career. It was this type of role that made Kay Francis an enormously popular star, adored by women who tried to emulate her on-screen courage and fashion sensibility.

A popular sub-genre of the women's picture was the maternal melodrama. In these movies, women have children out of wedlock and are forced to give them up so that the children can be reared with privileges the mother cannot offer. When mother and children are somehow reunited years later, the children do not recognize her. Though these women suffer terribly for others, they also offered female audiences a role model of heroic, courageous women, rather than one who needs to be saved. Other maternal melodramas include *Back Street* (1932), *I Found Stella Parish* (1935), and *Madame X* (1937).

Women's pictures often allowed audiences a glimpse at alternate choices that women could make if only society allowed. One such movie was Edmund Goulding's *The Great Lie* (1941), starring Mary Astor and Bette Davis, notable not for its convoluted and melodramatic plot but for showing a woman who is much more concerned with her career than her role as a mother. Astor's character is consumed with the desire to be a great concert pianist and shockingly uninterested in motherhood. Though such movies often seemed to undercut themselves with endings that forced the nontraditional woman to suffer, they also tantalized female audiences with alternate models of women who refused to play by the rules of society.

In the forties, as many women entered the workforce to take the place of men serving in World War II, women's pictures remained highly popular. The movies often featured sociopathic women, women with over-the-top desires (especially sexual) who presented dangers to both society and themselves. This type of role in women's pictures coincides with the rise of the femme fatale in film noir of the late forties and fifties. A superb example of mid-forties psychotic beauty is Gene Tierney in *Leave Her to Heaven* (1945). Tierney plays a jealous and murderous woman who is so intent on being the only person in her husband's life that she murders his wheelchair-bound brother. She is cruel, utterly beautiful, and without a heart.

All these films allowed female audiences an opportunity to vicariously experience excessive love, romance, and sexuality, to judge such behavior, and to consider society's sexual double standards and women's changing roles in American culture. The genre continued to be popular in the 1950s but survives today in only pale form as "chick flicks," focusing especially on teenage girls and young unmarried women for whom romance is paramount.

WALT DISNEY AND UB IWERKS

Walt Disney, more than any other animator, made the cartoon short an integral part of the motion picture experience. He also pioneered the feature-length animated film with the ambitious *Snow White and the Seven Dwarfs* (1937). Disney was not the sole creative force behind the production of his films, however. He started out teaming with Ubbe ("Ub" for short) Iwerks, who did the animation work on most of Disney's early films, including the *Alice in Cartoonland* series in 1923, a pioneering effort to mix live action and animation. The two then developed the character of Oswald the Lucky Rabbit in 1927 and launched a successful series of shorts until they lost the rights to the character in a corporate battle. Although they were left with neither a star nor financial backing, Iwerks and Disney responded by coming up with Mickey Mouse. The silent *Plane Crazy* (1928) became the first Mickey cartoon, and it was a hit.

But Disney, ever the innovator, wanted to work on a cartoon that used music, sound effects, and dialogue, and with Iwerks he created *Steamboat Willie* (1928), for which Disney himself provided Mickey's high, squeaky voice. The film was a smash success. Disney shrewdly resisted all attempts to buy out the character or his fledgling company, determined to control his own commercial and artistic destiny. Mickey Mouse memorabilia itself became an industry, with Disney supervising the licensing of Mickey's image on everything from wristwatches to coffee mugs. In 1930, however, Iwerks left Disney to pursue his own creative dreams, a move that stunned Disney and forced him to rely on other animators. Iwerks created two successful cartoon series on his own, Flip the Frog and Willie Whopper, both distributed through MGM, but although Iwerks's cartoons were fresh and funny, they never achieved the popularity of the famous mouse. By the late 1930s, it was obvious to Iwerks that his solo career was not going well and he rejoined Disney, although now only as a salaried employee; when he had left Disney in 1930, he sold out his interest in the company, thereby missing out on a fortune.

Disney continued experimenting in his short cartoons, using classical music in *The Skeleton Dance* (1929), the first of the "Silly Symphony" series, and producing the first cartoon in Technicolor, *Flowers and Trees,* in 1932. By 1933, his use of color and the fluidity of the animation had progressed to an astonishing degree, and his team scored a major hit with the short Technicolor cartoon *Three Little Pigs* (1933), featuring the Depression Era hit song "Who's Afraid of the Big Bad Wolf?" which rapidly became an international sensation.

At the same time, Disney introduced the rest of his most famous cartoon characters, including Donald Duck, Goofy, Pluto, and Minnie Mouse. He also continued experimenting with new processes, such as the multiplane camera, which used several layers of plastic cels on which the animated drawings were inked, to create a greater illusion of depth and perspective. He followed *Snow White* with *Pinocchio* in 1940 and *Bambi* in 1942, and also created what many consider his masterpiece, *Fantasia* (1940), a film that used classical music to illustrate a variety of animated sequences, some abstract, others more narrative-based. The film cost a fortune to produce and failed commercially when first released, but Disney's canny distribution practice of re-releasing his films every eight years or so for a new generation of youngsters assured that it would eventually turn a profit. He employed famed conductor Leopold Stokowski and the Philadelphia Orchestra to record the film's sound track, which included selections by Bach, Beethoven, Schubert, Tchaikovsky, Mussorgsky, and Stravinsky. But purists found the film vulgar and kitschy, and Disney's own comments on the film (seeing one sequence for the first time, Disney reportedly exclaimed, "This will *make* Beethoven!") did little to help critical reception. But despite these reservations the film was certainly a technical triumph, presented in a CinemaScope-like format a full thirteen years before that process was generally adopted, and employing multiple-channel stereophonic sound.

During the war years, Disney's company cranked out patriotic shorts and training films for the armed forces. But as the war ended, Disney's autocratic management style began to grate on his employees, who often remained un-credited, and they eventually went on strike for better pay, working condi-tions, and professional recognition. When the strike was eventually resolved, neither side was entirely satisfied with the result. The family atmosphere was gone, but Disney continued to produce a series of box office hits, moving into live-action features and television in the 1950s, with the daily "The Mickey Mouse Club" and "Disneyland," a weekly anthology series designed to exploit his vast library of old material and advertise new features from the company. In 1955, Disney opened Disneyland, a vast 160-acre amusement park in Anaheim, California, that rapidly became the most famous theme park on the planet. He kept planning new projects and films until his death in 1966, and he left behind a vast organization that bears his name.

LOONEY TUNES AND BETTY BOOP

Another notable animated cartoon entity during the 1930s and 1940s was Leon Schlesinger's "Looney Tunes and Merrie Melodies" unit, which started up in the early 1930s as a showcase for Warners' extensive library of popular songs. Early efforts, such as Tom Palmer's *I've Got to Sing a Torch Song* (1933), used former Disney animators as subcontractors to create musical cartoons with little plot or characterization. This changed when Warner Bros. decided to open their own animation unit and hired the groundbreak-ing directors Isadore "Friz" Freleng, Chuck Jones, Bob Clampett, Tex Avery, and others to crank out cartoons on a regular basis. Stuffed into a ram-shackle building at Warner Bros. dubbed "Termite Terrace," these animators created an anarchic world featuring Bugs Bunny, Daffy Duck, Elmer Fudd, and the rest of their rowdy characters. More than any other cartoon unit, Looney Tunes was aimed at an adult audience, with enough simple humor to keep children entertained. Emphasizing sight gags, violent slapstick, and breakneck pacing, the cartoons included Avery's *A Wild Hare* (1940), Jones's *Elmer's Pet Rabbit* (1941), and Clampett's *Wabbit Twouble* (1941). Jones spe-cialized in character-driven cartoons, building up gags through repetition and narrative development, while Clampett favored absurdity and wildly plastic exaggeration as his characters reacted to the zany world around them. Chuck Jones became the most famous of the Looney Tunes directors, and long after his retirement toured the country with 35 mm prints of his classic cartoons, delighting new audiences on a series of lecture tours.

Tex Avery was by far the most extreme animator of the group, employing

Tex Avery, the wildest of the classical Hollywood animators, sends up the western in *Wild and Woolfy* (1945).

sledgehammer violence and brutal pratfalls in a series of raucous cartoons that strained the limits of human credibility. Avery quit Warner Bros. at the height of the company's productivity and joined rival MGM (home of William Hanna and Joseph Barbera's "Tom and Jerry") to create Droopy, the Blitz Wolf, and Screwy Squirrel, among other outlandish characters, in such films as *Red Hot Riding Hood* (1943), a hopped-up fairy tale; *Wild and Woolfy* (1945), a western takeoff starring the Blitz Wolf; and *King-Size Canary* (1947), a variation on the classic cat-and-mouse chase. Avery continued in his idiosyncratic vein into the 1950s, doing exactly what he pleased, much to the dismay of MGM's cartoon producer, Fred Quimby. Avery's cartoons at MGM are now considered the high point of his chaotic career, and have an almost cult-like following among animation buffs.

Warner Bros. and MGM never made feature cartoons during their heyday, preferring to concentrate on short, seven-minute cartoons for theatrical release. This strategy left them out in the cold when the market for shorts collapsed with the decline in movie audiences in the 1960s and the demise of the double bill. The characters, however, live on in merchandising and new feature films produced with digital animation, and the classic Warner Bros. and MGM cartoons are regularly run on television, where they attract new generations of fans with each passing year.

In the late 1920s, Max and Dave Fleischer created Betty Boop, a caricature of a Jazz Age flapper, and enjoyed a wave of national popularity. Based in New York, Max had begun as a cartoonist for the *Daily Eagle* in Brooklyn, while Dave started working with his brother in 1920 to create the "Out of the Inkwell" series, a group of cartoons combining animation with live action, starring Koko the Clown. Their Betty Boop cartoons, such as *Betty Boop in Blunderland* (1934), *Betty Boop Snow White* (1933), and *Betty Boop for President* (1932), were wild, surrealist adventures, accompanied by jazz sound tracks by such luminaries as Louis Armstrong and Cab Calloway. The Fleischers also brought the popular comic strip Popeye to the screen, and in 1939 released their first full-length animated cartoon, *Gulliver's Travels,* a conscious attempt to imitate Disney's *Snow White*. The film failed to click at the box office, however, and the brothers moved to Florida to cut costs. There they produced one more feature, as well as a string of hyper-realistic cartoons featuring the comic book hero Superman, but financial strains forced them to close their studio soon after.

Mae West sizes up a possible conquest in Lowell Sherman's *She Done Him Wrong* (1933).

This was a period when the whole family went to the movies regularly, and cartoons were thus a family affair rather than entertainments aimed exclusively at children. Labor intensive to produce and requiring months to make, these films by the early 1960s simply did not make a profit anymore, due in part to declining theater audiences. MGM, among other studios, closed down their cartoon division, and unemployed artists eventually found a home for their animated shorts on television.

CENSORSHIP

The 1930s and 1940s witnessed major shifts in American culture, with both the Great Depression and America's entry into World War II, and Hollywood was quick to adapt to audience needs. The sexually charged Mae West, who sparkled in *Night After Night* (1932), *She Done Him Wrong* (1933), and *I'm No Angel* (1933), found herself stymied by the rigid imposition of the Motion Picture Produc-

Watched by Theresa Harris (left), Barbara Stanwyck (right) plots how to get ahead in Alfred E. Green's *Baby Face* (1933), one of the most sexually explicit pre-Code films.

tion Code on 1 July 1934, as pioneered by Will H. Hays and then administered by Joseph Breen. Although the Code had been around since the late 1920s, it remained largely unenforced until a plethora of suggestive films pushed audiences to protest that their children were being exposed to objectionable material. Prominent offenders included Mae West's early movies; William Dieterle's sexually charged drama *Grand Slam* (1933); *Baby Face* (1933), Alfred E. Green's racy tale of a young woman who sleeps her way to the top; Stephen Roberts's lurid *The Story of Temple Drake* (1933), based on William Faulkner's sensationalist novel *Sanctuary*; and Mitchell Leisen's bizarre musical *Murder at the Vanities* (1934), featuring a production number entitled "Sweet Marijuana." With the imposition of the Code, Hollywood, fearing government intervention if they did not comply, was brought to heel. Among the Code's many proscriptions were the warnings that "methods of crime shall not be explicitly presented," "illegal drug traffic must never be presented," "scenes of passion should not be introduced when not essential to the plot," "excessive and lustful kissing, lustful embracing, suggestive postures and gestures, are not to be shown," "miscegenation (sex relationships between the white and black races) is forbidden," "pointed profanity (this

131

Shirley Temple, perhaps the most popular of all child stars, in the late 1930s.

Chico, Zeppo, Groucho, and Harpo Marx strike a typically anarchic pose on the set of Leo McCarey's *Duck Soup* (1933).

includes the words God, Lord, Jesus, Christ—unless used reverently—Hell, S.O.B., damn, Gawd), or other profane or vulgar expressions, however used, is forbidden," and that "ministers of religion . . . should not be used as comic characters or as villains."

The Code had numerous other demands as well, but the effect on the American cinema was dramatic. Far from being a rating system (as today's G, PG, R, and so on), the 1934 Code covered all motion pictures and thus set definitive limits on what could be shown on the screen for any audience. Mae West was about to begin production of her next film, *It Ain't No Sin,* in 1934; by the time the Code had eviscerated her screenplay (West wrote many of the scenarios, as well as much of the dialogue, for her early films), the title had been changed to *Belle of the Nineties* (1934) and the film was a pale shadow of what it might have been. Similarly, the Jean Harlow sex comedy *Born to Be Kissed* was retitled *100 Percent Pure* to please the Hays/Breen office, and then finally released under the indifferent title of *The Girl from Missouri* (1934). Emblematic of the new regime was the astounding success of child star Shirley Temple, whose films *Little Miss Marker* (1934), *Captain January* (1936), and numerous others cemented her hold on the nation's box office as one of the top stars of the American cinema until 1940, when her popularity dwindled

as she approached her teenage years. Then there was the case of the anarchic Marx Brothers, who brilliantly lampooned society in *Animal Crackers* (1930) and *Horse Feathers* (1932), but when their satire of war and politics in *Duck Soup* (1933) left audiences cold, Paramount let the zany team go. They found a new home at MGM, where producer Irving Thalberg suggested that they counterbalance their patented brand of insanity by adding a love interest to their comedies, thus considerably diluting their impact in such films as *A Night at the Opera* (1935), *At the Circus* (1939), and *Go West* (1940).

GONE WITH THE WIND

The most famous film of the era is undoubtedly 1939's *Gone with the Wind*, based on Margaret Mitchell's page-turning best seller about the South during the Civil War. The production was the brainchild of independent producer David O. Selznick (in Hollywood fashion, the "O" stood for nothing; Selznick had no middle name but decided that the initial "O" added dignity to his screen credit). Selznick knew that only Clark Gable could play the role of Rhett Butler. After tortuous negotiations, Selznick struck a deal to borrow Gable from MGM in return for cash, a significant percentage of the profits, and Selznick's assurance that the finished film would be distributed through MGM.

The epic nature of the film required an enormous number of sets, and Selznick's insistence that the film be shot in Technicolor sent the budget still higher. Selznick also conducted a national talent search for the actress to play Scarlett O'Hara, testing everyone from Miriam Hopkins to Joan Bennett before deciding on Vivien Leigh at the last minute. By then production had already begun with the famous "burning of Atlanta" sequence, which consumed all existing sets on the Selznick lot left over from earlier productions.

At least four directors were involved with the film. George Cukor began to direct, but he was fired after Gable expressed his displeasure at the way Cukor was handling the project. Cukor was openly gay at a time when homosexuality was completely taboo in Hollywood, and the homophobic Gable felt that Cukor was spending too much time directing Vivien Leigh and not paying enough attention to his own character. Victor Fleming took over the reins after Cukor's departure, but when Fleming had a nervous breakdown, Sam Wood stepped in until Fleming was well enough to return. In addition, action director B. Reeves "Breezy" Eason handled many of the full-scale spectacle sequences, and a battalion of writers were assigned to the project, including (for a few days) novelist F. Scott Fitzgerald, with added daily rewrites by Selznick himself. The entire production was designed by the brilliant William Cameron Menzies, who had designed and directed the celebrated British science fiction film *Things to Come* (1936), based on an original screenplay by H. G. Wells. The strong supporting cast included Olivia de Havilland, Leslie Howard, and Hattie McDaniel.

The massive nature of the production drove everyone to the wall; Selznick was taking pep pills on a daily basis just to keep up with the killing pace of production, and the sheer physical size of the film required an army of extras, assistant directors, production assistants, and the services of at least three directors of cinematography, Ernest Haller, Lee Garmes, and Technicolor's houseman, Ray Rennahan. At a mammoth 222 minutes, the film was split in two sections and became an immediate sensation upon its release. Although Selznick toned down the racism in Mitchell's novel considerably, the film is still full of insulting racial stereotypes, and when the film had its world premiere in Atlanta, the film's African American stars, McDaniel and Butterfly McQueen, were not invited. The film's rose-colored view of slavery and the Reconstruction era uncomfortably recalls *The Birth of a Nation,* and yet the film has a hold on the collective national memory that refuses to fade.

HOLLYWOOD GOES TO WAR

In response to World War II, Hollywood produced a mix of escapist fare, political *agit-prop,* modulated social criticism, and, of course, war films. Tay Garnett's *Bataan* (1943) was a brutal war picture that brought the fight overseas back home to small-town American audiences. Mark Sandrich's *So Proudly We Hail!* (1943) was a patriotic paean to wartime nurses, starring Claudette Colbert. Zoltan Korda directed Humphrey Bogart in the hard-hitting war drama *Sahara* (1943), while Lloyd Bacon's *Action in the North Atlantic* (1943), also starring Bogart, was one of the best seagoing war movies, chronicling the work of the Merchant Marine. Billy Wilder directed *Five Graves to Cairo* (1943), featuring Erich von Stroheim as the famed German general Erwin Rommel, leader of Hitler's Afrika Korps.

Several films were made during this period that would later come back to haunt their creators. Lewis Milestone's *The North Star* (a k a *Armored Attack,* 1943), based on a screenplay by Lillian Hellman, tells the story of the inhab-

Dooley Wilson, Humphrey Bogart, and Ingrid Bergman in Michael Curtiz's *Casablanca* (1942).

itants of a small Russian village fighting against the Nazi onslaught, while Michael Curtiz's *Mission to Moscow* (1943) and Gregory Ratoff's *Song of Russia* (1944) highlight U.S.-Soviet wartime cooperation as one of the keys to victory in Europe. *Mission to Moscow* even portrays Stalin as a wise and benevolent leader.

In another vein, Curtiz directed *Casablanca* (1942), one of the most famous and beloved movies ever made, popular enough to be re-released theatrically half a century later. Humphrey Bogart and Ingrid Bergman star in this superb mix of romance, suspense, and political intrigue set in Nazi-occupied North Africa just prior to the U.S. entry into the war. The remarkable supporting cast included Paul Henreid, Claude Rains, Peter Lorre, Sydney Greenstreet, Conrad Veidt, and Dooley Wilson.

*   *   *

The films of the 1930s and 1940s in Hollywood thus consolidated an industry and gave rise to one of the most powerful and pervasive systems of image production and distribution that the world has ever known. The motion picture was still in its relative infancy, barely forty years old as a narrative entertainment medium. The pioneers who had built the industry watched in amazement as the Hollywood cinema became an international benchmark for glamour, star power, spectacle, action, and narrative compression. The motion picture industry was now a full-fledged business, with its own awards (the first Academy Awards ceremony was held in 1929), a stable studio system that was a community unto itself, and a worldwide distribution system that ensured Hollywood's continued international dominance.

The United States thus exported a way of life, a set of values and expectations, and a social order to the rest of the world, with the implicit suggestion that Hollywood's cultural dominance was yet another example of manifest destiny. The studios were designed, like an interlocking jigsaw puzzle, to dominate the industry as a whole. But even as Hollywood's pervasive influence increased, work abroad ensured that national film industries throughout the rest of the world would also have a lasting influence on the shape of the cinema. These are commercial pictures still ruled by a personal vision, expressing the needs, desires, and passions of those whom the Hollywood cinema too often marginalized. It is to these films and filmmakers that we now turn.

FIVE

INTERNATIONAL CINEMA THROUGH WORLD WAR II

Sound motion pictures had now been introduced throughout Europe and much of the world, and unlike England, which more or less followed the Hollywood model of genre-driven narratives, France, Germany, India, and Japan would all take highly individualized approaches to the sound film, reflecting their respective cultures. Filmmakers in France were especially adventurous. But as the shadow of world conflict fell over Europe and Asia, these artists were forced to make many painful choices. Jean Renoir, for example, fled Europe to make films in the United States after the fall of France to the Nazis, in 1940; René Clair left shortly earlier, but also spent the war years in the United States, working in Hollywood. Jean Cocteau, however, one of the most protean talents of the French cinema, decided to stay in France during the Nazi occupation and continued to make films of great power and beauty, managing to maintain a delicate balance between the interests of the Resistance and those of the Vichy government, the puppet French officials installed by the Nazis.

JEAN RENOIR

With the critical and popular success of *Boudu sauvé des eaux* (*Boudu Saved from Drowning*, 1932), Jean Renoir embarked upon *Madame Bovary* (1933), based on Gustave Flaubert's novel. The first cut of the film ran three hours and thirty minutes, but it was eventually sliced to 101 minutes. The film met with little commercial success; undeterred, Renoir began shooting *Toni* (1935) almost entirely on location in Les Martigues, using nonprofessional actors in most roles. *Toni* thus presages the Italian Neorealist movement by more than a decade, and in following his inherent bent for naturalism, Renoir created a beautiful and tragic film about doomed love, now recog-

A tense moment in Jean Renoir's pre-Neo-realist *Toni* (1935), shot on location in Les Martigues, France, using largely nonprofessional actors.

nized as one of his finest works. Nevertheless, the film found little public or critical favor, a pattern that was becoming increasingly familiar.

Renoir's next film, *Le Crime de Monsieur Lange* (*The Crime of Monsieur Lange,* 1936), marked the director's only collaboration with writer Jacques Prévert and gave ample evidence of the director's increasing politicization. Marked by beautiful, fluid, yet carefully precise camera work, as well as excellent acting by the theatrical ensemble Groupe Octobre, *The Crime of Monsieur Lange* is one of Renoir's finest and most accessible films. It was followed by *La Vie est à nous* (*People of France,* 1936), a political tract that bears a striking resemblance to Jean-Luc Godard's 16 mm *Cinétracts* of the late 1960s and early 1970s. Initially withheld by the censor, *People of France* enjoyed a limited release in the United States in 1937 but was not shown to the paying French public until 1969, following the May 1968 student riots there.

Renoir was now nearing the end of his first great stage of directorial activity, and in rapid succession he created a series of unforgettable films: *Partie de campagne* (*A Day in the Country,* 1936), based on a short story by Guy de Maupassant, completed in the face of considerable production difficulties, and not released in France until 1946 and the United States in 1950; *La Grande Illusion* (*The Grand Illusion,* 1937), one of the best-known and most

A courageous group of POWs keep up their spirits as they plot an escape in Jean Renoir's *La Grande Illusion* (*Grand Illusion*, 1937).

beloved films of all time, as compelling an antiwar document as any ever created; *La Bête humaine* (*The Human Beast*, 1938), an adaptation of Zola's novel (remade by Fritz Lang in 1954 as *Human Desire*); and finally, *La Règle du jeu* (*The Rules of the Game*, 1939), now universally recognized as the director's masterwork, although, amazingly enough, it was reviled at its initial release. This astutely observed tale of romance among the aristocrats and working class during a sporting weekend in

Marcel Dalio as the useless aristocrat Robert de la Cheyniest and Julien Carette as the poacher-turned-manservant Marceau, in Jean Renoir's comedy/drama of morals and manners, *La Règle du jeu* (*The Rules of the Game*, 1939).

Schumacher (Gaston Modot, far right), the violently jealous gamekeeper, threatens the poacher Marceau (Julien Carette, center) in the kitchen of Robert de la Cheyniest's palatial estate, while Lisette (Paulette Dubost, left), the object of both their affections, tries to remain neutral in Jean Renoir's *La Règle du jeu* (*The Rules of the Game*, 1939).

the country was withdrawn after a brief run and not revived until 1945, and later in 1948—and then only in a mutilated version that gave no sense of the original. It was not until 1961 that the "definitive" version of the film was painstakingly reconstructed from various archival materials.

Renoir spent much of 1939 in Rome, teaching at the Centro Sperimentale di Cinematografia. He co-wrote, with Carl Koch, Alessandro De Stefani, Carmine Gallone, and Luchino Visconti, a screen version of Puccini's opera *Tosca* and began production in the spring of 1940, only to be interrupted by Italy's entry into World War II. Koch completed the film (released 1941), and Renoir returned to France. In 1940, however, Renoir came to America at the behest of documentarian Robert Flaherty. His American period would be marked by a number of uneven films, but also some of great beauty and accomplishment. Meanwhile, Renoir's admirers in France were turning on him. At a crucial moment in his country's history, they complained, the director had "gone Hollywood." Renoir's next completed film was *This Land Is Mine* (1943), a story of the French Resistance shot entirely on studio sets. The film did acceptable business in the United States but received a truly hostile reception in France. Renoir then attempted to make amends with a thirty-four-minute short, *Salute to France* (1944), co-directed with Garson Kanin and produced by the Office of War Information from a script by Renoir, Philip Dunne, and Burgess Meredith, who also acted in the film. Though well received in the United States, the film did nothing to salvage Renoir's reputation at home. Renoir's next film was an independent production, *The Southerner* (1945).

Working with his old associate Eugène Lourié as set designer, future director Robert Aldrich as assistant director, and novelist William Faulkner as dialogue consultant, Renoir created one of his most satisfying American films, a tale of the trials and tribulations of a southern cotton farmer. *The Southerner* received the best contemporary critical notices of any of its director's American efforts.

Renoir's last American film was *The Woman on the Beach* (1947). He originally developed the idea with producer Val Lewton, famed for his horror films in the 1940s. Lewton, however, left the production before shooting commenced and the film was substantially cut prior to release. At least two versions now circulate; the more complete edition begins with a long undersea nightmare sequence reminiscent of Renoir's early *La Fille de l'eau*, in which the protagonists encounter each other at the bottom of the ocean. Jacques Rivette, Manny Farber, and other critics have hailed the film as a masterpiece. Mutilated as it is, it displays a maturity of vision equal to the precise grace of *The Rules of the Game* or *The Crime of Monsieur Lange*. In truncated versions running as short as seventy-one minutes, the film is only a fragment of what it might have been, but Rivette has aptly compared it to Erich von Stroheim's *Greed* (1924).

RENÉ CLAIR IN ENGLAND AND AMERICA

The career of René Clair followed a similar trajectory. After his initial sound films in France attracted international acclaim, Clair was lured to England in 1935 to direct the comedy *The Ghost Goes West* for producer Alexander Korda's London Films. The film tells the tale of an eighteenth-century Scottish laird who dies with his honor besmirched and so haunts his castle until the blot can be lifted from his name. Over a century later, his debt-ridden descendant sells the castle to an American businessman, who has it torn down and reconstructed in Florida. The ghost, however, continues to haunt the relocated castle, to the general consternation of all concerned. *The Ghost Goes West* was a substantial hit, and Clair, who at one point during production became so annoyed with Korda's interference that he threatened to bolt, soon set his sights on Hollywood, where he thought he would have more artistic freedom and better technical facilities and distribution.

It did not turn out that way. Clair's American films have their merits; *I Married a Witch* (1942) is a lighthearted forerunner to the long-running television series *Bewitched*: glamorous witch falls in love with unsuspecting mortal and predictable complications ensue. Much better was Clair's *And Then There Were None* (1945), based on the Agatha Christie mystery novel *Ten Little Indians*. Clair manages to make a potentially grisly situation into a light, frothy comedy; people are trapped on an island while a homicidal maniac kills them off one by one, the twist being that the killer is one of the ten, and a race soon develops to unmask the murderer's identity. Using his customary reliance on tightly synchronized musical cues and sight gags, and shooting almost entirely on indoor sets (even for the exterior sequences), as was Clair's custom, the director gives the film a light, fantastic touch that seems simultaneously unreal and yet beguiling.

The picture was Clair's most successful in the United States, and perhaps his most fully realized since *À Nous la liberté*. He stayed in America for the duration of the war, as did Renoir, but he returned to France in 1947, where he directed many more films including *Le Silence est d'or* (*Man About Town/Silence Is Golden*, 1947); *La Beauté du diable* (*Beauty and the Devil*, 1950); and *Les Belles de nuit* (*Beauties of the Night*, 1952), but never recapturing his former stature and success. In 1950, Clair recut *À Nous la liberté* to eliminate many of the film's most poetic and whimsical elements, in the process robbing it of much of its youthful innocence and charm. Unfortunately, this is the version that survives today on DVD. His work in France, in its original form, is playful, light, and graceful. His sound films after the early 1930s fail to live up to his early promise.

COCTEAU'S ORPHIC TRILOGY

Jean Cocteau is a very different case, a multitalented artist whose boldly Surrealist work in the theater, as well as his writings and drawings, defined the yearnings and aspirations of a generation. His groundbreaking sound feature film, *Le Sang d'un poète* (*The Blood of a Poet*, 1930), was not shown publicly until 1932 because of controversy surrounding the production of Dali and Buñuel's *L'Âge d'or* (1930), both films having been produced by the Vicomte de Noailles, a wealthy patron of the arts. Dispensing almost entirely with plot, logic, and conventional narrative, *The Blood of a Poet* relates the adventures of a young poet who is forced to enter the mirror in his room to walk through a mysterious hotel, where his dreams and fantasies are played out before his eyes. Escaping from the mirror by committing ritualistic suicide, he is then forced to watch the spectacle of a young boy being killed with a snowball with a rock center during a schoolyard fight and then to

142

play cards with Death, personified by a woman dressed in funeral black. When the poet tries to cheat, he is exposed, and again kills himself with a small handgun. Death leaves the card room triumphantly, and the film concludes with a note of morbid victory.

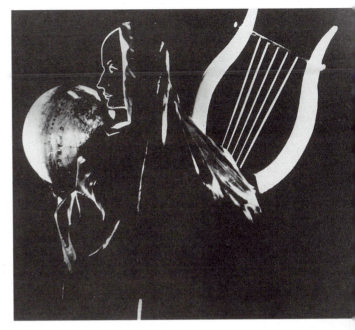

Jean Cocteau's classic first feature film, *Le Sang d'un poète* (*The Blood of a Poet,* shot in 1930 but released in 1932).

Photographed by the great Georges Périnal, with music by Georges Auric, *The Blood of a Poet* represented a dramatic shift in the production of the sound film. Though influenced by the work of Dali and Buñuel and the Surrealist films of Man Ray and René Clair, the picture represents nothing so much as an opium dream (Cocteau famously employed the drug as an aid to his creative process). Throughout, Cocteau uses a great deal of trick photography, including negative film spliced directly into the final cut to create an ethereal effect, mattes (photographic inserts) to place a human mouth in the palm of the poet's hand, and reverse motion, slow motion, and cutting in the camera to make people and objects disappear. For someone who had never before made a film, Cocteau had a remarkably intuitive knowledge of the plastic qualities of the medium, which he would exploit throughout his long career.

When the war broke out, Cocteau chose to stay in Paris with his lover, the actor Jean Marais, and work on his poems, plays, paintings, and sculptures under the noses of the Nazis. An instinctive politician, Cocteau managed to curry favor with both the occupying forces and the French Resistance, so that when the war ended he emerged socially and politically unscathed. It would not be until 1946 that he directed his second film, *La Belle et la bête* (*Beauty and the Beast*), easily the most poetic and sumptuous version of the classic fairy tale. In the late 1940s, he created a string of brilliant and often fantastic films, including *L'Aigle à deux têtes* (*The Eagle Has Two Heads*) and *Les Parents terribles* (released in the United States and the United Kingdom under the title *The Storm Within*), both adapted from Cocteau's own plays in 1948, as well as his undisputed masterpiece, *Orphée* (*Orpheus*, 1950), which

143

[LEFT] Left to right, Jean Marais, director Jean Cocteau, and Josette Day as Beauty on the set of Cocteau's fairy tale *La Belle et la bête* (*Beauty and the Beast,* 1946). [RIGHT] Jean Marais in full makeup as the Beast in Jean Cocteau's *La Belle et la bête* (*Beauty and the Beast,* 1946).

won the top prize at the 1950 Venice Film Festival and consolidated his reputation as one of the most original filmmakers of his generation. His last film, *Le Testament d'Orphée, ou ne me demandez pas pourquoi!* (*The Testament of Orpheus,* 1960), made shortly before his death, repeats many of the themes and motifs of *Orpheus* and *Blood of a Poet,* and together the films are known today as the Orphic trilogy.

Cocteau's dazzling visual sense, combined with his flair for the fantastic, created a world that belonged to him alone, a zone of spectacle, desire, and unfettered imagination. His imagery, especially his use of mirrors as portals that one may use to enter alternative worlds, has been appropriated by everyone from Andy and Larry Wachowski in *The Matrix* (1999) to television commercials, music videos, and numerous experimental films of the 1960s. Though Cocteau persistently returned to the myth of Orpheus and Eurydice, he created such a plethora of variations on this theme that his work was always original and startling. He also created the screenplays and/or dialogue for a number of classic films directed by others, most notably Robert Bresson's *Les Dames du Bois de Boulogne* (*Ladies of the Park,* 1945) and Jean-Pierre Melville's *Les Enfants terribles* (*The Strange Ones,* 1950), the latter based on a novel by Cocteau.

144

JEAN VIGO: SURREALISM AND ANARCHY

Jean Vigo's brief but incandescent career included two major sound films, *Zéro de conduite: Jeunes diables au collège* (*Zero for Conduct*, 1933) and *L'Atalante* (1934), which give only a hint of what he might have accomplished had he not died from tuberculosis at age twenty-nine. *Zero for Conduct*, especially, is a remarkable blend of fantasy and social criticism about a revolution at a boys' school, which tangentially served as the inspiration for Lindsay Anderson's 1968 movie *If. . . .* Vigo's film is revolutionary in its use of Surrealist imagery, fantasy sequences intercut with near-documentary location shooting, trick effects, and animation (a satirical drawing comes to life on a teacher's desk and transforms itself into an image of Napoleon). There is also a scene in which the sound track is run in reverse, creating an otherworldly effect as the boys engage in an epic, slow-motion pillow fight. At forty-one minutes, *Zero for Conduct* is really a featurette, but its impact was so intense that the French censors banned it until 1945 for fear that it would inspire similar rebellions at schools throughout the country. Indeed, Vigo's film seems absolutely prescient in presenting the tedium, mediocrity, and boredom of institutional education.

L'Atalante depicts a young couple's evolving romance on a houseboat in Paris. When the film initially received poor reviews, the distributor recut it and added a contemporary pop sound track. In the late 1990s, however, *L'Atalante* was restored to its original continuity and musical score and played in museums and art houses

The slow-motion pillow fight in Jean Vigo's surrealist anthem to childhood resistance to authority, *Zéro de conduite: Jeunes diables au collège* (*Zero for Conduct,* 1933).

Jean Gabin and Michèle Morgan in Marcel Carné's tragic *Quai des brumes* (*Port of Shadows*, 1938).

throughout the world. More than any of his works, the restored *L'Atalante* displays the bracing anarchy of Vigo's independent vision, as well as his deeply romantic and poetic sensibility. His impact continues to be felt today: in France the Prix Jean Vigo is awarded each year to young filmmakers who display a genuine "independence of spirit" in their art.

Other noted directors of the early sound era in France included Jacques Feyder, a leading light in the Poetic Realism school of cinema, creating films that spoke to the reality of everyday existence but retained an element of romanticism in their construction. Feyder's films *Le Grand Jeu* (*The Full Deck,* 1934) and *La Kermesse héroïque* (*Carnival in Flanders,* 1935) were joined by other works such as Julien Duvivier's most famous film, *Pépé le Moko* (1937), featuring French film star Jean Gabin as a doomed gangster, and Marcel Carné's fatalistic *Le Quai des brumes* (*Port of Shadows,* 1938) and *Le Jour se lève* (*Daybreak,* 1939), both of which viewed human existence as a brutal charade, devoid of hope or kindness. The most theatrical of the French early sound filmmakers, the writer and director Marcel Pagnol, created a well-regarded trilogy of films based on his plays: *Marius* (which Pagnol co-directed with Alexander Korda, 1931), *Fanny* (which was directed by Mario Almirante from Pagnol's script, 1932), and *César* (which Pagnol wrote and directed alone, 1936). As a whole, Pagnol's films are notable for their stately pacing and deliberate schematic structure.

FRENCH OCCUPATION CINEMA

In France during the war, with Paris under the Nazi occupation and the puppet Vichy government, only a few major filmmakers chose to stay behind and create a series of very subtly subversive films; otherwise, much of the

146

Vichy cinema was sheer escapism. Marcel Carné's *Les Enfants du paradis* (*Children of Paradise*, 1945), from a script by Jacques Prévert, was unquestionably one of the major films of the Resistance cinema, using the story of a group of theatrical performers to highlight the resilience of French national culture in the face of the occupying forces. Henri-Georges Clouzot created *Le Corbeau* (*The Raven*, 1943), a memorably vicious film documenting the effects of a series of "poison pen" letters on the inhabitants of a provincial French village. Like all of Clouzot's work, *The Raven* has a bleak view of humanity, and the town and its citizens in the film are viewed as a gallery of unscrupulous, gossiping, even drug-addicted miscreants. The film was viciously attacked in the Resistance press for its unflattering view of French society, and after the war Clouzot and the film's screenwriter, Louis Chavance, were banned from making films for a time, as retribution for their deeply misanthropic work. But the ban was soon lifted, and as later Clouzot films make clear, the director's pessimism was not directed at French society so much as against the human predicament in general; Clouzot was clearly a fatalist who saw life as a continuous battle. He would go on to create two of the French cinema's most acidulous films of the 1950s: the stunning *Le Salaire de la peur* (*The Wages of Fear*, 1953), about a group of down-and-out expatriates stranded in a South American hellhole who are hired to transport unstable nitroglycerine on a tortuous back-road route to help put out an oil well fire, and *Les Diaboliques* (*Diabolique*, 1955), a suspense thriller centering on murder and deception at a rundown French boarding school.

A more humane vision emerged in the superb *Les Dames du Bois de Boulogne* (*Ladies of the Park*, 1945), which Robert Bresson, one of the most important postwar directors, created in collaboration with Jean Cocteau, who wrote the dialogue for the film, with the story based on Diderot's classic "Jacques le fataliste et son maître." *Les Dames du Bois de Boulogne* is essentially an allegory centered on a young woman, Agnès (Elina Labourdette), whose economic circumstances have forced her into a life of high-level prostitution with her mother effectively serving as her pimp, but who is then "saved" by Hélène (María Casares), a wealthy woman who takes over her life, pays her debts, and installs her in a fashionable apartment. The luxurious domain, however, is really a prison. Hélène's true design is to marry off Agnès to her ex-lover, Jean (Paul Bernard), who has jilted Hélène after a long affair. Hélène wants revenge, and Jean's arranged marriage to a "fallen woman" will suit her purposes. Throughout the film, Bresson's impeccable camera movement and editorial style, coupled with Cocteau's sparkling and sardonic dialogue, bring this story of moral consequences into sharp detail, and the plight of Agnès is seen as emblematic of France's position under the Nazis; the illusion of freedom is present but at a terrible cost. Bresson's later films would be far more minimalist than *Les Dames du Bois de Boulogne*, but in this early masterpiece he created one of the treasures of world cinema.

Other notable films created under the Vichy regime include Jean Dellanoy's *L'Éternel retour* (*The Eternal Return*, 1943), a modern variation on the legend of Tristan and Isolde, with screenplay and dialogue by the ubiquitous Jean Cocteau. Marcel Carné's *Les Visiteurs du soir* (*The Devil's Envoys*, 1942) used life in fifteenth-century France to create a striking allegory on the predations of the Nazi regime, while 1943 also saw the creation of the Institut des Hautes Études Cinématographiques (IDHEC), the French national film school, which was founded by the French director and film theorist Marcel L'Herbier. After the war, the French cinema would go through a cataclysmic period of rejuvenation and change, spearheaded by the critical journal *Cahiers du Cinéma* (literally, "the notebooks of cinema"). *Cahiers* demanded an end to what it viewed as the "literary" nature of classical French cinema, and with the help of such theorists as Claude Chabrol, Jean-Luc Godard (often writing as Hans Lucas), Eric Rohmer, Jacques Rivette, François Truffaut, and others, set the stage for the creation of the New Wave (Nouvelle Vague) film movement in the late 1950s. All these critics would later become key directors in the New Wave movement, which would utterly transform the face of international cinema.

SOUND FILMS IN ENGLAND

In England, the development of the sound cinema was more directly tied to narrative exposition. Sir Michael Balcon, head of production for Gaumont-British until 1938, was a firm believer in giving the public entertainment films with no pretensions. But as we have seen, early English sound production was undermined by the creation of quota quickies, films shot in England to meet the government's demand that a percentage of all motion pictures shown in the country be homegrown productions. These quickies succeeded mostly in hampering the national cinema, outside of Alexander Korda's lavish productions and the revolutionary films of Alfred Hitchcock. Among the most popular English stars of the early sound period were the likes of Gracie Fields, a music hall singer, Tod Slaughter, who specialized in horror melodramas, and George Formby, a lowbrow comedian.

The other major business force during this era in the British film industry

Roger Livesey, as Dr. Reeves, addresses the heavenly tribunal in Michael Powell and Emeric Pressburger's lavish 1946 fantasy, *A Matter of Life and Death* (a k a *Stairway to Heaven*).

was J. Arthur Rank, who began in the film business in 1933 as a publicist and booker of Methodist films to churches and schools. In 1935 Rank embarked on an aggressive campaign of vertical integration, buying production facilities, film processing laboratories, theater chains, and distribution exchanges at a rapid clip. By 1945, the Rank Organisation was omnipresent, with more than a thousand theaters and half of England's film studios under its direct control. As with Sir Michael Balcon, J. Arthur Rank prized commercial considerations above all else, and his films catered to popular tastes and prejudices. However, Rank also offered finance and distribution to the Archers, the production company of Michael Powell and Emeric Pressburger, which created lavishly mounted films of epic scale and quality. Their output included Powell's *The Life and Death of Colonel Blimp* (1943), *A Matter of Life and Death* (a k a *Stairway to Heaven,* 1946), and *Black Narcissus* (1947); as well as the Two Cities unit, which produced Sir Laurence Olivier's *Henry V* (1944) and Sir Carol Reed's *Odd Man Out* (1947); and Cineguild, producer of Sir David Lean's *Brief Encounter* (1945), *Great Expectations* (1946), and *Oliver Twist* (1948).

Powell and Pressburger were perhaps the most eccentric and individual talents to come out of Britain during the war years. Their films were usually in sumptuous Technicolor and meticulously crafted. Pressburger generally performed the script chores; Powell, one of the great visionaries of the British cinema, handled direction. The Archers would continue as a produc-

Trevor Howard and Celia Johnson in David Lean's drama of illicit wartime romance, *Brief Encounter* (1945), based on Noel Coward's play *Still Life*.

tion entity after the war, but Powell's last film, the justly notorious *Peeping Tom* (1960), about a psychopathic sex killer who films his victims as he murders them, put a virtual stop to their careers. Though the film is a deeply considered meditation on voyeurism, violence against women, and the role of cinema in shaping dreams and desires, it was written off at the time as an unpleasant exercise in sadism, and has only recently been accorded the attention it deserves.

ALEXANDER KORDA

Other forces were also at work. London Films' Alexander Korda desperately wanted to create prestige pictures that could compete with their big-budget Hollywood counterparts, so he produced and directed *The Private Life of Henry VIII* (1933), which became the first British film to win an Academy Award for Best Actor (Charles Laughton in the title role). Korda's subsequent period costume dramas, such as Paul Czinner's *The Rise of Catherine the Great* (a k a *Catherine the Great*, 1934), Korda's *Rembrandt* (1936, again starring Charles Laughton), and his brother Zoltan Korda's racist paean to British colonial rule in Africa, *Sanders of the River* (1935), starring Paul Robeson, were part of the vanguard of the "quality British film" movement,

Charles Laughton in Alexander Korda's *Rembrandt* (1936), one of the films that began the British tradition of "quality" dramas.

Paul Robeson, center, in Zoltan Korda's ultra-colonialist *Sanders of the River* (1935).

films that were immensely popular adaptations of literary classics or historical dramas. By the time of William Cameron Menzies's spectacular *Things to Come* (1936), however, the formula was wearing thin, and Korda was facing bankruptcy. With Hitchcock about to depart for Hollywood, British cinema faced a dire situation.

DOCUMENTARY FILMS IN ENGLAND

The English documentary provided a brief ray of hope. Under the General Post Office and producer/director John Grierson, such films as Basil Wright's *Song of Ceylon* (1934) and Wright and Harry Watt's *Night Mail* (1936) demonstrated a new spirit of adventurousness in documentaries, which could not only report but also interpret events. *Night Mail*, for example, depicted the progress of an overnight mail train through England, with commentary by W. H. Auden and music by Benjamin Britten. As the war approached, Humphrey Jennings emerged as the leading light of the English documentary. Jennings and his associates created a memorable series of wartime films, from Harry Watt and Jennings's response to Hitler's nighttime bombings, *London Can Take It!* (1940), to Jennings's and Stewart McAllister's prescient slice of life, *Listen to Britain* (1942), a twenty-minute piece devoid of narration that simply shows everyday life in England at the height of the war. Jennings also directed a documentary feature, *Fires Were Started* (a k a *I Was a Fireman*, 1943), on the crews who cleaned up the damage from Hitler's bombings, and *A Diary for Timothy* (1945), emphasizing the importance of family in the face of war.

Working in a different area of documentary filmmaking, Mary Field specialized in nature and children's films. Born in Wimbledon, Field was a high school history teacher before she went to work for British Instructional Films in 1926, directing and producing the well-known series of shorts *The Secrets of Nature*. In 1933, Field began working for Gaumont-British Instructional Films, where she made educational films for eleven years. In 1944, she started up the Children's Entertainment Division of the Rank Organisation, over which she presided as executive producer until 1950. Field was a devoted activist for children's entertainment, and she argued for the establishment and development of the Children's Film Foundation. The foundation was ultimately set up by the British film industry to ensure the production of children's films, and Field served as the executive producer of the organization. She also directed propaganda films for the British government during World War II. Film historians and scholars have generally ignored Field's accomplishments as a documentarist, but her work touched the lives of British children for nearly three decades, and her many innovations, including popularizing the use of slow motion and telephoto (magnifying) lenses in nature films, merit attention.

EALING STUDIOS

Another important institutional shift took place in British cinema in 1938, when Sir Michael Balcon left Gaumont-British and became the head of production at Ealing Studios. Until then, Ealing had mostly been associated with musicals, but under Balcon's leadership the studio began to make films more intricately tied to British sensibilities. Balcon brought in a number of directors from the General Post Office documentary unit such as Alberto Cavalcanti and Charles Frend, and created the memorable war films *Went the Day Well?* (Cavalcanti, 1942) and *San Demetrio London* (Frend, 1943). In 1945, the studio pooled the talents of directors Cavalcanti, Robert Hamer, Basil Dearden, and Charles Crichton to create the first British postwar horror film *Dead of Night,* using five separate plot lines and a linking story to create one of the greatest of all horror films. After the war, Ealing began to specialize in a brand of fast-paced, cerebral, action-filled farces, such that the films became collectively known as "Ealing comedies."

GERMANY AND THE NAZI CINEMA

In Germany, the shift to sound was more sinister, with the indigenous film industries rapidly pressed into service of the Nazi regime. Joseph Goebbels created the Reichsfilmkammer (Reich Film Chamber) in 1933 and thus made himself the sole authority on what could and could not be shown on the screen. The following year saw the passage of the infamous Reichlichtspielgesetz (Reich Cinema Law), which made it illegal for Jews to work in the German cinema. Many talented film artists left the country almost immediately, most conspicuously Fritz Lang, but also directors Billy Wilder, Frank Wisbar (a k a Franz Wysbar), Douglas Sirk, and Robert Siodmak; actors Peter Lorre, Oskar Homolka, Anton Walbrook, and Albert Bassermann; composer Franz Waxman; and cinematographers Franz Planer and Eugen Schüfftan, as well as other gifted writers, directors, actors, and technicians.

153

Goebbels imported many Hollywood "B" films to meet immediate audience demand, but he also rapidly set about creating a new German cinema that would accurately reflect the dreams and ambitions of the new regime. Thea von Harbou, Fritz Lang's ex-wife, directed *Hanneles Himmelfahrt* (*Hannele Goes to Heaven*) and *Elisabeth und der Narr* (*Elisabeth and the Fool*) (both 1934), and also wrote the screenplays or dialogue for Hans Steinhoff's *Eine Frau ohne bedeutung* (*A Woman of No Importance*, 1936) and Harlan's *Jugend* (*Youth*, 1938), all of which enthusiastically supported the Nazi cause. Outright anti-Semitic propaganda was provided by Fritz Hippler's notorious *Der Ewige Jude* (*The Eternal Jew*, 1940), a scurrilous film that compared Jews to rats and then charged that they ruled the world's economy.

Tracked down by film historians in the 1980s, Hippler, who died in 2002, dismissively referred to *The Eternal Jew* as "the film that bears my name," as if the entire project had come to fruition without his help. In fact, Hippler was an aggressive Nazi supporter, and the film, one of the most vile documents ever created, helped to pave the way for the Holocaust, suggesting that the cure for "the Jewish problem" was their "elimination." Similarly despicable pro-Nazi films, such as Veit Harlan's *Jud Süß* (*Jew Süss*, 1940), which depicted Jews as rapacious rapists, usurers, and opportunists, as well as Hans Steinhoff's *Hitlerjunge Quex: Ein Film vom Opfergeist der deutschen Jugend* (*Our Flags Lead Us Forward*, 1933) and Franz Wenzler's *Hans Westmar* (1933), both essentially recruitment films for the Hitler Youth, were highly popular with German audiences. Amazingly, they were also shown in the United States by the German-American Bund, the then-rising American Nazi party. Shrewdly judging his audience, Goebbels, who nationalized the film industry entirely in 1942, also produced a large number of escapist musicals, melodramas, and comedies, in addition to weekly state-created and censored "newsreels," or *Deutsche Wochenschau*, which kept citizens apprised of the Reich's latest victories—vaguely real at first and later utterly fabricated, as the tide of war turned against the Reich in 1943.

Reinhold Schünzel's musical comedy *Amphitryon* (*Amphitryon—Happiness from the Clouds*, 1935) was one example of Goebbels's predilection for lighter, less demanding fare; as the war progressed, and the Nazis developed an early monopack color film process, Goebbels indulged in his taste for spectacle with Josef von Báky's color fantasy film *Münchhausen* (*The Adventures of Baron Munchausen*, 1943), which was designed as a prestige production to mark Universum Film Aktiengesellschaft's twenty-fifth anniversary as a production entity. Other "A" level Nazi films included Eduard von Borsody's *Wunschkonzert* (*Request Concert*, 1940) and Rolf Hansen's *Die Große Liebe* (*The Great Love*, 1942), which depicted home-front sacrifice in aid of the German war effort, while Wolfgang Liebeneiner's *Ich klage an* (*I Accuse*, 1941) presented a husband's murder of his wife as a noble act because of her lingering illness, essentially endorsing euthanasia as a national policy. Actor and director Kurt Gerron's *Theresienstadt* (*The Führer Gives a City to the Jews*, 1944) is particularly loathsome, because it falsely shows Jewish captives of the Nazi regime living in relative safety and comfort, when in fact the "city" cited in the film's title was built specifically for the film and destroyed the moment filming was completed. The town's inhabitants were then sent to their deaths in concentration camps, along with Gerron himself, who was Jewish, and who had been forced to write and direct *Theresienstadt* as his last act on earth. Hitler appears in the film, smiling broadly as he tours the mock city. The film was created under Goebbels's orders to counter reports of concentration camp atrocities that were then beginning to leak to the public.

Goebbels's dreams of grandeur inevitably led him to the production of Veit Harlan's epic historical war drama *Kolberg* (1945), designed to be the *Gone with the Wind* of the Nazi cinema; Goebbels himself was one of the screenwriters. Even as the perimeters of Germany were falling under the allied assault, Goebbels spent more than eight million marks on the color production and actually diverted troops from the battlefield to serve as extras in the film, which depicted German citizens in hopeless hand-to-hand combat against a ruthless enemy aggressor. After *Kolberg* was completed in the last days of the war, the finished film was first shown to German troops in occupied France and then screened in Hitler's private bunker in Berlin, even as Russian and American forces were only miles away. Goebbels's mad dream of cinematic power thus collapsed as did the regime that supported them; in one of his last speeches to his staff, Goebbels suggested that one day "a fine color film" would be made of the last days of the Reich, and that every man and woman should conduct themselves accordingly so that posterity could correctly report their allegiance to the Führer. In the end, as the final hours came and Hitler and his bride, Eva Braun, committed suicide, Goebbels poisoned his children and then killed himself and his wife, Magda, unable to imagine living in a world without Hitler. Thus, one of the most bizarre and death-obsessed cinematic regimes in history collapsed upon itself in an avalanche of lies, fantasies, and dreams of power. These films, both aesthetically mediocre and morally reprehensible, are almost never revived today.

LENI RIEFENSTAHL

Notable in the Nazi's use of the cinema to further their own ends was the career of propagandist and documentarian Leni Riefenstahl. Born in Berlin in 1902, Riefenstahl rapidly emerged as the foremost filmmaker of the Reich. A genuine artist, she gave her considerable skills to the Nazi cause, most notably in her "documentary" of the 1934 Nazi Party Congress at Nuremberg, *Triumph des Willens* (*Triumph of the Will*, 1935). Her unquestioned masterpiece, *Olympia*, a two-part record of the 1936 Olympic games, took her two years to edit before appearing in 1938.

Riefenstahl began her career as a dancer and painter and soon found her athletic, blonde good looks in demand for director Arnold Fanck's mountain films, which featured her in a variety of alpine settings, climbing from one adventure to the next. She soon became a star and was able to leverage her fame into a chance at directing with the mountain film *Das Blaue Licht* (*The Blue Light*, co-directed by Béla Belázs, 1932), which she also starred in, produced, and wrote. Drifting rapidly into the Nazi orbit, Riefenstahl found personal favor with Hitler as the personification of "Aryan perfection" and became active in fund-raising and other party affairs. In 1933, she created her first short film for the Reich, *Der Sieg des Glaubens* (*Victory of the Faith*).

Hitler then asked Riefenstahl to record the 1934 Nuremberg rallies and placed nearly unlimited resources at her disposal. The result was *Triumph of the Will*, for which she employed a crew of more than 120, including 30 cameramen. The sets were designed by the Nazis' in-house architect, Albert Speer, and the production included a vast amphitheater with camera cars moving up and down amid the swastika-emblazoned banners for spectacular crane and wide-angle shots. Most of the film was shot silently, with music added later; Riefenstahl not only edited the film herself but also supervised the music recording sessions. When she found that the conductor could not keep to the beat of the soldiers' marching feet on the screen, she pushed him from the podium and conducted the orchestra herself, achieving perfect synchronization. More than seventy years later, *Triumph of the Will* is still studied as a classic propaganda film, because it astonishingly manages to make both Hitler and the then-rising Third Reich seem simultaneously attractive and an agent for positive social change. Indeed, as the director Frank Capra and others discovered during World War II when they tried to reedit the film to discredit the regime, *Triumph of the Will* is "edit proof." It con-

156

Nazi spectacle dwarfs human scale in Leni Riefenstahl's 1935 propaganda film, *Triumph des Willens* (*Triumph of the Will*).

tains no scenes of book burning, speeches of racial hatred, or incitements to war; rather, it depicts the Nazi movement as an unstoppable juggernaut that everyone, seemingly, should embrace. The result is both hypnotic and repellent, and it is still screened at neo-Nazi rallies as a recruiting tool.

Riefenstahl followed this with two short films, a paean to the German Wehrmacht, *Tag der Freiheit* (*Day of Freedom*, 1935), and further Nazi Party rallies in *Festliches Nürnberg* (1937). With *Olympia*, however, she outdid herself. Again assembling an army of cameramen and technical assistants, she and her crew photographed every aspect of the 1936 Berlin Olympics, from the athletes relaxing in their guest quarters to the drama of the events themselves, linking the entire event (in a lengthy prologue) to the glories of ancient Greece. For *Olympia*, she used forty-five cameras, shot more than two hundred hours of film, and then locked herself in a cutting room for two years, editing the footage down to a 220-minute, two-part epic that employed slow motion, underwater photography, and even reverse motion to produce a kaleidoscopic hymn to the human body in motion, creating perhaps the greatest sports film ever made. Moving from personal athletic triumphs to scenes of epic spectacle, *Olympia* manages to be fairly evenhanded in its coverage of the event, even including footage of African American athlete Jesse Owens's victorious presence at the games, over Hitler's strenuous objections.

Goebbels had been adamantly opposed to the project, jealous of both Riefenstahl's personal access to Hitler and her artistic skill; in addition, she was a woman, and the entire Nazi culture viewed women as essentially inferior beings more suited to childbearing than creative endeavor. But when *Olympia* finally emerged to nearly universal praise, Goebbels became one of the film's most ardent supporters, and Riefenstahl was now considered untouchable within the Nazi film hierarchy. From this success, she spent some time as a photojournalist covering the Nazi invasion of Poland in 1939 and then began work on the project that would take her through the war, *Tiefland* (*Lowlands,* 1940–1944; released in 1954), based on the opera by Eugen d'Albert, with herself in one of the lead roles. She spent years meticulously working on this very minor, deeply artificial film, again displaying her insensitivity to humanity by using the Gypsy prisoners of one of the Nazi concentration camps as extras.

After the war, Riefenstahl was so identified with the Nazi regime that she found it impossible to obtain work, and even though she was formally cleared of charges of collaboration by a West German court in 1952, she remained an outcast in the international film world. She released *Tiefland* in 1954 to indifferent reviews and almost immediately withdrew it from circulation. In the 1970s, she began work on a long film about the Nuba tribe in Africa and published a coffee-table book of stills from the project, although the film itself was never completed. In her last years Riefenstahl supported herself by appearing on the lecture circuit with screenings of her films, and in 2002 actually released a new film, *Impressionen unter Wasser* (*Underwater Impressions*), which was essentially a documentary centered on her late-in-life passion (she was ninety-eight) for deep-sea diving and underwater photography. Keeping herself physically and mentally alert right up to the moment of her death in 2003, she ultimately seemed mystified at the furor that surrounded her career. In her memoirs, published in 1993, she argued that she would never have supported the Nazis if she had been aware of their ultimate aims. This claim was received with deep skepticism by most observers, however, and Riefenstahl remains a curious anomaly—a gifted artist who chose to work against the interests of humanity, to embrace evil rather than social justice. It is perhaps the most curious career in the history of the cinema, and one of the most deeply troubling.

FASCIST ITALY

While Germany under the Nazis was pursuing a cinematic strategy of escapist comedies, political propaganda, and epic spectacles, combined with liberal doses of "B" grade Hollywood films and Mickey Mouse cartoons (until 1939, when imports from the West were abruptly halted after the start of hostilities in Europe), Italy pursued a slightly different course. Benito Mussolini created the Ente Nazionale Industrie Cinematografice (ENIC) in 1934 and thus consolidated the production and exhibition of films into one gigantic entity. In 1935, Mussolini began construction of Cinecittà, the vast film studio near Rome that still stands today, and also created a film school for aspiring young directors, the Centro Sperimentale di Cinematografia. The key directors of the early sound period in Italy, Alessandro Blasetti and Mario Camerini, created a serviceable yet unremarkable series of films during this time, such as Blasetti's dramatic *Terra Madre* (*Motherland,* 1931) and Camerini's comedy *Gli Uomini che Mascalzoni!* (*What Scoundrels Men Are!,* 1932), starring a young Vittorio De Sica, who would later become one of Italy's greatest directors as part of the postwar Neorealist movement. Melodramas were especially popular with Italian audiences, particularly the sub-genre known as *telefono bianco,* or "white telephone" films, which depicted the emotional turmoil of Italy's upper classes in the manner of a contemporary nighttime soap opera, as in Guido Brignone's *Paradiso* (*Paradise,* 1932).

As the war approached, Cinecittà, then one of the most modern production facilities in Europe, with sixteen sound stages and generous state subsidies and tax breaks, began churning out a mix of escapist and frankly propagandistic films. These included Carmine Gallone's *Scipione l'Africano* (*Scipio Africanus: The Defeat of Hannibal,* 1937), a historical drama in the "sword and sandal" mode that sought to capitalize on Italy's past military glories to galvanize the public, and Gennaro Righelli's *L'Armata azzurra* (*The Blue Fleet,* 1932), which glorified the Italian air force. Blasetti's *1860* (1934) was another historical epic designed to inspire public support for Mussolini's regime, while Giovacchino Forzano's *Camicia nera* (*Black Shirt,* 1933) was even more direct in its admiration of Fascist ideology. But perhaps the most interesting aspect of the Italian wartime cinema, and its greatest legacy, comes from the many young directors who began their cinematic apprenticeship at Mussolini's state-run film school, including Renato Castellani, Vittorio De Sica, Roberto Rossellini, Pietro Germi, Giuseppe De Santis,

159

and Michelangelo Antonioni, all of whom would go on to great success in the postwar era. These talented cineastes directed films at Cinecittà before or during the war, some in direct support of Mussolini's regime, others merely designed as dramatic or comedic entertainment.

MAJOR ITALIAN FILMMAKERS

The great Luchino Visconti got his start when he directed an Italian version of James M. Cain's classic hard-boiled novel *The Postman Always Rings Twice* as *Ossessione* (*Obsession*) in 1943; with its dark and brooding vision of human existence, the film was not only out of step with Mussolini's war machine, but it also infringed on the literary rights to the source material, which MGM owned and would adapt to the screen in 1946. Banned in the United States for years, Visconti's film was ultimately released with official clearance in the 1970s and now appears on DVD as one of the most peculiar and fatalistic films produced in Italy during the war years. But the real breakthrough in the Italian postwar cinema would come with the production of Ros-

Anna Magnani fights for her freedom in Roberto Rossellini's Neorealist classic *Roma, città aperta* (*Open City,* 1945).

sellini's *Roma, città aperta* (*Open City*, 1945), an anti-Fascist film that was made in absolute secrecy in the last days of the war. The film tells of the Resistance movement in Rome against Fascism and details the daily travails that beset the underground combatants.

The raw realism of *Open City*—shot for the most part in the streets, apartments, garages, and cellars of Rome, using ordinary light bulbs and even car headlights for illumination, and featuring superb performances from a cast that comprised for the most part nonprofessionals—astounded audiences worldwide. The film ushered in the golden age of Neorealism, in which the cinema accurately reflected the concerns and vicissitudes of everyday life in stark newsreel fashion, without glamorous costumes, highly paid stars, or the certainty of a happy ending. Neorealist cinema, of which Rossellini, De Sica, and De Santis soon became the foremost exponents, was a conscious rejection of the Hollywood studio system and the production gloss traditionally associated with it. Thus Mussolini's real cinematic legacy is not the films he produced during his brief reign, but rather the film school and studio he created, which trained a group of directors who would go on to make some of the most important Italian films of the 1950s through the 1970s, all of whom were deeply opposed to Fascism.

JAPANESE FILMMAKING DURING WORLD WAR II

In Japan, war-themed films began appearing as early as 1938. One of the first such films was Tomotaka Tasaka's *Gonin no Sekkohei* (*Five Scouts*, 1938), which, despite its support of the Japanese war effort, seemed devoid of the blatant propaganda found in both Nazi and American war films of the period. Indeed, wartime propaganda "documentaries," such as *Five Scouts*, emphasized the importance of duty, honor, and country for Japanese soldiers, rather than glorifying war or inciting racial animosity. Kozaburo Yoshimura's *Nishizumi senshacho-den* (*The Story of Tank Commander Nishizumi*, 1940) is a much more straightforward battle film, while Kenji Mizoguchi created what is probably the best-known Japanese war film, the two-part *Genroku chushingura* (*The Loyal 47 Ronin*, 1941), a sweeping historical epic set in eighteenth-century Japan centering on a bank of Samurai warriors who remained steadfast in their devotion to their master even after his death. Akira Kurosawa, who would become one of Japan's most important postwar directors, made his cinematic debut with *Sugata Sanshiro* (*Judo Saga*, 1943), another historical drama, which focused on a nineteenth-cen-

161

tury judo champion as an example of personal selflessness and sacrifice. Kurosawa's first film was remarkably assured stylistically, evincing an almost Hollywood-like embrace of fluid camerawork, particularly in its abundance of deftly designed tracking shots.

Yasujiro Ozu, notably, managed to avoid being a significant part of the Japanese wartime motion picture industry, with the prewar *Shukujo wa nani o wasureta ka* (*What Did the Lady Forget?*) in 1937, and subsequently *Todake no kyodai* (*The Toda Brothers and Sisters,* 1941), a film of everyday life, and *Chichi ariki* (*There Was a Father,* 1942), which was also a typically intimate film about daily domestic life. After this, Ozu did not return to the director's chair until 1947, with *Nagaya shinshiroku* (*The Record of a Tenement Gentleman*). In all these films, he seemed more interested in the interior lives of his characters than in any external form that might affect their lives. He refined his use of off-screen space (significant action that occurs outside the frame, and is thus unseen by the audience) while further developing his predilection for what has been termed "pillow shots"—shots of the landscapes, billowing curtains, details of a building, or close-up street life, which have nothing to do with the film's narrative but which create a sense of atmosphere that punctuates and underscores the film's emotional center. As the war ended, Ozu's highly personal style became more and more sophisticated in its intricacy and structure. His pillow shots became his signature, along with his insistence on static setups, precise framing, and an avoidance of moving camera shots.

SOVIET WARTIME CINEMA

In the Soviet Union during the war, Sergei Eisenstein remained the only filmmaker of major cultural significance, while Boris Shumyatskiy, Stalin's cinematic watchdog, supervised the production of numerous mediocre propaganda films wholly lacking in visual or thematic originality. When Germany invaded in June 1941, Soviet filmmakers began producing a significant number of newsreel compilation films in support of the war effort. The most famous is probably Ilya Kopalin and Leonid Varlamov's *Razgrom nemetskikh voysk pod Moskvoy* (*Defeat of the German Armies Near Moscow,* 1942), which was screened in the West under the more commercial title *Moscow Strikes Back.* The film actually won an Academy Award for Best Documentary in 1942 (along with two American war films, John Ford's *The Battle of Midway* and Frank Capra's *Prelude to War*).

[ABOVE]: Early films were sometimes tinted, and then hand-colored for details a frame at a time, as in this scene from Edwin S. Porter's *The Great Train Robbery* (1903). [BELOW]: Rouben Mamoulian's *Becky Sharp* (1935) was the first feature shot in three-strip Technicolor.

Gone with the Wind (1939) was for many viewers the apotheosis of 1930s three-strip Technicolor.

Oscar Micheaux, an enterprising African American producer/director, created a large number of "race films" with all-black casts, such as *The Girl from Chicago* (1932).

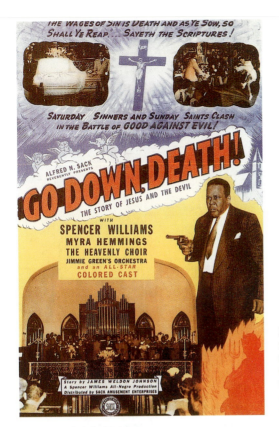

[LEFT]: Spencer Williams, another African American pioneer, created the religious melodrama *Go Down, Death* (1944) on a shoestring budget. [BELOW]: Bert Lahr (the Cowardly Lion), Judy Garland (Dorothy), Jack Haley (the Tin Man), and Ray Bolger (the Scarecrow) in Victor Fleming's *The Wizard of Oz* (1939), a film that pushed three-strip Technicolor to its visual limits.

[ABOVE]: Otto Preminger's *River of No Return* (1954) fused Technicolor and CinemaScope to create an eye-filling adventure film. [RIGHT]: André de Toth's *House of Wax* (1953), in the 3-D process Natural Vision, was a major commercial success, even though de Toth had vision in only one eye and thus had no idea what 3-D looked like, even in real life.

[ABOVE]: The muted tones of Alfred Hitchcock's *Vertigo* (1958): James Stewart and Kim Novak meet in the forest of giant redwood trees. [BELOW]: Jean-Paul Belmondo in Jean-Luc Godard's color-saturated political polemic, *Pierrot le fou* (1965).

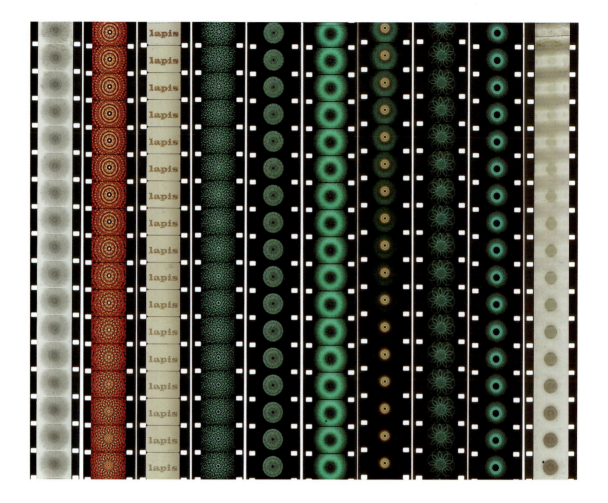

[ABOVE]: A series of frames from James Whitney's *Lapis* (1966), one of the first films to be entirely computer generated.
[BELOW]: Stanley Kubrick's *2001: A Space Odyssey* (1968) brought special effects to a new level.

[TOP]: Bruce Lee redefined the action film with his spectacular martial arts films from Hong Kong, such as *Fists of Fury* (Wei Lo and Jiaxiang Wu, *Tang shan da xiong,* 1971), shot in the French anamorphic process Dyaliscope. [BOTTOM]: *Yaaba* (*Grandmother*), a tale of family life in Burkina Faso, was directed by Idrissa Ouedraogo in 1989, and remains a classic example of contemporary African cinema.

[ABOVE]: Al Pacino blasts his way to the top of a cocaine cartel in Brian De Palma's *Scarface* (1983). [BELOW]: Denzel Washington stars as the charismatic *Malcolm X* in Spike Lee's 1992 biography of the famed civil rights leader.

[ABOVE]: Tim Burton's quirky fable *Edward Scissorhands* (1990) was a breakthrough film for Johnny Depp (left), as a young man with metal shears for hands who tries to find a place in society. [BELOW]: Casper Van Dien in Paul Verhoeven's *Starship Troopers* (1997), a stunning adaptation of Robert Heinlein's novel, with dazzling special effects by Phil Tippett, the twenty-first-century Willis O'Brien of CGI (computer-generated imagery).

[ABOVE]: Hayao Miyazaki's *Mononoke-hime* (*Princess Mononoke*, 1997) brought Japanese *anime* to the mainstream public, and became the biggest box office success in the history of Japan. [BELOW]: Tom Tykwer's race-against-the-clock
thriller *Lola rennt* (*Run Lola Run*, 1998), featuring red-haired Franka Potente in the leading role.

[ABOVE]: Color coordination indebted to Douglas Sirk: Todd Haynes's *Far from Heaven* (2002), with Julianne Moore and Dennis Haysbert in an interracial love story set in the 1950s, stylistically and thematically designed as an homage to Sirk's *All That Heaven Allows* (1955). [BELOW]: Wong Kar Wai's *Fa yeung nin wa* (*In the Mood for Love,* 2000), with Tony Leung and Maggie Cheung in another tale of forbidden romance, this time set in Hong Kong in the 1960s, with a very different palette of colors.

[ABOVE]: Gael Garcia Bernal (as Julio) and Diego Luna (as Tenoch) in Alfonso Cuarón's *Y tu mamá también* (*And Your Mother Too,* 2001), a road movie from Mexico that launched the career of its director and became an international art-house hit. [BELOW]: Fernando Meirelles and Kátia Lund's Brazilian film *Cidade de Deus* (*City of God,* 2002) documents the poverty and violence of Rio de Janeiro's slums in a brilliant blaze of color, light, and motion.

l as head of the Soviet film industry
Stalin's many purges, but the stamp
pedestrian films that continued to
f the era was Grigori Aleksandrov's
938), which recounts the adventures
ase after each other during a song-
film that he insisted that it be run
oom, much to the dismay of those
ilm screenings. As the war drew to a
Novye pokhozhdeniya Shveyka (*The
dravstvuy, Moskva!* (*Hello Moscow!,*
darity in the face of the enemy on-
nochi (*Days and Nights,* 1945) and
1944). After the end of the war, the
en steeper decline, both in terms of
vly began to improve with Stalin's
rough came only in 1957, with the
t zhuravli (*The Cranes Are Flying,*
during the World War II era that
tional success, winning the Grand

A

adapting both to the new technol-
l landscape created by the Depres-
tex of film production, centered in
that rivaled Hollywood, creating a
ideas as well as indigenous culture.
ety of national genres, among them
es of popular novels that promised
he dramas were also highly popular
's *Taqdeer* (*Destiny,* 1943) and *Hu-*
Nargis, a major figure in the Indian
d political activist who scored his
Raja Kumari (1947), specialized in
cals," films that drew on India's rich
markably popular—in fact, the first

Indian sound film, Ardeshir Irani's *Alam Ara* (*The Light of the World,* 1931), contains no fewer than a dozen production numbers, setting the pattern for much Indian film production since. Whether the film is a comedy or a drama, musical numbers are regularly inserted throughout many Indian films, even if they have little or nothing to do with the film's narrative. In 1934, Bombay Talkies, Ltd., was formed, creating commercial Indian films on a mass scale, while more thoughtful films, such as Debaki Bose's *Chandidas* (1932) and *Seeta* (1934) and P. D. Barua's *Devdas* (1935), tackled social issues. During World War II, the Indian cinema flourished, with its enormous market and enthusiastic audience demanding spectacle and escapism.

CHINA

In China, filmmaking got off to a late start, despite the fact that it is the most populous nation on earth. Production in China did not begin on a regular basis until the Asia Motion Picture Company was inaugurated in 1908, through a combination of American finance and local technicians. The first entirely Chinese-owned production company, Ming Hsing, was not incorporated until 1922. When sound came to China in the early 1930s, films like Bugao Cheng's *Kuang liu* (*Torrent,* 1933) dealt with current social issues, as did Yu Sun's *Dalu* (*Big Road,* a k a *The Highway,* 1934), about a group of men building a military road for the Chinese army, offering a mixture of Leftist political doctrine, comedy, and drama and striking an instructional, even didactic tone in their narrative construction. Other key films included Xiling Shen's *Shizi jietou* (*Crossroads*), about four young college graduates starting out their lives in Shanghai, and Mu-jih Yuan's melodrama *Malu tianshi* (*Street Angel*), both made in 1937. But with the Japanese invasion of Shanghai that year, the industry was thrown into turmoil. From this point on, China was essentially an occupied nation, and those technicians, actors, and directors who stayed in the industry found themselves producing propaganda films for the Japanese invaders. Those who fled the country settled in Taiwan, Hong Kong, or other outlying territories.

During the war, the Chinese film industry essentially remained a tool of the Japanese propaganda machine, but with Japan's defeat in 1945, civil war broke out between Chiang Kai-shek's Nationalist forces and Mao Tse-tung's Communist faction for control of the entire nation. As the internal war raged, Mao's forces gradually gained the upper hand, and the People's Republic of China, with a Communist government, was established in October 1949. Mao nationalized the Chinese film industry and began a cooperative program with the USSR to create highly politicized films that extolled the virtues of the new regime, such as Choui Khoua and Bin Wang's *Bai mao nu* (*The White-Haired Girl,* 1950), along with a regular "newsreel" that served to indoctrinate the public. Mao's government would go on through the 1950s to the late 1970s creating films that were little more than hard-sell commercials for the Communist Chinese government, devoid of originality, creativity, and often even basic entertainment value.

LATIN AMERICA

Mexico's cinema got off to a similarly slow start, but with the coming of sound the pace of production picked up rapidly, under the influence of several key figures of the early Mexican cinema, including the director Emilio Fernández and the cinematographer Gabriel Figueroa. Figueroa's career is particularly interesting. Born in Mexico City in 1907 into dire poverty, Figueroa began working as a still photographer. In 1935, after working as an assistant to cinematographer Alex Phillips, he won a scholarship to work and study in Hollywood with Gregg Toland, who only six years later would revolutionize the cinema with his cinematography in *Citizen Kane.* Returning to Mexico, Figueroa joined forces with Fernández to create a series of hypnotically beautiful films, perhaps none more enchanting and moving than Fernández's *María Candelaria* (1943), a compelling story of doomed love. *María Candelaria* went on to win the *Palme d'Or* at Cannes in 1946, and the Mexican cinema was truly launched.

In Brazil, the *chanchada* rapidly became the most popular cinematic product, an indigenous musical format that celebrated the lives of a gallery of ne'er-do-wells who spent much of their time lazing around, concocting foredoomed small-change con games, and drifting cheerfully from one romantic entanglement to another. One of the most important figures of this period, Humberto Maoro, created a series of genre films that copied American westerns, musicals, and crime dramas, such as his *Ganga Bruta* (*Brutal Gang,* 1933). The Brazilian Adalberto Kemeny, in creative partnership with Rudolf Rex Lustig, created a "city film" patterned after Walter Ruttman's *Berlin: Symphony of a Great City* entitled *São Paulo, Sinfonia da Metrópole* (*São Paulo, a Metropolitan Symphony*) in 1929, while Mario Peixoto used Eisensteinian montage techniques to great advantage in his experimental

165

The brutality of slum life in Mexico City in Luis Buñuel's unsparing *Los Olvidados* (*The Young and the Damned*, 1950).

feature film *Limite* (*Limit*, 1931), which he wrote and directed at the age of twenty-one, his only film as director.

But the Brazilian cinema failed to catch on, unlike the film industry in Mexico, which by the mid-to-late 1940s was turning out a wide variety of mysteries, dramas, musicals, and other genre films at a torrid pace, including early work by Luis Buñuel. After a disappointing period of nearly fifteen years trying to get a film off the ground in Hollywood and New York, Buñuel moved to Mexico in 1947 to jumpstart his career. He had been expelled from Spain after making his documentary film *Las Hurdes* (*Land Without Bread*, 1933), a film that unsparingly chronicled the widespread poverty and starvation in rural parts of the country. His first Mexican film, *En el viejo Tampico* (a k a *Gran Casino*, 1947), was a modest program picture, but by 1950, working with a group of nonprofessional slum actors, he created his masterpiece, *Los Olvidados* (*The Young and the Damned*, 1950), which launched him again on the international film scene. In its brutal depiction of the life of street children, fighting for survival on the mean streets of Mexico City, the film presented an unsettling mixture of newsreel reportage and dark Surrealist imagery to convey the innate fatalism and despair of slum existence. Much later, the film would serve as the model for Fernando Meirelles and Kátia Lund's equally brutal *Cidade de Deus* (*City of*

166

God, 2002), a Brazilian film also shot in the slums, this time in Rio de Janeiro, and again using nonprofessional actors.

*   *   *

In the United States, patterns of distribution were changing, and international films were having an increasing artistic and financial impact at the box office. National cinemas throughout the world were coming into being, rightly questioning the hegemony of Hollywood's dream factory. Hollywood would respond with the "problem film," tackling hard issues such as alcoholism (Billy Wilder's *The Lost Weekend* [1945]), racism (Elia Kazan's *Pinky* [1949]), mental illness (Anatole Litvak's *The Snake Pit* [1948]), and a host of others that had remained hitherto unexplored on the screen. The world had seemingly grown up overnight. The escapist antics of Abbott and Costello, Hollywood's most popular wartime comedians, rapidly dwindled in the face of the new social order. Musicals remained popular, but they too had to adapt to changing times with more realistic story lines and less reliance on the "let's put on a show" enthusiasm that had served the genre so well. Crime films became more bullet ridden, westerns more violent, and action thrillers added a new streak of sadism, to appeal to an audience that no longer believed in the Capraesque vision of small-town American life. Where would the postwar years take us? What sort of films would attract attention? How would the studio system adjust to a world in which actors were able to pick and choose their own projects? These were just some of the questions facing an industry that now found itself adjusting to a new world shaped by the tumult of global conflict.

SIX

POSTWAR CHALLENGES TO THE MOVIES

The first major postwar cinematic movement was Neorealism, which began in Italy with Rossellini's *Open City* (1945) but soon had an international impact. While Visconti's *Ossessione* (*Obsession*, 1943) was certainly a forerunner of the movement in terms of cinematic style and thematic outlook, *Open City* was a clarion call to the international film community that an entirely new set of values were now in play. Europe was in ruins and thus served as a spectacular backdrop for the uncompromising vision of the first Neorealists, as evidenced in such films as Visconti's *La Terra trema: Episodio del mare* (*The Earth Trembles,* 1948), Vittorio De Sica's *Ladri di biciclette* (*The Bicycle Thief,* 1948), and Rossellini's *Paisà* (*Paisan,* 1946) and *Germania anno zero* (*Germany, Year Zero,* 1948).

Of these, De Sica's *The Bicycle Thief* is undoubtedly the most famous, and deservedly so. Shot almost entirely on location, the film tells the story of Antonio (Lamberto Maggiorani), who supports his family by putting up posters around Rome. One day his bicycle, which Antonio desperately needs to keep his business going, is stolen while he works. Though Antonio tries to recover the stolen bicycle, descending into the depths of Rome's Black Market to do so, he finds that there is little that the police or his neighbors can do to help him. The bicycle, it seems, has probably already been "stripped" for parts, and Antonio is left without any means of transportation, bereft of hope. At the film's end, in an act of pathetic desperation, Antonio steals a bike himself, but is almost immediately caught. The owner refuses to press charges, but Antonio, now branded as a thief and seemingly out of options, sits down on a curb to assess his hopeless future. By his side, his son, Bruno (Enzo Staiola), who has accompanied his father on his downward social spiral, stares at Antonio with a mixture of fear and concern. What will happen to the family now? How will Antonio get work? The film ends on a note of complete despair, as passersby pay no attention

Bill-poster Antonio Ricci (Lamberto Maggiorani) and his son, Bruno (Enzo Staiola), try to find Antonio's stolen bicycle in the streets of Rome in Vittorio De Sica's *Ladri di biciclette* (*The Bicycle Thief,* 1948).

to the humiliated Antonio and his son. The system has failed Antonio, and De Sica refuses to give the audience the artificial luxury of a happy ending.

The Bicycle Thief and *Open City* were worldwide sensations. Neorealism was now recognized as a secure cinematic movement, an innovative way of looking at the world and seeing what was really there, as opposed to what one wished to see. For example, Rossellini's *Paisan* offered the public six vignettes of life in postwar Italy, depicting the tenuous relationship between Italian citizens and the occupying American forces at the end of the war. *Germany, Year Zero* is an even bleaker film, depicting life in bombed-out Berlin after the war, as a young boy scavenges on the streets for food, at one point joining a crowd as they strip the flesh from a dead horse in order to survive. Drawn in by early neo-Nazi ideology, the young boy murders his father, who is ill and therefore considered unfit to live, and at length kills himself in an act of supreme defeat.

By 1948, Rossellini was becoming more "theatrical" in his films, creating a two-part film, *L'Amore* (titled *Ways of Love* in the United States), which he designed as a vehicle for the star who had helped him bring *Open City* to

169

fruition, Anna Magnani. One section of *L'Amore* was a faithful presentation of Jean Cocteau's devastating playlet "*La Voix Humaine*" ("The Human Voice"), in which Magnani breaks up with her lover on the telephone but then is horrified to realize that he is already in the apartment of his new mistress. While Cocteau's scenario is superb, the film represents a departure from the everyday concerns of Neorealism, and as his career progressed Rossellini seemed increasingly interested in pursuing new avenues in his work. It was also during this period that the Swedish actress Ingrid Bergman wrote an admiring letter to Rossellini offering her services for one of his forthcoming films, and their relationship evolved into a love affair during the filming of *Stromboli* (a k a *Stromboli, terra di Dio,* 1950).

In the same month the movie was released, Bergman gave birth to a baby fathered by Rossellini. Since both were married to others at the time, the resulting scandal damaged their careers, especially in the United States. The bleak *Stromboli,* in which Bergman plays the wife of a brutal peasant fisherman living on a desolate island, was dismissed upon its initial release. Similarly, *Viaggio in Italia* (*Voyage in Italy,* 1954), featuring Bergman as the wife of a bored businessman (George Sanders) on a disastrous trip to Italy to clear up a family inheritance, was also poorly received but is now considered a classic, famous for its bizarre narrative structure. Bergman and Sanders are at each other's throats for nearly the entire film, trading insults, flirting with strangers, and it appears their marriage is in ruins. But in the last two minutes, they come upon a Catholic religious procession during a street fair and instantly renounce their bitterness, declaring their undying and passionate love for one another. Like many of his countrymen, Rossellini had an ambiguous relationship with Catholicism; as a realist, he seemed to reject it, but as a man of faith, he embraced it for the hope and comfort it offered. The sad, grinding death of the couple's marriage in *Voyage to Italy* is thus transformed through faith alone rather than by any machinations of the film's narrative. Rossellini has led us in one direction for nearly ninety-seven minutes and then gives us an ending that appears to defy logic. And yet, on a spiritual level, the ending makes sense and is completely satisfying.

MOTION PICTURES AND THE FIRST AMENDMENT

The Rossellini work that would have an even greater international impact was the second section of *L'Amore,* "The Miracle" ("*Il Miracolo*"), following Cocteau's "*La Voix humaine*" segment. With Tullio Pinelli and a young actor named Federico Fellini, soon to become one of the most important directors of the postwar Italian cinema, Rossellini co-wrote the story of a tramp (Fellini) who has an affair with a mentally unbalanced woman; when she gives birth to a son, she says he is the Messiah. The Catholic Church responded by mounting an aggressive campaign against the film. After it was finally released in the United States in December 1950, the New York State Board of Regents succeeded in banning it on the grounds that it was sacrilegious. But the film's American distributor took the case all the way to the Supreme Court, which in 1952 decided that the Regents' ruling had violated the separation of church and state.

This decision was enormously important for the future of motion pictures, because it was the first time that the medium had been ruled to be protected by the First Amendment to the Constitution. In 1915 the Supreme Court had ruled in a similar case that motion pictures were merely a form of interstate commerce, and as such were guaranteed no free-speech protection under the Constitution. Known as the Mutual Decision, that ruling had made it easier for the Hays/Breen office to control the production and exhibition of motion pictures. Now, in a single stroke, much of the Production Code's authority had been stripped away. It would be more than another decade before the Code collapsed completely, but the "Miracle" Decision of 1952 was a major step on the road to artistic freedom for the cinema.

Meanwhile, similar trouble was brewing in Italy, even as Neorealism was becoming influential internationally. In 1949, the Andreotti Law attempted to halt the production of films, specifically those of the Neorealist school, that did not serve "the best interests of Italy," and to remove state subsidies from films that failed to depict a thriving postwar Italian state. In some cases, the law even denied export licenses for international distribution. Many filmmakers found a way around the restrictions, but as the national economy regained its footing Italian producers and audiences began to turn to more traditional fare. As the 1950s dawned, new court rulings, technological advances, and changing audience tastes forced the studios to adapt in order to survive.

THE COLLAPSE OF THE STUDIO SYSTEM

In 1944, the U.S. Supreme Court handed down what became known as the de Havilland decision, ruling that the standard seven-year contract then given to most actors could not be indefinitely lengthened by suspensions caused when an actor balked at appearing in a particular project. Olivia de Havilland, best remembered for playing the sweet and gentle Melanie in *Gone with the Wind,* had brought the suit against Warner Bros. that would help lead to the eventual collapse of the studio system. Bette Davis had tried the same tactic in the early 1930s, but at the time did not possess the star power to make her rebellion successful. Now, under the de Havilland decision, actors would know exactly when their contract was up, and key players within the industry, no longer indentured servants to their home studios, began to look around for better scripts, directors, and projects.

Then came another ruling: in 1947, the Supreme Court declared that the long-approved practice of block booking, in which a studio could force an exhibitor to take an entire slate of films, many of them inferior, in order to get more desired films, violated federal antitrust laws. Again, the studios reeled. As a result, each film had to be sold solely on its individual merits. The distribution strong-arm tactics that had served the studios so well for nearly half a century were suddenly outlawed, and thus the studios cut back on production, making fewer films but with higher budgets and production values, signaling the beginning of the end for the "B," or "second," features. This was followed by yet another ruling: the government filed antitrust suits against Technicolor and Eastman Kodak, alleging that the companies held an effective monopoly on the production of color motion pictures. The industry had gradually begun to shift from three-strip Technicolor to Eastman's monopack system, using a single strand of film to record the full spectrum of color. By late 1948, Kodak agreed to make its color film patents available to competitors, ending Kodak's lock on raw stock production and color processing.

The same year, RKO Radio decided to sell its theaters, anticipating that the other studios would soon be forced by the government to take the same action. Owning production, distribution, and exhibition facilities clearly constituted an unfair business advantage that the studios had been taking for years. In May 1948, the Supreme Court ordered a district court to look into the possibility of forcing the other studios to sell their theaters, thus signaling an end (for the time being) to Adolph Zukor's master plan of vertical integration. Paramount, which had fought the government the hardest on this decision, finally signed a consent decree in 1949 that required it to sell its theaters and distribution exchanges, concentrating solely on the production of motion pictures. Soon Twentieth Century Fox, MGM, and Warners were forced to sell their theaters as well. No longer did the majors have a guaranteed market for their films. Now, theaters could play whatever films they wanted, and the majors had to compete in an open marketplace.

In the final analysis, however, the consent decree eventually favored the studios, who could now dictate the terms for their key films, forcing theater owners to increase concession prices to defray operating costs. The biggest studio blockbusters commanded enormous guarantees from the theater chains, which rapidly consolidated to offset their weak bargaining power. The studios also demanded a hefty percentage of the box office, often a 90–10 split in their favor for the first week of a major attraction. Despite this bargaining advantage, the studios were being backed into a corner by a combination of rising costs, shrinking markets, and new legal restrictions on their methods of doing business. To compete, the studios cut production costs to the bone, recycling scripts, sets, costumes, and musical scores to create cost-conscious films. Theater owners, with their new freedom to book whatever they wanted, began to turn to independent producers, who offered more favorable terms and reacted swiftly to fill the power vacuum left by the studios' loss of power.

With the abrogation of the seven-year contract, one-year contracts or multiple-picture deals (usually two or three films at a time) became the industry norm. James Stewart became the first actor to command a percentage of a film's gross with Anthony Mann's brutal 1950 western *Winchester '73*, part of a two-picture deal with Universal. The other film was Henry Koster's *Harvey* (1950), based on the Broadway play about a man whose best friend is an imaginary six-foot rabbit. Universal paid Stewart a straight salary for *Harvey*, but then gave him a huge chunk of the gross for *Winchester '73*, which the studio viewed as just another program western, unlikely to arouse much audience interest. The psychological penetration of Stewart's performance, however, coupled with Mann's aggressive visual style, made the film a breakout hit and turned Stewart into a millionaire almost overnight.

In the wake of Stewart's successful deal, arranged by legendary Hollywood agent Lew Wasserman, other actors began leaving the security of studio contracts to freelance on a picture-by-picture basis, selling their services to the highest bidder. Humphrey Bogart, for example, left Warner Bros. after more than twenty years to form his independent Santana Productions, releasing his films through Columbia Pictures and working on material that both deepened and enhanced the depth of his range as an actor, such as Nicholas Ray's superb Hollywood drama *In a Lonely Place* (1950).

FILM NOIR IN POSTWAR AMERICA

Film noir, which had been bubbling under the surface in Hollywood since the early 1940s in movies such as *Detour,* exploded into a major genre in the postwar era, with RKO Radio, "the house of noir," leading the way. The world of noir is a continual pattern of betrayal, deception, and violence in which no one can be trusted and everything is for sale at a price. Such films as Joseph M. Newman's *Abandoned* (a k a *Abandoned Woman,* 1949), a tale of murder, impersonation, and black market babies; Robert Siodmak's *The Killers* (1946), based on the Ernest Hemingway short story, with Burt Lancaster, in his first major role, as a doomed hoodlum; or Jean Negulesco's *Nobody Lives Forever* (1946), with a typically complex plot involving con men, murder, and a string of double crosses, perfectly captured the new mood of the nation. Noirs were cheap to make, requiring little in the way of sets or costumes, just a lot of shadows and dark alleyways. Neorealism's impact on noir was enormous; directors competed with each other to see how much filming could be done on location to increase authenticity, as in Jules Dassin's New York murder mystery *The Naked City* (1948), which prided itself on using nonprofessionals and actual street settings to enhance the grittiness and realism.

Adultery and murder were staples of the genre; in Henry Levin's *Night Editor* (1946), Tony Cochrane (William Gargan), a crooked cop, falls for the worthless Jill Merrill (Janis Carter) and leaves his faithful and trusting wife, Martha (Jeff Donnell), at home so he and Jill can park on lover's lane. One night, the two witness the murder of a young woman and clearly see the identity of the killer—Douglas Loring (Frank Wilcox), the vice president of a local bank—but Tony fears that an investigation would expose his illicit affair. For her part, Jill is sexually excited by the woman's brutal killing, much to Tony's disgust, but since the two now share the secret of both their affair and the young woman's murder, Tony has no choice but to cover up clues to the crime, while Jill returns to her palatial mansion and her much older husband, Ben (Roy Gordon). When Tony finally decides to make a clean break from their affair and to turn Loring in to the police, Jill stabs Tony in the back with an ice pick in a frenzy of jealousy; if she can't have Tony, no one can. *Night Editor* runs a tight sixty-six minutes, and no one can accuse it of being a lavish production. But the film struck a responsive chord in postwar audiences, who no longer trusted anyone or anything and wondered what they had actually accomplished by winning the war.

174

In George Marshall's *The Blue Dahlia* (1946), featuring hard-boiled novelist Raymond Chandler's only original screenplay for a film, war hero Johnny Morrison (Alan Ladd) returns home to find that his wife, Helen (Doris Dowling), has been unfaithful and in fact throws drunken parties on a nightly basis for a coterie of friends and hangers-on, all of whom are just looking for a good time. When Johnny confronts Helen, she tells him to get out and he leaves in a fury; thus, when Helen turns up dead shortly thereafter, Johnny is a prime suspect. With the help of two war buddies, Buzz (William Bendix) and George (Hugh Beaumont, who would later play the father on the television series "Leave It to Beaver"), Johnny tracks down the real murderer, a run-down detective named "Dad" Newell (Will Wright), who is also a Peeping Tom and a smalltime blackmailer—another authority figure proven bankrupt. Noirs continued to be produced through the early 1950s in abundance, as Cold War fears deepened, but without a doubt the Golden Age was the late 1940s, when those who had fought the war were coming home to a transformed society.

WOMEN AND FILM NOIR

Changes in gender roles during and after World War II had a tremendous influence on film and popular culture, particularly with regard to images of women. During the war, because so many men were called to active duty,

Housewife-on-the-make Phyllis Dietrichson (Barbara Stanwyck) hooks unscrupulous insurance salesman Walter Neff (Fred MacMurray) into a web of murder and deceit in Billy Wilder's noir classic *Double Indemnity* (1944).

Daughter Veda (Ann Blyth) doesn't approve of her mother, Mildred Pierce (Joan Crawford), in Michael Curtiz's acid look at postwar materialism, *Mildred Pierce* (1945).

women entered the workforce in unprecedented numbers. In fact, they were strongly encouraged to work for the war effort, which allowed them to step out of the traditional woman's role of homemaker. After the war, however, it was considered patriotic for women to give up their jobs for the returning vets. Though the change in gender roles might have appeared to be temporary, many men felt threatened by it, and anxiety toward strong, independent women was prominently displayed in the film noir genre. Hundreds of such films constitute a cinematic movement that spoke to a disillusioned, jaded, tired audience of mid-twentieth-century Americans with few ideals left.

Among the most celebrated was Billy Wilder's tale of murder and betrayal, *Double Indemnity* (1944), in which insurance salesman Walter Neff (Fred MacMurray) and vampish Phyllis Dietrichson (Barbara Stanwyck) plot to kill Phyllis's husband for the insurance money. Stanwyck's character was emblematic of film noir's manipulative and often vicious *femme fatale*.

Though the title role of *Mildred Pierce* (1945) is no such *femme,* the movie is perhaps director Michael Curtiz's darkest look at postwar American life, focusing especially on tensions between mother and daughter. Mildred (Joan Crawford) does whatever she humanly can to make her daughter, Veda (Ann Blyth), happy, but seemingly to no avail. When Mildred's second husband is found shot to death in her beach house, the police start asking questions, and Mildred is forced to recount her painful life story in a series of flashbacks. With first-class direction and impeccable acting—Crawford won an Academy Award—*Mildred Pierce* is one of the most brutal visions of American consumerism ever made in Hollywood.

THE SOCIAL PROBLEM FILM

In the postwar years, Neorealism crossed over into other genres as well, most notably the "problem film." Billy Wilder's harrowing tale of alcoholic writer Don Birnam (Ray Milland) in *The Lost Weekend* (1945) was partially shot on the streets of New York, in particular a memorable sequence in which Don, desperate for a drink, tries to hock his typewriter on the Jewish holiday of Yom Kippur, only to find that all the pawnshops are closed. As one Jewish store owner tells him, the pawnshops have reached an informal agreement—"they don't open on Yom Kippur, we don't open on St. Patrick's." Wilder stages the sequence in a series of seemingly endless tracking shots that highlight Don's Sisyphean trek through the city, as he meets rejection on all sides. Later, Don lands in the drunk tank at Bellevue, actually a studio set enhanced with judicious exterior shots of the real psychiatric hospital to lend veracity to the scene and embellished with a web of shadows to create a suitably ominous atmosphere.

Other problem films included Jules Dassin's brutal exposé of prison life, *Brute Force* (1947), featuring Hume Cronyn as a sadistic martinet who delights in dressing up in neo-Nazi regalia while torturing his prisoners to the strains of Wagner, and Anatole Litvak's *The Snake Pit* (1948), in which Olivia de Havilland descends into insanity and is committed to a public mental institution, with horrifying results. Without assistance from the public agencies that are supposed to help her, she is left to cope as best she can, though she is hardly able to care for herself. Also notable were two movies directed by Elia Kazan: *Gentleman's Agreement* (1947), dealing with ingrained anti-Semitism in postwar American society, and *Pinky* (1949), examining the problem of racial "passing" in an America still acutely color-conscious. In such films the endings are generally left unresolved, as if to say these were problems that could not be solved by the artificial narrative closure of a happy ending.

Neorealism, born out of the ashes of a defeated Italy, and film noir, created by the rising social tensions at the end of the war, and the problem film, which recognized that in the postwar world not all men and women were created equal after all, together created a late 1940s milieu in which the dominant social order was resoundingly called into question and found wanting, even if no solutions to the problems the films presented were forthcoming or even possible. We were living in a different world, and these films presented that world in a brutal and uncompromising fashion, in a radical departure from the films of more than a decade before, prior to the start of the war.

THE HOUSE UN-AMERICAN ACTIVITIES COMMITTEE

The American mood darkened even further with the investigations of the House Un-American Activities Committee (HUAC), which kicked into full gear in 1947. The results were disastrous for film as an art form, and equally grave for those caught in the net of hysteria and suspicion. The HUAC had been around since 1938, when a former Communist, James B. Matthews, named James Cagney, Bette Davis, Clark Gable, Miriam Hopkins, and even Shirley Temple as actors whose work unwittingly served Communist interests. At that time few people took the charges seriously. But in 1944, Walt Disney, aggravated by the 1941 animators' strike at his studios, helped to form the Motion Picture Alliance for the Preservation of American Ideals, aided by director King Vidor, actors Ward Bond, Gary Cooper, Robert Taylor, and John Wayne, novelist Ayn Rand, and gossip columnist Hedda Hopper, and matters began to get more serious.

In 1946, HUAC decided to hold formal hearings on the issue of Communist infiltration in Hollywood. At the dawn of the Cold War, with the Soviets gradually extending their influence throughout Eastern Europe, it was difficult to remember that Hollywood had produced films lauding the American-Soviet alliance during the war at the behest of the U.S. government. Now these films would be cited as proof of Communist influence in the motion picture industry. Those associated with the productions were brought to task by HUAC, creating an atmosphere of fear and distrust throughout Hollywood. When the committee asked him why he had participated in the making of *Song of Russia,* Robert Taylor said crisply that he had made the film under protest as an MGM contract performer. Subsequently Taylor became one of the first "friendly witnesses" to testify at the HUAC hearings on Communist infiltration in the film capital.

In May 1947, the committee held ten days of closed hearings in Los Angeles, where Taylor, Adolphe Menjou, and Jack Warner, as well as Leila Rogers, Ginger Rogers's mother and a virulent anti-Communist, all testified to the wide extent of Communist infiltration in Hollywood. Shortly thereafter, the Screen Actors Guild (SAG) instituted a loyalty oath that all members were asked to sign, although at this early stage participation was voluntary. In October 1947, HUAC held more hearings in Washington, where Walt Disney, as well as actors Robert Montgomery, Gary Cooper, George Murphy, and Ronald Reagan, testified to the immediate danger to the film community from Communist infiltration. Meanwhile, another group of actors, including Humphrey Bogart, Lauren Bacall, Danny Kaye, Gene Kelly, and Sterling Hayden, as well as lyricist Ira Gershwin and director John Huston, formed the Committee for the First Amendment to protest the hearings. The protests were soon drowned out by a chorus of disapproval, and Bogart and the others soon realized that the atmosphere of fear developing around the hearings could ruin their careers. Shortly thereafter, the Committee for the First Amendment was disbanded, and its former members returned to Hollywood to disavow their stand against HUAC.

THE HOLLYWOOD TEN AND THE BLACKLIST

Not everyone folded up their opposition to HUAC, however. In addition to the Hollywood Ten—ten writers, directors, and producers who protested the HUAC hearings—there were also hundreds of other actors, writers, directors, and producers who would be swept up in a frenzied wave of denunciations that would eventually cost them their jobs, their livelihoods, and in some cases their lives. In 1947, the Hollywood Ten—directors Herbert Biberman and Edward Dmytryk; screenwriters Alvah Bessie, Lester Cole, John Howard Lawson, Dalton Trumbo, Ring Lardner Jr., Albert Maltz, and Samuel Ornitz; and producer Adrian Scott—were charged with contempt of Congress for refusing to cooperate with HUAC and eventually served jail time as a result. On 24 November 1947, the chief executives of the major studios, fearful of government pressure, met at the Waldorf-Astoria Hotel in New York and issued a statement agreeing to fire or suspend without pay all the members of the Hollywood Ten and also to "eliminate any subversives in the industry." The blacklist had begun.

In 1949, the pro-blacklist Motion Picture Industries Council was created by director Cecil B. DeMille, producer Dore Schary, SAG president Ronald Reagan, and International Alliance of Theatrical Stage Employees (IATSE) chief Roy Brewer, giving the blacklist an official imprimatur to control the industry's destiny. The IATSE endorsement was particularly crucial to the formation of the new watchdog organization, as the IATSE was the key labor union of the motion picture business, representing everyone from cameramen to art directors, grips to gaffers (lighting assistants), set designers to screen cartoonists. Coupled with SAG's participation under Reagan, the blacklist now directly affected literally everyone who worked within the industry in any capacity, creating a climate of hysteria and persecution in which friends denounced friends, and enemies used the contentious atmosphere to advance their own careers at the expense of others. Actors Melvyn Douglas, John Garfield, Fredric March, Edward G. Robinson, Sylvia Sidney, and Paul Muni were named Communists or Communist sympathizers ("fellow travelers") by an FBI informant.

By late 1949, the California State Senate Committee on Un-American Activities identified such diverse personalities as Gene Kelly, Gregory Peck, Frank Sinatra, Orson Welles, Katharine Hepburn, and Charles Chaplin as Communist sympathizers. As the blacklist deepened, the HUAC began a second group of hearings into Communist infiltration within the film industry, this time convening in Hollywood. Now in full force, the blacklist, in both its 1947 and 1951 incarnations, dominated the entertainment industry for more than fifteen years, denying work to hundreds of talented writers, actors, and directors. Edward G. Robinson, who had been a fixture at USO bond rallies during World War II, was forced to attach his name to a ghost-written article asserting that he had been "duped" by the Reds.

Frank Sinatra, a vociferous supporter of the World War II effort, was suddenly unemployable and had to return to singing engagements to make a living. He was finally able to break back into acting in 1953 in Fred Zinnemann's epic war drama *From Here to Eternity,* in part by agreeing to work for a pittance. Gregory Peck and John Garfield also found it nearly impossible to get work, perhaps because of their involvement in films like *Gentleman's Agreement,* which was now denounced in some quarters as an attack on postwar American society. The harassment and stress endured by Garfield— who had also starred in Robert Rossen's *Body and Soul* (1947), another problem film that would soon cast doubts on his patriotism—contributed to his death from a heart attack in 1952 at the age of thirty-nine. His last film was the crime thriller *He Ran All the Way* (1951), directed by John Berry, whose own career came crashing to a halt when he was named a Communist. He had produced and directed a documentary, *The Hollywood Ten* (1950), denouncing the blacklist, and as a result was soon forced into exile. Charles Chaplin likewise fled the country, as did director Joseph Losey and numerous others. Losey, in particular, was a significant loss to the industry in the United States; he would direct some of the most brilliant British films of the 1960s.

As the blacklist continued, various members of the entertainment community appeared before the committee and "named names," including screenwriter Martin Berkeley, who on 19 September 1951 named more than one hundred members of the motion picture industry as Communists, Communist sympathizers, or "dupes." Numerous other "friendly witnesses," including Lloyd Bridges, Sterling Hayden, Roy Huggins, Lee J. Cobb, Elia Kazan, Larry Parks, Jerome Robbins, Frank Tuttle, and Robert Rossen (at first refusing to answer, then later recanting his earlier testimony and implicating more than fifty colleagues), all came before HUAC at various times to denounce their co-workers.

Edward Dmytryk had first appeared before the committee in 1947 and refused to answer questions, along with the rest of the Hollywood Ten, and he began serving a jail term for contempt in 1948 as a result. But prison life wore Dmytryk down, and in 1951 he appeared again before the committee, this time as a friendly witness, and named names. Dmytryk was immediately rewarded with a contract to direct *The Sniper* (1952), one of the most vicious films of his career, centering on a sociopathic serial killer (played by Arthur Franz) who targets young women as his victims. Perhaps not entirely coincidentally, the major star of the film was Adolphe Menjou, who had been one of the committee's staunchest supporters. It was a time of complete uncertainty and paranoia, when even a whispered innuendo could ruin a career.

Elia Kazan alienated many of his colleagues when he, too, testified as a friendly witness before the committee in 1952 and then published a newspaper display advertisement shortly thereafter to defend his decision. Kazan thus continued working through the 1950s and went on to make the now-classic film *On the Waterfront* (1954), which despite its directorial brilliance and Marlon Brando's magnetic performance in the leading role of dockworker Terry Malloy, is essentially a film that attacks labor unions as Communist fronts.

A Soviet atom bomb vaporizes Manhattan in Alfred E. Green's "Red Scare" film, *Invasion USA* (1952).

Such themes in movies were not new. In the wake of the first HUAC hearings on Hollywood, studios pumped out a host of "Red Scare" films, including the unsubtle *I Married a Communist* (a k a *The Woman on Pier 13,* 1949), directed by Robert Stevenson and produced by RKO Radio Pictures, controlled at the time by the eccentric Howard Hughes. Hughes forced all his employees to sign loyalty oaths and had the entire studio bugged to keep tabs on everyone. An odd series of anti-Communist thrillers followed, such as William Cameron Menzies's *The Whip Hand* (1951), which depicts ex-Nazi scientists working in the pay of the Kremlin to poison America's water supply; Alfred E. Green's *Invasion USA* (1952), which prophesizes a full-scale invasion of the United States by the Soviet Union, starting in Alaska; and perhaps most bizarre, Harry Horner's *Red Planet Mars* (1952), which posits that God is alive and well and living on Mars, sending out religious messages to all mankind that eventually lead to the downfall of the Soviet Union. Despite the ridiculousness of these films, they were taken seriously by a nation gripped by anti-Communist fervor. Indeed, with Stalin now busily enslaving Eastern Europe and the nuclear arms race well under way, the possibility of an all-out nuclear attack by either side, whether by design or accident, was very real.

THE RISE OF TELEVISION

In the midst of this atmosphere of distrust and paranoia, the advent of television also loomed as a threat to the industry. In 1939, television was a novelty in the United States, featured as a scientific wonder at the World's Fair in New York, but hardly a household item. The National Broadcasting Corporation began regular daily television broadcasts in 1939, but there were fewer than a million television sets in use nationwide, so it seemed that the new medium posed no serious threat to Hollywood dominance. In only ten years, however, the number of sets rose fivefold, and the studios were scrambling to lure back to the theater viewers who were staying home to watch Milton Berle for free. This meant a reversal of Hollywood's early strategy of simply ignoring television, in which networks were forbidden to employ studios' contract stars or to broadcast its older films. A new industry sprang up, however, providing viewers with such classic television series as *I Love Lucy, The Honeymooners,* and *Dragnet,* as well as an array of variety shows and sports programming, which were cheap to produce.

European producers were less afraid of the new medium than Hollywood, and foreign films, especially British productions, flooded the American airwaves, along with "B" films from Monogram, Eagle-Lion, PRC, and other smaller studios, plus Laurel and Hardy comedies and ancient black-and-white cartoon shorts. With television screening long-forgotten films to an entirely new audience, the studios realized the error of their ways and in 1956 began leasing their pre-1948 catalogue of films to the major networks and independent stations.

CINEMASCOPE, 3-D, AND CINERAMA

As for bolstering sagging theater attendance, Hollywood fought back against television with the foremost weapon in its arsenal: spectacle. This took several forms, the simplest of which was the almost universal introduction of color in motion pictures. In the late 1940s, nearly 90 percent of all feature films were in black-and-white; by 1957, roughly 50 percent of all films were shot in color; and by 1966, black-and-white movies had been phased out almost completely. Indeed, for years there were two categories for Best Cinematography at the Academy Awards, color and black-and-white, but these were consolidated after 1966.

The wide-screen CinemaScope process shaped the panoramic through the somewhat stage-bound spectacle of Henry Koster's biblical epic *The Robe* (1953).

In 1953 Twentieth Century Fox dusted off an old anamorphic photography and projection process the studio dubbed CinemaScope, which had been perfected by the Frenchman Henri Chrétien and first used by director Claude Autant-Lara in the experimental short film *Construire de feu* (*To Build a Fire*, 1928). Based on a process discovered in the 1860s and patented in 1898, Chrétien's technique essentially "squeezed" a long, rectangular image into a standard 35 mm film frame during shooting while another lens "unsqueezed" the image during projection. This created a panoramic image roughly two and a half times as wide as it is high for an aspect ratio of 2.35 to 1, compared to the standard Academy ratio of 1.33 to 1, which had been adopted in the early days of cinema as the industry standard.

Viewing CinemaScope as a cost-effective way of making films that were both highly exploitable and inherently spectacular, Twentieth Century Fox chief Darryl F. Zanuck decreed that from 1953 all the studio's films would be produced in CinemaScope, no matter what the subject matter, even travel shorts and other filler material. The first film presented in CinemaScope was Henry Koster's *The Robe* (1953), a biblical epic appropriately themed for the early 1950s. Within less than a year, the system was being copied by other studios, with names like WarnerScope. Though introduced as a gimmick, CinemaScope and its allied methods rapidly became industry standards that are still used today, although in the mid-1950s Fritz Lang famously complained that it was only suitable for photographing "snakes or funerals."

The same cannot be said of the brief 3-D craze that hit Hollywood in the early 1950s, the most successful process being Natural Vision, created by Milton L. Gunzburg. Using two frame-for-frame interlocked cameras "slaved" inside a single blimp, Natural Vision photographed films from two slightly different vantage points simultaneously, much as we view the world through two eyes. Polarizing filters then staggered one of these images to reach the brain a millisecond after the other, causing a sensation of depth perception. There was also a cheaper, competitive system using an anaglyph process, which melded red and green images printed on the same frame to create a black-and-white image that also produced an illusion of depth.

The first 3-D film was radio dramatist Arch Oboler's *Bwana Devil* (1952), a tepid tale of jungle adventure that nevertheless pulled in excellent grosses on the strength of the novelty of 3-D; Warner Bros. soon followed with André de Toth's infinitely superior *House of Wax* (1953), photographed in Gunzburg's Natural Vision process, which remains for many the most effective commercial 3-D film ever made. De Toth was an odd choice to direct the movie: he had only one eye, the other having been lost in an accident, and thus had no sense of depth perception, which he found highly amusing when Jack Warner assigned him to the project. But perhaps because of this, de Toth's use of the 3-D technique is generally restrained (except for one sequence, inserted at the studio's insistence, featuring a sideshow barker using a flyback paddle and ball, aimed directly at the audience). But despite this propitious beginning, and even though a number of major productions such as Alfred Hitchcock's *Dial M for Murder* (1954) employed the Natural Vision process, the resulting image caused a great deal of eyestrain, and by 1955 the 3-D fad was dead, its novelty exhausted.

Similarly evanescent was the Cinerama process, easily the most complex of the 1950s wide-screen formats. Originally developed by technician Fred Walker for Paramount for the 1939 World's Fair, Cinerama employed three cameras, all in frame-for-frame electronic synchronization, to photograph its epic scenes, and then three similar synchronized projectors, again in frame-for-frame interlock, to screen the finished film for audiences. Additionally, the cameras were positioned in a 165-degree arc during filming to create the widest possible panorama, with the three separate images melding on the screen to create one gigantic, overwhelming image, albeit with seams

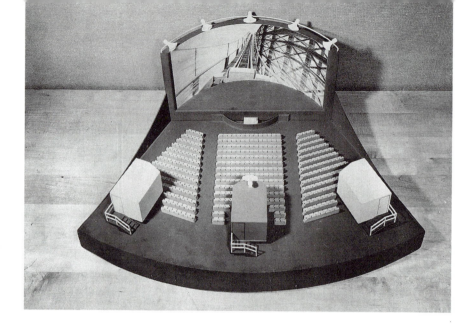

The three-projector Cinerama setup for theater screenings used three interlocking images to create one wide-screen whole and thus achieve a reasonable illusion of depth.

to the right and left of the screen's center, where the three images meshed. The projectors were positioned in a similar, arc-shaped arrangement in the projection auditorium, and stereophonic sound was added to complete the illusion of depth and audience participation.

Cinerama's debut film, *This Is Cinerama* (Merian C. Cooper, Gunther von Fritsch, Ernest B. Schoedsack, and Michael Todd Jr., 1952), employed first-person point-of-view sequences on a roller coaster and other shock techniques to thrill the viewer, and a number of Cinerama theaters were built throughout the

The audience is taken on a first-person roller-coaster ride in Merian C. Cooper, Gunther von Fritsch, Ernest B. Schoedsack, and Michael Todd Jr.'s *This Is Cinerama* (1952).

world to accommodate the new process. But the system was technically unwieldy and required constant maintenance; furthermore, if one frame was damaged in any of the reels for a particular segment of the film, all three reels had to be reprinted to maintain perfect picture synchronization. By the time of Henry Levin and George Pal's fairy tale extravaganza *The Wonderful World of the Brothers Grimm* and John Ford, Henry Hathaway, George Marshall, and Richard Thorpe's epic western *How the West Was Won* (both 1962), audiences had become tired of Cinerama and were more inclined to notice its imperfections than its visual grandeur. The Cinerama system was thus retired, and at this writing there are only a few Cinerama facilities left in the United States, including one in Los Angeles dedicated to keeping the process alive for scholars and archivists.

THE AUTEUR THEORY

In the midst of all this technological tumult, a new group of American directors came of age, eager to embrace the shift to color and CinemaScope. They were also bolstered by the critical cheerleading of the French journal *Cahiers du Cinéma,* begun in 1947 by writer and theorist André Bazin (then *La Revue du Cinéma,* changing its name in 1951). Co-edited by the French critic Jacques Doniol-Valcroze, *Cahiers du Cinéma* was the first publication to promote the auteur theory, or *le politique des auteurs,* which held that the director was the most important person involved in the creation of a film. Today, with the high profile enjoyed by such directors as Martin Scorsese, Woody Allen, Francis Ford Coppola, and other mainstream filmmakers, it seems impossible to imagine an era in which the director, for the most part, was considered a minor functionary in a film's creation, after the stars, the script, and the studio imprimatur.

Cahiers was the first major publication to recognize that the films of the great cinematic stylists—Hitchcock, Welles, Ophüls, Renoir, Ford, Hawks, and the rest—each had a distinctive visual signature and range of thematic interests or motifs that made every director an instantly recognizable individual, with his own set of values, levels of social engagement, and concomitant visual style. From the inception of the cinema through the 1950s, only trade papers such as *Variety* took note of the director for any given film, and with rare exception it was someone like Hitchcock or Welles, larger-than-life personalities who were indelibly stamped on the public consciousness.

More taciturn auteurs, such as Hawks, Ford, Lupino, Cukor, Lang, Arzner,

187

and others, created a body of work that was distinctively their own, but working without the acknowledgment that was afforded novelists, play-wrights, composers, and other major figures in the creative arts. *Cahiers* in-sisted that each director's body of work was unique and quantifiable; furthermore, as one can easily see in the early writings of such future direc-tors as François Truffaut, the *Cahiers* critics abolished the artificial line be-tween high and low art, praising the low-budget work of Edgar G. Ulmer, Samuel Fuller, and Anthony Mann as being on the same level as that of their more conventionally illustrious colleagues.

Finally, *Cahiers,* working in conjunction with the great champion of film and the New Wave Henri Langlois, curator of the Cinémathèque Française, insisted for the first time that American commercial films could also be per-sonal works of art, depending on the skill of their directors, and in addition that many of the films of the established directors were both uncinematic and literary, lacking in visual invention and imagination. Langlois, an obses-sive collector, was in love with the cinema in all its aspects, and over the years amassed one of the world's great film libraries, located in Paris. During the 1950s and 1960s, the screenings at the Cinémathèque Française served as a training ground for the young critics at *Cahiers,* who then went on to make groundbreaking movies of their own. In short, *Cahiers* rescued the Ameri-can cinema and its directors from critical oblivion, and forced a reassess-ment of the classical Hollywood cinema based not on stars or studio moguls but rather on the men and women who actually made the films under examination.

In recent years, it has been argued that the director, while an integral part of the film production process, is not necessarily the auteur of a film; coun-terexamples include the Marx Brothers, who exercised strong control over their films, or the comic actor W. C. Fields. Art director William Cameron Menzies, who designed *Gone with the Wind,* was so influential to the overall look of the final production that the film's principal director, Victor Flem-ing, offered Menzies co-credit as director. However, the film's producer, David O. Selznick, intervened with the suggestion that the movie carry the credit "production designed by William Cameron Menzies" in the opening titles, the first formal acknowledgment of the role of the production de-signer as an auteur in Hollywood history. Producers such as the visionary Val Lewton, whose atmospheric low-budget horror films at RKO in the 1940s all bore his individual stamp, no matter who directed the films, also can have a major influence on the look of a film. Cinematographer Gregg Toland, who shot Orson Welles's *Citizen Kane,* had such an impact on the

188

Sal Mineo, James Dean, and Natalie Wood in Nicholas Ray's classic film about teenage alienation, *Rebel Without a Cause* (1955).

film's visual design that Welles insisted on sharing with him the director's title card in the credits. For these reasons, a number of contemporary critics have argued that auteurism is reductive and oversimplifies the process of making a feature film. And certainly it's true: filmmaking is a team effort. But in most cases, it is the director who ultimately controls and shapes the visual, editorial, and aural world of a movie, working with the rest of the crew to achieve his or her vision.

1950S AMERICAN AUTEURS

Nicholas Ray made a name for himself with the gritty dramas *They Live by Night* (1948) and *Knock on Any Door* (1949), the latter one of the first films about juvenile delinquency. But his major film of the 1950s, and one of the key American films of the period, was *Rebel Without a Cause* (1955), a classic drama of teenage alienation featuring a stirring performance by James Dean as a disaffected teen at war with society and himself. Though the film was originally begun in black-and-white, Warner Bros. scrapped the first week's shooting and began again in CinemaScope and color. Ray takes full advantage of the panoramic CinemaScope image, balancing characters on oppo-

Outlaw motorcyclist Johnny (Marlon Brando) tries to impress small-town girl Kathie (Mary Murphy) in László Benedek's *The Wild One* (1953), the first of the biker-gang melodramas.

site ends of the screen, incorporating background images that comment on the main action within the frame, and carefully coordinating color, light, and shadow into a sinuous tapestry of emotion.

Teen rebellion was a potent theme of the early 1950s, as exemplified two years earlier by László Benedek's *The Wild One* (1953). The first of the biker-gang melodramas, *The Wild One* starred Marlon Brando as Johnny, a renegade motorcyclist who tries to make an impression on Kathie (Mary Murphy) when his gang comes to a small town and eventually starts a riot. Brando's performance as Johnny became almost instantly iconic, along with his insolent dialogue; when Kathie asks Johnny what he's rebelling against, Johnny immediately shoots back, "Whaddya got?" By the late 1960s, numerous studios and independent producers would create an entire series of biker films copying the Brando "rebel" formula, most notably Roger Corman's *The Wild Angels* (1966), but *The Wild One* remains the original.

Corman was one of the most unusual figures to surface in the 1950s; his low-budget crime, horror, and science fiction thrillers for the independent company American International Pictures in many ways defined the 1950s flight from studio domination. Corman's first film as a producer, Wyott Ordung's *Monster from the Ocean Floor* (1954), was made for the astoundingly low sum of $12,000, but Corman was dissatisfied with the result and felt that he could do a better job, so he took the helm for his 1955 production of *Five Guns West* and never looked back, directing more than fifty films by 1978. His key films include *Teenage Doll* (1957), a story of girls in a teenage gang war in New Orleans; *Sorority Girl* (1957), an exposé of the cruelties inherent in college sororities; the sick comedy *A Bucket of Blood* (1959), in which a hapless would-be sculptor accidentally becomes an art world sensation when his cat falls into a vat of cement, and he displays the result as a sculpture entitled "Dead Cat" (he soon moves on to human beings, which proves his undoing); *Machine-Gun Kelly* (1958), a psychological gangster film shot in black-and-white CinemaScope, with Charles Bronson in an early role; and perhaps his most famous film of the era, *The Little Shop of Horrors* (1960), which Corman shot in two days for roughly $27,000, about a man-eating plant named Audrey Junior, and which eventually became the basis for both a Broadway musical and a big-budget remake by Frank Oz in 1986. Corman has also served as the mentor for such figures as Francis Ford Coppola, James Cameron, Jonathan Demme, Ron Howard, Peter Bogdanovich, Martin Scorsese, and many others, all of whom Corman hired early in their careers.

Douglas Sirk began with a series of remarkable noirs, especially the brilliant psychological drama *Shockproof* (1949), before going on to direct a series of glossy Technicolor melodramas that were, in actuality, trenchant criticisms of the insularity of America in the 1950s, such as *Magnificent Obsession* (1954), *All That Heaven Allows* (1955), *Written on the Wind* (1956), and *Imitation of Life* (1959); again, the *Cahiers* critics were among the first to hail Sirk as a serious artist.

Samuel Fuller, another *Cahiers* favorite, created a frenzied universe of violence and anarchy in such deeply personal films as *Pickup on South Street* (1953), one of the best of the anti-Communist espionage thrillers; the bizarre CinemaScope western *Forty Guns* (1957), featuring Barbara Stanwyck as the matriarch of a renegade band of outlaws; and the ultra-violent crime film *Underworld U.S.A.* (1961), in which veteran screen villain Robert Emhardt presides over his criminal empire clad in a bathing suit and robe beside a luxurious indoor swimming pool, his greed and rapaciousness made all the more striking by the actor's enormous physical weight and his absolute refusal to exercise, or even to use the pool right next to his lounge chair. Fuller, a genuine outsider, wrote, produced, and directed most of his major films, in addition to providing occasional source materials for the noir films of others, such as Phil Karlson's memorably vicious newspaper drama, *Scandal Sheet* (1952), based on Fuller's novel *The Dark Page*. Fuller's apotheosis in the

The revisionist western: Helen Ramírez (Katy Jurado) confronts Amy Kane (Grace Kelly) as the two women in the life of besieged frontier marshal Will Kane (Gary Cooper) in Fred Zinnemann's *High Noon* (1952).

Cahiers critical pantheon came when he appeared as himself in critic-turned-director Jean-Luc Godard's 1965 masterpiece *Pierrot le fou* (*Pierrot the Fool*), holding forth on his theory of cinema during an upscale cocktail party for a generally mystified audience.

Phil Karlson was another original, whose films include *Kansas City Confidential* (1952), *99 River Street* (1953), *Tight Spot* (1955), and perhaps most memorably *The Phenix City Story* (1955), which chronicled the true story of a vicious murder and cover-up in a hopelessly corrupt Alabama town. With typical audacity, Karlson shot much of the film on location and even used clothing worn by the murder victim to add to the authenticity of the piece, which resulted in the case being reopened and the real killer being brought to justice.

Fred Zinnemann took a considerably more restrained approach to his work, creating the cautionary western *High Noon* (1952) in which frontier marshal Will Kane (Gary Cooper) discovers that an old nemesis, Frank Miller, is coming back to town to kill him. He attempts in vain to rally the townspeople to his side, and when everyone deserts him except for his new Quaker bride (Grace Kelly), Kane is forced to shoot it out with Miller and his gang in a climax that reveals the depth of his courage. With Miller dispatched, the townspeople again rally around the marshal, but he regards them with disgust, taking off his badge and dropping it in the dust as a gesture of contempt, just as he and his wife drive out of town for the last time. This clearly revisionist western infuriated many of Hollywood's old guard, particularly John Wayne, who thought it was a disgrace to the western genre

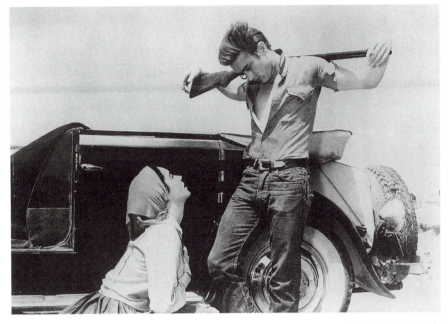

Elizabeth Taylor and James Dean in George Stevens's *Giant* (1956).

and frontier American values. Also shocking, in its display of brutality in the ranks, prostitution, and sexuality, was Zinnemann's *From Here to Eternity* (1953), a significant comment on the role of the military during World War II. Based on James Jones's novel about life on an army base in Hawaii in late 1941 and with a cast including Frank Sinatra, Montgomery Clift, Burt Lancaster, Deborah Kerr, and Donna Reed, the film won eight Academy Awards.

George Stevens directed *A Place in the Sun* (1951), a compelling modern version of Theodore Dreiser's novel *An American Tragedy* starring Elizabeth Taylor and Montgomery Clift; *Shane* (1953), in which a young boy (Brandon De Wilde) idolizes wandering gunman Shane (Alan Ladd); and *Giant* (1956), a sprawling saga set in Texas based on Edna Ferber's novel, with Elizabeth Taylor, Rock Hudson, and James Dean.

One of the key American western directors of the 1950s and 1960s was Budd Boetticher. During college he went to Mexico and saw his first bullfight. Entranced by the drama of the ring, Boetticher wanted to make a career for himself as a matador, but ended up in Hollywood through the influence of a friend, Hal Roach Jr., who got him a job working as a horse wrangler on the second unit of Lewis Milestone's *Of Mice and Men* (1939). This led to work as technical advisor on Rouben Mamoulian's *Blood and Sand* (1941), in which he coached Tyrone Power on the fine art of bullfighting, and also served as choreographer for the "El Torero" dance number. He drifted over to Columbia and was soon working as an assistant director until he got his first chance as solo director on the "B" film *One Mysterious Night* (1944). From then on, Boetticher made a name for himself as a reliable and inventive director in a variety of genres, especially with a remarkable series of westerns with Randolph Scott, including *Seven Men from Now* (1956), *The Tall T* (1957), *Ride Lonesome* (1959), and *Comanche Station* (1960).

In 1960 he left Hollywood for what should have been a brief trip to Mexico, to make a documentary feature on the life and career of matador Carlos Arruza, one of Boetticher's idols. As it turned out, Boetticher would run into numerous difficulties with the project, which would take many years to finish. Obsessed with completing the documentary, he turned down numerous other assignments, ran out of money, got divorced, and wound up spending one week in an insane asylum and another in a Mexican jail. To make matters worse, Arruza himself was killed in an automobile accident in 1966, forcing Boetticher to complete the film with the materials at hand. Finally, after various other production and financing problems, *Arruza* was released in 1972 to generally excellent reviews.

Another maverick filmmaker, Ida Lupino, emerged as one of the most interesting and individual directors of the era, tackling themes no other director would touch. During the 1950s, Lupino was the only female member of the Screen Directors Guild. Indeed, when she assumed the director's chair, a number of influential critics suggested that, as a woman, she had no business venturing into what they viewed as an exclusively male profession. But Lupino pushed ahead—"Believe me, I've fought to produce and direct my own pictures," she said in reflecting on her career—all the while being quite aware that it was important not to appear overly ambitious in order to fit into the gender constructions of 1950s Hollywood.

Her mastery of the Hollywood publicity machine is in itself fascinating, because she continually stressed her femininity and portrayed herself as a woman who accidentally assumed a directorial capacity, often saying that she "never planned to become a director." True enough, her first job as director, though uncredited, for *Not Wanted* (1949), seemingly fell into her lap when veteran Elmer Clifton became ill three days into shooting. But Lupino co-wrote the screenplay with Paul Jarrico (based on a story by Jarrico and Malvin Wald) and the film was released through Lupino's own production company, Emerald Productions (later known as The Filmakers [*sic*]); some have argued persuasively that she was angling for the director's chair from the start of preproduction.

Not Wanted is the story of a young woman who gives birth to an illegitimate child. Lupino attempted to cast the picture with a multicultural group of young women but had trouble getting her idea past producers; ultimately she was told by the production company that she "couldn't have the heroine in the same room with a Negro girl and a Spanish girl and a Chinese girl." Though shocked by the outright racism of the executive, she gave in, nevertheless telling him that someday she would be in a position to make a film without outside interference. True to form, Lupino still managed to cast a young Chinese woman in the film.

Never Fear (1949) is a study of a woman dancer fighting against polio. *Outrage* (1950) is one of the only movies of the period to directly represent rape and its aftermath. *Hard, Fast and Beautiful* (1951) is an acerbic study of a mother who tries to live her life through her daughter, a champion tennis player. The film attacks the model of motherhood championed in 1950s cultural ideology, comparable to Dorothy Arzner's critique of passive feminine roles in *Craig's Wife* (1936). *The Bigamist* and *The Hitch-Hiker* (both 1953) are film noir studies of masculinity and violence. Lupino's sometimes ambiguous feminism exemplifies the career of a woman director who refused to define herself in feminist terms, yet clearly employed a feminist vision in her films.

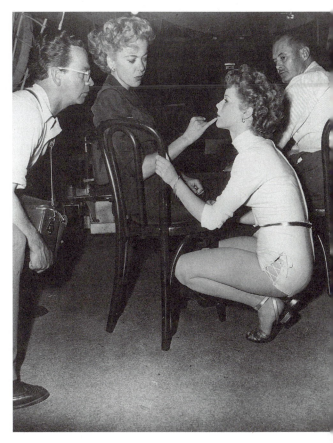

Director Ida Lupino instructs a technician on the proper way to light actress Sally Forrest on the set of *Never Fear* (1949), Lupino's groundbreaking film about the fight to conquer polio.

MUSICALS

At MGM, Gene Kelly and Stanley Donen contributed the pioneering shot-on-location musical *On the Town* (1949), as well as the much-beloved *Singin' in the Rain* (1952), about the early days of sound in Hollywood. Vincente

Fred Astaire and Judy Garland in Charles Walters's classic musical *Easter Parade* (1948).

Minnelli continued with his series of lavish musicals for the Arthur Freed production unit, such as *Meet Me in St. Louis* (1944), *An American in Paris* (1951), and *Gigi* (1958). Charles Walters emerged as a sort of second-string Minnelli who was nevertheless capable of excellence at times, with such musicals as *Easter Parade* (1948), starring Fred Astaire and Judy Garland, as well as *High Society* (1956) and *The Tender Trap* (1955).

Musicals of the 1950s existed in a peculiar state of flux, because as with the western, changing audience tastes were about to radically transform the genre. Musicals were an integral part of the 1930s and 1940s studio system, produced on an assembly line basis, as a reliable and profitable genre staple. In contrast, 1950s musicals were often aggressively lavish and laced with spectacular production numbers, as if trying to top themselves from scene to scene. Freed's MGM unit was almost an anachronism by 1955, as MGM's new production head, Dore Schary, eased out Louis B. Mayer to create a series of socially conscious films and ambitious biopics, such as Minnelli's *Lust for Life* (1956), starring Kirk Douglas as Vincent Van Gogh. The rock 'n' roll revolution was just over the horizon. Richard Brooks's *Blackboard Jungle* (1955) used Bill Haley and His Comets' "Rock Around the Clock" over its main titles; one year later, Fred F. Sears's film of the same title, starring Haley and his band, became the screen's first true rock 'n' roll musical. The big band era ended practically overnight, and traditional musicals, with a few exceptions, began to fade from the screen.

FIFTIES FATALISM

Fritz Lang continued with his brutal series of noirs and *policiers,* crime films that dealt with the dark and brooding side of human experience, the raw reality of the streets, and the criminals who plied their trade in the underworld. His films of the decade included *House by the River* (1950), a psychological murder mystery; *Clash by Night* (1952), a brooding melodrama; *The Blue Gardenia* (1953), an unrelentingly downbeat story of failed romance and murder; *The Big Heat* (1953), one of the screen's most vicious crime dramas; and *While the City Sleeps* (1956), a brilliant suspense film dealing with a teenage serial killer who stalks the streets of Manhattan.

Hollywood maverick Otto Preminger, who had burst into prominence with the mystery thriller *Laura* (1944), directed some of the best noirs of the era, such as the psychological thriller *Whirlpool* (1949), the hard-boiled crime drama *Where the Sidewalk Ends* (1950), and the brutally cynical *Angel Face* (1952) with noir icon Robert Mitchum. As his career progressed, Preminger challenged censorial taboos with such groundbreaking films as *The Moon Is Blue* (1953), *The Man with the Golden Arm* (1955), and *Anatomy of a Murder* (1959), which dealt, respectively,

Harry Belafonte and Dorothy Dandridge in Otto Preminger's *Carmen Jones* (1954), a modern version of Bizet's opera *Carmen* with an African American cast.

with adultery, heroin addiction, and rape, much to the consternation of those trying to enforce the Production Code. He also made a western, *River of No Return* (1954), in which a man with a past (Robert Mitchum) and his young son (Tommy Rettig) bond with a saloon singer (Marilyn Monroe) on a raft as they forge their way through danger on a raging river; *Carmen Jones* (1954), a modern version of Bizet's opera starring Harry Belafonte and Dorothy Dandridge with an African American cast; as well as *Advise & Consent* (1962), starring Henry Fonda, examining political power games in Washington.

SCIENCE FICTION

The 1950s science fiction movie became a signature genre of the era. Jack Arnold's parable of diminished American masculinity, *The Incredible Shrinking Man* (1957), tells the story of everyman Scott Carey (Grant Williams), who is exposed to a mysterious radioactive mist and gradually grows smaller

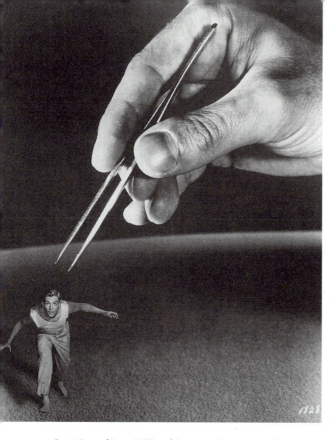

Scott Carey (Grant Williams) is exposed to a mysterious radioactive mist and then grows smaller and smaller in Jack Arnold's science fiction parable of American Cold War masculinity, *The Incredible Shrinking Man* (1957).

and smaller as a result. The movie is both chilling and poetic, filled with unforgettable set pieces in a nightmare vision of the familiar world turned into the unknown, as when, most memorably, Scott must fend off an ordinary spider that has emerged from behind a stale piece of cake.

Other science fiction movies specialized in malevolent aliens from other planets. Don Siegel, one of the most aggressive visual stylists of the era, created his acknowledged masterpiece, *Invasion of the Body Snatchers* (1956), a parable about the dangers of 1950s conformism in which humans are taken over by emotionless duplicates of themselves. The movie, shot in garish black-and-white on a minimal budget, is remarkably effective in its depiction of a sleepy suburb that at first appears pleasant but becomes increasingly threatening as the story unfolds.

Rudolph Maté's *When Worlds Collide* (1951) forecast the end of civilization when a rogue star collides with Earth; only a handful of survivors manage to escape the destruction by flying in a rocket to a new Eden, a hitherto unknown planet with conditions similar to those on Earth. As the ship glides into outer space on a gigantic ramp, we witness the destruction of Earth in a series of cataclysmic tidal waves, exploding volcanoes, and raging fires. The message at the end of the film is clear; some survivors of the human race may have made it to the new world, but will they manage to live in peace, or will they start the cycle of destruction all over again? A similar tone is evoked in Robert Wise's *The Day the Earth Stood Still* (1951), in which a flying saucer causes mass panic when it lands in Washington, D.C. Inside is the alien Klaatu (Michael Rennie) and his powerful robot, Gort. Klaatu looks perfectly human, so in order to better understand earthlings, he goes incognito and rents a room from Helen Benson (Patricia Neal) and her family, who befriend him. Though Klaatu's arrival on earth seems to bring nothing but chaos, his message urging peace is clear: we must all learn to live together, or perish.

The end of civilization in Rudolph Maté's *When Worlds Collide* (1951); 1950s science fiction as paranoid prophecy.

Howard Hawks had significant directorial input on one of the great science fiction classics of the 1950s, *The Thing from Another World* (1951), although the film is credited to Christian Nyby, Hawks's longtime editor. But according to all the cast and crew members, Nyby directed only one scene before turning to Hawks for help. Hawks's stamp is everywhere apparent in this superbly atmospheric and inventive film.

HITCHCOCK IN THE FIFTIES

Alfred Hitchcock created some of his most personal and deeply felt works in the decade, particularly *Rear Window* (1954), one of the cinema's great meditations on voyeurism and the supposedly detached observer. "Jeff" Jefferies (James Stewart), a photographer confined to a wheelchair as a result of an accident, stares idly out the back window of his Greenwich Village apartment and soon detects that his neighbor Lars Thorwald (Raymond Burr) has murdered his wife. Or has he? Jeff's other neighbors—an obsessive song-

Cary Grant as a victim of mistaken identity in Alfred Hitchcock's *North by Northwest* (1959).

writer, a pair of newlyweds, a scantily clad dancer, and a solitary woman Jeff dubs Miss Lonelyheart—all go about their business, oblivious to Thorwald's machinations. In the end it is up to Jeff to trap Thorwald, even while he is immobilized and unable to defend himself. In another collaboration with Stewart, Hitchcock directed what many consider to be his masterpiece, *Vertigo* (1958), the tale of ex-detective Scottie Ferguson, who falls in love with the mysterious Madeleine Elster (Kim Novak), only to witness her death in a fall from a bell tower. But nothing is what it seems in the film, and Scottie's obsession with the dead Madeleine and a woman he subsequently meets, Judy Barton (also Novak), tests his sanity until the final tragic irony.

Hitchcock ended the 1950s with *North by Northwest* (1959), a "wrong man" espionage thriller with Cary Grant as advertising executive Roger Thornhill, who is mistaken for George Kaplan, a government agent who does not in fact exist. But nefarious spies think he's real enough, and soon Thornhill is involved in an intricate tale of murder and deceit masterminded by the urbane Philip Vandamm (James Mason), who is determined to eliminate "Kaplan" at any cost. In all these films, Hitchcock remains as precise and calculating as he was in the 1930s and 1940s: a meticulous planner who executes his setups with cold brilliance, and a moralist who also believes that his first function is to entertain his audience.

BILLY WILDER'S AMERICA

Billy Wilder's 1950s films included some of the most famous sex comedies of the era, such as the raucous *The Seven Year Itch* (1955), in which a wandering husband (Tom Ewell) is smitten by the charms of his upstairs neighbor

(Marilyn Monroe), known simply as "the girl" throughout the film, while his wife is away. The scene of Marilyn cooling off over a New York City subway grate in the heat of summer is one of the cinema's most enduring images. As usual, Wilder manages to find just the right blend of comedy and innuendo to make the film a dazzling, playful treat. No less entertaining was the brilliant, gender-bending *Some Like It Hot* (1959), with Tony Curtis and Jack Lemmon in drag, on the run from the mob in an all-girl jazz orchestra, one of whose members is Marilyn Monroe. Other notable Billy Wilder films of the 1950s include the acidic Hollywood noir *Sunset Blvd.* (1950), a brutal study of faded glamour and ambition, with real-life silent-screen star Gloria Swanson in what was ironically her most famous role, as former silent-screen queen Norma Desmond, finally gone mad; as she informs her kept, much-younger lover, failed screenwriter Joe Gillis (William Holden), when he comments on her lost

Tom Ewell admires Marilyn Monroe's skirt in Billy Wilder's *The Seven Year Itch* (1955).

fame, "I *am* big! It's the *pictures* that got small!" In contrast, the lovely comedy/drama *Sabrina* (1954) features two wealthy brothers who couldn't be more different (Humphrey Bogart and William Holden), fighting for the attentions of a chauffeur's daughter (Audrey Hepburn) whose time in Paris has turned her into a very chic, lovely woman. Then there was the corrosive, bleak corporate love story *The Apartment* (1960), with Jack Lemmon, Shirley MacLaine, and Fred MacMurray. Truly, Wilder was a Renaissance man, with a mastery of many genres.

*   *   *

The cinema of the 1950s in the United States was simultaneously sophisticated, as with Hitchcock's and Wilder's films, and simplistic, as with the string of popular vehicles starring Dean Martin and Jerry Lewis (such as Norman Taurog's *Jumping Jacks* and Hal Walker's *Sailor Beware*, both 1952)

Dean Martin and Jerry Lewis, the most popular 1950s American comedy team, in Hal Walker's *Sailor Beware* (1951).

that were among the decade's most popular comedies. While these films accurately reflected the spirit of the times, so did the teen films from American International Pictures; the "Red Scare" films that dominated the first part of the decade; the lush, traditional Technicolor musicals of Vincente Minnelli; and the smaller rock 'n' roll musicals that were just beginning to appear. The fifties in the United States was a period of decisive change and stasis, of repression and liberation, of spectacle and gritty realism. Meanwhile, throughout the rest of the world, the cinema was also adjusting to the aftermath of the war, creating films that spoke directly to international postwar audiences on matters of vital importance. It is to these films, and filmmakers, that we now turn.

SEVEN

WORLD CINEMA IN THE 1950S

The cinema in Europe and Asia of the 1950s was in many ways changing more profoundly than the American cinema of the same era. Filmmakers were beginning to find their own national voices, in some cases as they began to break away from colonial rule. Improved distribution patterns also gave the international cinema greater visibility than ever before, thanks to the proliferation of film societies, museum screenings, and 16 mm non-theatrical prints of movies that could now reach a wide and enthusiastic audience worldwide.

JAPAN

Japan after World War II was a nation in ruins, with an Allied occupation government and a populace confused and dismayed by the Emperor's sudden insistence that he was not, in fact, a deity. As Japan began to rebuild, it rapidly threw off much of its military past and soon became an industrialized nation, adopting many of the customs and values of the West. Filmmaking, too, became more Westernized. Akira Kurosawa directed his first movie with the actor Toshirô Mifune, *Yoidore tenshi* (*Drunken Angel*, 1948), and then *Nora inu* (*Stray Dog*, 1949), a stark *policier*; both films signaled the future development of Kurosawa's mature style. Kurosawa's *Rashômon* (1950) was the first major Japanese production that broke out of its native country and into Western consciousness. It demonstrated to audiences that there was a vast literature of cinema in the world that had not yet been made available to the public, and further, that new national cinemas were creating some extraordinarily exciting work that should not, and could not, be ignored. *Rashômon* tells the tale of a young woman, Masako (Machiko Kyô), in eleventh-century Japan who is the victim of rape during an attack in the

Akira Kurosawa's *Shichinin no samurai* (*The Seven Samurai,* 1954), with Toshirô Mifune (center) as the warrior Kikuchiyo.

forest that also leaves her husband, Takehiro (Masayuki Mori), dead. The story is told from four conflicting points of view, each in turn calling into question the veracity of the other accounts. With Mifune, soon to become one of Japan's major stars, as the bandit Tajomura, *Rashômon* is a film about the unreliability of human memory and the uncertain quality of justice when all versions of a story are ultimately self-serving. Stunningly photographed and edited, *Rashômon* was Kurosawa's breakthrough in the West, and the term "the Rashômon effect" has now become a standard phrase describing cases in which differing eyewitness accounts cannot be reconciled.

Kurosawa followed *Rashômon* with *Ikiru* (*To Live,* 1952), in which a lowly clerk, Kanji Watanabe (Takashi Shimura), discovers that he is dying of cancer and is forced not only to face his mortality but also to interrogate the meaning and value of his life. Kurosawa's next venture, *Shichinin no samurai* (*Seven Samurai,* 1954), was an action vehicle that contained enough heart-pounding violent spectacle to become one of the first Japanese movies to be remade in America, as *The Magnificent Seven* (1960, directed by John Sturges). Kurosawa's most successful period as a director was in the late 1950s and early 1960s, with a series of brilliant works such as *Kumonosu jô* (*Throne of Blood,* 1957), a retelling of *Macbeth,* starring Toshirô Mifune as an overly ambitious warlord who is cut down by a hail of arrows that reduce

The intimate drama of family life, seen from the perspective of a *tatami* mat, in Yasujiro Ozu's *Banshun* (*Late Spring,* 1949).

him to a human pincushion in the movie's final minutes, and *Tengoku to jigoku* (*High and Low,* 1963), a contemporary story involving the kidnapping of an industrialist's son. Typically for Kurosawa, *High and Low* explores issues of moral ambiguity, when the tycoon (played by Mifune) discovers that it is his chauffeur's son who has mistakenly been kidnapped and not his own son. The film's descent into the Tokyo underworld is detailed and mesmeric, and Kurosawa uses the CinemaScope frame to create a gallery of claustrophobic compositions that effectively convey the squalor and density of criminal society.

Yasujiro Ozu, who had long established himself as a great director, kept up his leisurely pace of domestic dramas with *Banshun* (*Late Spring,* 1949), *Ochazuke no aji* (*Flavor of Green Tea over Rice,* 1952), and *Tokyo monogatari* (*Tokyo Story,* 1953), all shot in his signature sparse style. Kenji Mizoguchi created the period drama *Saikaku ichidai onna* (*The Life of Oharu,* 1952) and followed it up with perhaps his most famous film, *Ugetsu monogatari* (*Tales of Ugetsu,* 1953), a dreamlike ghost story in which two ambitious and greedy potters go off in time of war to sell their wares, leaving their families behind. Genjurô (Masayuki Mori) becomes romantically involved with a malevolent

205

female ghost, Lady Wakasa (Machiko Kyô), while Tôbei (Sakae Ozawa) dreams of becoming a samurai. Mizoguchi's deeply moving historical drama *Yôkihi* (*Princess Yang Kwei-fei*, 1955) is a tragic tale of a doomed royal love affair, shot in gentle pastel colors that evoke the hues of a Japanese screen print. Together, Kurosawa, Ozu, and Mizoguchi are three of the key Japanese directors of the early to middle 1950s.

SWEDEN

Sweden, which had largely escaped the most vicious depredation of World War II, emerged with a progressive, near Socialist political structure and a strong sense of national identity. Ingmar Bergman was becoming a one-man film industry, single-handedly putting the Swedish cinema before the public in a series of deeply allegorical films, beginning with the brutal drama *Kris* (*Crisis*, 1946), which he wrote and directed, and continuing at the rate of roughly a film per year until the late 1960s. Bergman, the son of a Lutheran minister whose discipline of the young boy was exceedingly strict, was tormented from his earliest years by issues of morality, conscience, belief in God, and personal responsibility, and these themes soon surfaced in his work as a filmmaker. In 1948, he directed the typically bleak *Musik i mörker* (*Night Is My Future*), about a young man who is blinded while in the military. *Fängelse* (*The Devil's Wanton*, 1949), about the suicide of a prostitute, was followed by numerous other somber works, including *Sommaren med Monika* (*Summer with Monika*, 1953), the story of an illicit summer romance that ends in tragedy, and *Gycklarnas afton* (*Sawdust and Tinsel*, 1953), an allegorical tale of sexual passion in a tawdry, third-rate circus. *Sommarnattens leende* (*Smiles of a Summer Night*, 1955) was an atypically lighthearted sex comedy, which first heralded Bergman's breakthrough to mainstream international audiences. *Det Sjunde inseglet* (*The Seventh Seal*, 1957) stars Max von Sydow as the medieval knight Antonius Block, who is visited by Death (Bengt Ekerot). The figure of Death wants to take Antonius to the next world, but the knight makes a bargain with him, and the two play a game of chess that will determine the knight's fate. Shot in stark black-and-white by the great Gunnar Fischer, *The Seventh Seal*'s central question, whether or not God exists, informs the structure of the entire work, as a variety of other characters drift through the movie either denying or endorsing belief in Divine power. Throughout the story, the plague ravages the

Medieval knight Antonius Block (Max von Sydow) plays a chess game with Death (Bengt Ekerot) in Ingmar Bergman's timeless allegory *Det Sjunde inseglet* (*The Seventh Seal,* 1957).

countryside and witch hunts are a pervasive social force; in short, Death is everywhere. Yet Bergman manages to remain both hopeful and humanistic despite his absolutely somber material. The film created a Bergman cult throughout the world, which ultimately had a limiting effect on the director's critical reception. Audiences wanted him to repeat the themes and visual conceits of *The Seventh Seal* in his subsequent films, but the director had moved on.

In such works as *Smultronstället* (*Wild Strawberries,* 1957), *Ansiktet* (*The Magician,* 1958), *Nära livet* (*Brink of Life,* 1958), and *Jungfrukällan* (*The Virgin Spring,* 1960), Bergman created a world that was at once sensuous and treacherous, developing a stock company of actors such as Max von Sydow (who later had a long career in American films), Bibi Andersson, Ingrid Thulin, and especially Liv Ullmann, who would fall in love with Bergman and have his child during a long relationship in the 1960s. Gentle, assured, and deeply reflective, *Wild Strawberries* focuses on a retired professor, Isak Borg (director/actor Victor Sjöström, in his last role), who agrees to accept an honorary degree on the occasion of the fiftieth anniversary of his graduation from the University of Lund. Professor Borg sets out by car to his destination, driven by his daughter-in-law Marianne (Ingrid Thulin), and along the way they meet a variety of people—some from the professor's past, some just traveling on the road, like himself—who cause him to examine his life in a new light. Set in the nineteenth century, *The Magician* is one of Bergman's most mysterious works, as the illusionist Albert Emanuel Vogler (von Sydow) travels with his troupe to a small Swedish village, where the town's officials meet him with skepticism. Is Vogler a fraud, or a genuine magician? By the film's end, Vogler emerges as either a hero or a charlatan, depending on your interpretation, and the cozy assumptions of the villagers have been seriously shaken. *The Virgin Spring,* one of Bergman's most emblematic films, deals with the rape and murder of a young woman, Karin (Birgitta Pettersson), by a group of shepherds in thirteenth-century Sweden; when her father, Töre (von Sydow), finds out, he exacts a violent revenge. The film won the Academy Award for Best Foreign Language Film in 1961, Bergman's first such honor; it was remade by horror director Wes Craven as *The Last House on the Left* in 1972, with much of its content stripped away and an emphasis on extreme violence. In the 1960s, Bergman moved away from the direct symbolism of his early works to a series of deeply personal and revelatory films, most notably *Persona* (1966).

LUIS BUÑUEL

Luis Buñuel remained a man without a country, continuing to make films for himself alone and seemingly trying to offend even his most ardent patrons. Buñuel's vision of man and society is, in many ways, even more nihilistic than Bergman's; after directing the brutal *Los Olvidados* (*The Young and the Damned*) in the slums of Mexico City in 1950, and rehabilitating his reputation as a director in the process, Buñuel went on to make a widely disparate group of deeply individual films as the decade progressed, such as *Susana* (*The Devil and the Flesh,* 1951), in which a young woman escapes from prison and then terrorizes a bourgeois Mexican household through a series of strategic seductions, nearly bringing about the collapse of the family until they finally expel her from their domain; and *El* (*This Strange Passion,* 1953), detailing the love life of a Mexican aristocrat who fetishizes women's feet to the point of insanity.

Buñuel's fascination with the moral hypocrisy of society continued in his typically bizarre *Ensayo de un crimen* (*The Criminal Life of Archibaldo de la Cruz,* 1955). The film's protagonist confesses in a series of flashbacks that all his life he has been obsessed with the thought of murdering those around him. As the plot progresses, Archibaldo watches as his intended victims meet accidental deaths just before he can kill them, falling out of windows or plunging down elevator shafts, literally just out of Archibaldo's grasp, in a shocking, twisted comedy. During this same period, Buñuel also created *Abismos de pasión* (1954), a typically idiosyncratic version of *Wuthering Heights,* and even *The Adventures of Robinson Crusoe* (1954), in English, starring the American actor Dan O'Herlihy as Crusoe. This version dwells on Crusoe's hallucinations while marooned on his desert island. The film, shot in garish color in Mexico, and ostensibly aimed at children, ranks as easily the most unusual version of Daniel Defoe's oft-told tale. In *Nazarín* (1958), Buñuel documents the life of a pious priest (Francisco Rabal) who ministers to his unwilling flock, attempting to inspire them to live a Christlike existence, while his parishioners do everything in their power to undermine his efforts.

In 1961, Buñuel was invited back to Spain to make *Viridiana* (1961) by the government of Generalissimo Francisco Franco as an apology for deporting him after the venomous documentary *Land Without Bread* in 1933. Buñuel cheerfully accepted and then created one of the most strongly anticlerical films of his career, in which the virtuous Viridiana (Silvia Pinal), a young woman about to take her vows as a nun, stops in to visit her only relative, Don Jaime (Fernando Rey), who lives on an isolated estate in wealthy seclusion. Don Jaime, who at first seems polite and welcoming, is actually obsessed with bedding Viridiana, who coincidentally looks like Don Jaime's long-lost wife who died thirty years earlier on their wedding night. Rebuffed by Viridiana, Don Jaime kills himself in a fit of self-loathing, and Viridiana inherits his estate. Still seeking to do good, Viridiana opens the doors of Don Jaime's mansion to the poor, who promptly move in and destroy the house, engaging in drunken revelry until all hours of the night.

Sardonic social criticism culminates in one particularly memorable sequence, in which the camera pulls back during a drunken dinner banquet to reveal a composition that is a searing parody of Leonardo da Vinci's *The Last Supper,* with drunks and beggars replacing Christ and the apostles, while Handel's *Messiah* plays in the background. To avoid government censorship, Buñuel edited it in Paris immediately after shooting and presented it at the Cannes Film Festival, where it won the *Palme d'Or* (Golden Palm), one of the festival's top honors, much to the consternation of the Spanish government, which immediately banned it. Buñuel shrugged off the controversy and returned to Mexico to direct several films in the early 1960s before moving to Europe, finally coming to rest in France, where he continued to direct until the late 1970s.

209

INDIA

India was throwing off the cloak of British colonialism in the 1950s, emerging as the world's most populous democracy, even as it confronted conditions of extreme poverty and privation at home. Satyajit Ray created a series of starkly personal films with his "Apu trilogy," which comprised the films *Pather Panchali* (*Song of the Road*, 1955), *Aparajito* (*The Unvanquished*, 1957), and *Apur Sansar* (*The World of Apu*, 1959). Ray, who graduated from the University of Calcutta with a degree in economics, soon changed his mind about joining the commercial rat race and studied art history and painting with the Hindu poet Rabindranath Tagore, who ran a small university in the town of Shantiniketan. Ray began illustrating books to make a living, one of them being the autobiographical novel *Pather Panchali*, which detailed the hardships of Bengali village life. Ray was immediately taken with the book and wanted to bring it to the screen, but with only Hollywood films and the endless procession of indigenous Indian musicals as a model, he didn't know how to approach the project.

In 1950, however, he saw Vittorio De Sica's *The Bicycle Thief* while on a trip to London and was stunned by the audacity of Neorealism's approach to the cinema: strip a film down to the basics, shoot on location, use nonprofessionals, and get to the truth. Returning to India, Ray fell in with director Jean Renoir, who was then shooting his film *The River* (1951) on location there and took him on as an informal assistant director and translator. He absorbed an enormous amount of technical knowledge from Renoir, as well as noting his mentor's skill with actors. And so, with De Sica's vision and Renoir's practical advice to guide him, Ray set out to adapt *Pather Panchali* to the screen. In true Neorealist fashion, he used all his savings, then sold all his possessions, and even pawned his wife's jewels to keep *Pather Panchali* moving forward, shooting the film entirely on location in a local Bengali village and using only the most meager technical resources to create a clear, direct, and deceptively artless tale.

After a year and a half of shooting, Ray ran out of money and was about to give up the project, when the Bengali government, impressed with his tenacity, gave him a grant to finish. Completed after years of arduous work, *Pather Panchali* was released in 1955 and screened at the Cannes Film Festival in 1956. The critical reception was rapturous, and Ray's career as a director was truly launched. *Aparajito* and *Apur Sansar*, the other two films in the trilogy, had the same simplicity of approach and stylistic integrity as *Pather Panchali*, as does his superb drama of a family in social collapse, *Jalsaghar*

210

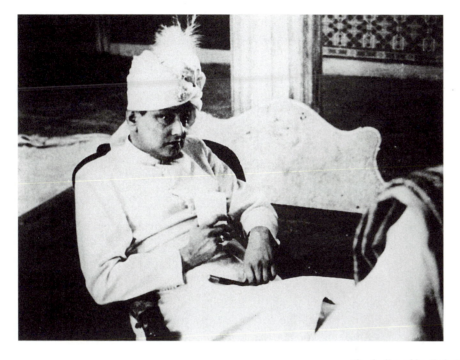

(*The Music Room,* 1958). *The Music Room* details the impending ruin of a once-distinguished family. Forced by pride to keep up the family name, an aging patriarch, Huzur Biswambhar Roy (Chhabi Biswas), presides over his ruined mansion as if living in an earlier, more affluent time, even though his funds have been exhausted. To keep up appearances, he throws a lavish party in his music room, a party that he can ill afford. The evening is a dazzling success, but the expense of putting on such a display bankrupts the patriarch, leading to the ruin of his house and the end of his aristocratic reign. Ray's subsequent films became more conventional and less personal, even as they attempted to recapture the magic of his earlier works. But his films in the late 1950s stand as a shining testament to one man's desire to bring his vision to the screen against seemingly insurmountable odds and to create a personal cinema that offered a more authentic picture of Bengali life than was being presented elsewhere.

A gifted but deeply troubled Indian auteur was Ritwik Ghatak, a radical playwright who made his first film as a solo director, *Nagarik* (*The Citizen*), in 1952. But Ghatak's career was sidetracked by alcoholism, as well as his decidedly unstable and volatile personality. Despite his undeniable brilliance as a director, he made only a few films, such as *Meghe Dhaka Tara* (*The Cloud-*

Capped Star, 1960) and the semi-autobiographical *Jukti, Takko Aar Gappo* (*Reason, Debate and a Story*, 1974) before succumbing to a variety of ailments at the age of fifty-one.

FEDERICO FELLINI

In Italy, in the wake of the Neorealist movement, Federico Fellini was the country's most visible director. Fellini began his career as a cartoonist and then enrolled in the University of Rome Law School in 1938 in order to avoid being drafted into Mussolini's army. He never actually took any classes, however, and instead spent his time as a court reporter, where he met the actor Aldo Fabrizi, who hired him at a nominal salary as an assistant. By the early 1940s, Fellini was writing scripts for Italian radio programs and developed an interest in film as a result of his work in the relatively new medium. In 1945, after the fall of Mussolini, he and some friends opened up a storefront business that he christened the Funny Face Shop, where, functioning as a sidewalk sketch artist, he drew caricatures of American soldiers. A chance meeting with Roberto Rossellini developed into a friendship, and Rossellini asked Fellini to help with the script for the film that became *Open City*. The success of the film encouraged Fellini to delve further into the cinema. He wrote several more scripts for Rossellini, including the scenario for the groundbreaking segment of *L'Amore*, "*The Miracle*," in which he also appeared.

Now working within the Italian film industry on a regular basis, Fellini served as an assistant director and/or scenarist for the young Italian directors Pietro Germi and Alberto Lattuada, both of whom had attended the Italian national film school Centro Sperimentale di Cinematografia. In 1950, Fellini made his first film as a director, *Luci del varietà* (*Variety Lights*, co-directed with Lattuada), but the modest comedy, about a vaudeville troupe, failed at the box office. His second film, now as solo director, was *Lo Sceicco bianco* (*The White Sheik*, 1952), a parody of the *fumetti* comic books then popular in Italy, which used captioned photos rather than drawings to tell their story. This film, too, failed to meet with public favor, but Fellini finally clicked with his next effort, the semi-autobiographical film *I Vitelloni* (*The Young and the Passionate*, 1953), about a group of young loafers who hang about a small Italian town waiting aimlessly for something to happen in their lives; the film would be remade by George Lucas as *American Graffiti* (1973), set in a small California town. *La Strada* (*The Road*, 1954) was an even bigger success, starring Fellini's immensely talented wife Giulietta Masina as Gelsomina, a sort of "holy fool" who tours the Italian countryside as an assistant to the strongman Zampanò (Anthony Quinn). Alternately heartbreaking and comic, this deeply perceptive film about the vagabond carnival life struck a chord with audiences worldwide and won an Academy Award for the Best Foreign Language Film.

Fellini's career, which had been negligible only a few years earlier, was now assured, and for the rest of the 1950s he created a series of unforgettable films, including *Il Bidone* (*The Swindle,* 1955), starring American actor Broderick Crawford as Augusto, a fast-talking con man who is not above donning a priest's collar to cheat his poverty-stricken victims, and *Le Notti di Cabiria* (*Nights of Cabiria,* 1957), starring Giulietta Masina as an eternally optimistic prostitute who perseveres in her faith in mankind, no matter how shabbily the fates and her various clients may treat her. *Cabiria* won Fellini another Academy Award for Best Foreign Language Film. In 1959, he

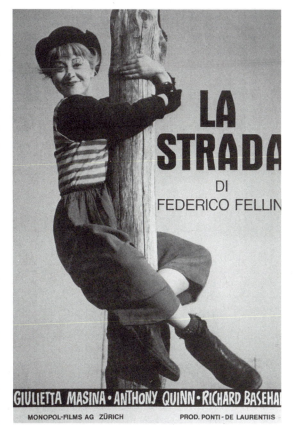

Federico Fellini's poetic drama *The Road* (*La Strada,* 1954), starring Fellini's wife, Giulietta Masina, as Gelsomina, a simple young woman who adores a brutal strongman, Zampanò, played by Anthony Quinn.

began shooting his most ambitious film yet, *La Dolce vita* (literally *The Sweet Life,* 1960), a biting condemnation of throwaway "pop" culture and the cult of celebrityhood, which also coined the term *paparazzi* for tabloid photographers.

Marcello Mastroianni, in the role that made him an international celebrity, plays Marcello Rubini, a scandal reporter for a sleazy Rome newspaper. Marcello spends his nights searching for gossip and scandal, going to endless, meaningless parties, hanging out on the Via Veneto in Rome, constantly looking for action. His sidekick, Paparazzo (Walter Santesso), is a stop-at-nothing photographer who specializes in catching stars in compromising situations. As the film progresses, Marcello sinks deeper into the

Sylvia (Anita Ekberg), an American actress on location in Rome, befriends a stray cat in Federico Fellini's epic drama of modern life, *La Dolce vita* (1960).

decadence of Rome's nightlife, although the few real friends he has left constantly tell him to quit writing for the "scandal sheets" and work on some project worthy of his undeniable talents. His best friend, Steiner (Alain Cuny), is an intellectual with a wife and two children who has nightly literary "salons" at his high-rise apartment, and urges Marcello to quit wasting his life. But when Steiner suddenly and inexplicably commits suicide, after killing his two infant children, Marcello feels there is no way out. The film's final sequence finds him drunk and unshaven, hanging out with a worthless group of party people, intent on momentary pleasure and nothing more. Marcello has now given up writing even for the gossip magazines; he has been reduced to being a publicist for hire, who dispenses instant, fraudulent celebrity—for a price.

Coming as it did at the end of the 1950s, *La Dolce vita* is a film that sums up the excesses and follies of the decade, and also gestures toward the on-rushing 1960s. With *La Dolce vita,* Fellini ended his first great decade as a filmmaker. Perhaps significantly, his next feature film, *Otto e mezzo* ($8^{1}/_{2}$, 1963), dealt with creative block, as film director Guido Anselmi (Mastroianni) cannot get his new film off the ground because he has run out of material from his own life with which to create. The sets are all built, the actors hired, the costumes prepared, and the money in place, but Guido has no idea what to shoot. The film ends with the situation unresolved, but by looking more intensively into his past, it is implied that Guido will find hope for his future work. $8^{1}/_{2}$ won Fellini his third Academy Award for Best Foreign Language Film, and he was soon involved in a series of captivating, dream-like projects that occupied his attention in the 1960s and 1970s.

MICHELANGELO ANTONIONI AND LUCHINO VISCONTI

An internationally recognized director of the period, Michelangelo Antonioni made his first mark as a cineaste writing film criticism for *Cinema,* the official film journal of the Italian Fascist government. Antonioni also attended the Italian national film school, the Centro Sperimentale di Cinematografia, and then worked as a co-screenwriter on Roberto Rossellini's early film *Una Pilota ritorna* (*A Pilot Returns,* 1942), and traveled to France to work with director Marcel Carné on his film *Les Visiteurs du soir* (*The Devil's Envoys,* 1942) as the official representative of Mussolini's government. He also began making short documentaries around this time; his first short, *Gente del Po* (*People of the Po River*), took only a brief time to shoot; but lack of funds and facilities postponed the completion of the film until 1943. In 1948, he made another short, *Nettezza urbana,* a k a *N.U.,* about a day in the life of Rome's street sweepers, and in 1950 directed his first feature film, *Cronaca di un amore* (*Story of a Love Affair*), a slight project that nevertheless recouped its small investment. It also contained the germ of Antonioni's later, distanced style, which would come to full flower in the 1960s, and set the stage for his 1955 film *Le Amiche* (*The Girlfriends*), with a script by Antonioni, Suso Cecchi d'Amico, and Alba De Cespedes from a short story by Cesare Pavese, whose bleak fascination with the despair of modern life perfectly matched Antonioni's own outlook. The title *The Girlfriends* is deeply ironic, for in Antonioni's world, friendship simply does not exist; all is expediency. People are used and then dropped. When Clelia (Eleonora Rossi-Drago) opens up a fashion salon in her hometown of Turin, she falls in with a fast set of "friends" whose meaningless pursuits of pleasure are merely a way to waste time. The members of the group, not surprisingly, are unprepared for the romantic vicissitudes of the real world, and the film ends with the "friends" turning on one another, with tragic consequences.

Antonioni's uncompromisingly alienated view of modern life would later find expression in his masterpiece *L'Avventura* (*The Adventure,* 1960), in which a group of friends sail to an uninhabited island and are forced to confront their own attitudes toward life when one of their group, a young woman named Anna (Lea Massari), mysteriously vanishes after a fight with her boyfriend, Sandro (Gabriele Ferzetti). Though the group searches for her, they never find her, and as the day goes on Anna's best friend, Claudia (Monica Vitti), finds herself becoming involved with Sandro, effectively re-

The difficulty of being: alienation and
isolation in Michelangelo Antonioni's
L'Avventura (*The Adventure*, 1960).

placing the missing Anna in his life. The film ends without an explanation for Anna's disappearance. Is it murder? Suicide? Or was she ever really there? Antonioni, as in his other films, plays with illusion and emotion to create a landscape of desolation and loss in which nothing is permanent, and everything, as well as everyone, remains a mystery.

Luchino Visconti's three films of the decade—*Bellissima* (1951), *Senso* (a k a *Livia*, 1954), and *Le Notti bianche* (*White Nights*, 1957)—all display the director's highly theatrical style. *Bellissima* is an unflinching and tragic dissection of the Italian film industry, as a mother sacrifices everything she has in the quest to make her daughter a star. *Senso* is a stunningly designed film shot in sumptuous color detailing the love affair between an Austrian military officer (played by American Farley Granger) and an Italian countess (Alida Valli, most famous for her role in Carol Reed's *The Third Man* [1949]). *White Nights* is an even more controlled film, signaling Visconti's final break with the Neorealist school, in a love story of deception and betrayal shot entirely on elegantly stylized sets—a complete departure from Neorealism's insistence on actual locations and nonprofessional actors. Vis-

216

conti's most noted films, however, were still to come in the 1960s and 1970s. Another important Italian film of the era was Vittorio De Sica's *Miracolo a Milano* (*Miracle in Milan,* 1951), a satirical fantasy that marked a departure from his Neorealist roots, from a screenplay by frequent De Sica collaborator Cesare Zavattini, who had written the screenplay for De Sica's *The Bicycle Thief.* An allegorical tale of a young man's picaresque voyage through life, *Miracle in Milan* ultimately emerges as a more positive and hopeful film than *The Bicycle Thief,* or the director's gloomy *Umberto D.,* although it was not well received when first released.

FILM IN 1950S ENGLAND

One of the major directors in postwar England was Sir Carol Reed, whose films included *The Third Man* (1949), a tense tale of espionage set in Vienna after the war. Although Joseph Cotten plays the lead in the film, Orson Welles steals the picture as Harry Lime, an unscrupulous black marketeer who eventually meets his end after a thrilling chase through the sewers of the city at night. Reed also directed a number of other classic films, including the IRA drama *Odd Man Out* (1947), with a young James Mason; the class-conscious murder mystery *The Fallen Idol* (1948), with Sir Ralph Richardson; and the Cold War spy satire *Our Man in Havana* (1959), based on the Graham Greene novel, with Alec Guinness and Noël Coward. Reed's most famous film is one of his last, *Oliver!* (1968), based on Lionel Bart's musical version of the Dickens novel, which won an Academy Award for Best Picture.

Orson Welles as Harry Lime in Sir Carol Reed's atmospheric drama of the Viennese postwar black market, *The Third Man* (1949).

Ealing Comedies

In the 1950s in Britain, comedy was one of the key cinematic genres. Ealing Studios excelled in a series of comedies of grace and sophistication that have become almost a genre unto themselves. With Sir Michael Balcon at the helm as producer, Ealing used the considerable talents of such actors as Alec Guinness, Stanley Holloway, Peter Sellers, Dennis Price, and others to create a dazzling array of comic gems. *Kind Hearts and Coronets* (1949), directed by Robert Hamer, is a cheerful black comedy about serial homicide, as Louis Mazzini (Dennis Price), the disgraced heir to a dukedom, methodically murders all the members of his estranged family line, the d'Ascoynes, who lie in his way to the title he "rightfully" deserves—each played, in a tour-de-force performance, by Alec Guinness. In all, Guinness plays no fewer than eight members of the d'Ascoyne family, one of them a woman, Lady Agatha d'Ascoyne. As Louis dispatches one unfortunate victim after another to attain his title, our sympathies remain entirely with him, as the d'Ascoynes are for the most part a thoroughly arrogant lot who deserve their respective fates. Scored with Mozart's *Don Giovanni, Kind Hearts and Coronets* is an elegant, civilized, and hilariously dark film, and Guinness's multi-role incarnations are astonishingly varied. Hamer's direction is equally assured, full of technical tricks and surprises. The remarkable scene in the church during which Louis sizes up his intended victims is one of the most cleverly realized examples of trick photography in the cinema, with six different versions of Alec Guinness on the screen in one shot, which was accomplished by running the same piece of film through the camera a total of seven times, with the aperture carefully masked off to photograph only one section of the frame for each exposure.

Charles Crichton's *The Lavender Hill Mob* (1951) features Guinness and Stanley Holloway as two bumbling dwellers of a boardinghouse who successfully steal a fortune in gold bars from the Bank of England; Alexander Mackendrick's *The Man in the White Suit* (1951) features Guinness again, this time as a man who invents a fabric that cannot be soiled, thereby putting laundries, dry cleaners, and tailors in jeopardy for their jobs; if the fabric is indestructible, who needs new clothing? Finally, in one of their few color productions, and also the last comedy the studio produced, Ealing introduced a young and rather chubby Peter Sellers to cinemagoers in Mackendrick's classic black comedy *The Ladykillers* (1955). Mrs. Wilberforce (Katie Johnson) runs a decrepit boardinghouse that, unbeknownst to her, is being used by a criminal gang—played by Alec Guinness, Cecil Parker, Herbert Lom, Sellers, and the loutish Danny Green—to plot a large-scale rob-

Alfred Pendlebury (Stanley Holloway) and meek bank clerk Henry Holland (Alec Guinness) try to steal a fortune in gold bullion in Charles Crichton's comedy *The Lavender Hill Mob* (1951).

bery. Masquerading as a string quartet, the gang pulls off the robbery after a series of misadventures, but in the end it is the landlady, Mrs. Wilberforce, who gets the money. Sadly, Ealing Studios closed shortly after the film's completion; it was remade under the same title, but with a radically different script, by Ethan and Joel Coen in 2004.

The St. Trinian Films and the Carry On Comedies

Another successful comedy series in 1950s and 1960s England was the St. Trinian films, based on the wildly popular satirical cartoons by Ronald Searle, which took England by storm in the early 1950s. Frank Launder was the director, starting with the unofficial predecessor *The Happiest Days of Your Life* (1950), and then moving on to *The Belles of St. Trinian's* (1954), *Blue Murder at St. Trinian's* (1957), *The Pure Hell of St. Trinian's* (1960), *The Great St. Trinian's Train Robbery* (1966, co-directed with Sidney Gilliat), and the final film in the series, *The Wildcats of St. Trinian's* (1980). The films gleefully burlesque the tradition of the English girls' boarding school, depicting both the school itself and the British Ministry of Education as corrupt and incompetent. The adolescent and teenage girls of St. Trinian's define poor sportsmanship and are often engaged in illegal activities (such as fixing horse races or making and then bottling bootleg gin). They gamble, smoke, drink, commit robberies and assaults with impunity, and even en-

219

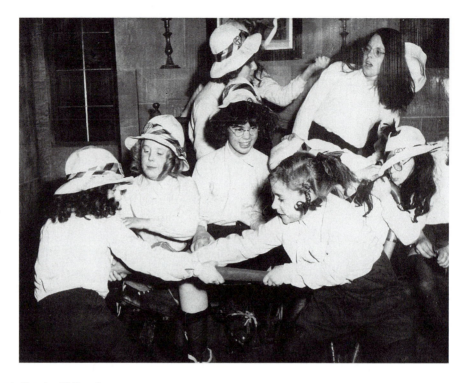

Anarchy in the U.K.: rebellion at a girls' boarding school in Frank Launder's *The Belles of St. Trinian's* (1954).

gage in prostitution if it helps them to achieve their ends.

Aided by a group of equally felonious staff members, especially the ubiquitous con man "Flash" Harry (George Cole), the girls of St. Trinian's set a new standard for the complete disregard of social norms and entranced the British public with images of feminine rupture and societal collapse in the otherwise staid 1950s.

Even more popular with contemporary audiences, although initially poorly received by the critics, were the Carry On comedies of producer Peter Rogers and director Gerald Thomas, specializing in lowbrow humor, sight gags, and slapstick. The first film, *Carry on Sergeant* (1958), was a modest success in England, but the second, the hospital comedy *Carry on Nurse* (1959), was an international hit and spawned a series of thirty-nine films, all directed by Gerald Thomas, that would end more than thirty years later with *Carry on Columbus* (1992). The Carry On films featured wheezy gags, "single-entendre" jokes, and a rotating cast of regulars, especially the gifted Sidney James and Kenneth Williams, essentially deriving their source material from the British music hall stage.

Hammer Horror

Horror was also a popular genre in the 1950s English cinema. Hammer Films began in 1934 as a small studio specializing in commercial genre movies, then moved into a series of taut noir films in the early 1950s, many with American actors. But in the late 1950s, Hammer found a winning new formula with horror and science fiction. This began when Hammer happened to adapt Nigel Kneale's popular BBC television series "The Quatermass Experiment" (1953) to the screen as *The Quatermass Xperiment* (1955), directed by Val Guest. The *X* in *Xperiment* was to capitalize on the fact that the British Board of Film Censors routinely gave an X, or "Adults Only," certificate to horror and science fiction films of the period, and thus the film had something of a forbidden air to it before it was ever released. The film was a massive success, and Hammer decided to concentrate entirely on graphic horror and science fiction films, after a poll discovered that audiences liked the horror aspect of *The Quatermass Xperiment* the most.

Hammer obligingly began creating a series of Gothic films that revitalized the genre, moribund since 1948, with generous doses of violence, sex, and bloodshed, all photographed in ravishing color. The Hammer look included lush cinematography, a tendency toward fluid camerawork, beautifully crafted period sets, and romantically suggestive clothing. Terence Fisher's *The Curse of Frankenstein* (1957) was the first pure horror film out of the studio's gate; it became an overnight sensation in both England and the United States, and made stars of Christopher Lee (as the Creature) and Peter Cushing (as Baron Victor Frankenstein). Universal Pictures, fearful of losing their franchise on movie monsters, initially opposed *The Curse of Frankenstein,* claiming that it infringed on their copyright for the character. Hammer responded that since their film was based on Mary Shelley's novel, which was in the public domain, they could do as they pleased. Despite the threat of a lawsuit Hammer pressed ahead, and when the film was a hit, Universal promptly struck a deal with Hammer giving them the rights to all their classic monsters. Hammer was transformed overnight from a small "B" production company into one of the most successful film studios in English history.

Fisher's *Dracula* (a k a *Horror of Dracula* in the United States) followed in 1958 and was an even bigger success both commercially and critically, with Christopher Lee as the bloodthirsty Count and Peter Cushing as his nemesis, Dr. Van Helsing. With that, Hammer began a seemingly endless cycle of horror and suspense films, relying on Fisher's considerable talent to create such

Christopher Lee as Dracula in Terence Fisher's *Dracula* (a k a *Horror of Dracula*), the film that started the modern Gothic horror tradition in 1958.

films as *The Revenge of Frankenstein* (1958), *The Hound of the Baskervilles* (1959), *The Mummy* (1959), *The Stranglers of Bombay* (1960), *The Brides of Dracula* (1960), *The Two Faces of Dr. Jekyll* (1960), and *The Curse of the Werewolf* (1961). Hammer continued the genre into the 1960s with other directors as well: *The Maniac* (Michael Carreras, 1963), *Paranoiac* (Freddie Francis, 1962), *The Kiss of the Vampire* (Don Sharp, 1962), and many others. Indeed, so successful was Hammer as a commercial proposition that the studio was eventually given the Queen's Award to Industry in April 1968 for their outstanding success in conquering overseas markets and successfully competing with Hollywood.

England's Women in Film

While Ida Lupino was the lone woman filmmaker working in Hollywood during the 1950s, at least three women were active within the industry during the same period in Great Britain. Muriel Box (born Violet Baker in 1905) worked her way into filmmaking through the ranks as a typist, "continuity girl," and finally screenwriter. After a great deal of success writing scripts for other directors, she finally directed *The Happy Family* in 1952, from a script co-authored with her husband, producer Sydney Box, based on a play by Michael Clayton Hutton. Released under the title *Mr. Lord Says No* in the United States, *The Happy Family* is a quietly amusing comedy that derives its humor from the class conflicts inherent in British society. *Street Corner* (1953) is one of Box's best efforts, a sort of forerunner of Kathryn Bigelow's police melodrama *Blue Steel* (1990); Box's version is a narrative about the lives of women in the police force, made as a response to Basil Dearden's *The Blue Lamp* (1950), a popular British *policier* that completely ignored the contributions of women police officers. *A Passionate Stranger* (1957) is an innovative comedy filmed in a mixture of color and black-and-white, while *The Truth About Women* (1957) is told in flashback, as Box presents the relationships between the sexes in a remarkably sophisticated light, atypical for its time period. *Too Young to Love* (1960), her most controversial film, an adaptation of Elsa Shelley's play *Pick-Up Girl*, deals frankly with pregnancy, societal views toward women, venereal disease, prostitution, and abortion. Box was thus able to infuse political statements into films that were billed as simple entertainment.

Wendy Toye began her career as a dancer and made her professional debut at the age of three at the Albert Hall in London. By the age of nine, she was choreographing a dance extravaganza at the London Palladium. In her teens, she danced at the Café de Paris in London and watched Sergei Diaghilev's famed Ballets Russes rehearse when the company was working with Jean Cocteau. In 1932, she appeared in a bit part as a dancer in Anthony Asquith's *Dance Pretty Lady*, which led to other film work as a dancer. In 1935, she worked as a choreographer on Paul Merzbach's *Invitation to the Waltz*, picking up valuable technical information along the way. From the 1930s to the 1950s she found regular work as a dancer, choreographer, and director, most notably with the Broadway production of *Peter Pan* in 1950–51, starring Boris Karloff and Jean Arthur, which put her firmly in the public eye.

Her break as a film director came when producer George Arthur asked her to direct the short *The Stranger Left No Card* (1952). Toye had originally been slated to do the choreography only, but she agreed to direct at the last minute when David Lean backed out of the project. Working with a budget of £3,000 and shooting without sync sound (using gramophone records to cue the actors), Toye finished on time and under budget. Cocteau, who was by this time chairman of the jury at the Cannes Film Festival, saw it and enthusiastically endorsed it. He awarded *The Stranger Left No Card* the prize for Best Short Film of the 1953 Cannes Festival, and Toye's career was off and running. Put under contract to Alexander Korda's London Films, she was next assigned to direct *The Teckman Mystery* (1954), then shifted to comedy with *Raising a Riot* (1955) and suddenly found herself with a substantial commercial hit on her hands. Her segment "The Picture" in the suspense omnibus *Three Cases of Murder* (1955) is a genuinely disturbing fantasy tale, while *All for Mary* (1955) and *True as a Turtle* (1956) followed in the light comedy vein. By her own admission, Toye was interested more in fantasy and suspense material, but up to and including her last feature, *We Joined the Navy* (1962), she was unable to break the stereotypical image that both the public and producers had of her as a comedy director.

Jill Craigie began her career as a journalist and then worked as a scriptwriter of documentaries for the British Council during World War II. Later she moved on to Two Cities Films, where she was offered the chance to write and direct documentaries, such as *Out of Chaos* (1944) and *The Way We Live* (1946). In 1948, Craigie formed her own production company, Outlook Films, and began planning to make *Blue Scar* (1949). The film is her only work that is not a documentary, instead a highly critical story about the life of a working-class Welsh mining family, set in the years of the nationalization of the coal industry. *Blue Scar* was censored and initially denied exhibition. A nationwide groundswell of public opinion, however, called for the release of *Blue Scar,* and it was finally shown to excellent reviews and enthusiastic audience response. Craigie returned to nonfiction with the 1951 documentary *To Be a Woman,* which argues for equal pay for equal work.

Also in Britain in the 1950s, the pioneer animator Joy Batchelor was refining the art of the cartoon in new and unexpected directions. Born in 1914 in Watford, England, Batchelor studied art and began a career as a commercial artist for cartoons. She worked on British cartoons such as *Music Man* (1938) and then met and married animator John Halas. In 1940 the partners formed their own production company, Halas & Batchelor Cartoon Films. During the war, Batchelor and Halas made public information and propaganda cartoons for the government, such as *Dustbin Parade* (1942), which stressed the importance of wartime recycling. Batchelor worked as a co-producer, co-director, and co-writer, and shared in all technical and aesthetic processes in their efforts, which included the first British full-length feature cartoon, *Animal Farm* (1954), adapted from the George Orwell novel. The production of *Animal Farm* during the Cold War era was a decided risk, as Orwell's pessimistic story of a group of farm animals ultimately dominated by the Fascist pig, Napoleon, was hardly standard children's fare. But Batchelor and Halas believed in the project intensely and spent nearly three years bringing it to life. By the mid-1950s, Halas-Batchelor was England's largest

224

animation house, and the team continued making short cartoons and industrials until the early 1970s. They were also among the first to use computer-assisted animation in their work, starting in the late 1960s.

Other important British films of the period were Laurence Olivier's adaptations of Shakespeare, *Hamlet* (1948) and *Richard III* (1955), which he directed and starred in to great acclaim. *Richard III* is especially interesting, employing heavily stylized color and an extensive use of interior sets to give the entire production an intentionally theatrical appearance, as if it is an illuminated manuscript come to life. For many, Olivier's films as a director came to epitomize the entire British cinema, although these high-profile films counted for just a fraction of the industry's total output. The equally irrepressible stylists Michael Powell and Emeric Pressburger continued their predilection for lavish spectacle with *Black Narcissus* (1947), a dazzling Technicolor film centering on a group of sexually repressed Anglican nuns attempting to start a school for the poor in an abandoned bordello in the Himalayan Mountains, and *The Red Shoes* (1948), the ultimate ballet film, which suggested that it was entirely worthwhile to sacrifice one's life in devotion to artistic endeavor. Powell and Pressburger continued making deeply individualistic films as the decade progressed.

FRANCE

It was in France in the mid-1950s that cinema was most enthusiastically debated and embraced, becoming almost a national obsession as the decade progressed. The French precedents to the Nouvelle Vague, or New Wave, include the satirist Jacques Tati, whose inventive visual comedies relied almost entirely on sight gags and required little dialogue, and the incomparable moralist Robert Bresson. Tati's eloquently sophisticated visual tropes in *Jour de fête* (*Holiday,* 1949), *Les Vacances de Monsieur Hulot* (*Mr. Hulot's Holiday,* 1953), *Mon oncle* (*My Uncle,* 1958), and his later films *Playtime* (1967), *Traffic* (1971), and *Parade* (1974), created a world of stand-alone sight gags that functioned without a plot, depending solely upon Tati's skill as a mime and *farceur* to create an intoxicating blend of reality and fantasy that also served as a subtle critique of conformity in modern society. *Playtime,* in particular, has much to say about the depersonalization of contemporary life, and since Tati not only directed but also starred in and scripted all his films, his creative control over the end product was absolute. Artistic freedom, however, came with a price; no matter how popular he was with critics and

The regimentation of modern life in Jacques
Tati's *Playtime* (1967).

audiences, Tati's painstaking approach and meticulous attention to detail created constant cash-flow problems. In his lifetime, Tati created only six feature films, from 1949 to 1974, but left an indelible mark, as worthy as Keaton or Chaplin, on the history of screen comedy.

Robert Bresson's work, after his early films of the mid-1940s, became progressively more severe, as he abandoned the use of professional actors and conventional mise-en-scène, preferring to work with "models" (his own term for the nonprofessional performers he used in his films from 1951 onward). He also developed a style of staging that utilized off-screen space, as his characters enter and exit the frame deliberately before and after each scene. After *Les Dames du Bois de Boulogne* in 1945, Bresson took six years off from filmmaking while he refined his mature style, evidenced for the first time in the contemplative *Journal d'un curé de campagne* (*Diary of a Country Priest*, 1951). His "models" deliver their lines without inflection or passion; the director often shot many takes of the same scene before attaining the absolute absence of emotion he was seeking; Bresson later explained that only without an actor's "tricks" could the "truth" of any situation come out. Bresson's films have a very distinctive look. Often shot on existing locations, either in sculptural black-and-white or sumptuously romantic color, they are edited with a careful, detailed precision, revealing only what is necessary to the audience and nothing more.

226

While at least one of his films is partly factually based, *Un condamné à mort s'est échappé, ou Le vent souffle où il veut* (*A Man Escaped,* 1956), from André Devigny's memoir of his year-long internment in a German prison during World War II, such later films as *Pickpocket* (1959), a loose adaptation of Dostoevsky's *Crime and Punishment,* are more like philosophical treatises than narratives, in which one's deeds are subject to constant scrutiny and all actions have almost immediate consequences. Every frame, every movement in his films is absolutely precise, as in *Pickpocket*'s extraordinary sequence of a gang of thieves working their way through a crowded train, picking the pockets of the unsuspecting passengers with effortless skill.

To stage this sequence, Bresson hired a professional pickpocket known only as Kassagi to choreograph the movements of the thieves. The result is astonishing; true sleight of hand without the aid of special effects or editorial trickery. *Pickpocket*'s plot, which involves a young man's descent into crime following the death of his mother, is seen as a series of conscious if ill-considered moral choices that eventually lead to his arrest and imprisonment. But even in prison, the possibility of redemption remains open. Bresson's cinema is

Two thieves work their way through a train stealing the possessions of the passengers in Robert Bresson's religious allegory *Pickpocket* (1959).

227

ultimately one of transcendence, as we move beyond our ordinary expectations as spectators and become one with his characters and their interior worlds.

Bresson was above all an individualist who created his own form of the cinema for himself rather than for audiences. He thus belonged not to the past, but to the present and future of cinema. The key New Wave figures—Jean-Luc Godard, François Truffaut, Eric Rohmer, Alain Resnais, and others—revered him and would use his model of independence, along with their own theoretical writings for *Cahiers du Cinéma,* as the springboard for their films, creating a new cinematic language that would drastically modify conventional rules of film grammar and syntax.

Agnès Varda

One of the first New Wave directors was Agnès Varda. Still active as a filmmaker today, and now part of the twentieth-century digital vanguard starting with her film *Les Glaneurs et la glaneuse* (*The Gleaners and I,* 2000), Varda was born in Belgium in 1928. She initially intended to become a museum curator, but due to her interest in photography she became the official photographer for the Theater Festival of Avignon, France, in 1947. In 1956, working with traditional 35 mm production equipment and relying solely on her experience as a still photographer, Varda successfully completed her first feature film, *La Pointe Courte,* several years before Godard, Resnais, or Truffaut made their feature debuts. Telling the tale of a young married couple in the fishing village of La Pointe Courte, France, the film was hailed for its freshness and its audacious film technique.

Indeed, future New Wave director Alain Resnais served as Varda's editor on *La Pointe Courte,* and when advised of her editorial strategy for the film he almost walked off the project: perhaps he was unhappy that her "parallel" editing style of pursuing two imagistic or narrative strands simultaneously so closely anticipated techniques that he himself would use in his debut feature *Hiroshima mon amour* (*Hiroshima, My Love* 1959). Varda next made a few documentaries, but *La Pointe Courte* would be her only feature film of the 1950s; despite the film's cultural impact, the innate sexism of the period prevented her from obtaining financing for a second film, *Cléo de 5 à 7* (*Cleo from 5 to 7*), until 1961, and then only because Godard, Truffaut, Resnais, and other New Wave luminaries had now established themselves as major cineastes, and Varda was swept along in their popularity. Told in near "real time," *Cleo from 5 to 7* (1961) is the story of a young woman waiting to hear whether or not she

Corinne Marchand as Cleo in Agnès Varda's New Wave classic, *Cléo de 5 à 7 (Cleo from 5 to 7,* 1961).

has cancer; we follow her after a doctor's appointment through a series of anxious meetings with friends. The film is remarkable for its near documentary flavor and montage editing, as well as its obsession with time.

Jean Rouch and Ethnographic Cinema

Jean Rouch was the foremost French documentary filmmaker of the era, most notably with *Les Magiciens de Wanzerbé* (*The Magicians of Wanzerbé,* 1948, co-directed with Marcel Griaule) and *Les Maîtres fous* (*The Mad Masters,* 1955), which depict the rituals and lifestyle of the Soughay people of West Africa. His style of detached observation sets his work apart from more participatory documentarians, with a minimum of interaction between himself and his subjects. The author of more than seventy-five ethnographic films, he documented not only the indigenous culture of West Africa but also the deleterious effects of colonialism on those whose lives he records. He also ventured into the area of "staged documentaries," such as *Moi, un noir* (*I, a Black Man,* 1958), which explores the consumerist fantasies of a group of West African citizens. Acutely conscious of his position as an outsider, Rouch went to great pains to depict the racial divide inherently present

229

as an underlying factor in all his work, as in *La Pyramide humaine* (*The Human Pyramid*, 1961), in which a group of African and French teenagers are thrown into close contact with one another, exposing the racist assumptions behind all colonial cinema.

Alain Resnais also made his initial reputation as a documentarian with the searing short film *Nuit et brouillard* (*Night and Fog*, 1955), one of the most effective examinations of the Holocaust ever made. Mixing black-and-white atrocity footage of the concentration camps taken by the Nazis themselves with color images of the death camps standing idle and overgrown with grass and weeds, Resnais weaves a haunting tapestry of memory and disaster, seamlessly moving back and forth in time to show the Nazis' mechanism of genocide in its full horror.

French Cinema Before the New Wave

Numerous other directors were active during this period in France. Jacqueline Audry worked as an assistant to directors Jean Delannoy, G. W. Pabst, and Max Ophüls before moving to the director's chair with *Gigi* (1949), *L'Ingénue libertine* (*Minne*, 1950), and *Mitsou* (1956), all based on novels by the French writer Colette. *Minne* was heavily censored because it depicted a young woman's sexual exploration outside of wedlock. In 1951, Audry directed her most famous film, *Olivia* (a k a *The Pit of Loneliness*), the story of a lesbian relationship, based on an autobiographical novel by Dorothy Strachey Bussy that examines life at an all-girls' boarding school, in which two girls compete for the love of the headmistress. René Clément's antiwar parable, *Jeux interdits* (*Forbidden Games*, 1952), is set in France in June 1940. A young girl's parents are killed in an attack on a bridge, along with her pet dog. The girl, Paulette (Brigitte Fossey), picks up the dog's body and meets the son of a local peasant couple, Michel (Georges Poujouly). Together, the two children conspire to create a graveyard for all the animals killed in the war, much to the displeasure of Michel's parents, who have taken Paulette in as a war orphan. But the improvised animal graveyard, decorated with crosses stolen from headstones of the graves of the town's dead, pushes Michel's parents over the edge. Angrily consigning Paulette to the authorities, Michel's mother and father essentially abandon the young girl to the fates of war, as she cries piteously for her dead mother. This moving and deeply troubling film won an Honorary Academy Award in 1953 for Best Foreign Language Film, and it retains much of its power to this day.

Easily the most bizarre film of 1950s French cinema is Isidore Isou's *Traité de bave et d'éternité* (*Venom and Eternity*, 1950), an experimental work of which only 111 minutes survive from a reputedly much longer film; it caused a scandal when it was screened at the Cannes Film Festival in 1951, where it won the Prix de l'Avant-garde as the most original and audacious film of the exhibition. The omnipresent Jean Cocteau, who once again found himself on the vanguard of cinema, awarded the prize. Isou's film, a product of the Letterist Movement, consists of randomly edited sections of blank film, "countdown" leader (also known as "Academy leader"), upside-down footage of military vehicles, scratched and out-of-focus stock footage, as well as commercials for Isou's numerous books, which interrupt the film at regular intervals. On the film's sound track, Isou insults the viewer, saying that he "wants to make a film that hurts your eyes," while a nearly thirty-minute section of the film offers heroic, angled shots of the director ambling around the streets of Paris, meeting various artistic luminaries at cafés and bars. The film ends with a long section of Letterist poetry, which takes the form of howls, grunts, screams, and guttural noises. Once seen, *Venom and Eternity* is never forgotten, one of the most confrontational films ever produced by the international avant-garde, and a testament to the continuously adventurous nature of the French cinema, even during the Cold War era.

Renoir

For his part, Jean Renoir continued his work as one of the foremost humanists of the cinema. His third and final period as a director begins with *Le Fleuve* (*The River*, 1951), an independently produced film based on Rumer Godden's novel and shot entirely in Calcutta. This relaxed and contemplative coming-of-age story, beautifully photographed in Technicolor, represented a return to the naturalism of Renoir's early work and won the International Award at the Venice Film Festival. *Le Carrosse d'or* (*The Golden Coach*, 1953), in contrast, displayed an intense interest in theatrical film style and gave Anna Magnani one of her greatest roles as Camilla, the fiery diva of a traveling theater troupe. Though Eric Rohmer has called *The Golden Coach* "the 'open sesame' of all of Renoir's work," it was not well received upon its initial release. Renoir was unable to find backing for another film until *French Cancan* (a k a *Only the French Can*, 1954), his first work made in France in fifteen years. This valentine to the Moulin Rouge nightclub met with great public success and featured a number of French music hall performers in cameo roles, including a very brief appearance by Edith Piaf.

Renoir's *Elena et les hommes* (*Paris Does Strange Things,* 1956) starred Ingrid Bergman, Jean Marais, and Mel Ferrer in a delicate love letter to a bygone age. *Le Testament du Docteur Cordelier* (*The Testament of Doctor Cordelier,* 1959) gave the director the chance to use multiple cameras for the first time, shooting the film in the manner long routinely used by television sitcoms. Loosely based on Robert Louis Stevenson's classic *Dr. Jekyll and Mr. Hyde, The Testament of Doctor Cordelier* stars Jean-Louis Barrault as Cordelier and his mad alter-ego, Opale, and is shot in stark black-and-white, in contrast to the lush color cinematography of Renoir's other films of his final period. *Le Déjeuner sur l'herbe* (*Picnic on the Grass,* 1959) is a topical fantasy shot partly in black-and-white and in delicious pastel colors; at once ephemeral and melancholic, it is as if the director were acknowledging his bewilderment in the face of the "civilizing" forces of modern society. *Le Caporal épinglé* (*The Elusive Corporal,* 1962) is a World War II tale of the numerous escape attempts of a corporal (Jean-Pierre Cassel) who is incarcerated in a series of German prison camps. In these films, we can see a mature, relaxed, contemplative Renoir, secure in his accomplishments and aware of his unique place in the cinematic pantheon, as one of the few classical French directors revered by the new criticism of *Cahiers du Cinéma.*

Vadim and Franju

Another important figure in France at this time was also highly influential and yet is largely forgotten today: Roger Vadim. Vadim's later work fell off badly into a sheen of commercialism and artistic compromise, but his early films, such as *Et Dieu . . . créa la femme* (*And God Created Woman,* 1956), *Les Liaisons dangereuses* (*Dangerous Liaisons,* 1959), and the sensuous vampire picture *Et mourir de plaisir* (*Blood and Roses,* 1960) contain sections of pure cinematic poetry that inspired the *Cahiers* critics to dare that they too might one day make movies. *And God Created Woman* also made a star out of Brigitte Bardot, Vadim's wife at the time. Shot in CinemaScope and Eastman Color with a small crew, the film demonstrated that a large budget was not essential to create a lushly beautiful work. *And God Created Woman* was one of the first French efforts of the 1950s to break out into an international hit—largely because of its mildly erotic subject matter—but the film now seems so innocent that it is hard to see what all the fuss was about. Nevertheless, Vadim led by low-budget example, and the directors of the French New Wave followed.

Another French documentarist of the 1950s who later went on to feature films with great success is Georges Franju, whose *Le Sang des bêtes* (*Blood of the Beasts,* 1949) gives an unsparing look at a Parisian slaughterhouse, as its workers go about their daily business with an air of businesslike detachment. Franju then began making equally disquieting fictional feature films, starting with *La Tête contre les murs* (*Head Against the Wall,* 1959), in which the director of an insane asylum thwarts the inmates' attempts to recover their sanity. His masterpiece, *Les Yeux sans visage* (*Eyes Without a Face,* 1960), centers on a crazed surgeon's attempts to keep his disfigured daughter eternally youthful and beautiful by transplanting the faces of a series of young women over her scarred visage.

GERMANY IN THE COLD WAR

In other parts of the world, film was undergoing a difficult transformation during the Cold War era. In the years immediately after the Second World War and Germany's defeat, the cinema in Germany, not surprisingly, underwent a major metamorphosis. The Allies broke up the giant film production consortium UFA, and many smaller production houses were licensed to make films. In addition, American movies, which had been banned for much of the war, now flowed freely onto German screens. Many of the German movies of the immediate postwar period were known as *Trümmerfilms* ("rubble films"). They depict a Germany in ruins following the collapse of the Third Reich, as ordinary citizens struggled simply to survive under the Allied occupation. Wolfgang Staudte's *Die Mörder sind unter uns* (*Murderers Are Among Us,* 1946) and Wolfgang Liebeneiner's *Liebe '47* (*Love '47,* 1949) are typical of the period in their bleak pessimism and acidulous view of the perils of human existence.

The vast majority of films of the 1950s in Germany were simply escapist entertainment, designed to take people's minds off the privations of daily living. But after 1955, as rearmament was finally permitted, German movies began to reflect a revisionist history of World War II, in which average citizens were simply the pawns of the Nazi hierarchy. Films that depicted acts of resistance against the Nazi regime, as well as the futility of war, were also being produced, as Germany struggled to find its moral compass in the Cold War era. One such antiwar film was Bernhard Wicki's *Die Brücke* (*The Bridge,* 1959), set in the last days of the Nazi regime, as a group of Hitler Youth try to defend a bridge from Allied attacks in an act of complete uselessness; the film won an Academy Award for Best Foreign Language Film. In

East Germany, a series of highly popular musicals kept audiences entertained, such as Hans Heinrich's *Meine Frau macht Musik* (*My Wife Wants to Sing,* 1958), which mixed escapist entertainment with mild doses of ideological propaganda. In addition, West Germany was becoming a thriving low-cost production center after the end of the war and hosted at least one American television series, "Flash Gordon," for thirty-nine episodes from 1954 to 1955.

THE EASTERN EUROPEAN BLOC

In Czechoslovakia, the animator Karel Zeman created a series of elegantly crafted feature films that deftly mixed live action, animation, and stop-motion figures to create a blend of realism and fantasy in *Poklad Ptacího ostrova* (*The Treasure of Bird Island,* 1953), *Cesta do praveku* (*Journey to the Beginning of Time,* 1955), and *Vynález zkázy* (*The Fabulous World of Jules Verne,* 1958), which received international distribution. The last film is an especially intriguing project, combining live action with a series of steel-engraved backdrops to give the illusion of a nineteenth-century illustration come to life. Also in Czechoslovakia, the puppeteer Jirí Trnka made a series of internationally

A mysterious submarine in Czech animator Karel Zeman's *Vynález zkázy* (*The Fabulous World of Jules Verne,* 1958).

234

Zbigniew Cybulski, "the Polish James Dean," as Maciek, a confused young partisan fighting against his own instinct for violence in Andrzej Wajda's *Popiól i diament* (*Ashes and Diamonds*, 1958).

renowned short films that featured state-of-the-art stop-motion animation along with live-action photography, such as *O zlaté rybce* (*The Golden Fish*, 1951), *Dobrý voják Svejk* (*The Good Soldier Schweik*, 1955), and *Sen noci svatojanske* (*A Midsummer Night's Dream*, 1959). In the Soviet Union, Stalin's death led to the beginnings of a new openness in Russian cinema, with Grigori Chukhrai's *Ballada o soldate* (*Ballad of a Soldier*, 1959) one of the most popular films of the era, both at home and abroad.

In Poland, Andrzej Wajda's *Popiól i diament* (*Ashes and Diamonds*, 1958) gave a new face to postwar alienation, that of Zbigniew Cybulski, whose brooding performance in the film earned him the nickname "the Polish James Dean." Set on the last day of the war in May 1945, *Ashes and Diamonds* focuses on the conflict between the Nationalists, guerrilla fighters who want to take back the country for Poles, and the Communists, who seek to add Poland to the ever-expanding Soviet Bloc. As the Nationalist triggerman Maciek, Cybulski conveys a sense of existential despair in all his actions, despite his love for another Nationalist sympathizer, Krystyna (Ewa Krzyzewska), with whom he spends a few stolen hours in a vain attempt to lend some meaning to his life. Maciek's assignment is to shoot Szczuka (Waclaw Zastrzezynski), the Communist Party secretary. When Maciek finally catches up with Szczuka and shoots him, the sky above Maciek suddenly explodes in a barrage of fireworks, as an ironic counterpoint to the murder Maciek has just committed. At the film's end, however, Maciek falls to his death in a gesture of ultimate futility; in Wajda's film, violence begets only violence and solves nothing. Wajda's other 1950s films in Poland, including his debut film *Pokolenie* (*A Generation,* 1955) and *Kanal* (1957), are similarly fatalistic. *A Generation* deals persuasively with the alienation of postwar Polish youth, while *Kanal* deals with the last days of the September 1944 Warsaw uprising against the Nazis in a typically brutal fashion. Wajda would later become a key filmmaker in Poland's Solidarity movement in the early 1980s with his film *Czlowiek z zelaza* (*Man of Iron,* 1981), which favorably depicted the pro-democracy movement's formative days.

CANADA

Canada remained a minor force in film production in the 1950s, due in part to its proximity to the United States and access to Hollywood product. Seeing that it could not compete in the feature-film market, Canadians instead focused on documentaries, shorts, and cartoons created by the National Film Board of Canada, which was inaugurated in 1939 under the leadership of John Grierson, the British documentarist who had been the director of the General Post Office film unit in England in the 1930s. In the 1950s, the National Film Board's biggest star was Norman McLaren, a Scottish animator who emigrated to Canada in 1941 after living in the United States. McLaren's specialty was what he termed "direct cinema," painting directly on clear 35 mm film with a variety of paints and inks to create a series of sensuous, simmering abstract animations. His 1952 anti-nuclear war film *Neighbours* (a k a *Voisins*) won an Academy Award for the Best Documentary (Short Subject), much to the surprise of many observers at the time. In the atmosphere of paranoia and mistrust that typified Cold War tensions, McLaren's parable of two neighbors who come to blows over a flower located on a property line conveyed an unambiguously pacifist message. To make the film, he used live actors but treated them like stop-motion puppets, manipulating their hands, heads, and feet to create jerky, uneven movements. McLaren's other key films of the 1950s in Canada include *Blinkity Blank* (1955), *Rhythmetic* (co-directed with Evelyn Lambart, 1956), *A Chairy Tale* (a k a *Il était une chaise,* co-directed with Claude Jutra, 1957), and *Short and Suite* (1959).

236

EGYPT

In Egypt, 1950 saw the country's first color production, *Baba Areess* (*Father Wants a Wife*), directed by Hussein Fawzi, a typically escapist light comedy. However, the revolution of 23 July 1952 brought the collapse of the exceptionally corrupt reign of King Farouk, and almost immediately a new cinema sprang up, reflecting a renewed spirit of hopeful nationalism. Such films as the bluntly titled *Yascot el istemar* (*Down with Imperialism*, 1953), directed by Hussein Sedki, signaled a new sense of cultural identity in the Arab world, and Youssef Chahine, who would later go on to a major career in the Arab cinema, also directed films designed to raise the country's political consciousness, such as *Siraa Fil-Wadi* (*Struggle in the Valley*, 1954), which starred a young Omar Sharif. At the same time, quickly produced comedies, thrillers, and crime films were also popular with audiences, as a respite from the more overtly political films. The Egyptian industry dominated Arab film of the early 1950s, partly because the technical facilities used to make Egyptian films had been commandeered from the British government as a side effect of the 1952 revolution. Musical comedies with a romance theme remained enormously popular with local audiences, along with melodramas, farces, and comedy revues, essentially photographed music hall variety shows.

*   *   *

The 1950s was thus a decade of dynamic change on the international scene, marked by technological and artistic advances as well as changing political alliances and the beginning of the end of colonial rule. Eastern Europe was still firmly under the thumb of the Soviet bloc, and Chinese cinema was relegated for the most part to Maoist propaganda. But in Italy, France, Great Britain, Japan, and elsewhere, the cinema was undergoing a process of intense nationalization, in which countries vied with each other to create an individual cinema that spoke to each country's sovereign interests, in a way that was both commercially and aesthetically viable. Monopack color film freed the world's filmmakers from reliance on three-strip Technicolor, and lighter cameras capable of producing studio-quality imagery proliferated. The national film schools in Italy, the Soviet Union, and France churned out hundreds of graduates, eager and ready to make their marks on the cinema.

In a world before the Internet and the Web, where telephones and telegrams were the speediest methods of communication and the fax had not yet been invented, cinema offered an immediacy of ideas and entertainment that no other medium could match. Although television was ubiquitous in the United States, the rest of the world was only beginning to use the new technology; even as late as 1960, American television was still mostly in black-and-white, with color reserved for special programming. Videotape was in its infancy, using enormous machines that ran two-inch tapes in a straight run without editing; the technology had only existed in the United States since 1954, the same year that color first came to American television. The hold of the cinema on the world's populace was absolute, and a clamoring international audience demanded increased production. But in many ways, cinema had yet to break free of the syntax imposed upon it by the introduction of sound; the visual element, in many cases, was employed almost exclusively in the service of the narrative. The 1960s would change all that, with a revolution in cinema that would spread throughout the world, literally changing the language of film. This revolution would start in France, with the creation of the Nouvelle Vague, better known as the New Wave.

EIGHT

THE 1960S EXPLOSION

THE FRENCH NEW WAVE

The 1960s really began in 1959 with the films of the French New Wave, which had been in its formative stages since Agnès Varda's *La Pointe Courte* and Roger Vadim's *And God Created Woman* (both 1956). The first time the term "New Wave" appeared was on 3 October 1957 in *L'Express,* as the title of Françoise Girond's article on French youth. The following year, Girond published a book entitled *The New Wave: Portrait of Today's Youth,* dealing not with cinema but with political and social issues. Pierre Billard also used the term in the journal *Cinéma 58,* as a means to describe the fervor for a rejuvenated cinema. By 1959, the expression "the New Wave" was used repeatedly at the Cannes Film Festival. By 1960, it was a fully popularized term that described an important film movement originating in France.

It is impossible to name the first French New Wave film, much less the first French New Wave director, because the New Wave exploded simultaneously with the production of a number of short films and features, many of which did not receive wide distribution. But despite the complexity of the birth of the New Wave, most historians agree that within France, at least, a burgeoning collection of talented young critics-turned-filmmakers began producing a new kind of cinema. In particular, Pierre Braunberger, who ran a small production studio called Les Films de la Pléiade, played a strong role as a nurturer and backer of short films produced in the late fifties and directed by the likes of Jean Rouch, Alain Resnais, François Truffaut, Maurice Pialat, Jacques Rivette, and Eric Rohmer. Braunberger had known these and other young cinema critics since his involvement with film "cine-clubs" such as Objectif 49, and later he was close with the staff of *Cahiers du Cinéma,* which in turn inspired the work of Truffaut and Godard. Other groundbreaking New Wave directors include Varda, Vadim, Alexandre Astruc, Claude Chabrol, Louis Malle, Chris Marker, and Georges Franju.

The feature films these directors created were simultaneously original and daring, changing audience expectations almost overnight. Because of their international acclaim the explosion hardly stopped in France; instead, it spread throughout the world, fueled by the availability of cheap 16 mm prints, lightweight sync-sound cameras, portable projectors, and a network of film societies and film journals that encouraged nearly everyone to pick up a camera. Soon, national cinemas were springing up throughout the world.

François Truffaut

François Truffaut was the supreme romanticist as well as the most commercially successful director of the movement. After a series of short films, he made his first feature, *Les Quatre Cents Coups* (*The 400 Blows*), in 1959, a semi-autobiographical account of his own childhood. Starring the talented Jean-Pierre Léaud, the film deals frankly with the joy and pain of adolescence in which the lead character struggles to find his own identity in a world of uncomprehending parents, hostile teachers, and intractable authority. With an immediate success, Truffaut went on to create the existential gangster comedy *Tirez sur le pianiste* (*Shoot the Piano Player*, 1960), the ineffably romantic love story *Jules et Jim* (*Jules and Jim*, 1962), the revenge drama *La Peau douce* (*The Soft Skin*,

François Truffaut (third from left, foreground) shooting on location in Paris in the early 1960s.

1964), and then went to England to create his only English-language film, the futuristic science fiction parable *Fahrenheit 451* (1966), based on the Ray Bradbury novel.

Truffaut's visual style is a combination of experimental and classical techniques, and like all the directors of the New Wave, he relied on handheld cinematography, location shooting, and sophisticated editorial structures—freeze-frames, optical zooms, and rapid intercutting—to create a new, more self-conscious, cinematic grammar. Ultimately he came to embrace the domain of classical studio cinema in such films as *La Nuit Américaine* (*Day for Night*, 1973), about the behind-the-scenes world of the cinema. Truffaut's other films of note include the homage to Hitchcock,

Linda (Julie Christie) and her husband, Guy Montag, the fireman (Oskar Werner), at home in François Truffaut's adaptation of Ray Bradbury's classic *Fahrenheit 451* (1966), depicting a future society in which books are outlawed.

La Mariée était en noir (*The Bride Wore Black*) and *Baisers volés* (*Stolen Kisses*), both from 1968; *L'Enfant sauvage* (*The Wild Child,* 1970), in which Truffaut also starred as a sympathetic doctor trying to teach basic social skills to a child raised outside of civilization; *Les Deux Anglaises et le continent* (*Two English Girls,* 1971), a romantic period piece in the spirit of *Jules and Jim; L'Histoire d'Adèle H.* (*The Story of Adele H.,* 1975), a story of obsessive love set in nineteenth-century Halifax; the French Resistance drama *Le Dernier Métro* (*The Last Metro,* 1980), one of Truffaut's finest late films; and the thriller *Vivement dimanche!* (*Confidentially Yours,* 1983), his last production. He also collaborated with his idol Alfred Hitchcock on a superb 1967 book-length interview entitled *Hitchcock/Truffaut,* analyzing Hitchcock's films using hundreds of photos and frame enlargements, and played the role of Professor Claude Lacombe in Steven Spielberg's *Close Encounters of the Third Kind* (1977). Truffaut's romantic vision in all his films is one of love, loss, and remembrance, a vision that gives us the world not necessarily as it is, but as we would like to have it.

Jean-Luc Godard

Jean-Luc Godard was the firebrand of the movement. His first feature film, *À bout de souffle* (*Breathless,* 1960), was shot for a pittance, using natural lighting, wheelchair dollies (Godard simply put his cameraman in a wheel-

Director Jean-Luc Godard, one of the major architects of the New Wave, in the early 1960s.

chair and pushed him around the set to create tracking shots), and fragments of a script to tell the story of a smalltime punk (Jean-Paul Belmondo) who kills a policeman and must run for his life until he is betrayed by his girlfriend (Jean Seberg). Dedicated to the Hollywood studio Monogram Pictures, famous for its low-budget films, *Breathless* was Godard's most successful film commercially, but it is also his most conventional. Almost immediately, he began to abandon narrative and traditional Hollywood syntax to create a political cinema.

Jean-Paul Belmondo and Jean Seberg in Jean-Luc Godard's groundbreaking New Wave debut, *À bout de souffle* (*Breathless*, 1960).

243

Le Petit Soldat (*The Little Soldier*, 1960; released 1963) is a political thriller about French involvement in Algeria, shot (like *Breathless*) in 35 mm silent black-and-white with sound added in post-synchronization. The stark, newsreel look of the film, plus the explicit torture sequences, signaled that Godard was interested in being much more than an entertainer; in this, his second feature, he was already engaged in serious social commentary. The film was shot on the rain-swept streets of Geneva and Zurich in April and May 1960 and was immediately banned by both the French Censor Board and the Minister of Information; finally, after cuts and intense negotiations, the film was released three years later. It was still so incendiary, however, that no U.S. distributor would touch it; it was two more years before its American premiere at the New York Film Festival.

With typical perverseness, Godard's next feature, *Une femme est une femme* (*A Woman Is a Woman*, 1961), is a Techniscope, Eastman Color romantic comedy, about as far away from *Le Petit Soldat* as one can get, but not surprisingly Godard undermined the inherent artificiality of the genre by insisting that all the performers use their street clothes in the film, keeping music to a minimum, and shooting the entire film in a rather drab, flat style, essentially cutting against the grain of the material. *Vivre sa vie: Film en douze tableaux* (*My Life to Live*, 1962), however, is a much more deeply considered film, detailing the life of a prostitute, Nana Kleinfrankenheim (Anna Karina, Godard's wife at the time). Structured as a series of vignettes, the film charts Nana's initiation into "the life," her downward spiral, and eventually her murder, as part of an underworld deal gone wrong. Much of the material in the film is clearly improvised, as in *Breathless*, but in these early works Godard abandoned traditional narrative structure to present a series of incidents that, when viewed together, offer greater insight and are far more compelling in their intensity than the usual three-act screenplay structure.

Les Carabiniers (*The Soldiers*, 1963), on the other hand, is a return to political commentary, as two mercenaries, Ulysses (Marino Masé) and Michel-Ange (Albert Juross), sign up to fight in an absurdist war and send back home cryptic postcards with Nazi slogans as a record of their adventure. Again, the film aroused a storm of protest, and it was not screened in the United States until 1967 at the New York Film Festival. With *Le Mépris* (*Contempt*, 1963), one of his most dazzling early films, Godard documents the collapse of the marriage of screenwriter Paul Javal (Michel Piccoli) and his wife, Camille (Brigitte Bardot). Paul works as a writer-for-hire on a film version of Homer's *Odyssey*, which is directed by Fritz Lang (playing himself)

and produced by the egomaniacal Jeremy Prokosch (Jack Palance). Godard's intense admiration for Lang's films is clearly evident in *Contempt;* indeed, Godard appears as Lang's assistant director on the *Odyssey* film-within-the-

Michel Piccoli, Fritz Lang, and Jack Palance relax on the set of Jean-Luc Godard's *Le Mépris* (*Contempt,* 1963), a film about the pressures of filmmaking and the collapse of a marriage that has been tested by modern life.

film, bustling about the set, barking orders to the crew. Shooting on location in Rome and Capri during the spring and summer of 1963 in Technicolor and Franscope (similar to CinemaScope), Godard made full use of his lavish budget (about $900,000, his most expensive film to date), and created one of the most penetrating films ever made about the difficulties of relationships between women and men, as well as one of the finest films about the making of a film. Although the film was butchered upon its release in Italy, the original film has now been restored on DVD.

Alphaville, une étrange aventure de Lemmy Caution (*Alphaville,* 1965) is a science fiction parable about a world ruled by a giant computer that deprives citizens of free will and turns them into ideological zombies. *Pierrot le fou* (*Pierrot the Fool,* 1965) marks a return to color, in a tale of love on the run in the south of France, as Ferdinand (Jean-Paul Belmondo) and Marianne (Anna Karina) attempt to escape from Ferdinand's wife and a group of shadowy gangsters in pursuit of Marianne. The film is stunningly designed in bold, primary colors, and is again composed in set pieces rather than as a

Natacha Von Braun (Anna Karina) meets secret agent Lemmy Caution (Eddie Constantine) in Jean-Luc Godard's political science fiction film *Alphaville, une étrange aventure de Lemmy Caution* (*Alphaville*, 1965).

linear narrative. American director Samuel Fuller plays himself in a famous party scene, in which he expounds on his theory of cinema. Most of *Pierrot le fou* was improvised, with very little in the way of a script; as Godard said, "I just write out the strong moments of the film, and that gives me a kind of frame of seven or eight points. . . . The whole ending was invented on the spot. . . . Two days before I began I had nothing, absolutely nothing." And yet the finished film is powerful, cohesive, and very funny.

In the summer of 1966, Godard agreed to make two films almost simultaneously, one shot in the morning, and the other in the afternoon, to satisfy producers and distributors who were hungrily awaiting his next film; by this time, Godard had become a cult figure. In fact, the shooting of the films overlapped only by about a week, but it was still a remarkable achievement. The first, *Made in U.S.A.*, was ironically never generally distributed in the United States (with but one screening at the New York Film Festival in 1967), because Godard based the film on a book for which he did not have the rights. The second, *2 ou 3 choses que je sais d'elle* (*Two or Three Things I Know About Her*, 1967), explores the life of a Parisian housewife who turns to prostitution to make ends meet; this film also never received commercial American distribution, except for a screening at the New York Film Festival in 1968. Both, however, were widely shown clandestinely on college campuses, as well as in museums, art galleries, and film societies, and had a pro-

246

Corinne (Mireille Darc) is held at gunpoint by a band of cannibalistic revolutionaries in Jean-Luc Godard's violent satire of modern life, *Weekend* (1967).

found effect on filmmakers worldwide. *Two or Three Things* is particularly interesting because of its direct political commentary, the absolute fragmentation of narrative, and Godard's increasing impatience with any aspect of traditional film form, using slogans, intertitles, product shots as in a commercial, and voiceovers to create a scathing critique of consumer society.

Godard's *La Chinoise* (literally, *The Chinese Girl,* 1967), a political tract about a group of young university students in Paris who have fallen under the sway of Maoist Marxism, is thought by many observers to have been a harbinger of the "Events of May" in 1968, when students and workers rioted against the government of Charles de Gaulle and brought the country to a complete standstill. In *Weekend* (1967), Godard created his most ambitious vision of modern life as hell on earth, a savage satire in which a husband, Roland (Jean Yanne), and wife, Corinne (Mireille Darc), who are trying to kill one another, travel the length of France in an apocalyptic near-future to extort some money from a dying relative. The roads, streets, and highways are littered with dead bodies and wrecked cars; in one scene with a grisly traffic pileup, Corinne and Roland pass by without even looking back.

In the 1970s Godard temporarily abandoned commercial filmmaking to form the Dziga Vertov Collective (or Groupe Dziga Vertov, named after the famed Soviet political filmmaker of the 1920s), creating a series of 16 mm agit-prop films. It was not until the early 1980s that he returned to his former milieu. But in the sixties it was Godard, more than any other director, who defined the era as a rebellious, adventurous decade of social, sexual, political, and artistic exploration; his films were shown around the world as political tracts, organizing manifestoes, and provocative artistic statements that galvanized a new generation of filmmakers.

Alain Resnais

Alain Resnais made his first feature, *Hiroshima mon amour* (*Hiroshima, My Love*, 1959), from a script by the gifted Marguerite Duras, about a young man and woman who meet in Hiroshima by chance and have a brief affair. He is Japanese and she is French. Throughout *Hiroshima mon amour*, the characters are referred to only as "she" and "he." As the film concludes, we realize that both are really the embodiment of their respective countries; she is Nevers, in France, and he is Hiroshima, in Japan; the figurative embodiment of two cultures that collided with devastating consequences during World War II.

Resnais followed this with the memorable cinematic puzzle *L'Année dernière à Marienbad* (*Last Year at Marienbad*, 1961), in which a man and woman meet in a grand, mysterious hotel and engage in a series of reminiscences about their past affair—or did the affair ever occur? Structured in a series of flashbacks and designed

Emmanuelle Riva and Eiji Okada as two lovers in Alain Resnais's *Hiroshima Mon Amour* (*Hiroshima, My Love*, 1959).

Delphine Seyrig as "A" and Giorgio Albertazzi as "X" in Alain Resnais's existential parable *L'Année dernière à Marienbad* (*Last Year at Marienbad*, 1961).

as a series of elegant tracking shots through the palatial grounds of the cavernous, crumbling hotel, *Last Year at Marienbad* is ultimately a riddle without a solution. It was nominated for numerous awards and won the Golden Lion at the 1961 Venice Festival. Resnais's other great film of the 1960s, *Muriel ou Le temps d'un retour* (*Muriel, or The Time of Return*, 1963), is an oblique commentary on France's involvement in Algeria, in which a young man can't forget his complicity in the torture and subsequent death of a young woman, Muriel, during the war in Algeria. Again manipulating space and time, Resnais uses what he termed "memory editing," cutting between the past and the present, memory and reality, to create a haunting document of conscience and loss that lays bare the mechanisms of war, colonialism, and suppressed atrocity. *La Guerre est finie* (*The War Is Over*, 1966) and *Je t'aime, je t'aime* (*I Love You, I Love You*, 1968) are more conventional and do not approach the power of his earlier work.

Claude Chabrol

Known informally as "the French Hitchcock," Claude Chabrol, another member of the *Cahiers du Cinéma* group, entered filmmaking promisingly with *Le Beau Serge* (*Bitter Reunion*, 1958) and *Les Cousins* (*The Cousins*, 1959), but he soon became identified with a string of stylish, highly commercial thrillers. Films such as *Le Scandale* (*The Champagne Murders,* 1967, shot in both French and English versions), *Les Biches* (*The Does,* 1968), and *La Femme infidèle* (*The Unfaithful Wife,* 1969) were marked by technical mastery and a certain cool precision that made Chabrol perhaps the most traditional of all the New Wave directors.

His other key films include the psychological crime thriller *Le Boucher* (*The Butcher,* 1970), in which a young schoolteacher, Hélène (Stéphane Audran, then married to Chabrol) meets a lonely butcher, Popaul (Jean Yanne), in a small French village. While their relationship deepens, Chabrol frames this unlikely romance against a series of murders of young girls, in which Popaul rapidly becomes a suspect. Is he guilty, or is it circumstance? Chabrol keeps the audience on the edges of their seats, offering tantalizing clues that may or may not implicate Popaul. Another major Chabrol film, *La Rupture* (*The Breakup,* 1970), presents a brutally funny examination of family life in which a young housewife (Stéphane Audran again) is nearly strangled by her out-of-control husband (Jean-Claude Drouot) during breakfast, only to respond by hitting him over the head with a frying pan to protect her young son from her husband's violence. Chabrol weaves a complex tapestry of sinister family interconnections as the film progresses, even tossing LSD into the mix in the final moments. All this is played for mordant humor, with an air of cynical detachment, as if Chabrol is almost fond of the monsters he presents on screen. His cold, calculating vision is centered on the family as the root of all evil, and in later works, such as *La Cérémonie* (*The Ceremony,* a k a *A Judgment in Stone,* 1995) and *La Fleur du mal* (*The Flower of Evil,* 2003), he continued his investigation into the dark regions of the heart while maintaining his position as a highly bankable and somewhat old-school director. Chabrol died in 2010; his last film was *Bellamy* (2009).

Other New Wave Directors

Eric Rohmer, perhaps the most cerebral of the New Wave directors, made his feature-length directorial debut in 1959 with *Le Signe du lion* (*The Sign of the Lion*), but found his mature, contemplative style in such later films as *La Collectionneuse* (*The Collector,* 1967), *Ma Nuit chez Maud* (*My Night at Maud's,* 1969), and *Le Genou de Claire* (*Claire's Knee,* 1970), in which his characters are involved in complex moral and romantic situations that typically resolve themselves in an unexpected manner. His films were created in cycles: his "Six Moral Tales" runs from 1962 to 1972, and his "Comedies and Proverbs" group was completed between 1980 and 1987. Rohmer's camera movement recalls the rigorous compositions of Ozu and Bresson. He was as romantic and precise in his scenarios (he wrote the screenplays for all his films) as either of these two great directors, and he allowed his actors great latitude to get to the emotional core of the material. Like Chabrol, Rohmer, sadly, died in 2010.

Documentarist Chris Marker made a definitive mark with *La Jetée* (*The Pier*, 1963), a short time-travel science fiction film composed almost entirely of still photographs (there is only one "moving" shot in the film, which is almost imperceptible) that delivers a fatalist message about the circular inevitability of nuclear war. *La Jetée* won the Prix Jean Vigo for its daring theme and inventive structure, and later served as the basis for Terry Gilliam's *Twelve Monkeys* (1995). Marker continued with such films as *Le Joli Mai* (*Lovely May*, 1963), a documentary questioning average Parisians about the effects of the Algerian War; *Le Mystère Koumiko* (*The Koumiko Mystery*, 1965), a deeply personal documentary view of a young Japanese woman's life during the 1964 Tokyo Olympics; and such later films as the spellbinding *Sans soleil* (*Sunless*, 1983), a sort of ritualized documentary in which the camera travels to the four corners of the earth to bring back images and words that evoke the essence of time, reflection, and memory.

After her groundbreaking work on *La Pointe Courte* and her follow-up *Cleo from 5 to 7*, Agnès Varda made the beautiful but chilling *Le Bonheur* (*Happiness*, 1965), in which a young couple lives an idyllic life in the French countryside until the husband falls in love with another woman. He tells his wife and she drowns herself in a lake as a result. Then Varda presents us with the shocking conclusion: the husband marries his mistress, who takes the place of his wife as though she had never existed. The children adore their new "mother," her husband worships her, and life goes on much as before. Varda is clearly suggesting that in contemporary French society, women are merely replaceable objects, to be dispensed with at whim. Shot in richly saturated color, bursting with light and sunshine, *Le Bonheur* may be the most beautiful "horror" film ever made.

Louis Malle began his career with underwater explorer Jacques-Yves Cousteau's documentary *Le Monde du Silence* (*The Silent World*, 1956), which Malle co-directed. After working as Robert Bresson's assistant on *A Man Escaped* (1956), he made his feature debut with the complex crime thriller *Ascenseur pour l'échafaud* (*Elevator to the Gallows*, a k a *Frantic*, 1958), with Jeanne Moreau and Maurice Ronet. The film was largely shot on the streets of Paris and sports a gorgeous score improvised by Miles Davis in one all-night jam session. A bizarre comedy, *Zazie dans le métro* (*Zazie in the*

A "perfect murder" starts to unravel in director Louis Malle's first feature film, *Ascenseur pour l'échafaud* (*Elevator to the Gallows*, a k a *Frantic*, 1958).

Subway, 1960), followed, and then the English language *A Very Private Affair* (*Vie privée*, 1962), a part-fiction, part-fact biography of Brigitte Bardot's rise to stardom, starring Bardot as herself.

But these films were overshadowed by the triumph of Malle's 1963 film *Le Feu follet* (*The Fire Within*), a stark drama dealing with the last days of a self-destructive alcoholic, Alain Leroy (Maurice Ronet), who decides to kill himself after one last trip to Paris to see his friends, all of whom try to distance themselves from Alain's suicidal mission. In the end, as promised, Alain makes good on his threat, leaving a simple note: "I have killed myself because you have not loved me." Few films have so effectively conveyed the despair and alienation of modern life, and *The Fire Within* won the Special Jury Prize at the Venice Film Festival. After several lighter films, Malle created an epic seven-part television documentary, *L'Inde fantôme* (*Phantom India*, 1969), and then began to make a series of deeply individualistic films in the early 1970s, including the coming-of-age story *Le Souffle au coeur* (*Murmur of the Heart*, 1971) and the drama *Lacombe Lucien* (1974), about a young boy who joins the occupying Nazi forces in France during World War II when the Resistance turns him down. Louis Malle died in 1995.

Jacques Rivette is one of the most uncompromising of the classical

252

French New Wave directors; he is also one of the most prolific. His first mature film, *Paris nous appartient* (*Paris Is Ours*, 1960), tells the tale of group of young intellectuals in the 1950s caught up in a mysterious tale of suicide, madness, and a production of Shakespeare's *Pericles*. *La Religieuse* (*The Nun*, 1966) was a more mainstream film, starring Anna Karina as a young woman forced into a life in the church, but *L'Amour Fou* (*Mad Love*, 1968) marked a return to Rivette's earlier, uncompromising form. Centering on the disintegrating marriage of a theater director and his wife, with a running time of nearly four hours, *Mad Love* is as unsparing in its chronicle of a relationship in collapse as Godard's *Contempt*. For many, however, Rivette's equally epic *Céline et Julie vont en bateau* (*Celine and Julie Go Boating*, 1974) is the director's key film, a hallucinatory tale of two young women and their evanescent fantasy universe. Rivette had an art house hit with *Va savoir* (*Who Knows?* 2001), another examination of life and theatricality, playing with games of reality and illusion in much the same manner as his earlier work. As with the best New Wave directors, Rivette is absolutely uncompromising in bringing his vision to the screen; the fact that he is able to continue to produce such idiosyncratic films in the hyper-commercial world of the twenty-first century is a testament to his perseverance and artistry.

Beyond the New Wave

In 1968, Jean Renoir appeared in and directed a short film, shot in half a day, *La Direction d'acteur par Jean Renoir* (*The Direction of the Actor by Jean Renoir*). In it, he directs the actress Gisèle Braunberger (to whom the directing credit is sometimes given) in a scene from a Rumer Godden novel, *Breakfast with Nicolaides*. The following year, Renoir directed his final feature, *Le Petit Théâtre de Jean Renoir* (*The Little Theater of Jean Renoir*), released in 1971, with Jeanne Moreau in four sketches that Renoir wrote, directed, and narrated for French television. It was warmly received in the United States, though it was far from the director's most accomplished work. Renoir accepted an honorary Oscar in 1975 for his lifetime achievement in the cinema and in 1977 was inducted into the French Legion of Honor; he died in 1979. His career, stretching from silents to television movies, had encompassed every genre. Along with Jean Cocteau, he remained one of the touchstones of the New Wave filmmakers.

Although not considered a New Wave director, Jean-Pierre Melville had a considerable impact on the filmmakers of the period. His independent films were shot on shoestring budgets, on actual locations, with skeleton crews, and Melville often served as his own cameraman and art director. Melville's noirish *policier Bob le flambeur* (*Bob the Gambler*, 1955), a gritty film about a thief, is alluded to in Godard's *Breathless*. Godard also took note of the economic editing and the stylized violence of *Bob the Gambler*. He admired the seediness of Melville's mise-en-scène, which includes deserted streets, grimy gambling halls, and a dark, urban atmosphere that was both moody and sophisticated. Melville even makes a brief appearance in *Breathless* as a novelist being interviewed by Jean Seberg. Like *Breathless, Bob the Gambler* omits the action sequences that audiences were accustomed to seeing. Off-screen gunshots cleverly suggest a shootout, for example, while careful editing often cuts out violent gunplay. *Bob the Gambler* is a rather flat, cool, and precise *policier* that clearly had a major impact.

Melville's first feature films were about the period of the French Resistance, of which he had been an active member. Made entirely independently, *Le Silence de la mer* (*The Silence of the Sea*, 1949) is an adaptation of a novel about the Resistance. *Léon Morin prêtre* (*Leon Morin, Priest*, 1961) deals with the story of a priest during the Occupation. In 1969, Melville returned to the same territory with *L'Armée des ombres* (*The Shadow Army*). Regarded by some as one of the most historically accurate screen versions of the Resistance, *The Shadow Army* was not screened commercially in the United States until 2006. Inspired by Joseph Kessel's 1943 novel, the film exposes the mixture of courage, tragedy, and often inhumane choices that the members of the Resistance made in order to survive the war. Celebrated for avoiding clichés of the war film, *The Shadow Army* is in many ways Melville's personal story. At the time of its release, however, some critics declared that his actors lacked emotion, and the film was generally panned. Nevertheless, it is remarkable for its lack of melodrama and subdued psychological mood, marking the film with the cold style that distinguishes Melville's oeuvre. It is this cool, flat, almost abstract style that attracted Godard and other New Wave filmmakers and critics.

In 1967, *Le Samourai* (*The Samurai*) was acclaimed as among the finest international thrillers, considered a favorite by directors such as Martin Scorsese, John Woo, and Quentin Tarantino. In the tradition of American film noir, *The Samurai*, about a hit man hired by a mobster to assassinate a nightclub owner, takes place on gray and wet Parisian streets, mostly at night. Jazz musicians are expressionless and police stations are deserted and gloomy. No one can trust anyone and the plot has all the requisite twists, turns, and double crosses expected from Melville's bleak worldview. Though some are turned off by Melville's coldness, most celebrate the film for its distinctively cruel and dark pessimism. Like many Melville films, *The Samurai* omits exciting visuals such as car crashes and explosions, thus allowing viewers to use their own imaginations. It is an existential gangster movie that is very much about the psychology of the outsider figure.

INGMAR BERGMAN

Sweden's Ingmar Bergman continued his exploration of the depths of the human psyche in a stunning series of films that included *Såsom i en spegel* (*Through a Glass Darkly*, 1961), *Nattvardsgästerna* (*Winter Light*, 1962), and *Tystnaden* (*The Silence*, 1963), a trilogy that interrogates the meaning of human existence in a hostile and uncomprehending world. Bergman then took a giant step forward with the shattering *Persona* (1966), in which two women engage in a life-or-death battle of wills. Elisabeth Vogler (Liv Ullmann), a stage actress of great renown, suddenly and for no apparent reason stops speaking in the

The mute actress Elisabeth Vogler (Liv Ullmann, foreground, in profile) and Nurse Alma (Bibi Andersson) in Ingmar Bergman's psychological study *Persona* (1966).

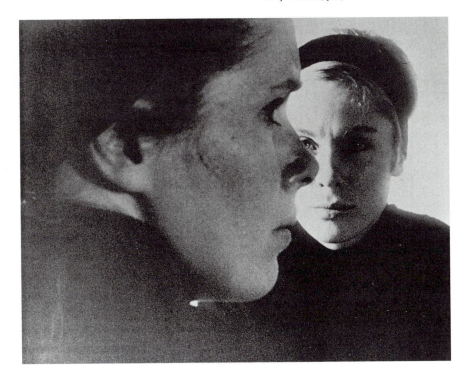

255

middle of a performance. A psychiatrist concludes that since there is nothing physically wrong with Elisabeth, she must simply be refusing to speak, and so sends her home to convalesce with Nurse Alma (Bibi Andersson). Alma, a young and charmingly naive woman, is no match for Elisabeth's strength of will. Treating Elisabeth more as a confidante than as a patient, she incessantly chatters on about her many problems, including an unexpected sexual encounter with a stranger, her subsequent pregnancy, and an abortion. All the while, Elisabeth coolly observes her as if studying for a future role. After Elisabeth writes a letter to a friend detailing Nurse Alma's past sins and childish vulnerability, Alma reads the letter on the way to the post office and realizes that Elisabeth is out to destroy her. From this point on, the film becomes a brutal psychological battle in which the personalities of both women blend into one identity and teeter on the brink of madness.

For Bergman, this is typically harrowing psychic terrain, but what sets *Persona* apart is his unexpectedly audacious visual presentation of the film's narrative. Usually a highly theatrical director, he uses freeze-frames, film rips, shock cuts, slow motion, shot repetition, and clips from classic Swedish films to distance viewers and remind them that the movie is, above all, a visual and aural construct. But more than this, Bergman clearly incorporates the self-reflexivity and cinematic liberation of the New Wave in *Persona*, which opens with the image of the projector's carbon arc lamp being ignited and ends with the arc being extinguished.

Bergman had started shooting the film on a studio set, as was his usual custom, but soon realized that the results were unsatisfactory and began all over again, moving the entire cast and crew (including his superb cinematographer, the gifted Sven Nykvist) to his island home on Fårö, using a local museum to double for the interior hospital sets. The results are remarkable, suggesting an entire break from the past for the director, who now embraced a new intimacy in his work.

In 1970, Bergman made his only English-language film, *The Touch* (*Beröringen,* 1971), starring Max von Sydow, Bibi Andersson, and Elliot Gould, but the film failed to connect with audiences. When Bergman tried to line up an American distributor for his next film, he found, much to his surprise, that he was "unbankable" in the United States because of the commercial failure of *The Touch*. Never mind that he had created a gallery of superb films; in true Hollywood fashion, all that mattered was his last project. After taking *Viskningar och rop* (*Cries and Whispers*) to all the major studios and being turned down flat, Bergman, in a gesture of despair, contacted Roger Corman, who was then running his own company, New World Pictures, out of a small office in Venice, California. Shocked that the majors had turned away one of the cinema's most accomplished artists, Corman immediately agreed over the phone to advance Bergman $100,000 plus a percentage of the profits for the North American distribution rights. Armed with this financing and additional support from the Swedish national film studio, Bergman shot *Cries and Whispers* at a country house for a minimal budget and then turned it over to Corman for American release. To Bergman's delight and astonishment, *Cries and Whispers* (1972) became the biggest financial success of his career to date and reestablished him as a director of the first rank, both critically and commercially. Bergman was then able to continue making films that won him more international acclaim, including the Academy Award winning *Fanny och Alexander* (*Fanny and Alexander*, 1982), which was Bergman's last major work. Retiring to his small house on the island of Fårö, Bergman lived there in relative seclusion until his death in 2007. For his part, Corman continued to serve as the American distributor for foreign films that were being shut out of the increasingly restricted U.S. market, including Fellini's *Amarcord* (1973), Truffaut's *L'Argent de poche* (*Small Change,* 1976), Volker Schlöndorff's *Die Blechtrommel* (*The Tin Drum,* 1979), and Bruce Beresford's *Breaker Morant* (1980).

OTHER SWEDISH DIRECTORS

Another important Swedish director of the 1960s was Mai Zetterling. After an extensive career as an actress, Zetterling made her first short film, *Wargame* (1962) (not to be confused with Peter Watkins's 1965 film *The War Game*), which won a prize at the Venice Film Festival. The film is a brief but effective antiwar parable, as two young boys fight over a toy pistol on the roof of a skyscraper. *Älskande par Loving* (*Couples,* 1964), in which three pregnant women remember, through flashbacks, their past love affairs, and *Nattlek* (*Night Games,* 1966), a dark and brooding film about human sexuality, brought her international recognition as a practitioner of personal cinema. In 1968, Zetterling directed *Flickorna* (*The Girls*), a feminist exploration of three actresses in a production of Aristophanes' *Lysistrata* who become obsessed with the theme of women's oppression off the stage.

Two additional Swedish filmmakers made their mark in the 1960s, Bo Widerberg and Vilgot Sjöman. Widerberg's long career as a director was highlighted by the international success of his tragic nineteenth-century love story, *Elvira Madigan* (1967), in which two young lovers, army officer

Lieutenant Sixten Sparre (Thommy Berggren) and Hedvig Jensen (Pia Degermark), a famous tightrope walker who performs professionally under the name Elvira Madigan, abandon their former lives to run away together. Their romantic idyll starts out in the beauty of full summer, but as the leaves turn Sixten realizes that he must make a choice between life on the run with Elvira or returning to his wife and children. But a return home is impossible: as a deserter from the armed forces, Sixten is subject to court-martial. At length, the two run out of money and Sixten is reduced to stealing food to live. Realizing that their situation is desperate, the couple takes a drastic step in the film's shocking conclusion. Gorgeously photographed by Jörgen Persson in the bucolic Swedish countryside and perfectly matched with music of Mozart, *Elvira Madigan* was a surprise international hit.

Vilgot Sjöman is a different case altogether. He was initially a writer; one of his novels was filmed by Swedish director Gustaf Molander as *Trots* (*Defiance*) in 1952. In 1956, Sjöman attended UCLA's film school on a scholarship. Returning to Sweden, he served as an assistant to Ingmar Bergman on *Winter Light* in 1963 and then began making feature films with *Älskarinnan* (*The Mistress*, 1962) and the taboo-breaking *491* (1964), whose title refers to the number of times Christ told his disciples to forgive those who transgressed against them, "seven times seventy," or 490 times. The 491st sin, however, is another matter. *491* deals with a social worker, Krister (Lars Lind), who is forced to supervise a group of worthless, violent youthful offenders. Despite all efforts, the young men continually violate the rules of society, with disastrous results. *Jag är nyfiken—en film i gult* (*I Am Curious [Yellow]*, 1967) ignited an international debate when it became the first film to graphically depict sexual intercourse as part of a fictional narrative. It was initially banned in both Sweden and the United States, but after a lengthy court battle it was released theatrically, and led to the explicit presentation of sex in American cinema. Sjöman died in 2006.

ITALIAN CINEMA IN THE 1960S

In Italy, Federico Fellini made his first color film, the beautiful *Giulietta degli spiriti* (*Juliet of the Spirits*, 1965), again starring his wife, Giulietta Masina, this time as a woman who is alone and unloved in her marriage while her husband is off having an affair. *Juliet of the Spirits* is deeply sympathetic to the powerlessness of women in 1960s Italian society, but perhaps for this reason it was not well received critically or commercially and failed to make

Giulietta Masina (right), as Juliet, comes to terms with her fantasies in Federico Fellini's first color film, the hallucinatory and gorgeous *Giulietta degli spiriti* (*Juliet of the Spirits*, 1965).

back production costs, nearly bankrupting its producer. Fellini closed out the decade with *Fellini Satyricon* (1969), a hallucinating vision of first-century Rome, in which two young men, Encolpio (Martin Potter) and Ascilto (Hiram Keller), give themselves over to a life of endless decadence. The film's look is sumptuous, but for many it was an empty spectacle, more interested in visual excess than any thematic content.

Michelangelo Antonioni created a series of deeply despairing films of triumphant nihilism during this decade: *L'Avventura* (*The Adventure*, 1960), *La Notte* (*The Night*, 1961), and *L'Eclisse* (*Eclipse*, 1962), in which his protagonists fitfully struggle against the society in which they live in a futile attempt to break free and better their emotional and spiritual condition. Even in his first film in color, *Il Deserto rosso* (*The Red Desert*, 1964), Antonioni suggests that alienation and isolation are the predominant state in the modern world and that all attempts at "meaning" are a waste of time—which is just what his characters do: waste time. Whether watching the approach of dusk in Rome (in *L'Eclisse*), wandering through the city at night in search of something to do (in *La Notte*), or destroying the interior of a boat as a perverse game out of sheer boredom (in *The Red Desert*), his protagonists are possessed of an air of predestined fatalism, born into a world they neither understand nor control. Power, money, influence, friendship, love: all are fleeting, precious, and ultimately unattainable. Like the characters in Samuel Beckett's play *Waiting for Godot*, Antonioni's men and women must wait, and wait, and wait—but for what, they have no idea.

Pier Paolo Pasolini, on the other hand, was just beginning his career, with the near-Neorealist *Accattone* (1961) and *Mamma Roma* (1962), both gritty slices of Italian life with a typically uncompromising view of human existence. Pasolini's breakthrough film, however, was *Il Vangelo secondo Matteo* (*The Gospel According to St. Matthew*, 1964), which stunned critics with its bold, newsreel approach to the life of Christ; many feel it is the most expressive religious film ever made. Shot using nonprofessional actors on the simplest of locations, *Gospel* gives us a Christ at once fiery and compassionate, in touch with the concerns of the world but still not of it, who deals with matters directly and aggressively, sure of his heavenly vocation. As portrayed by nonprofessional Enrique Irazoqui, Pasolini's Christ is above all a man of action whose words flow from his deeds. Pasolini also cast his own mother as the Virgin Mary and surprised viewers of his earlier works with the reverent humanism of his approach to the material. This is all the more surprising when one considers the fact that Pasolini was an atheist, a Marxist, and an early and outspoken gay activist; he dedicated *The Gospel According to St. Matthew* to Pope John XXIII, whom the director felt had brought the Church into the modern era. Honored with three Academy Award nominations, and winner of a Special Jury Prize at the Venice Film Festival, *The Gospel According to St. Matthew* is a direct and accessible life of Christ, as a savior who is open to all.

After creating a violent version of *Edipo re* (*Oedipus Rex*, 1967), Pasolini turned to another religious parable, *Teorema* (*Theorem*, 1968), based on his own novel, and then to versions of *Il Decameron* (*The Decameron*, 1971), *I Racconti di Canterbury* (*The Canterbury Tales*, 1972), and finally, his most despairing film, *Salò o le 120 giornate di Sodoma* (*Salo, or The 120 Days of Sodom*, 1975), a brutal, openly sadistic allegory set in Fascist Italy in 1944. Pasolini was murdered on 2 November 1975 under mysterious circumstances; the violent manner of his death (he was repeatedly run over by his own car) provides an ironic postscript to his controversial career.

Another important Italian director of the period was Pietro Germi, director of *Divorzio all'italiana* (*Divorce, Italian Style*, 1961), a delicious satire of conventional marital values, as well as *Signore & signori* (*The Birds, the Bees*

Oedipus (Franco Citti) in Pier Paolo Pasolini's violent adaptation of Sophocles' *Edipo re* (*Oedipus Rex*, 1967).

and the Italians, 1965). Elio Petri's *La Decima vittima* (*The 10th Victim*, 1965) is a futuristic science fiction comedy that takes place in a world where war has been outlawed, but not murder—provided, that is, that both parties agree to try to murder each other as part of an international game called "The Hunt." Marcello Mastroianni and Ursula Andress appear as veterans of the game, chasing each other through a variety of homicidal escapades, only to fall in love at the last possible moment.

Petri's *Indagine su un cittadino al di sopra di ogni sospetto* (*Investigation of a Citizen Above Suspicion*, 1970) is a much more somber work, which won an Academy Award as Best Foreign Language Film. Gian Maria Volontè plays an unnamed police inspector in Fascist Italy who kills his mistress, then misdirects the official inquiry into her murder with false evidence. The police suspect the inspector but fail to arrest him because of his social position. Gillo Pontecorvo's *La Battaglia di Algeri* (*The Battle of Algiers*, 1966) is an Italian/Algerian co-production that examines the Algerian War against French colonialism, told in flashbacks to 1954, when the battle began in earnest. Shot in a grainy, black-and-white newsreel style, *The Battle of Algiers* looks more like a documentary than a staged film. Attacked by many as being

The old aristocracy fades in Luchino Visconti's *Il Gattopardo* (*The Leopard,* 1963), featuring Burt Lancaster.

Dirk Bogarde as the doomed Gustav von Aschenbach in Luchino Visconti's *Morte a Venezia* (*Death in Venice,* 1971).

too explicit in its methodology, as if it were intended to be a blueprint for revolutionary resistance, the film uses nonprofessional actors to create a realistic and devastating effect. Indeed, looking at many of the films in this section, we can see that the influence of Neorealism remained strong twenty years after Rossellini's *Open City*; the use of actual locations, black-and-white film, nonprofessional actors, and handheld camerawork lends *The Battle of Algiers, The Gospel According to St. Matthew,* and other 1960s Italian films a veracity and authenticity that more polished films lack.

Luchino Visconti continued his fascination with corruption, decadence, and power in *Il Gattopardo* (*The Leopard,* 1963), in which Burt Lancaster plays an aging nobleman whom time has passed by, and *La Caduta degli dei* (*The Damned,* 1969), which documents the downfall of a German munitions dynasty during the Third Reich, featuring Dirk Bogarde. As the decade came to a close, Visconti would cast Bogarde as the aging Gustav von Aschenbach in his adaptation of Thomas Mann's novella *Death in Venice* (1971). Von Aschenbach, on vacation in Venice, becomes hopelessly obsessed with the handsome young man Tadzio (Bjørn Andresen), failing to notice that all around

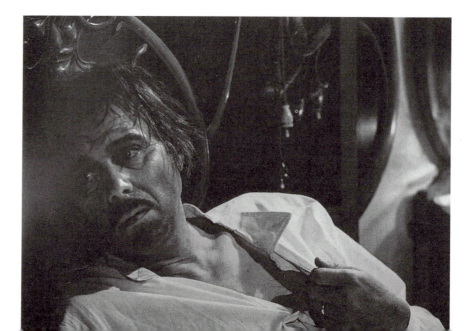

Clint Eastwood shoots it out in Sergio Leone's *Per un pugno di dollari* (*A Fistful of Dollars,* 1964), the film that kicked off the spaghetti western cycle in the early 1960s, immediately established Eastwood as a star, and revitalized the western genre.

him the other resort guests are dying off one by one as the result of a cholera epidemic. Bogarde's performance is a model of tact and humility, and Visconti brings the period alive with just the right amount of Baroque orna-mentation. Regarded as a disappointment when first re-leased, the film, like so many others, has attained classic status over the years. Visconti died in 1976.

On a more commercial level, Mario Bava and Sergio Leone stand out. Bava, originally a cameraman from the 1930s onward, created some of the most beautifully photographed horror and fantasy films of the era, such as *Black Sunday* (*La Maschera del demonio,* 1960), *Blood and Black Lace* (*Sei donne per l'assassino,* 1964), and *Planet of the Vampires* (a k a *Planet of Blood;* original title *Terrore nello spazio,* 1965). This last film's phantasmal sets seem to be an inspiration for the look of Ridley Scott's *Alien* (1979), particularly in the design of the alien spaceship. Sergio Leone, on the other hand, made his name by reinventing the western genre with a series of brutal films star-ring Clint Eastwood that came to be known as "spaghetti westerns," such as *Per un pugno di dollari* (*A Fistful of Dollars,* 1964), which was a remake of Akira Kurosawa's *Yojimbo* (1961). The spaghetti western revived the mori-bund American frontier myth-cycle of the traditional western; Leone's for-mula was to strip the dialogue and motivation down to nothing and simply allow events to happen, with massive doses of sadism and violence. His bravura style in *A Fistful of Dollars* depended on exaggerated wide shots and extreme close-ups, which edited together creates a tension that brings the film's brutality to the forefront. Leone's subsequent films, *Per qualche dollaro in più* (*For a Few Dollars More*, 1965) and *Il Buono, il brutto, il cattivo* (*The Good, the Bad, and the Ugly*, 1966), carried on the operatic tradition of the first film in the "Man with No Name" series, a group of exceptionally violent and aggressively visual westerns with little dialogue or character motivation that made Eastwood, then a relatively unknown television actor, into an international star.

As his style matured, Leone became more elegiac and sweeping in his embrace of the western formula, reaching his apotheosis in the epic *Once Upon a Time in the West* (1968), a 165-minute paean to the genre (reduced to 140 minutes for its original U.S. release) with an enormous cast, including Charles Bronson, Claudia Cardinale, Jason Robards, Woody Strode, and Henry Fonda cast against type as a ruthless killer. Leone followed this film with a series of increasingly personal projects, culminating in the similarly ambitious *Once Upon a Time in America* (1984), an epic gangster film starring Robert De Niro, James Woods, Tuesday Weld, and Joe Pesci. Originally clocking in at 227 minutes, the film was savagely cut to 139 minutes for its first U.S. release but still retained much of the grandeur of the material. (Both *Once Upon a Time* movies have been restored to their original lengths for DVD release.) Leone died in 1989.

ENGLAND IN THE 1960S

In England, the Free Cinema movement, pioneered by Lindsay Anderson, Karel Reisz, and Tony Richardson, was a direct response to the New Wave in France. The movement had been inaugurated in 1954, and as with the *Cahiers du Cinéma* group, all three men began their careers as critics and then branched out into documentaries dealing with emerging postwar British society. Anderson, one of the most idiosyncratic and individual directors of the movement, directed *O Dreamland* (1953), about Margate, a British amusement park; *Every Day Except Christmas* (1957), depicting the Covent Garden market; and *Thursday's Children* (1954), about a school for deaf children, which won an Academy Award for Best Documentary Short. Reisz and Richardson co-directed *Momma Don't Allow* (1955), about a night at a jazz club. Next came the "Kitchen Sink" dramas, such as Jack Clayton's

Youthful rebellion: a boarding school student fires on his schoolmasters in Lindsay Anderson's apocalyptic fantasy of British boarding school life, *If . . .* (1968).

Room at the Top (1959), featuring Laurence Harvey as an amoral social climber, and Richardson's *Look Back in Anger* (1958), starring Richard Burton, from the play by John Osborne.

These corrosive views of British working-class life soon became a thriving subgenre, with such films as Reisz's *Saturday Night and Sunday Morning* (1960) and Anderson's brutal soccer drama *This Sporting Life* (1963), starring a young and athletic Richard Harris; *If . . .* (1968), a political fantasy set in a boarding school; and *O Lucky Man!* (1973), a satire of contemporary social mores. *If . . .* is undoubtedly Anderson's most famous film, chronicling the adventures of young Mick Travis (Malcolm McDowell) as he attempts to keep his individuality intact in a society bent on repressing individual impulse, with apocalyptic results. Another key film, Richardson's *The Loneliness of the Long Distance Runner* (1962), is a boys' prison drama in which delinquent teenager Colin Smith (Tom Courtenay) is caught after a robbery and sent to a harsh reformatory run by the spit-and-polish "Governor" (Michael Redgrave). Obsessed with sports, the Governor sees in Colin a promising candidate for an upcoming long-distance running contest between the inmates of the reform school and the boys of a privileged private school. Colin trains aggressively, all the while flashing back to the events that got him into prison in the first place and developing a hatred for all authority, especially the Governor. On the day of the big race, Colin runs easily, but stops short of the finish line by only a few feet to humiliate the Governor, looking at him with a triumphant smile. At the film's end, Colin is back in the reformatory disassembling gas masks—one of the most menial and filthy jobs at the school. But by not "winning," Colin has shown that he refuses to be crushed by the system, and the film became a cult hit among youth of the period.

Swinging London

In the early 1960s, gay rights began to emerge as a social issue, and a small group of films began to champion the cause of the gay, lesbian, and bisexual community. Basil Dearden cast matinee idol Dirk Bogarde in *Victim* (1961), one of the first British films about closeted homosexuality in a society where being gay was a criminal offense. The film was so direct and unapologetic for its time that it was refused a code seal by the Motion Picture Association of America when Dearden refused to edit it. A movement of similarly themed films would explode in the late 1960s and early 1970s, including works of Derek Jarman, but the roots of this tradition began here. Sidney J. Furie, who directed the Canadian drama *A Cool Sound from Hell* (1959), moved to Britain in the early 1960s and directed the pioneering Queer biker drama *The Leather Boys* in 1964, starring Colin Campbell as the straight-arrow motorcyclist Reggie, and Dudley Sutton as Pete, a gay biker who falls in love with Reggie and tries to seduce him.

In 1965, Furie went on to direct one of the most intelligent Cold War spy thrillers, *The Ipcress File*, the film that shot Michael Caine to stardom. Designed as an antidote to the gloss and chic sadism of the James Bond films, *The Ipcress File* ably displays Furie's considerable gifts as a visually dazzling director, who also gets the most out of his thematic interest in the grimier side of espionage. The Bond films, of course, became a national industry that is still an ongoing franchise, with Terence Young's *Dr. No* (1962) and *From Russia with Love* (1963), and Guy Hamilton's excellent *Goldfinger* (1964), which remains the high point of the series. In a more realistic vein, Bryan Forbes dealt with racial prejudice and unwanted pregnancy in the pioneering drama *The L-Shaped Room* (1962), while Basil Dearden also tackled British racism and "passing" in the crime thriller *Sapphire* (1959).

On a more cheerful note, the American expatriate Richard Lester made the short *The Running Jumping & Standing Still Film* (1959) for a few hundred pounds, featuring Peter Sellers and members of the "Goons," a zany comedy troupe whose off-the-wall humor inspired the later Monty Python television shows and films. The Beatles saw the film, loved it, and insisted that Lester direct their films, both *A Hard Day's Night* (1964) and *Help!* (1965), which met with great success. Lester also directed the brilliant comedy of the sexes *The Knack . . . and How to Get It* (1965), which won the top prize at Cannes and established 1960s British humor as surreal, offbeat, and irreverent. Lester's visual inventiveness (freeze-frames, sped-up motion, repeat montages, inserted titles, slow motion, and reverse motion, along with dissolves, wipes, and other camera tricks) became his trade-

Gert Fröbe as Goldfinger and Sean Connery as James Bond in Guy Hamilton's *Goldfinger* (1964), arguably the best of the Bond films.

mark, though in later films such as *Petulia* (1968), *The Bed Sitting Room* (1969), *Juggernaut* (1974), and *Robin and Marian* (1976) he displayed a considerably more restrained approach.

Other important films of the British New Wave include John Schlesinger's *Billy Liar* (1963), about a compulsive liar stuck in a small British town which he will never leave, and *Darling* (1965), featuring Julie Christie as a ruthless model and social climber who will stop at nothing to get to the top of the celebrity-driven world of "Swinging London." David Lean created the spectacular *Lawrence of Arabia* (1962), which made Peter O'Toole a star, and *Doctor Zhivago* (1965), which did the same for Omar Sharif. Tony Richardson's *Tom Jones* (1963), based on Henry Fielding's novel about a worthless but charming ne'er do well who makes his way from one misadventure to another in eighteenth-century England, won multiple Academy Awards. Peter Watkins created a terrifying vision of worldwide nuclear holocaust in his newsreel-like fiction film *The War Game* (1965), released in 1967, which used nonprofessional actors and crude handheld camera work to give the feel of a documentary film. Ironically, the film won an Academy

Peter O'Toole as T. E. Lawrence in David Lean's epic adventure film *Lawrence of Arabia* (1962).

Award as Best Documentary in 1968 for its depiction of the outbreak of World War III. The American musical director Stanley Donen traveled to London to make the satiric comedy *Bedazzled* (1967), in which short-order cook Stanley Moon (Dudley Moore) sells his soul to the Devil (Peter Cook) for a chance at the woman of his dreams. The film is smart, funny, and sharp; it was remade by director Harold Ramis under the same title in 2000. Joseph Losey, who fled America during the years of the blacklist in the mid-1950s, established himself as one of England's most perceptive social critics with *The Servant* (1963) and *Accident* (1967), both starring Dirk Bogarde, and both dealing with the inequities and suppressed passions of the British class system, with superb scripts by the playwright Harold Pinter.

Jonathan Miller, though more famous as an opera director, also made black-and-white films in the mid-1960s that capture an era now vanished forever. *Alice in Wonderland* (1966), a seventy-two-minute film boasting a cast that includes Peter Sellers, Michael Redgrave, John Gielgud, Leo McKern, Peter Cook, and Wilfred Brambell, has a remarkably lavish look, enhanced by Dick Bush's deep-focus, wide-angle cinematography. The climactic trial sequence was filmed on a specially designed set at Ealing Studios, but for the most part, *Alice in Wonderland* makes the everyday world surreal, producing a realistic document of unreal events. The result is an intelligent film easily appreciated by adults, shot in a dreamy, almost hallucinatory style in which fantasy and reality are mingled together in a feverish dream of adolescence. A final touch is Ravi Shankar's mesmeric sitar and oboe score, which effectively evokes the colonial past of the British Empire.

Michelangelo Antonioni went to London in 1966 to shoot *Blowup*, another of his films depicting alienation. A shallow, selfish London fashion photographer, Thomas (David Hemmings), accidentally witnesses two lovers having a quarrel in a park and takes a series of photographs that seems to suggest the argument is really a murder in progress. Jane (Vanessa Redgrave) chases after Thomas and demands the film back, offering to have sex with him in exchange for the undeveloped roll of film. But Thomas tricks her and develops the roll, blowing each image up progressively until he thinks he sees a corpse at the edge of one image, almost obscured by the foliage. Returning to the park he finds the body, but for some reason fails to report it to the police; the next day, the body has vanished. Did the murder happen? Was there ever a body? As with Antonioni's *L'Avventura,* we will never know. In the film's tantalizing final shot, Thomas himself vanishes before our eyes, as if he had never existed. An enormous commercial and critical success when first released, *Blowup* is perhaps the key film of swinging London in the 1960s, and boasts a superb sound track by Herbie Hancock and Jimmy Page, who also appears in the movie with his band, the Yardbirds.

Stanley Kubrick

Stanley Kubrick, one of the best-known filmmakers in the history of the medium, was born in the Bronx, New York, in 1928, and began his career as a still photographer for *Look* magazine, the now-defunct American weekly picture journal. In 1950, he made a short film entitled *The Day of the Fight,* based on a pictorial he had done for *Look* and sold it to RKO (released in 1951); in 1953 he directed his first feature, *Fear and Desire,* followed by *Killer's Kiss* in 1955. For reasons of economy and control, Kubrick's involvement in both these productions was total: he served as screenwriter, cameraman, director, editor, sound dubber, and mixer in each case, making the films for only $20,000 and $75,000 each. After modest success, he directed the racetrack robbery drama *The Killing* (1956), the antiwar film *Paths of Glory* (1957), and the Roman drama *Spartacus* (1960, begun by Anthony Mann, who quit over creative differences).

In 1961, Kubrick moved permanently to England; he would never return to America, gradually becoming more reclusive as his career progressed. His adaptation of Vladimir Nabokov's *Lolita* (1962) was well received, but his 1964 nightmare comedy, *Dr. Strangelove or: How I Learned to Stop Worrying and Love the Bomb,* earned him a permanent place in the cinematic pantheon. This brilliant black comedy of all-out nuclear warfare features Peter Sellers in no fewer than three roles—Group Captain Lionel Mandrake, President Merkin Muffley, and the sinister Dr. Strangelove himself—and manages to highlight both the horror and the inherent absurdity of the prospect

Peter Sellers as Dr. Strangelove in Stanley Kubrick's nightmare comedy *Dr. Strangelove or: How I Learned to Stop Worrying and Love the Bomb* (1964).

of thermonuclear war. From Sterling Hayden's performance as the utterly mad General Jack D. Ripper to Keenan Wynn's turn as Colonel "Bat" Guano and Slim Pickens's once-in-a-lifetime role as Major T. J. "King" Kong (he rides a nuclear warhead like a bucking bronco to its final target, thus triggering the Doomsday Machine that will destroy all life on earth in a wave of multi-megaton nuclear blasts), *Dr. Strangelove* is a catalogue of apocalyptic absurdities, a no-holds-barred satire that is both brutal and topical. Kubrick's poker-face visual style works perfectly with such supercharged material, and Ken Adam's grandiose sets (he also designed the James Bond movies in the 1960s) create a sense of realism in situations that are simultaneously grotesque and surreal.

After the international success of *Dr. Strangelove*, Kubrick could write his own ticket, which is exactly what he did for the rest of his career. *2001: A Space Odyssey* (1968) was the result of four years of intense labor and research and marked a new maturity for the science fiction film, as well as a new benchmark for special effects. *A Clockwork Orange* (1971) vividly adapted Anthony Burgess's dystopian novel about teenage hoodlums on the rampage, while *Barry Lyndon* (1975) redefined the historical epic with Kubrick's insistence on period illumination only—candles, lamps, and the like—for all interior scenes. In *Full Metal Jacket* (1987), he showed the dehumanizing horror of basic training and hand-to-hand combat in the Vietnam War. If his last film, *Eyes Wide Shut* (1999), was problematic for many viewers, Kubrick had long since discharged his debt to the cinema. Kubrick died in 1999.

Perhaps the film that put an end to the 1960s in Britain with the utmost finality is Nicolas Roeg and Donald Cammel's justly notorious *Performance* (1970), in which ex-pop star Turner (Mick Jagger) lives in a dilapidated house in a rundown area of London, presiding over a peculiar ménage, including Pherber (Anita Pallenberg) and Lucy (Michèle Breton). When

270

Stanley Kubrick (with beard, standing directly to the right of the camera) on the set of his film *A Clockwork Orange* (1971).

hoodlum-on-the-run Chas (James Fox) comes into Turner's life unexpectedly, Turner drugs the gangster with hallucinogenic mushrooms and momentarily delights in dressing him up in a variety of disguises, ostensibly to obtain a camouflaged passport photo, so that Chas can leave the country. It is at this point that Chas's old associates finally discover his hiding place. Making no attempt to escape, Chas asks his captors for one last favor—a final chat with Turner. In Turner's bedroom, Chas responds to Turner's unspoken wish to be murdered and shoots a bullet into the dissipated pop star's brain, killing him instantly. Brilliantly photographed, with dazzling optical effects at every turn, the film indelibly chronicles the end of an era in London, when English pop music and film electrified a generation. *Performance* is a one-of-a-kind production, which signaled that the 1960s era of excess and experimentation had come to a screeching halt.

DAS NEUE KINO IN GERMANY

In the 1960s, the German cinema was still trying to rebound from the war. Two filmmakers of the period are of immense importance, partly because

271

they paved the way for one of the key directors of Das Neue Kino (New Cinema) in Germany in the 1970s, Rainer Werner Fassbinder. But Jean-Marie Straub and Danièle Huillet's work is in a class by itself, among the glories of modern formalist cinema. Indeed, Straub and Huillet formed one of the few husband-and-wife production teams of true equality. Together they created some of the most demanding and interesting films of the 1960s and 1970s, beginning in 1963 with their short film *Machorka-Muff* (sometimes spelled *Majorka-Muff*). Straub ran a local cine-club in his birthplace of Metz, France, and later worked in various assistant capacities for such directors as Jean Renoir, Abel Gance, and Robert Bresson, all of whom had an enormous influence on his work.

Straub and Huillet met in 1954 in Paris and immediately became artistic partners. In 1958 Straub, fleeing conscription into the French armed forces, moved to Munich, Germany, with Huillet, where they became involved with radical theater groups. Among Straub's early collaborators was Rainer Werner Fassbinder, who appears in Straub's short film *Der Bräutigam, die Komödiantin und der Zuhälter* (*The Bridegroom, the Comedienne, and the Pimp*, 1968). The movie combines the story of the murder of a pimp (Fassbinder) with a drastically condensed theatrical piece and a lengthy tracking shot from an automobile of prostitutes plying their trade on an ill-lit German thoroughfare. Perhaps the couple's most famous early film is *Chronik der Anna Magdalena Bach* (*The Chronicle of Anna Magdalena Bach*, 1968), which the directors shot on actual locations of Johann Sebastian Bach's life, featuring Gustav Leonhardt, the renowned harpsichordist, as Bach, and Christiane Lang, also a classical musician in real life, as Anna.

With period instruments borrowed from various museums for a historically accurate sound, as well as costumes and props gleaned from a variety of private collections for added authenticity, the film nevertheless almost collapsed before production. Huillet and Straub insisted on recording all the sound live on location, eschewing the use of any post-dubbing, to get the most natural and authentic performances from the ensemble of excellent musicians they had assembled, as well as to re-create the original acoustics. But this horrified the original backers, who withdrew their funding a few days before shooting was to begin. Jean-Luc Godard came through with emergency funding, but the reduced budget meant that the film had to be shot in black-and-white rather than in color, which the directors would have preferred. Nevertheless, *The Chronicle of Anna Magdalena Bach* was a surprise hit at the 1968 New York Film Festival and remains a stunning artistic achievement.

Christiane Lang as J. S. Bach's wife in Jean-Marie Straub and Danièle Huillet's minimalist masterpiece *Chronik der Anna Magdalena Bach* (*The Chronicle of Anna Magdalena Bach,* 1968).

In *Chronicle,* as in all their works, Huillet and Straub insisted upon lengthy takes, some nearly ten minutes long, which were used virtually without editing in the final print. Coupled with the use of natural lighting, austere sets, and subdued performances, this minimalist shooting technique results in an extraordinary sense of place, as if one is watching the incidents of Bach's life as they occur rather than a re-creation. Other early successes include an adaptation of Heinrich Böll's novel *Billiards at Half Past Nine,* which became the astoundingly rich and perverse *Nicht versöhnt oder Es hilft nur Gewalt wo Gewalt herrscht* (*Not Reconciled, or Only Violence Helps Where Violence Rules,* 1965). By the late 1960s and early 1970s, Straub preferred to function more as a producer than a director. Often working in 16 mm film, Huillet and Straub directed such works as *Geschichtsunterricht* (*History Lessons,* 1972) and *Moses und Aron* (*Moses and Aaron,* 1975). In all these films, the team demands a great deal from the viewer, using stylized sets, static camerawork, and spare visual compositions that avoid spectacle or artifice. Given the proper attention, however, Straub-Huillet films remain among the most haunting and visually resonant of the German filmmaking renaissance. Their partnership came to an end when Huillet died in

273

2006; without her guiding hand, Straub's future as a filmmaker seems uncertain.

THE HOLLYWOOD NEW WAVE

In America, the lessons of the French New Wave were being absorbed by Hollywood, along with the influence of the British Free Cinema Movement. Perhaps the most direct evidence of this is *Bonnie and Clyde* (1967), a Depression-era crime drama about Clyde Barrow (Warren Beatty) and Bonnie Parker (Faye Dunaway), two bank robbers in the Midwest who pursue their trade for fun as well as profit. When *Bonnie and Clyde* was first proposed, both Godard and Truffaut were seriously considered as directors, and Truffaut did a good deal of work on at least one draft of the script. When the film was finally handed to American director Arthur Penn, he appropriated various New Wave visual techniques for the look of the film, such as slow motion, romantic deep-focus shots, abrupt editorial transitions (courtesy of the brilliant editor Dede Allen), and a lyrical approach to the material that seems deeply indebted to Truffaut's sensibility in *Jules and Jim*. In addition, the film's star, Warren Beatty, believed so deeply in the effort that when an initial series of screenings flopped, he put in his own time and money to

"They're young, they're in love, and they kill people"—the advertising tag line for Arthur Penn's New Wave–influenced *Bonnie and Clyde* (1967), with Warren Beatty as Clyde Barrow and Faye Dunaway as Bonnie Parker.

get the film out to a more receptive audience—young, college-age viewers—and *Bonnie and Clyde* became not only a hit, but the touchstone work of the new Hollywood.

Nevertheless, it is important to remember that Hollywood in the early 1960s was still deeply conservative, with such films as William Wyler's *Ben-Hur* (1959), Jerome Robbins and Robert Wise's *West Side Story* (1961), Joseph L. Mankiewicz's *Cleopatra* (1963), George Cukor's *My Fair Lady* (1964), Robert Stevenson's *Mary Poppins* (1964), and Wise's *The Sound of Music* (1965) topping both the box office and critical polls. Then, too, Elvis Presley, who had shaken up the music scene so decisively in the late 1950s with such rock 'n' roll classics as "Heartbreak Hotel" and "Hound Dog," was now reduced to a string of tepid musical pictures that were out of step with both the pop music of the era and changing audience tastes. Films such as *Girls! Girls! Girls!* (1962), *Fun in Acapulco* (1963), *Girl Happy* (1965), and *Harum Scarum* (1965) were so formulaic that they gave rise to the oft-repeated film genre joke: "When is a musical not a musical?" Answer: "When it's an Elvis Presley movie." But these straightforward commercial films were all but swept away in the tidal wave of innovation that was to follow.

A few of the old masters of the trade were able to keep step with the changing times. In particular, Alfred Hitchcock created *Psycho* (1960), a film justly famous for its unprecedented level of graphic violence, and also for the manner in which it was shot, quickly and cheaply. Hitchcock had worked steadily throughout the 1950s on a variety of glossy entertainments; they had a distinctly personal edge, yet all were large-budget films with "A" casts, shot in color with generous production schedules. In 1955, he moved into the relatively new medium of television with the creation of *Alfred Hitchcock Presents*, an anthology series of thirty-minute mysteries he personally introduced but which were largely directed by others, including the talented noir specialist John Brahm. When on occasion he directed one of the series' playlets himself, Hitchcock was impressed with the speed and facility with which television crews worked; the half-hour shows were usually shot in little more than two days.

Aware of the stripped-down, back-to-basics work of Truffaut, Godard, and other New Wave artists, Hitchcock was determined to shoot *Psycho* with a television crew, in black-and-white, on the Universal lot, using contract players and a minimal budget. The result was astonishing: *Psycho* became the biggest hit of his long career and forever typecast Anthony Perkins in the role of repressed psychotic Norman Bates. The film's set piece, of course, is the infamous shower scene, in which Marion Crane (Janet Leigh) is stabbed to death

The silhouette of a deranged killer in Alfred
Hitchcock's *Psycho* (1960).

with a large kitchen knife, in a blizzard of
rapid cuts that recall nothing so much as
Sergei Eisenstein's editorial structure in
Strike or *Battleship Potemkin.*

By shooting, as he always did, from a storyboard, co-designed with
graphic artist Saul Bass, Hitchcock enhanced the violence of the attack with
a barrage of camera angles, cut together in brief bursts of imagery, for a sequence that lasts only forty-five seconds yet took a full week to shoot. Indeed, the entire sequence is a masterpiece of deception; close-ups of Janet
Leigh during the attack were duly photographed, but some close-ups of her
torso during the stabbing and an overhead shot of her naked body in the
shower required a body double. In addition, although much of the attack is
suggested by montage—shots of the knife stabbing at the air are intercut
with shots of Marion screaming, blood running down the drain, and so
on—there is one shot in the middle of the sequence that shows the knife
clearly penetrating Marion's abdomen. For years, theorists and critics argued that the murder scene was an illusion, accomplished solely by editing
rather than a kitchen knife, but a frame-by-frame blowup of the sequence
published in 1974 by Richard J. Anobile conclusively demonstrated that
Hitchcock had indeed put in one direct point of contact on the screen for
several seconds to solidify the visual impact of the scene.

THE PRODUCTION CODE COLLAPSES

Another interesting aspect of *Psycho* was Hitchcock's insistence to exhibitors that absolutely no one be admitted to the theater after the film had begun. By exerting this degree of control over his audience, Hitchcock managed to dictate not only every aspect of the film itself, but also the conditions under which it was viewed. Finally, *Psycho* marked, in a very important sense, the beginning of the end for the Motion Picture Production Code. Contemporary audiences are by now accustomed to the current rating system of G, PG, PG-13, R, and NC-17 to classify the content of a film; when *Psycho* came out in 1960, the Production Code was theoretically still intact, all films were subject to the code in a supposedly uniform manner, and films were not individually rated. Many traditional reviewers, accustomed to Hitchcock's intricately plotted thrillers of an earlier era, reacted violently to the film, dismissing it as a cheap shocker of no distinction. But younger audiences embraced the film for its visual daring, its unexpected plot twists, and the brutality of its mise-en-scène.

In 1966, Warner Bros. released Mike Nichols's *Who's Afraid of Virginia Woolf?* starring Richard Burton and Elizabeth Taylor, with a budget of roughly $7 million. Adapted from Edward Albee's play, the film had a great deal of censorable language, much of which Nichols refused to cut. Finally Jack Valenti, head of the Motion Picture Association of America, crafted a solution: one phrase, "screw you," would be removed, but the rest of Albee's text would remain intact. The film was released with a Code Seal, with the sole prohibition that it was designed for "mature audiences only," which in some theaters meant under eighteen not admitted; in other, more conservative areas, no one under twenty-one.

But the real death knell for the MPAA Code was the American release of Antonioni's *Blowup,* just a few months after *Who's Afraid of Virginia Woolf?* Antonioni's film features full frontal female nudity, drug use, and profanity, and the MPAA told the distributor, MGM, that even with cuts the film would be nearly impossible to approve. To get around this, MGM created Premiere Sound Films as a front company to release the film; since Premiere was not a signatory to the Code, they were not required to adhere to it. Both films were enormous commercial and critical successes and demonstrated that audiences were tired of being told what they could and couldn't see on the screen.

Shortly thereafter, the old Code was abandoned. In 1968, the MPAA instituted the rating system as we know it today with G, PG (briefly known as GP), R, and X ratings to classify a film's content. In 1984, the PG-13 rating was created for Garry Marshall's comedy *The Flamingo Kid* and John Milius's violent thriller *Red Dawn*; after that, the PG-13 rating was used on Steven Spielberg's *Indiana Jones and the Temple of Doom* and several other near-R rated films that year. In September 1990, the MPAA introduced the NC-17 rating to replace the X rating, which was then consigned to films that were sheer pornography. The first NC-17 rated film was Philip Kaufman's sexually explicit *Henry & June* (1990), about notorious writer Henry Miller and his wife, based on a book by their friend Anaïs Nin.

Other adventurous American films of the period included British director John Boorman's *Point Blank* (1967), a sleek thriller starring Lee Marvin as a mobster mysteriously resurrected from the dead who systematically works his way to the top of an organized crime syndicate in search of a bundle of money owed him from a robbery gone wrong. Casually killing and maiming his opponents as he searches for the loot—in one instance he tosses a particularly obnoxious villain off a hotel balcony with nary a backward glance— Lee Marvin's Walker is a combination of Orpheus and Avenging Angel. Boorman directs the film with an obvious debt to Alain Resnais, as the past and present fuse together in a maelstrom of violence.

John Schlesinger's *Midnight Cowboy* (1969) became the first film in history with an X rating to win the Academy Award for Best Picture; today it would probably be an R. Schlesinger's tale of failed hustler Joe Buck (Jon Voight) and his erstwhile pimp, Enrico "Ratso" Rizzo (Dustin Hoffman), also captures, for better or worse, a part of New York now gone forever: Forty-second Street's grimy chain of movie theaters where prostitutes, junkies, winos, and drug dealers congregated with impunity, creating a subcultural city-within-a-city in which violence and money ruled. The area has now been cleaned up and made tourist-friendly, but the movie captures the real grime and danger of the place and reminds us that not everyone in Manhattan lives in a penthouse apartment. As a tale of despair and sadness and yet, in the end, hope, *Midnight Cowboy* is a one-of-a-kind film, which brings to life a vision of Manhattan as an earthly hell, populated by people who will do anything to get out of the city and "the life."

Dennis Hopper's *Easy Rider* (1969) was a countercultural hit, with the first wall-to-wall rock 'n' roll sound track in Hollywood history. Shot for a bit less than $350,000, partially financed by co-star Peter Fonda's trust fund, and photographed in a mix of 16 mm and 35 mm for a grainy, funky look, the movie made biker movies respectable and transformed what might have

been a routine genre picture into a compelling tale of a personal cross-country odyssey. Mike Nichols's *The Graduate* (1967) exposed the alienation and uncertainty of youth in an exploitational adult world and made an overnight sensation out of Dustin Hoffman. For many, *The Graduate*, with its signature Simon and Garfunkle sound track, is one of the most influential American films of the 1960s, one of the few to deal sympathetically with the plight of young adults trying to make their way in the modern world. Audiences flocked to see both films; *Easy Rider* grossed more than $30 million in the United States alone.

THE NEW AMERICAN DOCUMENTARY FILM

The documentary film that set the pace for the new decade was *Primary* (1960), which covered the 1960 U.S. presidential race, made by four men who would become the key players of the new, handheld, sync-sound documentary tradition: Albert Maysles, Robert Drew, D. A. Pennebaker, and Richard Leacock. Working as Drew Associates, the four created a new style of documentary production that simply observed their subjects with an almost constantly running camera, following them everywhere. The key principle was not to interfere, to keep shooting even when things got dull (you never knew what might happen next), and to stay with your subject all the time for total emotional and physical intimacy. In addition, there was no narration, and the resulting films had a rough, raw look, which made them seem like newsreels more than anything else. This new method of cinéma vérité, known as "direct cinema" in Britain, became the dominant documentary style of the 1960s, films that were unvarnished reports of events rather than interpretations of them.

After *Primary*'s success the four split up, with brothers David and Albert Maysles pairing off, and Pennebaker and Leacock working as a duo particularly interested in pop music and culture. D. A. Pennebaker's 16 mm documentary *Monterey Pop* (1968) was blown up to 35 mm and released to theaters to rapturous reviews, capturing Jimi Hendrix, Otis Redding, Janis Joplin, the Who, and other pop artists at their peak. Two years later, Michael Wadleigh's *Woodstock* (1970) accomplished much the same thing on a larger scale, using a battery of more than twenty 16 mm cameras to capture the epic 1969 pop music festival at Woodstock in all its incandescent glory. But the peace, love, and harmony of Woodstock proved short-lived; later in 1969, the Rolling Stones played the Altamont Speedway in California to a violent, stoned audience of dazed hippies and Hell's Angels. The concert ended in a stabbing death, captured on film by the Maysles brothers in their brutal documentary *Gimme Shelter* (1970).

Other key documentaries of the period came from the prolific Frederick Wiseman, whose *Titicut Follies* (1967), about life in a Massachusetts mental hospital, followed by *High School* (1968), *Hospital* (1970), and *Welfare* (1975), all depicted the American social system in crisis. Wiseman became famous for his style of relentless yet unobtrusive camera work and his absolute refusal to add any voiceover narration or music during editing to guide the viewer, resulting in raw and uncensored documents that capture the stripped-down essence of his numerous subjects. D. A. Pennebaker's *Don't Look Back* (1967) chronicled Bob Dylan's first British tour as a folk troubadour, using a lightweight sync-sound 16 mm camera that gave him the ability to shoot almost anywhere. Albert and David Maysles's *Salesman* (co-director, Charlotte Zwerin, 1969) is one of the bleakest films of the new documentary movement, following four Bible salesmen around the country as they peddle their wares to the poor and indigent who can't even afford to put food on the table. Documentarist and cinematographer Haskell Wexler directed the fiction feature *Medium Cool* (1969), about a TV news cameraman's crisis of the soul as he struggles to decide whether or not he should in-

The American documentary comes of age in Frederick Wiseman's *Welfare* (1975).

tervene when filming scenes of riots and political demonstrations at the 1968 Democratic National Convention in Chicago.

AMERICAN MAVERICKS

On a more commercial front, the boundaries were also being tested. Russ Meyer's *Vixen!* (1968) pushed soft-core pornography to new extremes, while Roger Corman, who began the decade with a series of inventive horror films loosely based on the works of Edgar Allan Poe, such as *The Pit and the Pendulum* (1961), ended the decade with socially conscious (and highly profitable) youth films such as *The Wild Angels* (1966), centering on the exploits of the Hell's Angels motorcycle gang, featuring real members of the club as extras in the film, and *The Trip* (1967), the first Hollywood film to seriously explore the use of LSD.

Through his connections as a director and producer, Corman also continued to give younger filmmakers a shot at directing their first films, so long as they stayed on time and under budget. In 1968, Corman gave film critic

Peter Bogdanovich the chance to make his debut film, *Targets*, based on the real-life Texas Tower sniper killings by Charles Whitman in 1966. With only $130,000 at his disposal and a minimal schedule, Bogdanovich, who deeply admired the work of Howard Hawks, crafted an elegantly structured narrative centering on aging horror star Byron Orlok (Boris Karloff in his last truly distinguished role) doing a press junket for his final film, while clean-cut American boy Bobby Thompson (Tim O'Kelly) goes on a shooting rampage, killing his family one by one and then picking off strangers from the top of a huge oil tank. The fading star and the sniper cross paths in the final moments of the film, as Orlok attends a drive-in screening of his film while Thompson shoots at the patrons from behind the screen. The sharp, spare film was a revelation, launching Bogdanovich's career and earning the respect of the Hollywood veterans he idolized.

Michelangelo Antonioni's first Hollywood film was *Zabriskie Point* (1970), a flawed but ambitious attempt to examine America's youth culture that used many of the techniques of the Hollywood independent film (location shooting, nonprofessional actors, minimal script) to become Antonioni's most quintessentially American production. Mark (Mark Frechette) goes on the run after killing a policeman during a demonstration, stealing a light plane to escape to the desert. There he meets the disenchanted Daria (Daria Halprin), who is disgusted by her job as secretary for the relentlessly corporate Lee Allen (Rod Taylor), who also implicitly wants to keep Daria as his mistress. After a brief romantic interlude, Mark and Daria are separated, and Mark is subsequently killed by the police. Disconsolate, Daria gazes off into the distance, looking at the enormous, ultra-modern desert house that serves as the conference center for Lee's company. In a stunning final sequence, Daria watches as the enormous glass house explodes over and over again, symbolizing Antonioni's rejection of materialist culture. To the sounds of Pink Floyd's mesmeric "Careful with That Axe, Eugene," we see the house repeatedly self-destruct from numerous vantage points, and then we move inside to watch a television set, a refrigerator, racks of clothing, and other consumer goods explode in super slow-motion, as chunks of food, shreds of clothing, and bits of glass and metal drift serenely off into space. In the film's final shots, we see that the house is actually intact; the entire series of explosions has occurred solely in Daria's mind. While marred by the uncertain performances of the two leads (both nonprofessionals) and some rather unconvincing dialogue, the film is visually stunning. Antonioni continued with his thematic preoccupations of loneliness and loss of identity in such later films as *Professione: reporter* (*The Passenger*, 1975) and *Al di là delle nuvole* (*Beyond the Clouds*, 1995), despite a debilitating stroke in 1985. He died in 2007.

John Cassavetes, an intense young actor who was deeply impatient with what he viewed as the mediocrity of the many Hollywood films in which he appeared, shocked audiences with *Shadows* (1959), his first film as director, a 16 mm feature shot for less than $40,000. He went on to direct the dramas *Faces* (1968), *Husbands* (1970), and many more deeply personal films in the 1970s, all made entirely according to the dictates of his own conscience while still appearing in more conventional films to fund his work as a director. Using improvisatory techniques and a handheld camera, Cassavetes made decidedly independent films that were uniquely his own and existed entirely outside the Hollywood mainstream. Cassavetes died in 1989.

THE NEW AMERICAN CINEMA

Another important school of noncommercial filmmaking was the New American Cinema, a loosely knit group of artists who made experimental or underground movies in 16 mm on nonexistent budgets. These movies nevertheless profoundly influenced the language of cinema, in everything from MTV videos in the 1980s to television commercials, as well as the editorial and visual style seen in such television series as "24" (premiered 2001). The American experimental film was pioneered in the 1940s and 1950s by the independent filmmaker Maya Deren, whose *Meshes of the Afternoon* (co-director, Alexander Hammid, 1943) and *Ritual in Transfigured Time* (1946) first introduced audiences to an authentically American avant-garde filmic vision. By the 1960s, an entire underground movement had developed in New York and San Francisco as a part of the emerging counterculture of the period. Scott Bartlett was one of the first to mix video and film in his electric love poem *OffOn* (a k a *Off On*, 1972), and Stan Brakhage, one of the most prolific members of the movement, directed

Experimental filmmaker Maya Deren at work in the 1940s.

283

Homoerotic fetishism in *Scorpio Rising* (1964),
Kenneth Anger's film about American motorcycle culture.

the epic *Dog Star Man* (1961–65), *Scenes from Under Childhood* (1967–70), and the sensuous, shimmering ode to physical love, *Lovemaking* (1968).

Bruce Conner specialized in violent collage films, using found footage with original material to create *Cosmic Ray* (1962), a four-minute visual assault on the viewer that many consider the prototype of the MTV video, set to the beat of Ray Charles's "What'd I Say?" Conner also directed *Report* (1967), a brilliant compilation film that interrogates the assassination of John F. Kennedy. James Whitney's *Lapis* (1966), one of the first computer-generated films, featured mathematically precise, circulating forms of a mandala set to classical Indian music. Other notable films of the New American Cinema include Jack Smith's Queer classic *Flaming Creatures* (1963), a transgendered orgy set in an Orientalist fantasy world, and Kenneth Anger's homoerotic *Scorpio Rising* (1964), which links the members of an outlaw biker gang to Christ and the twelve apostles, cut to the beat of a sound track of early sixties rock. Shirley Clarke directed numerous short films as well as several features, the most famous of which is *The Connection* (1962), based on the play by Jack Gelber, in which a group of jazz musicians in a loft wait for their "connection," a heroin dealer, to arrive.

284

Alternative visions: director Shirley Clarke at work on the set of her film *The Connection* (1961).

The most famous filmmaker of this movement was undoubtedly pop artist Andy Warhol. Warhol began turning out films at a staggering rate in the early 1960s, starting with a series of three-minute silent screen tests of celebrities and fellow artists who passed through his New York studio, dubbed "the Factory." He then moved on to the epic *Sleep* (1963), a five-hour, thirty-five-minute film of the poet John Giorno sleeping, and *Empire* (1964), an eight-hour film of the Empire State Building from dusk to dawn, both silent. Later sync-sound films, such as *Vinyl* (1965), Warhol's version of Anthony Burgess's novel *A Clockwork Orange,* and *Chelsea Girls* (1966), a three-and-a-half-hour, split-screen, color and black-and-white voyage into the depths of the New York art world scene, are vigorously framed, nearly formalist works, part documentary and part fiction. After his near-fatal shooting by Valerie Solanis in 1968, Warhol retired from filmmaking but continued painting, leaving it to his associate, Paul Morrissey, to direct such films as *Flesh* (1968) and *Trash* (1970).

Gerard Malanga (center, holding chains) as the juvenile delinquent Victor, with onlooker Edie Sedgwick (right, seated), in Andy Warhol's *Vinyl,* shot in one afternoon in 1965.

285

The beginnings of Structuralist cinema: Michael Snow's *Wavelength* (1967).

The California dream goes worldwide: Bruce Brown's *The Endless Summer* (1966).

Near the end of the 1960s, a new trend emerged in the cinematic avant-garde: the structural film. Its foremost proponent was Michael Snow, whose *Wavelength* (1967) is basically a forty-five-minute zoom across an empty loft while Snow manipulates the image using various stocks and color filters. It created a sensation and attracted an entire school of filmmakers in its wake, such as Ernie Gehr, Hollis Frampton, and Joyce Wieland, who made films that were concerned primarily with the formal properties of the film medium, such as grain, duration of shots, framing, light, color filters, and camera movement.

Bruce Brown created a new genre in the 1960s, the surfing movie, with his crossover hit *The Endless Summer* (1966), originally intended for fellow surfers but eventually emerging as an independently produced commercial movie. *The Endless Summer* is essentially a travelogue, filmed around the world, and structured without much planning. Mike and Robert are fixated on their quest for the best surf, and Brown simply sets up his camera on a tripod to record the two young men's exploits, intercut from time to time with some clumsy comedy segues that help to bridge the gaps between the disparate sequences. What is most

Robert Downey Sr.'s corrosive satire of the advertising industry, *Putney Swope* (1969).

striking about *The Endless Summer* is its inherent artlessness, but the film was a breath of fresh air for audiences, particularly in those areas where surfing was just a dream.

The iconoclastic Robert Downey Sr. made a series of brutally satirical films in the early 1960s as a writer/director, starting with the improvised feature film *Babo 73* (1964), which cast underground film icon Taylor Mead as "President of the United Status [*sic*]," and *Chafed Elbows* (1966), a warped musical comedy about a mother and son who fall in love and go on welfare. His most successful film is undoubtedly *Putney Swope* (1969), a savage satire on American racial attitudes and the advertising business, as token African American advertising executive Putney Swope (Arnold Johnson) is accidentally elected the head of a top Madison Avenue ad agency and turns the company upside down. Firing most of the agency's staffers, Putney renames the shop the Truth and Soul agency, and begins creating a series of TV ads that are both brazen and effective. Soon, all of corporate America is flocking to Putney's door, but ultimately the temptation of easy money is too pervasive and Putney sells out, fleeing the agency with a briefcase full of cash. Downey went on to write and direct the allegorical western *Greaser's Palace* (1972), and has since written and directed a number of equally idiosyncratic features such as *Rented Lips* (1988) and *Too Much Sun* (1991).

THE OLD MASTERS

The 1960s also saw the final films of many of the classical Hollywood directors who had worked in the industry since its infancy. Alfred Hitchcock's last films were among his best, including the European-influenced horror picture *The Birds* (1963), in which large groups of birds attack a small California town without explanation, and *Marnie* (1964), a psychological study of a kleptomaniac that was unjustly dismissed when first released. *Torn Curtain* (1966) and *Topaz* (1969), both political thrillers, were perhaps less successful, but Hitchcock returned to form with the murder mystery *Frenzy* (1972), shot on location in England, before ending his career with the gently comic caper *Family Plot* (1976). Hitchcock died in 1980.

John Ford's epic work came to a graceful close with the racial drama *Sergeant Rutledge* (1960); the elegiac western *Two Rode Together* (1961); the remarkable "chamber western" *The Man Who Shot Liberty Valance* (1962), a film shot almost entirely on interior sound stages for precise control of camera movement and lighting; the knockabout comedy *Donovan's Reef* (1963); *Cheyenne Autumn* (1964), one of Ford's most sympathetic films on the plight of Native Americans in the

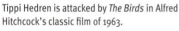
Tippi Hedren is attacked by *The Birds* in Alfred Hitchcock's classic film of 1963.

288

early western United States; and *7 Women* (1966), a tragic and intimate drama superbly played by Anne Bancroft, Anna Lee, Woody Strode, and Mildred Dunnock. Ford died at the age of seventy-nine in 1973.

Howard Hawks, Hollywood's most reliable multigenre director, ended his career with an African big-game safari film, *Hatari!* (1962), followed by the comedy *Man's Favorite Sport?* (1964), the stock-car racing drama *Red Line 7000* (1965), and two economical westerns, *El Dorado* (1966), one of his finest films in any genre, and *Rio Lobo* (1970). Hawks died in 1977.

Fritz Lang, who had worked in America since 1936's *Fury*, returned to Germany to make his final films, the two-part *Das Indische Grabmal* (*The Indian Tomb*) and its companion, the epic costume drama *Der Tiger von Eschnapur* (*Tiger of Bengal*) in 1959, as well as the prescient crime picture *Die Tausend Augen des Dr. Mabuse* (*The Thousand Eyes of Dr. Mabuse*, 1960), in which Lang's arch criminal now uses a deluxe hotel for his base of operations, in which every room is under surveillance. Lang died in 1976.

Orson Welles, the aging *enfant terrible* of the American cinema, wandered through Europe in the 1950s and early 1960s making *Othello* (a k a *The Tragedy of Othello: The Moor of Venice*, 1952), *Mr. Arkadin* (1955), *The Trial* (*Le Procès*, 1962), and *Chimes at Midnight*, a k a *Falstaff* (*Campandas a medianoche*, 1965), with whatever materials came to hand. Although all show flashes of brilliance, they are to some extent compromised by the lack of sufficient financing and inferior production facilities. Welles's virtuoso 1958 picture *Touch of Evil* turned out to be his last American film; in 1968 he directed the slight romance *The Immortal Story* (*Une Histoire immortelle*) in France, and in 1974 the semidocumentary *F for Fake* (*Vérités et mensonges*), with additional footage by François Reichenbach. Welles died in 1985.

George Cukor, the supreme Hollywood stylist, continued his long career in the cinema in the 1960s with the romantic comedy *Let's Make Love* (1960); the rather sensationalistic *The Chapman Report* (1962), which was recut by censors before receiving a desultory release; *My Fair Lady* (1964), which was one of the late triumphs of the classic musical and Cukor's career; the U.S./Soviet Union cultural exchange project *The Blue Bird* (*Sinyaya ptitsa*, 1976), which failed to ignite despite an all-star cast; and his last movie, in 1981, *Rich and Famous,* a remake of Vincent Sherman's 1943 drama *Old Acquaintance.* Cukor died in 1983.

Samuel Fuller shocked audiences with his independent, low-budget thriller *Underworld U.S.A.* (1961), one of the most brutal crime films ever made, as well as the psychiatric hospital drama *Shock Corridor* (1963), the bizarre sex tragedy *The Naked Kiss* (1964), and his last major film, the deeply personal World War II drama *The Big Red One* (1980), which was finally restored to its director's original cut on DVD. Fuller died in 1997.

BEYOND WESTERN EUROPE AND THE UNITED STATES

In Japan, the cinema was rapidly becoming more sexually graphic and violent, with the *pinku eiga,* or "pink" film, dominating the marketplace in the late 1960s. "Pink" films were near-pornographic conflations of sex and sado-masochistic violence, such as Kôji Wakamatsu's *Okasareta hakui* (*Violated Angels,* 1967) and *Yuke yuke nidome no shojo* (*Go, Go Second Time Virgin,* 1969); these and the equally violent *yakuza,* or gangster films, attracted much of the nation's film-going audience. The Japanese New Wave was unlike any other, often steeped in brutality and nihilism. Films such as Nagisa Oshima's *Seishun zankoku monogatari* (*Cruel Story of Youth,* 1960) were stylistically audacious but treated sex as a bartered commodity and displayed a deep misogyny. *Cruel Story of Youth* is typical of Japanese New Wave cinema of the period, depicting a world bereft of hope, ambition, or even a shred of compassion. Shohei Imamura's *Nippon konchuki* (*The Insect Woman,* 1963) is a similarly bleak story of a prostitute surviving in an unforgiving world, while Seijun Suzuki's aptly titled *Tokyo nagaremono* (*Tokyo Drifter,* 1966) and Imamura's *Jinruigaku nyumon: Erogotshi yori* (*The Pornographers,* 1966) are equally matter-of-fact in their depiction of a universe in which all is violence, greed, and objectification. Perhaps much of this despair and alienation stems from the bitterness of Japan's war effort and subsequent defeat in 1945; one of the most famous films of the early 1960s in Japan was Masaki Kobayashi's epic *Ningen no joken I, II, III* (*The Human Condition,* 1959–61), which used its nine hours-plus running time to examine the war and its aftermath for contemporary audiences.

At the same time, the Japanese cinema gave the world one authentically new monster to deal with, the prehistoric, radioactive dinosaur *Gojira* (*God-*

The violence of passion in Nagisa Oshima's *Seishun zankoku monogatari* (*Cruel Story of Youth,* 1960).

zilla in the West), whose debut film, directed by Ishirô Honda in 1954, led to a wave of sequels and companion "behemoth" films also directed by Honda, such as *Sora no daikaijû Radon* (*Rodan,* 1956, a giant flying reptile), *Mosura* (*Mothra,* 1961, a huge flying moth), and *Kingu Kongu tai Gojira* (*King Kong vs. Godzilla,* 1962, in which Kong and Godzilla battle to a draw, destroying much of the Japanese countryside in the process), the aptly titled *Kaijû sôshingeki* (*Destroy All Monsters!* 1968), and numerous others. So popular were Honda's films with international audiences that for many years in the 1960s, a standing miniature set of Tokyo existed at Toho Studios in Japan, ready to be demolished at a moment's notice. For many years, Honda also functioned as Akira Kurosawa's second-unit or "action" director, working on the director's more spectacular epic films.

LATIN AMERICA AND CINEMA NOVO

Mexican cinema in the 1960s was in a period of artistic and commercial decline, unusual for such an otherwise rampantly productive decade throughout the rest of the world. Luis Buñuel continued his string of highly idiosyncratic films with the political satire *La Fièvre monte à El Pao* (*Republic of Sin,* 1959) and the disturbing *La Joven* (*The Young One,* 1960). Then, as noted, he took a quick trip to Spain to make *Viridiana* in 1961 and promptly got kicked out of the country. Returning to Mexico, he made the scathing comedy of manners *El Ángel exterminador* (*The Exterminating Angel,* 1962), in which a group of bourgeois Mexico City residents find themselves unable to leave a dinner party and are compelled by some mysterious force to stay in the dining room for days until finally the spell is broken. Following this was the allegorical featurette *Simón del desierto* (*Simon of the Desert,* 1965), in which a religious fanatic stands on top of a giant pillar in the desert for years on end to prove his religious faith, until the Devil finally tempts him into renouncing his claim to near-sainthood and whisks him off to a cavernous New York nightclub. But Buñuel was practically the sole exception to the general rule of mediocrity. Indeed, the quality of Mexican films in the 1960s was so poor, with a wave of cheap horror films, comedies, and musicals, that the Arieles, the Mexican Academy Awards, were canceled from 1958 to 1971. Buñuel himself soon left the country, finding greener pastures in France for his final group of films, such as his late Surrealist masterpiece *La Charme discret de la bourgeoisie* (*The Discreet Charm of the Bourgeoisie,* 1972). After a long and prolific career, Buñuel died in 1983.

291

Fernando Rey as Don Rafael in Luis Buñuel's late surrealist masterpiece, *Le Charme discret de la bourgeoisie* (*The Discreet Charm of the Bourgeoisie*, 1972).

Outside of Mexico, Latin American cinema in the 1960s was overtly political; the most engaged cinema was probably in Brazil, home of the Cinema Novo (New Cinema) movement. Its foremost exponent was Glauber Rocha, who was born in Brazil in 1938. Attracted to the cinema at an early age, Rocha became a journalist and then studied law, but soon abandoned both professions to pursue film full time. In 1962, after making several short movies, he took over the direction of the feature film *Barravento* (*The Turning Wind*), which examined the plight of Brazil's poor black fishermen in a direct and accessible manner. But Rocha was more of a mystic, and his first wholly personal feature was *Deus e o Diabo na Terra do Sol* (*Black God, White Devil*, 1964), which he directed at the age of twenty-five. In this cinematic allegory, a young man named Manuel kills his boss and then flees with his wife, Rosa, to follow the messianic preacher Sebastiao and meets the notorious hired gun, or *jagunço*, Antonio das Mortes. What follows is a series of brutal encounters that suggest that only violence will help those who are sorely oppressed, a theme Rocha embellished in *O Dragão da Maldade contra o Santo Guerreiro* (*Antonio das Mortes*, 1969), his first film in color, in which the hit man of *Black God, White Devil* becomes a hero by joining a peasant war against a brutal landlord. The Marxist implications of Rocha's cinema are hard to miss; sick of a society that placated its citizens with an endless procession of genre films and *chanchada* (musicals), he posited the existence of a cinema that would instruct and enlighten the public. But political conditions in Brazil meant that he was always working in an unstable environment, and he left Brazil to work abroad, making one of his finest late films, *The Lion Has Seven Heads* (*Der Leone have sept cabeças*, 1971), on location in the Congo with Jean-Pierre Léaud in a pivotal role as a possessed cleric. Other key films of the Cinema Novo movement include Ruy Guerra's *Os Fuzis* (*The Guns*, 1964) and Nelson Pereira dos Santos's *Como Era Gostoso o Meu Francês* (*How Tasty Was My Little Frenchman*, 1971).

In Argentina, Santiago Álvarez, Octavio Getino, and Fernando E. Solanas created *La Hora de los hornos: Notas y testimonios sobre el neocolonialismo, la violencia y la liberación* (*The Hour of the Furnaces*, 1968), an epic paean to revolution. In Cuba, the new government of Fidel Castro encouraged filmmakers such as Santiago Álvarez, who directed the political documentaries *Hanoi, martes 13* (*Hanoi, Tuesday the 13th*, 1967) and *LBJ* (1968), as well as the earlier, controversial short *Now* (1965), which used images of race riots in the United States, underscored with a Lena Horne vocal, to urge violent resistance to police brutality in the battle for civil rights; the film ends with the word "Now" spelled out in a hail of machine gun bullets. Other important Cuban filmmakers included Humberto Solás, director of *Lucía* (1968), as well as Tomás Gutiérrez Alea, whose *Memorias del subdesarrollo* (*Memories of Underdevelopment*, 1968) was also an impassioned plea for social equality.

THE EASTERN EUROPEAN NEW WAVE

In the countries of the Eastern Bloc, the culture was still coming out from the Stalinist deep freeze. We have already discussed many of the most important figures in this cinematic thaw, such as Poland's Andrzej Wajda and the Soviet filmmakers Mikheil Kalatozishvili and Grigori Chukhrai, whose films in the late 1950s set the stage for further developments in the 1960s. But two figures in the 1960s took matters much further, Poland's Roman Polanski and Jerzy Skolimowski. Polanski attended the Polish Film School at Lodz and made several shorts, including the farcical *Dwaj ludzie z szafa* (*Two Men and a Wardrobe*, 1958), before shooting his first feature, *Nóz w wodzie* (*Knife in the Water*), in 1962. *Knife* takes place almost entirely on a small pleasure boat, as a married couple, Andrzej (Leon Niemczyk) and Krystyna (Jolanta Umecka), picks up a nameless young hitchhiker (Zygmunt Malanowicz) to

Roman Polanski (back to camera) is about to carve up private eye Jake Gittes (Jack Nicholson) in Polanski's *Chinatown* (1974).

join them for a short cruise. Sexual jealousy soon disrupts the holiday as Andrzej becomes envious of the young man's good looks and youthful vigor. At a spare ninety-four minutes, the film attracted enough attention to garner Polanski an Academy Award nomination for Best Foreign Language Film, and his career was suddenly quite a public affair. Interestingly, Jerzy Skolimowski collaborated with Polanski on the script of *Knife in the Water,* along with writer Jakub Goldberg.

Almost immediately, Polanski moved to the West, stopping in London to direct *Repulsion* (1965), a searing drama of an unstable young woman, Carole Ledoux (Catherine Deneuve), who is left alone in an apartment in London for a weekend and gradually descends into homicidal madness. Marked by moody black-and-white cinematography and superb performances from Deneuve and the supporting cast, the film was a substantial hit, as was Polanski's next British film, *Cul-de-sac* (1966), a brutal thriller starring Donald Pleasence as George, the jealous, possessive husband of Teresa (Françoise Dorléac), who resents the fact that they are forever hidden away from the world in a remote castle on the northeast coast of the British Isles. Polanski left England for the United States, where he directed several very successful films, including the haunting *Rosemary's Baby* (1968), where witches apparently inhabit an apartment building on New York's Upper West Side and have designs on the pregnant Rosemary (Mia Farrow), and *Chinatown* (1974), a brilliant noir set in a corrupt 1930s Los Angeles, with Jack Nicholson as

294

private eye Jake Gittes, who is drawn deeper and deeper into a mystery involving millionaire Noah Cross (John Huston) and his daughter Evelyn Mulwray (Faye Dunaway). However, in March 1977 Polanski was arrested on a charge of statutory rape and subsequently fled the United States to avoid prosecution. Since then, he has worked in Europe, creating films such as *Tess* (1979) and *Bitter Moon* (1992), but the highlight is doubtless the World War II drama *The Pianist* (2002), the moving, true story of a classical pianist, a Polish Jew, who struggles to survive the Holocaust and goes into hiding from the Nazis in Warsaw. The project was especially personal for Polanski, as he himself survived the Nazi occupation of Poland as a young boy. *The Pianist* won Academy Awards for Best Director, Actor, and Writing (Adaptation) and the Palme d'Or at the Cannes Film Festival. His latest films are *The Guest Writer* (2010) and *Carnage* (2011).

Jerzy Skolimowski had a much lower profile but produced several interesting films of youthful social protest, such as *Walkower* (*Walkover,* 1965) and *Bariera* (*Barrier,* 1966); he left Poland soon after to create the mysterious thriller *Deep End* (1971), shot in London and Munich with U.S. and German financing. He then moved on to create what many consider his signature film, *Moonlighting* (1982), with Jeremy Irons as the foreman of an illegal Polish work crew in London renovating the luxurious flat of a wealthy man, in an effectively realized allegory of wealth versus privation. He then took a long hiatus from diecting but reemerged triumphantly with the stunning political thriller *Essential Killing* (2010), among several other films.

In Hungary, Miklós Jancsó stood out as the most influential filmmaker of the 1960s, followed by András Kovács and István Gaál. Kovács pursued a documentary style in his films *Nehéz emberek* (*Difficult People,* 1964), *Falak* (*Walls,* 1968), and *Staféta* (*Relay Race,* 1971), and Gaál worked on a thinly disguised autobiographical trilogy of films detailing his early life under the Stalinist regime. But Jancsó emerged as the boldest visual stylist of the group, with such films as *Szegénylegények* (*The Round-Up,* 1965), *Csillagosok, katonák* (*The Red and the White,* 1967), and *Még kér a nép* (*Red Psalm,* 1972), in which he used a ceaselessly tracking camera to create strongly political films that dealt with issues of responsibility in wartime, mob violence, and military behavior.

In Jancsó's films, the camera is an impassive observer that sees, records, and moves on with a clinical formalism that is simultaneously distancing and unnerving. Often we might wish to linger on a particular scene, but as his camera keeps moving, we know that we will only have a brief time to view each image before the eye of the lens moves on. *The Round-Up* set the

Director Miklós Jancsó (right, pointing), one of the most important directors of the Hungarian cinema in the 1960s.

tone for Jancsó's later work after a rapturous reception at the 1966 Cannes Film Festival; in 1972 his *Red Psalm* won for Best Direction at Cannes. A meticulous planner, Jancsó shoots his films quickly; he uses as few as twelve takes to create an entire film, because his lengthy tracking shots are so detailed and so elegantly executed.

Vera Chytilová was one of the most important directors of the Czechoslovakian New Wave. She began her career as a university student, emphasizing philosophy and architecture, then worked as a model, script clerk, and draftsperson, among other jobs, before she fought her way into the Prague Film School (FAMU). Working at Barrandov Studios, Chytilová encountered problems distributing her difficult, feminist work. Her early films were shot in the style of 1960s underground films in America, gritty cinema verité–like works that featured non-actors in philosophical investigations into the nature of power over women in Czech culture. Her formalism met with approval from Western critics, but it caused her to be completely silenced for several years by the political machine in her native country.

Sedmikrasky (*Daisies,* 1966) is Chytilová's best-known work abroad, although it was banned in her native country for several years. It can be aptly described as a Brechtian comedy, in which two young women loll around, often semi-nude, as they talk directly to the audience about philosophical and political questions. *Daisies* is thus a prototypical New Wave feminist film, with Brechtian political statements ("Everything is spoiled for us in this world"), jarring editing (the women are intercut with stock footage of buildings falling apart), and existential ponderings (at one point, the women ruminate that if "you're not registered, [there is] no proof you exist").

Jan Schmidt's absurdist, apocalyptic tragic comedy *Konec srpna v Hotelu Ozon* (*The End of August at the Hotel Ozone,* 1967) is an appropriate coda to this brief survey of Czech films; in August 1968 Soviet tanks rolled into Prague to crush a regime that was becoming too liberal for the Soviet rulers. The Czech cinema came to an abrupt end for the time being.

In Yugoslavia, Aleksandar Petrovic's romantic *Dvoje* (*And Love Has Vanished,* 1961) is generally considered the first film of that country's New Wave movement. Petrovic followed it up with his most commercially successful film, *Skupljaci perja* (*I Even Met Happy Gypsies,* 1967), a love story that ends in murder, set among the gypsy tribes of the region. Dušan Makavejev, however, soon emerged as the most visible proponent of the Yugoslavian New Wave, with the love story *Covek nije tica* (*Man Is Not a Bird,* 1965); the neo-Godardian *Ljubavni slucaj ili tragedija sluzbenice* (*P.T.T. Love Affair; or The Case of the Missing Switchboard Operator,* 1967), which uses stills, interviews, clips from documentaries, and other

A scene from Vera Chytilová's *Sedmikrasky* (*Daisies,* 1966), a groundbreaking film of the Czech New Wave.

Brechtian devices to tell the story of the murder of a young woman and the political, social, and sexual attitudes that led to her demise; and *W.R.— Misterije organizma* (*W.R.: Mysteries of the Organism,* 1971), a paean to the human spirit and a rejection of both Stalinist ideology and American commercial society.

In East Germany, personal visions had a harder time coming to the surface, as everything was subject to the strictest censorship possible and had to conform to the Communist Party line. Nevertheless, some remarkable films were made. Joachim Kunert's *Die Abenteuer des Werner Holt* (*The Adventures of Werner Holt,* 1965) details that country's struggle to survive at the end of World War II. Konrad Wolf's *Sterne* (*Stars,* 1959), the story of a young Jewish woman who becomes romantically involved with a German prison guard during the same era, effectively interrogates the anti-Semitism of the period.

Political theater in Dusan Makavejev's *W.R.—Misterije organizma* (*W.R.: Mysteries of the Organism*, 1971).

But these were exceptions to the general run of careful, commercial films favored by the government.

Vulo Radev, one of the key directors of the Bulgarian cinema, created the political allegories *Kradetzat na praskovi* (*The Peach Thief,* 1964) and *Nay-dalgata nosht* (*The Longest Night,* 1967), both set in wartime and examining the mechanics of human responsibility when all other social structures collapse. Also in Bulgaria, Grisha Ostrovski and Todor Stoyanov made *Otklonenie* (*Detour,* a k a *Sidetracked,* 1967), a film dealing with a romantic reunion, shot in the "memory editing" style of Alain Resnais, mixing past, present, and future into one seamless, dreamlike whole. Gueorgui Stoyanov's *Ptitzi i hratki* (*Birds and Greyhounds,* 1969) is an even more experimental work, intercutting the trial of a group of Resistance fighters during World War II with fantasy sequences that picture an idyllic earthly paradise, juxtaposing graphic violence with dreams of youthful abandon to create an unsettling commentary on social and political corruption.

In the USSR, Sergei Parajanov's *Tini zabutykh predkiv* (*Shadows of Forgotten Ancestors,* 1964) was a bold symbolic break from the tradition of safe literary adaptations and light romantic comedies. Parajanov employed plastic use of the cinematic medium—zoom shots, wide-angle lenses, and a richly detailed color scheme—to tell the story of a tragic love affair set in nineteenth-century Carpathia. The film was so visually dazzling that it immediately attracted international attention, winning a BAFTA (the British equivalent of the Academy Award) as the Best Foreign Film of the year. But Parajanov rapidly fell into disfavor with the ruling Soviet authorities, much as Eisenstein had in the early 1930s, for his baroque approach to the cinema, which reveled in light, shadow, color, and spectacle to push the power of film to its limits. As a result, he was only able to complete one more film entirely on his own, *Sayat Nova* (*Color of Pomegranates,* 1968), which was banned almost immediately upon its release and issued in a limited fashion with heavy cuts in 1972.

In 1974, Parajanov's resistance to the Soviet regime led to a five-year prison sentence at hard labor, on charges that were entirely fabricated. Released in 1978 as a result of an international outcry by members of the film community, Parajanov made a short film, *Return to Life* (1980), by way of celebration. But by 1982 he was back in jail, again on trumped-up charges, although he served only a short sentence before being released. Finally, under Mikhail Gorbachev's new regime, he was able to make two final feature films, *Ambavi Suramis tsikhitsa* (*The Legend of the Suram Fortress,* 1984) and *Ashugi-Karibi* (*The Lovelorn Minstrel,* 1988), both co-directed with Dodo Abashidze, but the imprisonment and suffering he had undergone left him a broken man. When Parajanov died in 1990 of lung cancer at the age of sixty-six, the Soviet Union lost the most inventive director to work in the USSR since Eisenstein's blaze of glory in the 1920s. After his death, the Armenian documentarist Mikhail Vartanov created *Parajanov: Verjin garun* (*Parajanov: The Last Spring,* 1992), which contained fragments of the director's last, unfinished work, *The Confession* (1990).

AFRICA

In Senegal, the director Ousmane Sembène, a former dock worker who became a full-time novelist when a back injury forced him to abandon manual labor, made a short film, *Borom Sarret* (1963; often miscredited as 1966), about a day in the life of a poor cart driver who barely makes a living transporting passengers around the streets of Dakar. As Senegal, and Africa, passed from colonialism into an era of self-rule, budding filmmakers searched for schooling to bring their visions to the screen, and Sembène found his teacher in Mark Donskoy, the Soviet filmmaker, who trained him in the Moscow Film School. Later, Sembène apprenticed under director Sergei Gerasimov at the Gorky Film Studio and then returned to Senegal to

African cinema breaks through the barriers of colonialism at last in Ousmane Sembène's *La Noire de . . .* (*Black Girl*, 1966).

make films of his own. *Borom Sarret* was shot with a 35 mm silent newsreel camera, with minimal sound effects, music, and dialogue dubbed in after the fact, and voiced in French, the colonial language of Senegal, rather than Wolof, an indigenous tongue. But it was, at twenty minutes, an impressive start.

Sembène followed it up with *La Noire de . . .* (*Black Girl*, 1966), an ambitious attack on French racism and colonialism, in which a bourgeois French couple hires a young Senegalese woman to be their live-in maid at their apartment on the French Riviera. Showing no concern for her dignity, her cultural heritage, or even her humanity, the couple treats the young woman with callous indifference. She soon feels socially isolated, and in desperation takes her own life. *Black Girl* was an immediate international success, establishing Sembène as the foremost film director of sub-Saharan Africa. *Black Girl*, too, was shot in French, but with *Tauw* (1970), a twenty-four-minute color movie shot in 16 mm sync sound, Sembène embraced the language and culture of his home country, shooting primarily in the Wolof language; *Tauw* documents one day in the life of a dock laborer in Senegal who can't get work. When his girlfriend becomes pregnant, Tauw leaves his family home to start a new life with her, much to his mother's sorrow. Tauw's future is uncertain, but the film has an optimism that suggests he will find his place in the world, despite many difficulties.

From this promising start, Sembène went on to shoot numerous features, such as *Mandabi* (*The Money Order,* 1968), in which a man attempts to cash a money order but encounters an intimidating government bureaucracy that thwarts him at every turn; and *Emitai* (*God of Thunder,* 1971), which documents the war between French colonial forces and the Diolas, a Senegalese tribe, in the final days of World War II. Other films, such as *Xala* (*The Curse,* 1975), *Ceddo* (*Outsiders,* 1977), *Camp de Thiaroye* (*The Camp at Thiaroye,* 1987, co-directed with Thierno Faty Sow), and *Guelwaar* (1992), consolidated his international reputation, and his work remains a vibrant

voice of social commentary as well as a barometer of the effects of political change in Senegal and Africa as a whole. One of his final films, *Moolaadé* (2004), criticized the practice of female genital mutilation and was well received at the Cannes Film Festival. Sembène continued to work until his death in 2007; with his passing, the African cinema lost one of its most authentic and vigorous social critics.

*　　*　　*

The 1960s were thus a crucible of international change in the cinema, in which the styles and values of the previous sixty years of film were called into question. Around the world, people saw the chance to create films that related directly to their own lives and spoke to the realities and dreams of their varying situations. Hollywood's representational lock on world cinema was shaken by the artists of the French New Wave, who spread their message of hope, diversity, and change to the filmmakers of other countries; these directors in turn picked up cameras to create a cinema of their own. Films became political statements, and radical departures in both style and content became the norm. If the filmic revolution of the 1960s proved anything, it demonstrated conclusively that anyone with the will to do it could make a movie, no matter how meager his or her resources. Informal distribution networks sprang up around the world, bypassing the traditional cinematic marketplace and bringing films directly to a widely diverse audience. The 1970s would be a different era altogether, but for the moment, the cinema was a universal language that reached out across cultural boundaries and spoke to the human condition in a more inclusive fashion than ever before.

NINE

WORLD CINEMA 1970 TO THE PRESENT

DAS NEUE KINO

If the 1960s marked a period of nearly limitless expansion in world cinema, the 1970s was, to a degree, an era of retrenchment. The most significant artistic movement of the early 1970s was Das Neue Kino, the New German Cinema that flourished under the auspices of Jean-Marie Straub, Danièle Huillet, Rainer Werner Fassbinder, Wim Wenders, Werner Herzog, and others. These directors all came to the cinema as the result of the Oberhausen Manifesto, published in spring 1962, which declared that the old German cinema was dead and that only a decisive break with the past would bring about a new vision of film. Behind all this activity was the figure of filmmaker and producer Alexander Kluge, who was the first to successfully persuade the German government to fund the young German Film Board, a state-run subsidy that successfully bankrolled nineteen feature films, as well as to start film schools in Berlin and Munich and create a national film archive. Straub and Huillet, discussed earlier, can be seen as the founding figures of Das Neue Kino, leading us to Fassbinder, the most incandescent and prolific figure of the New German Cinema.

Rainer Werner Fassbinder

Born in 1946 in Bavaria, Fassbinder worked at a variety of odd jobs while absorbing as many films as he possibly could, particularly the 1950s Technicolor melodramas of European émigré Douglas Sirk. Dropping out of high school, he applied to the prestigious Berlin Film School but was turned down. Unperturbed, Fassbinder began making short films, as well as doing work in the theater with the Munich Action Theater group, where he had the opportunity to observe Jean-Marie Straub. Straub filmed one of his condensed theater pieces as a twenty-three-minute production, *Der Bräutigam, die Komödiantin und der Zuhälter* (*The Bridegroom, the Comedienne, and the Pimp*, 1968), which consisted of only twelve shots. Fassbinder was impressed

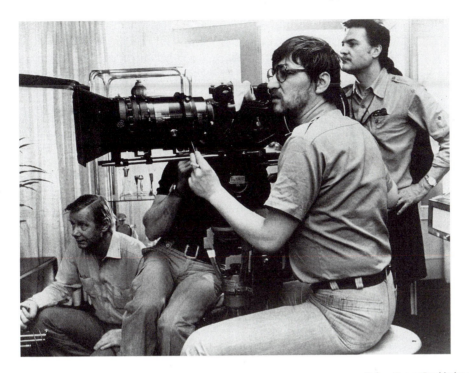

Rainer Werner Fassbinder on the set in the mid-1970s, his most prolific period as a filmmaker.

with the speed with which Straub worked, the simplicity of his camera setups, and the bold originality of his vision.

The Bridegroom, the Comedienne, and the Pimp tells (in a typically fragmented way) the story of James (Jimmy Powell), a young African American soldier living in Munich who falls in love with Lilith (Lilith Ungerer), a prostitute who wants to escape her sordid life. The film is one of the classics of the New German Cinema, and like Straub and Huillet's *The Chronicle of Anna Magdalena Bach,* it had an electrifying effect on young filmmakers. Straub proved that one could make films cheaply and effectively with a minimum of financing, sets, or other physical properties. Fassbinder used his experience as an actor in the film to launch his own career, shooting in much the same manner: quickly, cheaply, and with a high degree of theatricality. His 1969 feature debut *Liebe ist kälter als der Tod* (*Love Is Colder Than Death*), a downbeat crime drama with a typically pessimistic worldview, was shot on a shoestring budget of 95,000 marks, roughly equivalent to the spare production costs of *Breathless* or *The 400 Blows.* But where Godard and Truffaut seemed to be drunk with the plastic and kinetic possibilities of cinema, Fassbinder staged his scenes in long, flat takes, with the characters speaking in an equally disengaged fashion, and editing reduced to a minimum. *Katzelmacher* (1969) was shot in a mere nine days, telling the tale of a Greek immigrant who falls in with a group of slackers in Munich. Fassbinder began to churn out feature films with astonishing rapidity, often making three or more a year. Typically using a stock company of actors, he soon assumed an almost mythic status among its members.

As Fassbinder's films began to form a clear identity, he became a favorite at international cinema festivals, reveling in the attention he was receiving even when his work was met with boos. *Warnung vor einer heiligen Nutte* (*Beware of a Holy Whore*, 1971) is a backstage look at the mechanics of his filmmaking style, as the cast and crew of a movie wait around on location in a Spanish hotel for the arrival of their star and director so that shooting can begin. Eddie Constantine, so memorable as private eye Lemmy Caution in Godard's *Alphaville*, plays himself as the star everyone is waiting for, while Lou Castel plays the director, Jeff, who is clearly modeled on Fassbinder himself, right down to Fassbinder's signature leather jacket.

In 1972 Fassbinder scored one of his key early international successes with the fatalistic *Händler der vier Jahreszeiten* (*The Merchant of Four Seasons*), which centers on the hapless Hans Epp (Hans Hirschmüller), once a member of the French Foreign Legion and now a door-to-door greengrocer. When his wife tries to leave him, he has a minor heart attack and becomes increasingly despondent about the failure of his life to amount to anything. Hans finally goes to a bar and drinks himself to death, suffering a fatal heart attack as the other patrons watch with detachment.

In the next few years, Fassbinder created a series of polished, Sirk-influenced films such as *Die Bitteren Tränen der Petra von Kant* (*The Bitter Tears of Petra von Kant*, 1972), about the love life of a fashion designer; the five-part television series *Acht Stunden sind kein Tag* (*Eight Hours Are Not a Day*, 1972), a family drama centering on the workplace; and a riff on Sirk's 1955 *All That Heaven Allows, Angst essen Seele auf* (*Ali: Fear Eats the Soul*, 1974), in which a white sixty-year-old German cleaning woman, Emmi (Brigitte Mira), falls in love with a young black immigrant, Ali (El Hedi ben Salem). (Director Todd Haynes also paid homage to Sirk's film in *Far From Heaven* [2002], with Julianne Moore, Dennis Quaid, and Dennis Haysbert.)

Success as a filmmaker did little to temper Fassbinder's view of life. Although he kept up the rapid pace of production, causing one critic to jokingly observe that Fassbinder and his colleagues made whole films on their lunch breaks, Fassbinder now began a downward personal spiral, drinking heavily and abusing drugs. His later work, such as the television movie *Ich will doch nur, daß ihr mich liebt* (*I Only Want You to Love Me*, 1976), *Satans-*

304

braten (*Satan's Brew*, 1976), and the aptly titled English-language feature *Despair—Eine Reise ins Licht* (*Despair*, 1978), starring Dirk Bogarde, continued the militantly gay director's preoccupation with lost love, romantic betrayal, dissatisfaction with one's life, and the seeming impossibility of happiness in the modern world.

Fassbinder's famously epic *Berlin Alexanderplatz* (1980), based on Alfred Döblin's novel, chronicles the life of average man Franz Bieberkopf (Günter Lamprecht), who is released from prison but finds that he cannot reintegrate himself into society, due to forces seemingly beyond his control. At 941 minutes, or more than fifteen and a half hours, this monumental project took a full 154 days to film and was screened on German television in fourteen parts. The slight yet elegiac *Lili Marleen* (1981) followed, an elegantly staged period piece set in Nazi Germany, as a cabaret singer (Hanna Schygulla) becomes a Nazi icon when her hit single, "Lili Marleen," becomes a sort of national anthem for the Nazi movement. *Die Sehnsucht der Veronika Voss* (*Veronika Voss*, 1982) is about a fading Nazi movie star who after the war becomes a morphine addict. The director's last film, *Querelle* (1982), based on the novel by the French writer Jean Genet, deals with a French sailor who comes to terms with his homosexuality after a visit to a spectacular brothel that fulfills his

Rainer Werner Fassbinder's *Die Sehnsucht der Veronika Voss* (*Veronika Voss,* 1982) follows the postwar career of a fading Nazi movie star in Fassbinder's signature sardonic style.

every fantasy. By this time, Fassbinder's high-speed lifestyle was catching up with him. Overweight, drinking and smoking heavily, Fassbinder died of an overdose of cocaine and sleeping pills in a Munich apartment at the age of thirty-seven.

At the same time, Fassbinder's contemporaries were making their mark. Hans-Jürgen Syberberg made his first feature, *Fünfter Akt, siebte Szene. Fritz Kortner probt Kabale und Liebe* (*Fritz Kortner Rehearses*), in 1965; this was followed by Alexander Kluge's *Abschied von gestern—(Anita G.)* (*Yesterday Girl*) and Volker Schlöndorff's *Der Junge Törless* (*Young Torless,* both 1966). Wim Wenders's directorial debut was the drama *Summer in the City* (1970), and in 1978 Syberberg created one of the most ambitious films of the movement, *Hitler–ein Film aus Deutschland* (*Our Hitler: A Film from Germany*), a seven-hour work that compares Hitler to King Ludwig of Bavaria and argues that both men were mad, with obsessive dreams of world conquest. Thus Syberberg seeks to interrogate the soul of Germany, arguing that there is something inherent in the German psyche that dreams of limitless dominion. Using a wide variety of theatrical devices, such as rear-screen projection, obvious studio sets, and minimalist props, Syberberg's best films are ruminations on the desire for conquest and the chains forged by a nation's history.

Kluge, who started as an assistant to Fritz Lang in 1958 when Lang returned to Germany to make his last two films, also directed the political allegory *Die Artisten in der Zirkuskuppel: Ratlos* (*Artists under the Big Top: Perplexed,* 1968), the equally activist *Gelegenheitsarbeit einer Sklavin* (*Part-Time Work of a Domestic Slave,* 1973), and the twelve-part investigative tract *Die Macht der Gefühle* (*The Power of Emotion,* 1983), which examines how emotion operates in human relations. Like Fassbinder, Kluge is an intensely political filmmaker, and Fassbinder even dedicated one of his later films, *Lola* (1981), to him. He is also responsible for coordinating the production of the omnibus film *Germany in Autumn* (*Deutschland im Herbst,* 1978), which incorporated the talents of Fassbinder, Schlöndorff, Edgar Reitz, and other Neue Kino directors in a meditation on the political, social, and artistic climate of Germany in the late 1970s.

Volker Schlöndorff is one of the most commercially successful directors of the New German Cinema, and, not surprisingly, his films are more traditional. *Der Plötzliche Reichtum der armen Leute von Kombach* (*The Sudden Wealth of the Poor People of Kombach,* 1971), from a script by the actor and writer Margarethe von Trotta, was a substantial commercial and critical success and proved to be a turning point in Schlöndorff's career. He and von Trotta, who also appeared in the film, fell in love during production, and they married shortly after the shooting wrapped. Afterward they worked together on several projects, co-directing *Die verlorene Ehre der Katharina Blum oder: Wie Gewalt entstehen und wohin sie führen kann* (*The Lost Honor of Katharina Blum*, 1975). In 1979, Schlöndorff's *Die Blechtrommel* (*The Tin Drum*, 1979) became the first film from post–World War II Germany to receive an Academy Award as Best Foreign Language Film, signaling that the New German Cinema had finally broken through to mainstream audiences. He has since moved into more commercial fare with *The Handmaid's Tale* (1990, based on the Margaret Atwood novel), *Die Stille nach dem Schuß* (*The Legend of Rita*, 2000), and *Der Neunte Tag* (*The Ninth Day*, 2004).

In 1978 Von Trotta directed her first full-length solo project, *Das Zweite Erwachen der Christa Klages* (*The Second Awakening of Christa Klages*). This film, like most von Trotta films, focuses on a female protagonist. Based on a true story, *The Second Awakening of Christa Klages* is the story of an unlikely trio of thieves who pull off a robbery to aid an alternative day-care center. Her next film, *Schwestern oder Die Balance des Glücks* (*Sisters, or the Balance of Happiness*, 1979), also met with great success, telling the tale of two sisters' individual struggle for identity, each polarized by her associations with home and career. Both *Die Bleierne Zeit* (*Marianne and Juliane*, 1981) and *Die Geduld der Rosa Luxemburg* (*Rosa Luxemburg*, 1986) demonstrate von Trotta's persistent and continued interest in issues of female identity and the philosophy of filmic "reality." *Marianne and Juliane* is a narrative of two sisters' lives in 1968 Germany as they fight for women's rights in a revolutionary period of modern history, while *Rosa Luxemburg* re-creates (and, to a large extent, reinvents) the history of the revolutionary Rosa Luxemburg, a leading political activist of the Spartacus League, a splinter group of the Social Democrats in Germany in the early part of the twentieth century.

WERNER HERZOG

Werner Herzog directed his first short film, *Herakles*, using a stolen camera in 1962, when he was a freshman at the University of Munich. His first feature film, *Lebenszeichen* (*Signs of Life*, 1968), deals with the loneliness and isolation of three German soldiers who must guard an old bunker on a remote Greek island, while his second full-length film, *Auch Zwerge haben klein angefangen* (*Even Dwarfs Started Small*, 1970), uses a riot by a group of dwarfs locked in an institution to draw attention to the materialism of daily life. But Herzog's *Aguirre, der Zorn Gottes* (*Aguirre: The Wrath of God*, 1972),

Klaus Kinski as the mad, charismatic Don Lope
de Aguirre in Werner Herzog's *Aguirre, der Zorn
Gottes* (*Aguirre: The Wrath of God*, 1972).

starring the cult actor Klaus Kinski as a crazed conquis-
tador who searches for a treasure trove of gold in six-
teenth-century South America, was the film that put Herzog on the map.
Shot in both English and German versions, the manic Kinski is superb as the
crazed visionary who will let nothing stand in the way of his insane quest,
no matter what the cost. Subsequent films consolidated Herzog's reputation
as an uncompromising and individualistic artist, such as *Nosferatu: Phantom der Nacht* (*Nosferatu the Vampyre*, 1979), with Kinski in the title role, in
a remake of F. W. Murnau's classic *Nosferatu* of 1922, and *Fitzcarraldo*
(1982), in which an obsessed colonialist (Kinski again) determines to develop a trade route for ships in the Amazon jungle as well as to establish a
grand opera company there. For *Fitzcarraldo,* Herzog took his crew on location for the shoot, which was insanely difficult; at one point in the film, Kinski's character hauls a ship over the Andes Mountains, and to film it Herzog
did just that. More recently, Herzog scored a commercial and critical hit
with the bizarre documentary *Grizzly Man* (2005), which he created from
existing archival footage, documenting the life of a young man obsessed
with wild bears and their habitat, and the 3-D *Cave of Forgotten Dreams*
(2010), one of the most visually sensuous documentaries ever made.

WIM WENDERS

Wim Wenders's early films include the allegorical murder drama *Die Angst des Tormanns beim Elfmeter* (*The Goalie's Anxiety at the Penalty Kick*, 1972) and the equally cerebral *Alice in den Städten* (*Alice in the Cities*, 1974), about an epic case of writer's block. He later collaborated with Nicholas Ray on *Lightning Over Water* (1980) before coming to America to direct *Hammett* (begun in 1980, completed in 1982) for Francis Ford Coppola's Zoetrope Studios; Coppola eventually took over production and reshot part of it, which ultimately satisfied no one. Wenders's next American film, however, *Paris, Texas* (1984), was a commercial and critical hit, after which Wenders returned to Germany for the triumphal *Der Himmel über Berlin* (*Wings of Desire*, 1987), in which a group of angels look after the destiny of a man in postwar Berlin. The film is shot in gorgeously saturated black-and-white and color by Henri Alekan, who, among many other projects, had also shot Jean Cocteau's *Beauty and the Beast* in 1946.

Wenders's remarkable documentary *Chambre 666* (*Room 666*, 1982) stems from placing a camera in a room during the 1982 Cannes Film Festival and then asking a wide range of directors, including Steven Spielberg, Rainer Werner Fassbinder, Chantal Akerman, Michelangelo Antonioni, Jean-Luc Godard, Yilmaz Güney, Susan Seidelman, Paul Morrissey, and others to speculate on the future of cinema. Spielberg delivers an earnest monologue, while Godard, after delivering a few pointed observations, gets up and turns off the camera. Wenders has since directed the feature *Am Ende der Gewalt* (*The End of Violence*, 1997), an examination of brutality in the Hollywood cinema; the documentary *Buena Vista Social Club* (1999); one of the videos for the rock documentary *U2: The Best of 1990–2002* (2002); the fatalistic drama *Land of Plenty* (2004); and a omnibus, multipart film, *8* (2007), which he co-directed with Jane Campion, Jan Kounen, and Gaspar Noé. In 2011, Wenders directed the 3-D documentary *Pina*, on the life and work of choreographer Pina Bausch.

NEW GERMAN VISIONS

In the years since the New German Cinema first exploded, a number of talented directors have appeared on the scene, such as Tom Tykwer, whose *Lola rennt* (*Run Lola Run*, 1998) is a race-against-time thriller in which Lola

309

(Franka Potente) must save her boyfriend from assassination by drug dealers. Deftly mixing animation, live action, digital special effects, and a lively rock score, *Run Lola Run* is notable for telling its story with three different scenarios. Doris Dörrie is best known for her feminist comedy *Männer . . .* (*Men . . .*, 1985); her earlier films, such as *Im Innern des Wals* (*In the Belly of the Whale*, 1985), represented a strong feminist vision within a more serious context. *In the Belly of the Whale* opens with the violent beating of teenager Carla (Janna Marangosoff) by her policeman father, Erwin (Peter Sattmann), who alternates between brutalizing her and buying her expensive presents to compensate. Fed up, Carla leaves home to search for her mother, Marta (Silvia Reize), who ran away ten years earlier after also being repeatedly beaten by Erwin. When Carla finally tracks her down, she discovers Marta has become a prostitute. Returning home in despair, Carla is murdered by her father. The film's uncompromising scenario reflects Dörrie's own jaded view of relationships between men and women. Her other films include *Paradies* (*Paradise*, 1986), *Ich und Er* (*Me and Him*, 1988), and the tragic romance *Cherry Blossoms* (2008).

CHANTAL AKERMAN

While the New German Cinema was a key movement in the period from 1970 to the late 1990s, spreading its stripped-down style around the world, filmmakers elsewhere were re-creating the cinema in yet another new form. The Belgian director Chantal Akerman came to the United States after quitting film school at home. Her first job was as a cashier for a porno theater in New York. Profoundly influenced by Jean-Luc Godard's *Pierrot le fou* (1965), Akerman was determined to direct; she claimed to have stolen the money to finance her early film, *Hotel Monterey* (1972), a grim, completely silent look at a shabby welfare hotel. Here she expressed an interest in the transient nature of modern urban life, with an eye toward spaces that underscore the discord of mobility; hotels, train stations, and the people who move within these spaces.

Je, tu, il, elle (*I, You, He, She*, 1974), shot in stark black-and-white on a minimal budget, was Akerman's breakthrough feature-length film, for which she also wrote the screenplay and played the lead role. The camera follows a woman, Julie, who seems lost in a modern industrial world. In one scene, Julie sits at a table compulsively eating piles of sugar for no apparent reason; in the next scene, she hitchhikes, gets a ride from a trucker (Niels Arestrup),

Delphine Seyrig as Jeanne in Chantal Akerman's study of modern alienation, *Jeanne Dielman, 23 Quai de Commerce, 1080 Bruxelles* (1976).

and seduces him. Back in her apartment, she makes love to a woman (Claire Wauthion). Because the camera records the action in a detached, almost clinical manner, this scene has often been noted for its unusual portrayal of sexuality.

But the film was merely a curtain raiser for her next effort, the groundbreaking *Jeanne Dielman, 23 Quai du Commerce, 1080 Bruxelles* (1976), about the daily activities of a Belgian housewife and prostitute. For much of the story Jeanne (Delphine Seyrig) lives her life alone, compulsively cooking, cleaning, and entertaining her son, living a life of quiet desperation. All the while, she welcomes customers into her home. This routine existence is finally punctuated by a scene in which Jeanne suddenly, and without warning, kills a client with a pair of scissors after having sex with him, in a gesture of disgust and despair. The film ends with an almost unendurably long take of Jeanne sitting at her dining room table after the murder, listlessly staring out the window into the night, as the glare of a neon sign washes over her impassive face. *Jeanne Dielman*'s depth and detail are the work of a great auteur fully in control of the medium (indeed, many people still regard the film as the high point of Akerman's career), and its solid critical reception afforded Akerman the power to make projects of her own choosing.

311

Stanislas Merhar and Sylvie Testud in *La Captive* (*The Captive*, 2000) by Chantal Akerman.

News from Home (1977) and *Les Rendez-vous d'Anna* (*The Meetings of Anna*, 1978) are equally personal in their intent and execution. In *News from Home*, Akerman lets the camera stare at urban spaces, while off-screen she reads letters from a mother to an absent daughter. Similarly, *Les Rendez-vous d'Anna* uses sameness to create drama. The camera follows director Anna Silver (Aurore Clément) as she travels through a series of empty spaces—hotels, train stations, underground railways—on a promotional tour for her latest film. *Les Rendez-vous d'Anna* contains Akerman's signature long takes, avoidance of close-ups, naturalistic sound, and lack of conventional narrative. *Toute une nuit* (*All Night Long*, 1982) continues this theme of personal solitude, as it follows a series of random sexual encounters during one particular night. In 2000, Akerman created the stunning story of love and obsession *La Captive* (*The Captive*) based on a narrative by Marcel Proust, which documents a rich young man's passion for a young woman he wants to possess body and soul.

Akerman proved herself able to swing easily between genres and moods with the searing documentary *South* (*Sud*, 1999), about the brutal 1998 lynching of James Byrd Jr. in Jasper, Texas. The film was shot on location shortly after the murder took place. Typically for Akerman, she simply records the places and the people, both black and white, who were part of the lynching, refusing to make obvious judgments and firmly acknowledging her outsider status. But the film's last shot, in which the camera retraces the route by which Byrd was dragged to his death by a chain attached to the back of a pickup truck, is an ample indictment of the social attitudes that allow such atrocities to persist. In 2011, Akerman directed the equally uncompromising *La folie Almayer* (*Almayer's Folly*), an unflinching study of prejdice and greed.

312

THE DARDENNE BROTHERS

Jean-Pierre and Luc Dardenne began making short video documentaries together in the 1970s, and then shot their first fiction film in 1987, *Falsch* (*False*), in which the ghosts of a Jewish family, reunited after World War II in a deserted airport, are forced to deal with their past. The work is atypical for the Dardenne brothers in that it is highly stylized, with vibrant colors and theatrical staging, and while it is an excellent film, it does not really anticipate their later work. Their second film, *Je pense à vous* (*You're on My Mind*, 1992), is also a surprise, in its narrative of a factory worker photographed with conventional cinematic imagery, using crane shots, a sweeping music track, and rather contrived performances.

However, the Dardennes' *La Promesse* (*The Promise*, 1996), a handheld documentary-like tale of a man and his young son who are engaged in an illegal immigration scheme in contemporary Belgium, hit a nerve with audiences and critics alike, confirming that the brothers had returned to their bare-bones roots. This was followed by the equally compelling *Rosetta* (1999), about a young girl who lives with her alcoholic mother and is desperate to hang onto her job. In 2005, the brothers completed *L'Enfant* (*The Child*), in which a desperate young father sells his infant son for cash because he lives in a world in which everything is for sale. When the father changes his mind and retrieves the child, he finds that his complications have only begun. With *Lorna's Silence* (*Le Silence de Lorna*, 2008) and *The Kid with a Bike* (*Le Gamin au Vélo*, 2011), the Dardennes continued their unsparing view of a cruel and often indifferent world.

NEW CINEMA IN ITALY

In Italy, the Neorealist school had long since evaporated. Vittorio De Sica acted in and/or directed a long series of conventional romantic comedies simply to keep working, although he did complete one final masterpiece, *Il Giardino dei Finzi-Contini* (*The Garden of the Finzi-Continis*), in 1971. However, Roberto Rossellini, ever adaptable, reinvented himself completely with a string of remarkable television movies for RAI, Italian television, beginning with the historical drama *La Prise de pouvoir par Louis XIV* (*The Rise of Louis XIV*, 1966), a French-Italian co-production, and continuing with many similar films, including *Atti degli apostoli* (*The Acts of the Apostles*, 1969),

Socrate (*Socrates*, 1970), *Blaise Pascal* (1971), and *Il Messia* (*The Messiah*, 1976). What makes these movies remarkable is their vibrant use of color, their long and complex tracking shots, often lasting as long as ten minutes, and the painstaking degree of historical accuracy that the director insisted upon in their creation. For many viewers, they remain the most satisfying and intellectually challenging historical dramas made for the screen.

Lina Wertmüller, born in Rome in 1926, initially produced a number of avant-garde plays and worked as a puppeteer, stage manager, set designer, and writer for radio and television. Her first major break into the film industry came when she worked as an assistant on Federico Fellini's *8 ½* (1963). Fellini financed Wertmüller's first film, *I Basilischi* (*The Lizards*), in 1963. Both *The Lizards* and her second film, *Questa volta parliamo di uomini* (*Let's Talk About Men*, 1965), examined male gender roles. She then teamed up with actor Giancarlo Giannini for many of her most famous films, notably *Mimi metallurgico ferito nell'onore* (*The Seduction of Mimi*, 1972), nominated for the *Palme d'Or* at the 1972 Cannes Film Festival. *Film d'amore e d'anarchia, ovvero stamattina alle 10 in via dei Fiori nella nota casa di tolleranza* (*Love and Anarchy*, 1973) was a commercial and critical success for the director, who became a cult figure in the United States after the film's release in 1974.

Many of Wertmüller's films are comic sociocultural studies of Italian machismo and sexuality; she has been consistently interested in sexuality and leftist political activism, especially in her early work. This is aptly demonstrated by *Travolti da un insolito destino nell'azzurro mare d'agosto* (*Swept Away*, 1974), a socialist comedy in which a rich woman, Raffaella (Mariangela Melato), and some friends rent a yacht to sail the Mediterranean; one of the sailors on the boat, the socialist Gennarino (Giancarlo Giannini), finds Raffaella and her friends spoiled and overbearing. When Rafaella impulsively decides to visit a small island, she orders Gennarino to take her in a little motorboat, which promptly conks out in the middle of the trip. The two seek shelter on another island, which is completely uninhabited. Gennarino, used to fending for himself, quickly adapts to the situation, while Rafaella can do nothing for herself and must now beg for Gennarino's aid. The tables have thus quite neatly turned, and the two begin a dance of sexual attraction with decidedly political overtones.

Pasqualino Settebellezze (*Seven Beauties*, 1975) is a bizarre comedy set in a Nazi concentration camp, starring Giancarlo Giannini as a ladies' man who suddenly has to deal with the horror of battle in World War II; when captured, he learns to survive in the camp no matter what the cost. But as the 1970s progressed, Wertmüller seemed to have lost her edge. A brief flirtation with Hollywood in the late 1970s produced the English-language *The End of the World in Our Usual Bed in a Night Full of Rain* (*Fine del mondo nel nostro solito letto in una notte piena di pioggia*, 1978), which was neither a commercial nor critical success. In 1992, she wrote and directed *Io speriamo che me la cavo* (*Ciao, Professore!*), a sentimental comedy about poor schoolchildren in Naples, considerably less compelling and challenging than her earlier work. In 2004, Wertmüller directed the English-language comedy *Too Much Romance . . . It's Time for Stuffed Peppers* (*Peperoni ripieni e pesci in faccia*) with Sophia Loren and F. Murray Abraham.

Bernardo Bertolucci came to prominence with *Il Conformista* (*The Conformist*, 1970) and *La Strategia del ragno* (*The Spider's Stratagem*, 1970), compelling political dramas remarkable for their penetrating social insight. *Ultimo tango a Parigi* (*Last Tango in Paris*, 1972), with Marlon Brando and Maria Schneider, was scandalous in its day for its frank sexuality, while *Novecento* (*1900*, 1976), *The Last Emperor* (*L'Ultimo imperatore*, 1987), and *The Sheltering Sky* (*Il Tè nel deserto*, 1990) showed the director moving into the realm of epic spectacle. In his *Stealing Beauty* (*Io ballo da sola*, 1996) and *The Dreamers* (*I sognatori*, 2003), Bertolucci seems to be trying to recapture his youth, with narratives that recall the spirit of unbridled optimism present in his early films, especially his hymn to youthful rebellion, *Prima della rivoluzione* (*Before the Revolution*, 1964).

The flamboyant Franco Zeffirelli, renowned for his work in opera, directed a series of popular successes, such as *The Taming of the Shrew* (1967), *Romeo and Juliet* (1968), *Endless Love* (1981), and, with Mel Gibson delivering a creditable performance, *Hamlet* (1990). He also contributed a well-received look at Fascist Italy, *Tea with Mussolini* (1999). Other key Italian figures of the period include Dario Argento, whose smart and violent thrillers such as *L'Uccello dalle piume di cristallo* (*The Bird with the Crystal Plumage*, 1970) brought a new level of graphic bloodshed to the screen, and Lucio Fulci, whose *E tu vivrai nel terrore—L'aldilà* (*The Beyond*, 1981) is a surrealistic series of gory set pieces centering on a decaying Louisiana hotel. Fulci rapidly developed a cult following among horror enthusiasts and enjoyed a prolific career as a director. The veteran master Federico Fellini directed the social satires *La Città delle donne* (*City of Women*, 1980) and *Ginger e Fred* (*Ginger and Fred*, 1985), while such up-and-coming auteurs as Maurizio Nichetti, with *Ladri di saponette* (*The Icicle Thief*, 1988), a parody of De Sica's *The Bicycle Thief*, and Giuseppe Tornatore, with *Nuovo cinema Paradiso* (*Cinema Paradiso*, 1989), attempted to revive an industry that had lost much of its commercial vitality. Roberto Benigni created the crowd-pleasing

315

comedies *Il Piccolo diavolo* (*The Little Devil*, 1988), *Johnny Stecchino* (*Johnny Toothpick*, 1991), and the enormously successful World War II comedy fable *La Vita è bella* (*Life Is Beautiful*, 1997), which won the Academy Award for Best Foreign Language Film.

ENGLAND

In England, the habitually excessive Ken Russell made a name for himself as a purveyor of over-the-top spectacle. Among his works are his adaptation of D. H. Lawrence's *Women in Love* in 1969; his sensationalized biography of Tchaikovsky, *The Music Lovers* (1970); *Tommy* (1975), based on the Who's rock opera of the same name; an *outré* biography of composer Franz Liszt, aptly titled *Lisztomania* (1975), with Roger Daltrey of the Who as Liszt; and the science fiction thriller *Altered States* (1980), which deals with experiments in a sensory deprivation tank that predictably go horribly wrong. In 1991, Russell made the exploitation drama *Whore*, but it seemed to most observers that he was playing to diminished returns by this point in his career.

Queer activist Derek Jarman, who had worked as production designer on Russell's semi-historical splatter film *The Devils* (1971) and *Savage Messiah* (1972), a typically overheated biopic on the life of the sculptor Henri Gaudier-Brzeska, emerged to become one of the most distinctive

Gay British activist Derek Jarman produced a series of sensuous films in the 1980s and early 1990s, such as *The Last of England* (1988), an examination of the collapsing British empire.

Derek Jarman's *Edward II* (1991), a modern adaptation of Christopher Marlowe's 1592 play, with surrealist imagery and copious amounts of violence.

voices of the new era, directing such films as *Sebastiane* (1976), *Jubilee* (1977), and *The Tempest* (1979). The gorgeous biographical film on the painter *Caravaggio* (1986) was followed by the allegorical *War Requiem* (1989), with music by Benjamin Britten and a brief appearance by Sir Laurence Olivier as an old soldier, in his final appearance on the screen. *The Last of England* (1988) gave a surrealistic dark view of declining England under Prime Minister Margaret Thatcher. The sexually graphic and violently inventive *Edward II* (a k a *Queer Edward II,* 1991) followed, loosely based on Christopher Marlowe's 1592 play, but by this time Jarman was ill with AIDS and needed the assistance of a "ghost director" to help him get through the shooting. Jarman's quiet, meditative study of the philosopher *Wittgenstein* (1993) was followed by *Blue* (1994), the director's final *cri-de-coeur,* in which the viewer is confronted by nothing more than a blue screen for approximately seventy-nine minutes, as Jarman furiously laments his onrushing death on the film's chaotic sound track. *Glitterbug* (1994), a compilation of early Super 8 mm home movies with a suitably shimmering sound track by Brian Eno, was released posthumously.

317

Ken Loach created a series of rough-and-tumble films about working-class England, the most compelling of which is *Riff-Raff* (1990). Mike Leigh, always his own master, also chronicled the perils of the class system in the appropriately titled *Bleak Moments* (1971), *High Hopes* (1988), *Life Is Sweet* (1990), *Naked* (1993), *Secrets & Lies* (1996), and *Career Girls* (1997) before doing an abrupt about-face and tackling a large-scale historical drama, *Topsy-Turvy* (1999), based on the lives of the comic opera masters Gilbert and Sullivan. Despite a multimillion-dollar budget, two Academy Awards, and sustained critical praise, the film failed to click at the box office. *Vera Drake* (2004) is about a back-alley abortionist in 1950s England; typically, Leigh never condemns his characters but rather concentrates on the social issues around them. In addition to directing, Leigh also writes the scripts for all his movies in concert with his actors, creating the scenario for each in a series of intensive rehearsals before shooting starts. Terence Davies, another master of drab British realism, scored with the semi-autobiographical film *Distant Voices, Still Lives* (1988), then continued his examination of British working-class life with *The Long Day Closes* (1992). In 2000, he succeeded admirably with an adaptation of Edith Wharton's novel *The House of Mirth* and in 2011 directed the tragic romance *The Deep Blue Sea*, set in 1950s London.

Channel Four Films, a commercial British broadcasting company, commissioned a large schedule of 16 mm television features in an attempt to jumpstart the moribund English film industry, which had fallen a long way from its glory days of the 1960s as an international commercial force. The increasing stranglehold of Hollywood on the international box office had brought about a crisis that only aggressive government subsidies and strategic low-budget production campaigns could hope to counteract. Many of Channel Four's modestly budgeted films played as theatrical presentations in other countries, such as Stephen Frears's comedy *My Beautiful Laundrette* (1985), and increased the visibility of English films abroad. Frears, for one, took this opportunity and ran with it, going on to make some of the most individual films of the period, such as *Sammy and Rosie Get Laid* (1987), *Dirty Pretty Things* (2002), *Mrs. Henderson Presents* (2005), and *The Queen* (2006). Mike Newell's *Four Weddings and a Funeral* (1994) was a surprise comedy hit, and Peter Greenaway, after a strong beginning with *The Draughtsman's Contract* in 1982 and *Drowning by Numbers* in 1988, confounded critics and audiences alike with his sexually explicit and brutally violent *The Cook, the Thief, His Wife and Her Lover* (1989). Guy Ritchie's *Lock, Stock and Two Smoking Barrels* (1998) was a cleverly made heist thriller; Mike Hodges's intricate *Croupier* (1998), the film that first brought actor Clive Owen to the

Sally Potter's stunningly beautiful *Orlando* (1993), with Tilda Swinton in the title role, here in a moment of repose with actor Billy Zane.

public's attention, was an existential and downbeat crime drama. Sally Potter offered the elegant *Orlando* (1992), a feminist period piece based on the Virginia Woolf novel, with brilliant performances from Tilda Swinton and Quentin Crisp. Despite financial reversals and rising production costs, innovative films continue to be made in Britain, along with a string of popular commercial comedies, such as Peter Cattaneo's *The Full Monty* (1997) and Chris and Paul Weitz's *About a Boy* (2002).

FRANCE

The French cinema kept expanding on both the commercial and personal horizons, as former New Wave directors pursued their own objectives. Meanwhile, a new wave of highly commercial filmmakers, who championed what became known as "cinema du look," made more accessible, mainstream films, with a highly polished sheen of technical execution. One of the key inspirations for the French New Wave, the classicist Robert Bresson, made his final film during this period—*L'Argent* (*Money*, 1983), a superb psychological study of the effects of a 500-franc counterfeit note on the lives of a number of unsuspecting victims.

319

Jean-Luc Godard's controversial updating of the story of the birth of Christ, *Je vous salue, Marie* (*Hail Mary,* 1985), with Myriem Roussel as Mary.

The most popular French film of the early twenty-first century was arguably Jean-Pierre Jeunet's charming *Le Fabuleux Destin d'Amélie Poulain* (*Amélie,* 2001), starring Audrey Tautou as a young woman looking for love in Paris. Visually inventive and photographed in dazzling color, *Amélie* was a surprise breakout hit for the French film industry internationally.

The astoundingly prolific Jean-Luc Godard directed *Passion* (1982), *Prénom Carmen* (*First Name: Carmen,* 1983), *Je vous salue, Marie* (*Hail Mary,* 1985), *King Lear* (1987), *Allemagne 90 neuf zéro* (*Germany Year 90 Nine Zero,* 1991), *For Ever Mozart* (1996), *Éloge de l'amour* (*In Praise of Love,* 2001), and *Notre musique* (*Our Music,* 2004), all riveting personal statements. In 2010, Godard's *Film socialisme* demonstrated that he was still at the top of his game as a social critic and provocateur.

The relaxation of censorship allowed for a more frank depiction of sex and violence. In the late 1990s and the early part of the new century, Catherine Breillat's explicit *Romance* (1999) and Gaspar Noé's drama of rape revenged, *Irreversible* (*Irréversible,* 2002), were among several European films that demanded the right to depict the entire range of human experience on the screen without censorship. These demanding movies were often a trial for audiences, and yet they told a simple truth: the cinema was no longer a place of refuge in the world. Instead, it now reflected our deepest fears, and confronted, rather than comforted, the viewer.

ELSEWHERE IN WESTERN EUROPE

The reigning king of contemporary Spanish cinema, and the spiritual heir to Buñuel's spirit of anarchy, is Pedro Almodóvar, who attracted international attention with *Mujeres al borde de un ataque de nervios* (*Women on the Verge of a Nervous Breakdown*, 1988), a screwball comedy about extremely dysfunctional family life, and *La Ley del deseo* (*Law of Desire*, 1987), a freewheeling romantic comedy with a transsexual twist. Almodóvar, who is openly gay, generally celebrates the absurdities and excesses of modern life in his films, but in *Todo sobre mi madre* (*All About My Mother*, 1999), *La Mala educación* (*Bad Education*, 2004), *Volver* (*Return*, 2006), and *The Skin I Live In* (*La Piel que habito*, 2011), he has moved away from the freneticism that marked his earlier efforts into more serious territory.

In Portugal, the unstoppable Manoel de Oliveira, who began his career as a director in 1931 and is still going strong in his second century, created an astonishing series of rigorously personal films, such as *Viagem ao Princípio do Mundo* (*Voyage to the Beginning of the World*, 1997), *Um Filme Falado* (*A Talking Picture*, 2003), and the enigmatic fable *O Estranho Caso de Angélica* (*The Strange Case of Angelica*, 2010) using CGI imagery for the first time.

Holland's Paul Verhoeven, after earning a Ph.D. in mathematics and physics, began his career with a series of documentaries for the Royal Dutch Navy and Dutch television. His early

Antonio Banderas in Pedro Almodóvar's gender-bending comedy *La Ley del deseo* (*Law of Desire*, 1987).

feature film *Spetters* (1980) examined a group of teenagers, gay and straight, who are caught up in the world of motorcycle racing, while *De Vierde Man* (*The Fourth Man*, 1983) is a macabre comedy about a woman who may or may not have murdered her three previous husbands for their money. By 1987, Verhoeven had moved to Hollywood, where he directed the violent action thriller *RoboCop* (1987), followed by *Total Recall* (1990), *Basic Instinct* (1992), *Showgirls* (1995), *Starship Troopers* (1997), and *The Hollow Man* (2000), before returning to Holland for the World War II thriller *Black Book* (2006).

A more romantic note was struck by Swedish director Lukas Moodysson, whose *Fucking Åmål* (*Show Me Love*, 1998) is, despite the title, a gentle and tender love story of a young girl's battle to find her sexual identity in a small Swedish town. In *Tillsammans* (*Together*, 2000), Moodysson casts a nostalgic eye on Swedish youth in the 1970s, as the members of a commune fight among themselves in the quest for a Utopian existence that predictably eludes them. Moodysson's *Lilja 4-ever* (*Lilya 4-ever*, 2002) is a more somber film, in which a sixteen-year-old girl (Oksana Akinshina) lives in a small town in post-Soviet Russia and dreams of a new life elsewhere. After this film, which has some echoes of *Show Me Love* (albeit in a much darker hue), Moodysson turned to increasingly experimental works, such as *Ett Hål i mitt hjärta* (*A Hole in My Heart*, 2004) and the absurdist black-and-white film *Container* (2006).

LATE SOVIET AND POST-SOVIET CINEMA

The Soviet power structure, along with its attendant censorship on all foreign and domestic films, was firmly in place through the end of the 1980s. Despite this interference, a number of interesting filmmakers began creating work in the 1970s and 1980s; films included Elem Klimov's brutal war drama *Idi i smotri* (*Come and See*, 1985), Grigori Chukhrai's Russian-Italian spy thriller *Zhizn prekrasna* (*Life Is Wonderful*, 1979), and Andrei Tarkovsky's science fiction allegory *Stalker* (1979). Tarkovsky is perhaps the most important director of this era of Soviet cinema, but state censorship drove him from the country into self-imposed exile for two years, until Mikhail Gorbachev's policy of *glasnost* (openness) arrived in the Soviet Union.

Tarkovsky had a long and distinguished career in Russian filmmaking from the late 1950s onward; his early film *Ivanovo detstvo* (*Ivan's Childhood*, 1962) tracked the adventures of a twelve-year-old Russian spy during World

War II as he slips across German lines to collect information for his country. The film was begun by director Eduard Abalov, who was abruptly fired; Tarkovsky was brought in to finish, though initially he received no screen credit. The movie is a somewhat sentimental drama, firmly in step with Soviet Cold War policy. But *Andrey Rublyov* (*Andrei Rublev*, 1969), a violent historical drama about fifteenth-century Russian religious life and warfare, centering on a particularly ascetic monk, was so stark in its depiction of medieval hardship that, though made in 1966, it was held from release by the authorities until 1969 and then shown only in a severely edited version (the cuts have since been restored).

Solyaris (*Solaris*), a mystical science fiction film, followed in 1972; it was remade by Steven Soderbergh in the United States in 2002. Tarkovsky further tweaked authority with his radically structured semi-autobiographical film *Zerkalo* (*The Mirror*, 1975), and after completing *Stalker* (1979), he shot the dreamlike *Nostalghia* (*Nostalgia*, 1983) during a sojourn to Italy. After his defection from the USSR in 1984, Tarkovsky made one final film before his death, the Swiss/French production *Offret* (*The Sacrifice*, 1986), in which Alexander, an aging journalist (beautifully played by Erland Josephson), confronts his lack of faith on the eve of World War III.

Tarkovsky's death, and the many prizes his films had won in international festivals, ironically accelerated the rebirth of filmmaking in Russia. In addition, films that had been suppressed for years finally received a belated release. Aleksandr Askoldov's gently critical film about the Russian Revolution, *Komissar* (*The Commissar*), for example, which had been sitting on the shelf since its production in 1967, was finally released in 1988. A greater frankness about sex and drugs was apparent in Vasili Pichul's *Malenkaya Vera* (*Little Vera*, 1988), while Pavel Lungin's *Taksi-Blyuz* (*Taxi Blues*, 1990) presented contemporary Moscow as a neon wilderness of alcohol and poverty, albeit with a darkly humorous tone. Pavel Chukraj's *Vor* (*The Thief*, 1998) was even more provocative, telling the tale of a Soviet mother and child who are held in thrall by a charismatic con man in the Stalin-era 1950s. In 2002, Alexander Sokurov's *Russkiy kovcheg* (*Russian Ark*) marked a turning point in the cinema: a digital movie shot in one continuous take, recorded directly onto a digital hard drive imbedded in the camera. For ninety minutes, Sokurov's camera prowls through the Hermitage, the great Russian art museum in St. Petersburg, as a fabulous gallery of historical personages drift in and out of the film in one spectacularly extended traveling shot. Sokurov got the film on the second take, despite the freezing weather, and thus on 23 December 2001 a new era in the movies was born.

POLAND

In Poland, the documentary and feature filmmaker Krzysztof Zanussi's *Struktura krysztalu* (*The Structure of Crystal*, 1969) and *Iluminacja* (*Illumination*, 1973) were bold cinematic experiments, while Andrzej Wajda contributed to the birth of the Solidarity Movement with the production of increasingly political films, particularly *Czlowiek z zelaza* (*Man of Iron*, 1981). Despite a military crackdown in the last days of 1981 in opposition to the Solidarity labor movement, Wajda, Zanussi, and Krzysztof Kieslowski continued to work in Poland, creating movies of originality and beauty. Kieslowski's last great work, his epic *Trzy kolory* (*Three Colors*) trilogy, *Blue* (1993), *White* (1994), and *Red* (1994), was shot in Poland and France and dealt with the pressures of life in materialistic modern French society.

One of the most enigmatic and influential figures of the Polish cinema is Agnieszka Holland, whose career began in Poland; later she moved in succession to Germany, France, and finally the United States. Born in Warsaw in 1948, Holland experienced firsthand the horrors of anti-Semitism, as her entire family on her father's side was murdered under the Nazi regime in World War II. Educated in Czechoslovakia, she graduated in 1971 from the Prague Film School and made her first films for Czechoslovakian television. As a screenwriter, Holland became closely associated with Andrzej Wajda beginning in 1977 and co-wrote the screenplays of many of his films, including *Bez znieczulenia* (*Without Anesthesia*, 1978) and *Danton* (1983).

In 1979, Holland directed and co-wrote the feature *Aktorzy prowincjonalni* (*Provincial Actors*), which won the Critics' Prize at the Cannes Film Festival. *Provincial Actors* displays an early use of Holland's poetic realism in a political tract loosely allegorized in the play-within-a-film form. The company of players in the film put on the Polish play *Liberation*, yet Holland shows the stifling atmosphere of conformity and yearning for freedom that the players experience. Abused by a tyrannical director who obviously represents a figurehead of the colonizing forces ruling over Poland, one actor experiences a breakdown; as a result, his relationship with his wife becomes unbearable. Holland's next feature film, *Goraczka* (*Fever*, 1981), was banned by the Polish government. Based on a story by Polish writer Andrzej Strug, *Fever* tells of the political struggle at the turn of the twentieth century when Poland fought for independence. Released right after the imposition of martial law in Poland, the film was almost immediately banned because of its brutally realistic portrayal of the occupying Soviet forces. Holland's next film, *Kobieta samotna* (*A Woman Alone*, 1981), was the last film she directed in Poland, chronicling the plight of an unmarried mother employed as a letter carrier who embezzles the money of old-age pensioners to make ends meet when unexpected expenses arise.

After the imposition of martial law, Holland emigrated to Paris, where she began planning *Bittere Ernte* (*Angry Harvest*, 1986), produced in West Germany, drawing upon her experience as a Polish Jew for the screenplay. Set during World War II, the film examines the problematic love affair between a Jewish woman, Rosa Eckart (Elisabeth Trissenaar), and the Christian German farmer Leon Wolny (Armin Mueller-Stahl), who hides her from the Nazis. Holland's next two films, *Europa, Europa* (1990) and *Olivier, Olivier* (1992), return to the inevitable themes of moral ambiguity, violence, and power. *Europa, Europa*, based on actual events, tells the story of a Jewish teenager in Nazi Germany who poses as a member of the Hitler Youth in order to survive the war. *Olivier, Olivier* is a deeply disturbing film about a mother whose son disappears at the age of nine and then resurfaces six years later in Paris. But is it her son, or is it an imposter?

YUGOSLAVIA AND HUNGARY

Other Soviet Bloc countries have also had an uneasy time creating new work in an atmosphere of political turmoil, but the Yugoslavian filmmaker Emir Kusturica created a sensation with *Otac na sluzbenom putu* (*When Father Was Away on Business*, 1985), in which a man is arrested for a chance political remark and thrown into prison; his family, and in particular his son, Malik, waits outside for his release. *Dom za vesanje* (*Time of the Gypsies*, 1988) is the story of a young Gypsy, Perhan, who is seduced into a life of crime, while the sprawling epic *Bila jednom jedna zemlja* (*Underground*, 1995) is a surreal war film centered in Belgrade, in which the war is artificially prolonged by ambitious black marketeers amid a series of bizarre incidents. *Crna macka, beli macor* (*Black Cat, White Cat*, 1998) is a much lighter work, a romantic comedy of chaotic family life.

In Hungary, István Szabó's *Mephisto* (1981), *Oberst Redl* (*Colonel Redl*, 1985), and *Hanussen* (1988) are potent political parables with a distinctively graceful touch. Márta Mészáros emerged as another talented feminist filmmaker of note, who learned her trade from her former husband, director Miklós Jancsó. Her films *Kilenc hónap* (*Nine Months,* 1976) and *Napló gyermekeimnek* (*Diary for My Children,* 1984) tackle issues of feminine identity in an overwhelmingly patriarchal society and offer an individual perspective of the problems of a woman living in contemporary Eastern Europe. Ildiko Enyedi's offbeat *Az Én XX. Századom* (*My Twentieth Century,* 1989) charts the picaresque adventures of twin sisters born in Budapest in the late nineteenth century. Separated shortly after birth, the two take decidedly different career paths—one becomes a violent political activist, the other a playgirl. Their life journey is linked to the introduction of electricity, which is seen as offering a new world of industrial promise at the expense of a breakdown in the nineteenth century's social fabric. Progress, in short, comes with a price tag.

THE AUSTRALIAN RENAISSANCE

Australia, where some of the earliest feature films had been produced, had long fallen into a creative slump. But in the 1970s, a combination of favorable tax breaks and government incentives allowed a new generation of "down under" filmmakers to break through to international prominence. Bruce Beresford's *The Adventures of Barry McKenzie* (1972) was an early hit, followed by his *Breaker Morant* (1980), a military period drama. Subsequently, Beresford went to the United States to direct *Driving Miss Daisy* (1989), following in the steps of other indigenous filmmakers who leave their native countries to make bigger but perhaps less adventurous films in Hollywood. George Miller made the violent action film *Mad Max* (1979), propelling the Australian-born Mel Gibson to instant stardom; Miller's *Mad Max 2: The Road Warrior* (1981) was an even greater success. Miller, too, moved to Hollywood, to direct such films as *The Witches of Eastwick* (1987) and *Babe: Pig in the City* (1998).

Other Australian directors of note in this period include Fred Schepisi, whose *The Chant of Jimmie Blacksmith* (1978) addressed racial problems at home, and Gillian Armstrong, whose breakthrough film was the feminist-inflected *My Brilliant Career* (1978). Peter Weir's fortunes took off beginning with the mysterious, Antonioni-like parable *Picnic at Hanging Rock* (1975), and he moved on to the equally ambiguous allegory *The Last Wave* (a k a *Black Rain,* 1977), the historical drama *Gallipoli* (1981), and the action thriller *The Year of Living Dangerously* (1982). But Weir, too, succumbed to the lure of Hollywood, continuing his career with such mainstream fare as

The Australian cinema began its modern renaissance with Peter Weir's evocative and mysterious *Picnic at Hanging Rock* (1975).

Dead Poets Society (1989), *Green Card* (1990), and the maritime epic *Master and Commander: The Far Side of the World* (2003).

Philip Noyce began his career with the racial drama *Backroads* (1977), then moved on to a sentimental story about Australian newsreel cameramen in the 1940s and 1950s, *Newsfront* (1978). This was followed by the expert thriller *Dead Calm* (1989), loosely based on Roman Polanski's *Knife in the Water,* which offered a very young Nicole Kidman one of her first leading roles. Since then, Noyce's work has fluctuated wildly, from the straightforward Hollywood thrillers *Patriot Games* (1992) and *Sliver* (1993) to *The Saint* (1997), an unsuccessful revival of the 1960s television series. He then turned in some of his finest work to date, particularly *The Quiet American* (2002), based on Graham Greene's novel, starring Michael Caine as a weak-willed journalist in Saigon at the beginning of the Vietnam War, and *Rabbit-Proof Fence* (2002), a historical drama featuring Kenneth Branagh as a vicious racist who attempts to reeducate Aboriginal children against their will. Baz Luhrmann's *Strictly Ballroom* (1992), *Romeo + Juliet* (1996), and *Moulin Rouge!* (2001) are spectacular paeans to excess, both visual and narrative, making him probably the most commercial director of the Australian New Wave. Luhrmann's lastest projects include the epic drama *Australia* (2008), and a 3-D version of *The Great Gatsby* (2012).

327

NEW ZEALAND

In New Zealand, where the film industry had long been marginal, Peter Jackson first came on the scene in 1987 with his twisted science fiction gore film *Bad Taste,* which he also acted in, photographed, and edited. Next were the puppet horror film *Meet the Feebles* (1989) and the darkly humorous splatter film *Dead Alive* (a k a *Braindead,* 1992), all of which were commercial successes. But these offbeat films were just the curtain raiser for *Heavenly Creatures* (1994), a recounting of one of New Zealand's most famous murder cases, in which two teenage girls form an unnaturally close attachment and are forcibly separated by their parents; furious at the intrusion into their lives, they go on a murderous rampage. The film offered an important early role to Kate Winslet as Juliet Hulme, one of the two girls, and garnered Jackson worldwide attention. After a brief sojourn in Hollywood, Jackson returned to his native land and launched into the films that would put both him and New Zealand cinema firmly in the public eye—the spectacular three-part *Lord of the Rings* series (2001–03) and the digital remake of *King Kong* (2005).

Jane Campion is another talented New Zealand cineaste, whose early subjects included the semi-autobiographical *Sweetie* (1989), which documents a dysfunctional family in full flower, and *An Angel at My Table* (1990), a biography of the noted New Zealand writer Janet Frame. *The Piano* (1993), with Holly Hunter and Harvey Keitel, was an international success, and allowed Campion the freedom to create her controversial version of Henry James's novel *Portrait of a Lady* (1996), criticized for its use of deliberate anachronisms as a framing device for the film's central narrative. *Holy Smoke* (1999) is a feminist take on the mechanisms of relationships between men and women, while *In the Cut* (2003) is a sexually charged suspense film. In 2011, Campion produced director Julia Leigh's feminist fable *Sleeping Beauty,* in which a young woman, Lucy (Emily Browning), works in a mysterious "sex club" to pay for her college tuition.

CANADA

Canada had a resurgence of cinematic activity in the 1970s thanks to a generous subsidy program to encourage national filmmaking. The two major

Jane Campion's *Sweetie* (1989), a tale of sibling rivalry between Sweetie (Geneviève Lemon, left) and Kay (Karen Colston), is one of the most personal films of the New Australian cinema.

filmmakers to emerge from this scheme are completely different in taste and style: the crowd-pleaser Ivan Reitman, whose comedy horror film *Cannibal Girls* (1973) was made almost entirely on credit, using the cast members of the long-running Canadian television comedy series *SCTV* as its principals, and David Cronenberg, maker of violent but deeply introspective films. Where Reitman frankly went for the bottom line and rapidly moved to the United States with such films as *Meatballs* (1979), *Stripes* (1981), and *Ghost Busters* (1984), all three starring Bill Murray, Cronenberg's cerebral horror and suspense films *Shivers* (1975, co-produced by Reitman), *Scanners* (1981), *The Dead Zone* (1983), *Dead Ringers* (1988), *Crash* (1996; not to be confused with Paul Haggis's 2005 film of the same name), *eXistenZ* (1999), and *A History of Violence* (2005) created a world of paranoia and uncertainty that was simultaneously seductive and threatening.

Denys Arcand is a significant Canadian filmmaker of the late 1980s through the present, with the satiric *Le Déclin de l'empire américain* (*The Decline of the American Empire*, 1986), *Jésus de Montréal* (*Jesus of Montreal*, 1989), *Amour et restes humains* (*Love & Human Remains*, 1993), and *Les Invasions barbares* (*The Barbarian Invasions*, 2003). In addition, the eccentric Atom Egoyan made a series of unsettling low-budget features dealing with themes of sexual obsession, voyeurism, and questions of identity in *Speaking Parts* (1989), *Exotica* (1994), *The Sweet Hereafter* (1997), *Felicia's Journey* (1999), and *Where the Truth Lies* (2005).

329

INDIA

For the hypercommercial Indian film industries, the musical romance film still reigns supreme, yet alternative visions continue to challenge their dominance. Whereas the musicals were surefire box office propositions, more marginal Indian movies relied on private financing and government grants to defray production costs. We have already traced the career of director Ritwik Ghatak, one of the more adventurous Indian filmmakers; in the late 1960s, Mrinal Sen, another excellent contemporary director, began what many consider the Indian New Wave with *Bhuvan Shome* (*Mr. Shome*, 1969), the tale of an officious older man whose interaction with a young peasant girl completely alters his life. The film marked a break from Sen's earlier, more traditional style (he made his first film, *The Dawn*, a k a *Raat Bhore*, in 1956). Sen pressed on with this new direction in his film work with *Interview* and *Calcutta 71* (both 1971), and he later created the self-reflexive *Akaler Sandhane* (*In Search of Famine*, 1980) in which a film crew making a historical drama about the 1943 famine in Bengal runs afoul of the local citizens, who do not wish to be reminded of the past. Other active Indian directors include Aparna Sen, who directed the romantic drama *36 Chowringhee Lane* (1981), which deals with the end of the British empire in India, and Satyajit Ray's son, Sandip Ray, who scored with *Uttoran* (*The Broken Journey*, 1994), based on a script by his father, in which a wealthy doctor is forced to come to terms with his ethical standards when confronted with the poverty of rural India.

Deepa Mehta began her career as a director working for her father, an Indian film distributor, then honed her craft working on documentary films in the late 1960s and early 1970s. After a sojourn in Canada, where she directed television programs, Mehta made her first feature, *Sam & Me*, in 1991, before embarking on her ambitious trilogy *Fire* (1996), *Earth* (1998), and *Water* (2005), which explore the rapidly changing roles of women in contemporary Indian society. *Fire* centers on two women, Sita and Radha, who are both stuck in loveless marriages and eventually find some measure of solace in a lesbian relationship. *Earth*, set in 1947, deals with a family's troubles against the backdrop of civil war, and the long-delayed *Water*, another period piece, details the plight of a young girl who is married and then widowed by the age of eight and forced to live a life of privation as a result. Set in 1938, as the British grip on India was faltering, the film is unrelenting in its exposé of the brutal conditions that marginalized women in India during this period, and Mehta received death threats as she struggled to complete the project, one of the most uncompromising visions of Indian life ever filmed. In a similar vein, Shekhar Kapur's *Bandit Queen* (1994) details the life of the bandit renegade Phoolan Devi, a real-life female outlaw who survived grinding poverty and brutal sexism to become a notorious criminal, implicated in a string of kidnappings, robberies, and other crimes, yet emerged as a triumphant feminist heroine for daring to defy the patriarchal power system.

But without a doubt the most influential contemporary Indian director is Mira Nair, whose early films have blossomed into a career that is already rich in accomplishment and promises much for the future. Born in Bhubaneswar, India, in 1957, Nair worked as an actress in the theater community in New Delhi for three years before coming to the United States to study at Harvard. *Jama Masjid Street Journal* (1979), a documentary on cultural life in India, was her student thesis film, later screened at New York's Film Forum in 1986. In 1982, Nair directed *So Far from India*, an hour-long documentary about a subway newsstand salesman in New York whose wife waits for his return to India. Nair's third film, *India Cabaret* (1985), reveals the marginalized existence of strippers, a unique presentation of the lives of those who work in an industry that most people never discuss; it won several international awards. *Salaam Bombay!* (1988), a drama centering on Bombay's street people, won numerous awards and an Oscar nomination for Best Foreign Language Film in 1989.

Nair's next film, *Mississippi Masala* (1991), is an interracial love story in which Demetrius, an African American man (Denzel Washington), falls in love with Meena (Sarita Choudhury), the daughter of an Indian motel owner who strenuously objects to their match. Set in the cultural melting pot of the southern United States, the film is a refreshingly frank look at the politics of racism in America. Nair then made a more conventional Hollywood film, *The Perez Family* (1995), but returned to India to make the lavish historical spectacle *Kama Sutra: A Tale of Love* (1996) and the equally colorful *Monsoon Wedding* (2001), both of which were substantial successes. This was followed by Nair's adaptation of Thackeray's novel *Vanity Fair* (2004), and then the "culture clash" family drama *The Namesake* (2006), starring Kal Penn, which was also a commercial success.

Nair was also one of many filmmakers who contributed to *11'09''01—September 11* (2002), an omnibus film about the world's response to the events of 9/11. Her segment, "India," joined contributions by Ken Loach ("United Kingdom"), Shohei Imamura ("Japan"), Iran's Samira Makhmalbaf

Mira Nair's *Mississippi Masala* (1991), with Denzel Washington and Sarita Choudhury, about
love, racism, and ethnic pride among immigrants from India and African Americans.

("God, Construction and Destruction"), Sean Penn
("USA"), Claude Lelouch ("France"), Amos Gitai ("Israel"), Youssef Chahine ("Egypt"), Idrissa Ouedraogo
("Burkina Faso"), and Alejandro González Iñárritu ("Mexico"). As a window into what the rest of the world thinks about the issues of international
terrorism, *11'09''01—September 11* is an invaluable document for anyone
interested in twenty-first-century global politics. In homage to the events of
9/11, each segment is precisely 11 minutes, 9 seconds, and 1 frame long;
taken as a whole, the film is sad, angry, and deeply moving. Mira Nair's most
recent film as a solo director is *Amelia* (2009), a biopic on aviator Amelia
Earhart.

AFRICAN VOICES

In Egypt, Youssef Chahine continued as one of the country's most important directors, with *al-Asfour* (*The Sparrow,* 1972), *Awdat al ibn al dal* (*The
Return of the Prodigal Son,* 1976), *Hadduta misrija* (*An Egyptian Story,*
1982), *al-Massir* (*Destiny,* 1997), and other works. One of the most mysterious and experimental films of the Egyptian cinema in the last several

decades is Chadi Abdel Salam's *al-Mummia* (*The Night of Counting the Years,* 1969), a dreamlike narrative centering on the robbery of ancient artifacts from Egyptian tombs. Since then, the Egyptian government has withdrawn state support from filmmaking, but newer directors have still made interesting contributions, such as Daoud Abdel Sayed's *al-Sa Alik* (*The Bums,* 1985), *al-Bahths an Al-Sayyid Marzuq* (*The Search of Sayed Marzouk,* 1990), and *Kit Kat* (1991). A feminist director, Asmaa El-Bakry, shooting her films in French rather than Arabic, has attracted considerable attention with *Mendiants et orgueilleux* (*Beggars and Proud Ones,* 1991). In Tunisia, director Moufida Tlatli directed the remarkable feminist historical drama *Samt el qusur* (*The Silences of the Palace,* 1994), in which she contrasts the present with flashbacks of Tunisia's colonial past and reflects upon the subservient status of women in the Arab world.

Idrissa Ouedraogo, born in Burkina Faso in 1954, began a distinguished career after studying film at the African Institute of Cinematography in Ouagadougou, and later in Kiev and Paris. After a number of short films, his feature film *Yam Daabo* (*The Choice,* 1986) met with critical acclaim, and his next film, *Yaaba* (*Grandmother,* 1989), about two young children who befriend an old woman whom the villagers consider to be a witch, secured his reputation.

Also in Burkina Faso, Gaston Kaboré directed the quietly dramatic *Wend Kuuni* (*God's Gift,* 1982), about a dying boy who is adopted by a passing merchant and nursed back to health, and *Zan Boko* (1988), in which a native villager, Tinga (Joseph Nikiema), fights against the gradual Westernization of his culture. Souleymane Cissés's films of African social life in his birthplace of Mali, such as *Baara* (*Work,* 1978), *Finyé* (*The Wind,* 1982), and *Yeelen* (*Brightness,* 1987), are carefully detailed examinations of cultural identity. In Mauritania, Med Hondo (born Abid Mohamed Medoun Hondo) made a riveting series of deeply personal films with the documentary *Soleil O* (1967), the political drama *West Indies ou les nègres marrons de la liberté* (*West Indies,* 1979), and *Sarraounia* (1986), again critiquing the lingering effects of colonial rule in Africa for the past century.

In Algeria, Mohammed Lakhdar-Hamina made a highly successful drama of the Algerian revolution, *Chronique des années de brais* (*Chronicle of the Years of Embers,* 1975), while Mohamed Bouamari directed *El Faham* (*The Charcoal Maker*) in 1973, also concerned with the impact of postcolonial times on a man and his family, as gas begins to supplant the fuel he makes. Désiré Ecaré made the highly sexually charged drama *Visages de femmes* (*Faces of Women*) in the Ivory Coast in 1985, while in Angola, Sarah

Maldoror directed the compelling political drama *Sambizanga* (1972), about a young woman's search for her imprisoned husband.

Tunisia's Nouri Bouzid's *Man of Ashes* (*Rih essed*, 1986) is a drama of an approaching wedding day with unexpected ramifications, as sexual molestation incidents from the distant past surface to cause havoc in the lives of a young man and his best friend.

In Morocco, Souheil Ben-Barka's early film *Les Mille et une mains* (*The Thousand and One Hands*, 1972) led to a long career, including the Soviet/Spanish/Italian/Morrocan co-production *La Batalla de los Tres Reyes* (*Drums of Fire*, 1990), which he co-directed with the Russian Uchkun Nazarov. A lavish historical spectacle made for international consumption, this epic war film boasts a cast including Claudia Cardinale, Fernando Rey, Harvey Keitel, and F. Murray Abraham, shot on location in Morocco, Spain, and Ukraine. In 2002, Ben-Barka wrote and directed *Les Amants de Mogador* (*The Lovers of Mogador*), starring Max von Sydow. In nearly all these films, colonialism is the villain, separating wife from husband, children from family, and families from their cultural heritage. The new African cinema's theme is social and personal independence, as the continent's citizens shake off the chains of hundreds of years of exploitation, slavery, poverty, and ignorance.

The distribution many of these films receive outside Africa is sparse at best, and local audiences often dismiss thoughtful works in favor of genre videos. Shot cheaply in a few days, such videos—particularly in the burgeoning "Nollywood" cinema of Nigeria, where literally thousands of low-budget films are produced each year—have proliferated with the advent of digital video, making movie production populist. But only the more cerebral films attract foreign distribution, however limited.

The highly experimental feminist director Safi Faye has been luckier than many in this regard. Born in Dakar, Senegal, of Serer origin, Faye has strong links to her cultural heritage, which she records in *Fad'jal* (*Grand-père raconte*, 1979), named after the village where Faye's parents were born. Safi Faye began as a teacher in Dakar. Though she has traveled and studied abroad, she maintains close ties with her family and cultural roots. Faye studied ethnology in France in the 1970s and worked as an actor and model to support her studies. In her early short film *La Passante* (*The Passerby*, 1972), Faye plays an African woman living in France who becomes the object of romantic interest from two men, one French, one African, creating a study of the different cultural expectations of women. After gaining experience as a student filmmaker, Faye found support from the French Ministry

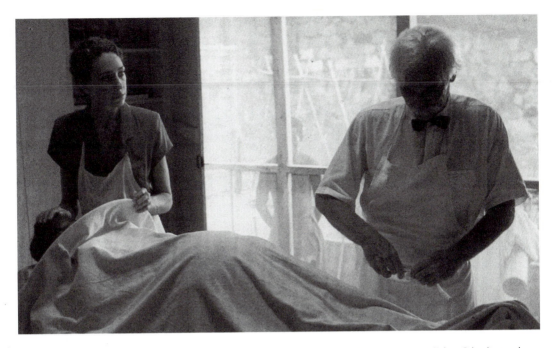

Marisa Berenson as Helene Schweitzer and André Wilms as Albert Schweitzer in Bassek Ba Kobhio's *Le Grand Blanc de Lambaréné* (*The Great White of Lambaréné*, 1995). Courtesy of California Newsreel, www.newsreel.org.

of Cooperation to make *Kaddu Beykat* (*Letter from My Village*) in 1975, thus becoming the first sub-Saharan African woman to make a feature film. *Kaddu Beykat* is a semi-autobiographical, fictionalized study of a village that suffers economically because its people refuse to go along with colonial demand for single-crop cultivation. *Les Âmes au soleil* (*Souls under the Sun*, 1981) documents the difficult conditions that women face living in Africa in times of drought and poor health. Faye's *Selbe et tant d'autres* (*Selbe: One Among Many*, a k a *One and So Many Others*, 1982) records the lives of women who are left behind in villages when men migrate to the city in search of employment.

In Cameroon, director Bassek Ba Kobhio created a fine film on the lingering effects of French colonialism with *Le Grand Blanc de Lambaréné* (*The Great White of Lambaréné*, 1995), a not particularly sympathetic view of the paternalistic life and work of Albert Schweitzer in Africa. Schweitzer (André Wilms) and his wife, Helene (Marisa Berenson), run their jungle hospital like a fortress in which Schweitzer's word is law. We follow his career through the eyes of Koumba (Alex Descas), a young African who grows up working in Schweitzer's hospital. When independence comes, Schweitzer is unable to make the shift from colonialism to self-government and is rejected by the very people he tried to help, who are tired of his self-imposed godlike status.

THE ASIAN ACTION FILM

Asian cinema saw an enormous renaissance, creating everything from routine action thrillers to deeply moving and intimate dramas. Bruce Lee was born in San Francisco, spent much of his youth in Hong Kong, and went back to America to work in the television series "The Green Hornet" (1966–67) and Paul Bogart's film *Marlowe* (1969) before returning to his homeland and reclaiming his cultural heritage. Lee redefined the action genre with a string of balletic action films such as Wei Lo and Jiaxiang Wu's *Tang shan da xiong* (*Fists of Fury*, 1971), Wei Lo's *Jing wu men* (*Fist of Fury*, a k a *The Chinese Connection*, 1972), Robert Clouse's *Enter the Dragon* (1973), and Lee's own *Meng long guojiang* (*Return of the Dragon*, 1972) before his sudden death in 1973 at the age of thirty-two, just as his international career was taking off.

In the wake of Lee's meteoric success and untimely death, a host of imitators sprang up, but none was more inventive or successful than Jackie Chan. Chan started as a child actor, then was tapped as a Bruce Lee clone in Wei Lo's *Xin ching-wu men* (*New Fist of Fury*, 1976). He soon developed his own personality based on the acrobatic fight gags of the classic Hollywood comedians Harold Lloyd, Buster Keaton, and Charles Chaplin. In such Hong Kong–produced films as Jackie Chan and Sammo Hung Kam-Bo's *'A' gai waak* (*Project A*, 1983), Chan's *Ging chaat goo si* (*Police Story*, 1985), and Jing Wong's *Sing si lip yan* (*City Hunter*, 1993), Chan perfected his comic timing, performing stunts that set the bar for a new generation of action stars. Both Chan and Lee often worked for the two most prolific studios in Hong Kong, the Shaw Brothers Studio, operated as a twenty-four-hour film factory by brothers Run Run and Run Me Shaw, and the Golden Harvest Studios. These facilities churned out an enormous amount of commercial product and dominated Hong Kong cinema in the 1970s and 1980s.

It was also during this period that the action director John Woo emerged as a fierce visual stylist, starting with a string of low-budget action films for the Shaw Brothers and Golden Harvest, including *Dinü hua* (*Princess Chang Ping*, 1975), *Liang zhi lao hu* (*Run Tiger Run*, 1985), and *Ying xiong wei lei* (*Heroes Shed No Tears*, a k a *The Sunset Warrior*, 1986). He made his first major impact with *Ying hung boon sik* (*A Better Tomorrow*, 1986), a violent, hard-boiled crime drama starring Chow Yun-Fat, and followed it with *Dip hyut shueng hung* (*The Killer*, 1989), *Die xue jie tou* (*Bullet in the Head*, 1990), and *Laat sau sen taan* (*Hard Boiled*, 1992), all bravura action pieces. Since 1993, Woo has worked in Hollywood with less passion and originality, making big-budget thrillers and action films such as *Broken Arrow* (1996), *Face/Off* (1997), and *Mission: Impossible II* (2000).

The twin brothers Oxide Pang (a k a Oxide Pang Chun) and Danny Pang first teamed as co-directors on *Bangkok Dangerous* (1999), a violent action film, but then went on to create their signature work, *Gin gwai* (*The Eye*, 2002), an unsettling psychological horror film, in which a blind girl gets a cornea transplant with unexpected results. The film was so successful that it almost immediately spawned a sequel, *Gin gwai 2* (*The Eye 2*, 2004). Tsui Hark, another Hong Kong action specialist, created his own brand of cinematic mayhem in *Die bian* (*The Butterfly Murders*, 1979), *Suk san: Sun Suk san geen hap* (*Zu: Warriors from the Magic Mountain*, 1983), *Shanghai zhi ye* (*Shanghai Blues*, 1984), and many others, while also producing films by other directors. But Hong Kong's future as a vibrant cinematic center was put in doubt when the British handed over the tiny nation to mainland China in 1997, and many of its most talented directors, actors, and technicians fled to the West. Jackie Chan, for example, went on to a long and profitable career as an action/comedy star in Hollywood.

TAIWAN

In Taiwan, Edward Yang, director of *Qingmei Zhuma* (*Taipei Story*, 1985), and Hou Hsiao-hsien were both prolific social commentators. Hsiao-hsien's *Tong nien wang shi* (*A Time to Live, a Time to Die*, 1985), *Lianlian fengchen* (*Dust in the Wind*, 1986), and *Beiqing chengshi* (*A City of Sadness*, 1989) strike a personal and meditative note in Taiwan's rapidly emerging cinema. Taiwanese cinema in its early stages was really a reflection of Japanese culture, inasmuch as Taiwan was really a Japanese colony during the early part of the twentieth century. As with Japan, sound came late to Taiwan because of the popularity of the *benshi* or narrators of silent films, who were often more popular than the stars of the films they presented to the public. However, with the Second Sino-Japanese War (1937–45), the Japanese took over Taiwan directly and attempted to force the Taiwanese to completely subjugate their culture. Much later, in 1993, Hou Hsiao-Hsien would make *Hsimeng jensheng* (*The Puppetmaster*) about this dark period in Taiwanese history, which came to an end only with the collapse of the Japanese empire at the end of World War II and the dawn of the Chinese Nationalist government. Thus the Taiwanese movie industry was almost moribund until 1950. Films after that period were rigidly controlled by the government, and by 1960 Taiwan was entering a rapid period of growth as a nation, with the government sponsoring what were known as "Health Realism" films, "moral uplift" tracts that sought to convince viewers to aspire to a better life. At the same time, romantic melodramas were also popular, as were martial arts films.

The Taiwanese New Wave dates from the early 1980s and the introduction of videocassettes on a large scale. Low-cost video films became a popular genre, and more ambitious filmmakers soon learned to use these tools to make movies not unlike the Italian Neorealist films of the late 1940s. Hou Hsiao-Hsien's *A City of Sadness* dealt with the coming of the Chinese Nationalist rules after the end of the Japanese era and the problems of the locals in dealing with their new "masters." Yang's *Taipei Story* examines the new materialism of the era, as Taiwanese are exposed to a more commercial lifestyle that tugs against the roots of their cultural traditions. In the 1990s, as the Taiwanese New Wave gathered force, Tsai Ming-liang's *Aiqing wansui* (*Vive L'Amour,* 1994) won the Golden Lion at the Venice Film Festival, presenting an almost Antonioniesque vision of modern city life as a nightmarish world of social alienation. Using long takes and an unsparing camera style that strips away the surfaces of urban existence like a scalpel, Ming-liang's film demonstrated that life in a prosperous society often came at the price of personal isolation and loneliness.

THE FIFTH GENERATION IN CHINA

In mainland China, the end of Mao Tse-tung's Cultural Revolution paved the way for a new group of filmmakers. The Beijing Film Academy, which had been closed from 1966 to 1976, finally reopened in 1978. The graduating class of 1982 became known as the Fifth Generation, and their first major work was *Huang tu di* (*Yellow Earth,* 1984), directed by Chen Kaige and photographed by Zhang Yimou. A gentle tale of cultural transition set in the 1930s, *Yellow Earth* was pictorially stunning and set the style for a more meditational cinema in which the landscape is a central character. Zhang Yimou's *Qiu Ju da guan si* (*The Story of Qiu Ju,* 1992) continued the trend of stark pictorial beauty, coupled with a delicate adherence to the Communist Party line in which some criticism is tolerated, but only if placed in either a historical context or presented as part of an abstract allegory. Many of China's most popular directors have begun working outside the country, and a number of China-produced films have been funded with outside money, such as Chen Kaige's *Bian zou bian chang* (*Life on a String*, 1991), with financing from Germany and Britain, and Zhang Yimou's *Da hong deng long gao gao gua* (*Raise the Red Lantern*, 1991), financed by a Taiwanese company, shot in China, and distributed through a firm in Hong Kong to circumvent Chinese censors. Few in China actually get to see these films; the movie theaters still operating in China are rundown, and the favorite venue of exhibition is the traveling caravan, roaming from village to village, for screenings in the vast territorial boundaries.

The new generation of Chinese filmmakers includes Zhang Yimou, with the historical drama *Da hong deng long gao gao gua* (*Raise the Red Lantern*, 1991), starring Gong Li.

JAPAN

In Japan, the cinema in the 1970s went through a period of crises, after a boom period in the 1960s. Television viewing, coupled with increasing Hollywood imports, led to a drastic drop in production, causing the Japanese government to introduce a plan in 1972 that gave financial incentives to films of clearly artistic intent. As a result, in the 1980s and 1990s Japanese cinema began a remarkable resurgence, led by filmmakers such as Sogo Ishii, whose *Gyakufunsha kazoku* (*The Crazy Family*, 1984) documents in wildly satirical fashion the collapse of a traditional Japanese family under intense social pressure. Also, *animé,* or highly stylized animated cartoons, began to proliferate with such lavishly designed epics as Hayao Miyazaki's *Mononoke-hime* (*Princess Mononoke,* 1997), which became the highest-grossing film in Japanese history.

A new genre was also developing in Japan that became known informally as "J-Horror." These films were deeply disturbing, often extremely violent movies that would build up a mood of mounting dread and suspense rather than deliver a series of shocking sequences every ten minutes or so. Many observers compared these atmospheric psychological horror films to the works of producer Val Lewton at RKO in the 1940s, and the comparison has merit, up to a point. Where J-Horror departs from the Lewton formula of understated menace is in its embrace of extravagantly violent visuals at key points in the film's narrative, usually saving the most shocking sequence for the film's conclusion.

Two of the genre's most proficient directors are Hideo Nakata and Takashi Miike. Nakata's *Ringu* (*The Ring*, 1998), which was remade by Gore Verbinski in the United States in 2002 under the same title, dealt with a videotape that curses all who watch it with death within a week. The film was so successful that it spawned an immediate sequel, *Ringu 2* (*The Ring 2*, 1999). Nakata went on to create the equally effective supernatural thriller *Honogurai mizu no soko kara* (*Dark Water*, 2002), remade in the United States by Walter Salles in 2005 with the same title, in which a young woman and her daughter move into an apartment in which it always seems to be raining. Takashi Miike's *Ôdishon* (*Audition*, 1999) is an even more disturbing film, in which a young woman, seemingly shy and modest, is actually a serial killer who mutilates her male victims purely for pleasure. Takashi Shimizu's *Ju-on: The Grudge* (2003) has gone through several remakes in Japan and an American version directed by Shimizu himself in 2004; the film centers on a cursed house that drives its inhabitants insane with a series of bizarre hallucinations. All these films depend on mood, lighting, and a leisurely construction to achieve their unsettling effect; as the many remakes attest, the genre has given new life to the horror film.

Kinji Fukasaku's filmmaking career began in the mid-1960s. Most of his early films were violent *yakuza* gangster dramas, science fiction films, and Samurai action dramas, but in his final years he created the controversial and very violent *Batoru rowaiaru* (*Battle Royale*, 2000) and *Batoru rowaiaru II: Chinkonka* (*Battle Royale II*, 2003), both based on a best-selling novel by Koushun Takami. *Battle Royale* depicts a near-future Japan in which high school students have become violent and unmanageable. The government then starts a program that abducts one group of high school students each year and puts them on an island. There they are forced to systematically kill each other one by one, until one lone victor emerges. The entire event is televised and becomes a national craze. Causing a firestorm of government protest in Japan, the film was a runaway success. Fukasaku began shooting the sequel but died before he could complete it; his son, Kenta, who wrote the screenplays for both movies, took over. Quentin Tarantino was so impressed with *Battle Royale*, and Fukasaku's career as a whole, that he dedicated *Kill Bill: Vol. I* (2003) to Fukasaku's memory.

"Beat" Takeshi Kitano's violent gangster films also rapidly developed a cult following. Moody and introspective, Kitano's films intersperse long sections of psychological tension with acts of utter brutality. Kitano began his career as a comedian, then as an omnipresent television host, and finally agreed to star in a feature film, *Sono otoko, kyôbô ni tsuki* (*Violent Cop*, 1989), which Kinji Fukasaku was slated to direct. Fukasaku bowed out at the last minute and Kitano took over, creating a film that set the bar still higher for violence. In the film's opening scene, a gang of juvenile delinquents beats up an elderly man, but Kitano's character, Detective Azuma, does nothing to prevent the crime. Later, however, Azuma tracks one of the young boys to his home and beats him up, as if to exact some retribution. Subsequent films consolidated his reputation as a sort of ultra-violent Jackie Chan, who mixed everyday tedium with outbursts of violence and bizarre comedy, seemingly schooled more in the ethos of comedy than in the *yakuza* genre, though his brutal movies often have crime at their forefront.

FILM IN KOREA

Korea came to the cinema relatively late, with its first silent film not being produced until 1923. In 1935, the sound film was introduced, but any further artistic development was cut short when Japan invaded China in 1937 and the Korean cinema was given over to outright propaganda. In 1945, with the surrender of Japan, Korean film began a renaissance, although the country was soon split into two. The first Korean color film didn't appear until 1949, and for the most part the Korean cinema of the 1950s and 1960s was given over to escapist genre films. One of the most popular directors of this period was Kim Ki-young, whose film *Hanyo* (*The Housemaid*, 1960) tells the almost Buñuelian tale of a young woman who enters the house of an esteemed and happily married composer and soon has an affair with him that brings pain to all concerned. The director of more than thirty films from 1955 onward, Kim was one of the most prolific genre filmmakers of the 1960s, although his work was unknown outside Korea. It was not until 1974, when the Korean National Film Archive was finally established, that these historic postwar Korean films finally found a permanent home.

Modern Korean cinema is dominated by the figure of Im Kwon-taek, an

341

incredibly prolific director with more than 100 films to his credit since 1962, although his work has received, as with so many other excellent Asian filmmakers, scant attention in the West outside of film festivals. Born in Jangsung, Cholla Province, in 1936, Im is known for his careful examination of Korean life, but he takes his vision and expands it beyond the boundaries of Korea into something that becomes universal to the human condition. Beginning with *Dumanganga jal itgeola* (*Farewell to the Duman River,* 1962), a film that dramatized the lives of a group of young students who fought against the Japanese in Manchuria, Im began making films at a furious pace, many of them action films but with deep psychological penetration, dealing with the events of Korea's war-torn past. Initially considered to be a reliable genre director who could bring projects in on time and on budget, Im began to move outside genre norms with his breakthrough film *Mandala* (1981), a more contemplative work about the hard lives of two Korean monks. Since then, he has directed *Seopyeonje* (known as *Sopyonje* in the West, 1993) and *Chunhyang* (2000), both of which deal with "pansori," a style of nineteenth-century popular music that specializes in love stories or satiric narratives.

THE CINEMA IN LATIN AMERICA

Brazil's Bruno Barreto created the raucous comedy *Dona Flor e Seus Dois Maridos* (*Dona Flor and Her Two Husbands*) in 1976, while Carlos Diegues scored with the colorful *Bye Bye Brasil* (*Bye Bye Brazil,* 1979), an examination of circus life in the Amazon, as a rag-tag troupe competes with the encroaching influence of television. Hector Babenco made an interesting homage to American "B" films of the 1940s with *Kiss of the Spider Woman* (*O Beijo da Mulher Aranha,* 1985), starring William Hurt, Raul Julia, and Sonia Braga. Brazil's Walter Salles began his cinematic career with the documentary short *Socorro Nobre* (*Life Somewhere Else,* 1995), which led to his first fiction feature, *Central do Brasil* (*Central Station,* 1998), in which a hardened, cynical woman takes in a young boy after his mother dies and regains some of her lost humanity as they search for the boy's absent father. The film was a surprise art-house hit throughout the world and eventually brought Salles to the United States. Fernando Meirelles and Kátia Lund's *Cidade de Deus* (*City of God,* 2002) is a brutal slum drama set in the shanty towns of Rio de Janeiro, as gangs of young kids battle for survival in a world of drugs, guns, and sudden death; it owes much to the spirit of Buñuel's *Los Olvidados.*

Argentine cinema underwent a resurgence in the 1980s and 1990s. In the 1950s and 1960s, Argentina's leading force in the cinema was the prolific Leopoldo Torre Nilsson, whose films *La Casa del ángel* (*The House of the Angel,* 1957), *Fin de fiesta* (*The Party Is Over,* 1960), and *El Ojo de la cerradura* (*The Eavesdropper,* 1964) were well received at international film festivals. María Luisa Bemberg became one of the most important directors of the new era with the passionate historical romance *Camila* (1984), which was the biggest box office hit in Argentine history, while her film *De eso no se habla* (*I Don't Want to Talk About It,* 1993) became an international success at the box office and Bemberg's most influential film. This whimsical tale of Charlotte (Alejandra Podesta), a woman who is born a dwarf and brought up by her mother, Leonor (Luisina Brando), to ignore her condition entirely, and then falls in love with the dashing Ludovico D'Andrea (Marcello Mastroianni), is funny, sad, and wise.

Bemberg died in 1995; since then, such directors as Fernando E. Solanas, Lucrecia Martel, Juan José Campanella, Fabián Bielinsky, and Luis Puenzo have contributed to some of Argentine cinema's most prolific years. Solanas, the oldest of the group, directed the exquisite musical drama *Tangos, el exilio de Gardel* (*Tangos, the Exile of Gardel,* 1985), in which a group of Argentine exiles in Paris gather together to celebrate the tango in a series of staged performances, dedicated to Carlos Gardel, a legendary Argentine tango star. An outspoken political activist who is often critical of the government, Solanas survived a shooting attack in May 1991 when he was struck by two bullets during an ambush. Solanas continued to make films, however, and became even more involved in political causes. *La Dignidad de los nadies* (*The Dignity of the Nobodies,* 2005), for example, details the economic crisis of Brazil in the early part of the twentieth century, brought about by inflation and predatory bank policies.

Lucrecia Martel's *La Ciénaga* (*The Swamp,* 2001) is a stunning film about the complicated lives of two women and their respective families who live in a small town. Juan José Campanella's *El Hijo de la novia* (*Son of the Bride,* 2001) is a tale of midlife crisis in which forty-two-year-old Rafael Bielvedere (Ricardo Darín) struggles with his relationship with his overbearing father and elderly mother. After twenty years as an assistant director, Fabián Bielinsky's first film as a director, *Nuevas reinas* (*Nine Queens,* 2000), was a fast-paced and wildly popular caper comedy that relied on deception and comic confusion; sadly, Bielinsky succumbed to a heart attack shortly after the completion of his next film, the hauntingly enigmatic *El Aura* (*The Aura,* 2006), about a low-level government worker who inadvertently becomes involved in a high-stakes casino robbery. Luis Puenzo's *La Historia oficial* (*The Official Story,* 1985) is a complex tale of love and memory, as a couple in Buenos Aires realize that their adopted daughter may be the child of a woman who vanished from her home in the wave of terror from 1976 to 1983, known as the "Dirty War," when Argentina was under the rule of a brutal military dictatorship. The film was a remarkable success both critically and commercially and won the Academy Award for Best Foreign Language Film.

Mexican cinema, moribund from the 1960s through the 1980s, began to show signs of a resurgence with such films as María Novaro's *Danzón* (1991), an exquisite film about love, dancing, and Mexican cultural life, and Alfonso Arau's delicate love story *Como agua para chocolate* (*Like Water for Chocolate,* 1992). Arturo Ripstein, who started his career as an uncredited assistant director to Luis Buñuel, directed his first feature, *Tiempo De Morir* (*Time to Die*), in 1965. Since then, Ripstein has been remarkably prolific, with more than fifty feature films to his credit. He is also known for embracing digital filmmaking in his more recent works, stating flatly in an interview that " the future of cinema is digital."

Alejandro González Iñárritu's *Amores perros* (*Love's a Bitch,* 2000) was a breakthrough film that became a substantial hit internationally, painting a violent picture of modern life in Mexico City in a series of interlocking stories, not unlike Tarantino's *Pulp Fiction* (1994). With *Amores perros,* the Mexican cinema returned to its commercial, populist roots, with movies that were simultaneously exploitable at the box office and yet undeniably rich in personal expression. The film was Iñárritu's feature film debut after a long apprenticeship directing television commercials and established him as a front-rank artist in a single stroke. Alfonso Cuarón's *Y tu mamá también* (*And Your Mother Too,* 2001) is one of the ultimate road movies of all time, as two young boys take to the highway with an older woman for a voyage of pleasure, introspection, and personal discovery. The film was an unexpected international hit. Cuarón almost immediately left Mexico for Hollywood, where he directed the highly successful *Harry Potter and the Prisoner of Azkaban* (2004) and then went to England to direct the dystopian science fiction parable *Children of Men* (2006), a film notable for its stunning handheld cinematography and oppressively bleak production design. But as these artists leave Mexico, the country's indigenous film industry suffers. Such migration has been part of a recurring pattern that has drained the Mexican cinema of much of its promising talent.

IRAN'S REVOLUTIONARY CINEMA

The Iranian cinema went through a true renaissance as a result of the Islamic revolution in 1979 that brought Ayatollah Khomeini into power. Under the previous regime of Mohammed Reza Shah Pahlavi, which lasted from 1941 to 1979, films were mostly a commercial affair. With the revolution, however, filmmaking came to a halt until 1983, when the Farabi Cinema Foundation was created by the new government to encourage the production of Islamic films that were both artistically and politically engaged.

The new government's strict censorship drove many filmmakers into exile or out of the industry, but some stayed and adapted while a new generation was trained to put the government's message before the public. One of the most effective films was Bahram Beizai's *Mosaferan* (*Travelers*, 1992), in which a wedding ceremony is tragically disrupted when the bride's sister and her entire family are killed in a horrific automobile accident en route. Beizai introduces a Brechtian note early on, when the sister turns directly to the camera and announces that she and her entire family will be killed shortly. When news of the crash is received, the wedding is transformed into a wake, as mourning relatives gather to comfort the family in their time of grief. The grandmother, however, refuses to believe that the accident has happened and argues that the sister and her family will still attend the wedding. In the film's transcendent climax, the dead relatives float into the house holding a large mirror in front of them, seemingly resurrected from the dead in a blaze of blinding blue light.

Other key directors of the new Iranian cinema include Mohsen Makhmalbaf, whose *Nun va Goldoon* (*A Moment of Innocence*, 1996) deals with his own teenage years as an anti-Shah firebrand, when he was arrested and jailed for stabbing a policeman. Years after being freed as a result of the revolution in 1979, Makhmalbaf decided to make a film of the incident. But in an unexpected touch, the policeman Makhmalbaf stabbed appears out of nowhere for a casting call, hoping to get a part in the film. Makhmalbaf uses this material to weave a complex tapestry of past and present, real and imagined, and of what was and what might have been.

Makhmalbaf's wife, Marzieh Meshkini, directed an elegant three-part film about the life of women in Iran, *Roozi ke zan shodam* (*The Day I Became a Woman*, 2000). The movie was shot as three shorts to escape government censorship, then shipped out of the country and assembled in Paris into

Marzieh Meshkini (right, foreground) directs *Roozi ke zan shodam* (*The Day I Became a Woman*, 2000), one of the key feminist films of the new Iranian cinema.

final form. Harshly critical of the sexism of the Iranian government, the film was denounced at home, though it won numerous awards abroad. Another director working with stories of women and the Islamic regime is the couple's daughter, Samira Makhmalbaf, whose films include *Sib* (*The Apple*, 1998, when she was eighteen) and *Panj é asr* (*At Five in the Afternoon*, 2003).

Abbas Kiarostami is another leading exponent of the post-revolutionary Iranian cinema, exploring the harsh realities of daily life in films such as *Khane-ye doust kodjast?* (*Where Is the Friend's Home?* 1987) and *Zendegi va digar hich* (*Life, and Nothing More*, 1991) in near-documentary style. *Zire darakhatan zeyton* (*Through the Olive Trees*, 1994) completed this Kiarostami trilogy, self-reflexively presenting a dramatic account of the filming of the first movie, using its own actors to re-create the production process. *Ten* (2002), an even more rigorous work, is composed entirely of shots of a woman driving a car and, in reverse-angle shots, her various passengers.

Jafar Panahi's *Ayneh* (*The Mirror*, 1997) is the story of a lost young girl, Mina, who searches the streets of Tehran for her mother. With her arm in a cast, Mina hitches rides from various buses and taxis, but just when she seems on the verge of finding her mother she suddenly steps out of character. The real Mina (also the actress's name) removes the prop cast and walks off the set in disgust, complaining, "All they want me to do is cry all the time." Members of the crew attempt to coax her back to work, but the real

The "Vow of Chastity," signed by von Trier and Vinterberg, contained ten rules that aimed at simplifying the cinema, as part of a self-described "rescue action" to return motion pictures to their most basic origins. The rules were these:

1. Shooting must be done on location. Props and sets must not be brought in. (If a particular prop is necessary for the story, a location must be chosen where this prop is to be found.)
2. The sound must never be produced apart from the images or vice versa. (Music must not be used unless it occurs where the scene is being shot.)
3. The camera must be handheld. Any movement or immobility attainable in the hand is permitted. (The film must not take place where the camera is standing; shooting must take place where the film takes place.)
4. The film must be in color. Special lighting is not acceptable. (If there is too little light for exposure the scene must be cut or a single lamp be attached to the camera.)
5. Optical work and filters are forbidden.
6. The film must not contain superficial action. (Murders, weapons, etc., must not occur.)
7. Temporal and geographical alienation are forbidden. (That is to say that the film takes place here and now.)
8. Genre movies are not acceptable.
9. The film format must be Academy 35 mm.
10. The director must not be credited.

Part joke, yet deadly serious at the core, the Dogme movement took Europe by storm, requiring a new level of authenticity that had all but been wiped out by decades of bloated spectacles, predictable genre films, and lackluster star vehicles. Note, too, the final rule: von Trier and Vinterberg decisively rejected the idea that the director could be the unspoken "star" of his or her film, a radical notion in itself.

The first Dogme film was Vinterberg's *Festen* (*The Celebration*, 1998), a handheld digital film about a disastrous family celebration in an enormous Danish mansion, with a large cast of characters, no conventional plot, and production values that bordered on the nonexistent. Nevertheless, the film was a compelling and harrowing experience, displaying considerable sophistication in its construction and execution. Von Trier's *Idioterne* (*The Idiots,* 1998) was a more experimental film, with a group of actors performing grotesque bodily gestures in public. Søren Kragh-Jacobsen's *Mifunes sidste sang* (*Mifune,* 1999) was a fairly traditional narrative in which a man returns home to help his mentally challenged brother after the death of their father. In 1999, Harmony Korine directed *Julien Donkey-Boy,* chronicling the daily life of a decidedly unhappy family, featuring Werner Herzog as the father of a young abused boy; it was the first American Dogme film.

Rules, of course, are made to be broken, and even on the first Dogme film, *Celebration,* Vinterberg confessed to covering up a window during one scene in the film, a direct violation of the rules. As the Dogme films continued to roll out, the novelty of the experiment began to wear off, and Lars von Trier pretty much abandoned Dogme's strict rules to create such films as the minimalist social fable *Dogville* (2003), the anguished personal drama *Antichrist* (2009), and his most ravishing film to date, the apocalyptic *Melancholia* (2011), which von Trier describes as "a beautiful film about the end of the world." With these films, von Trier has emerged as one of the world's foremost directors, and one of the medium's most ferociously individualistic talents.

*   *   *

If one considers that the first experiments in motion pictures as a visual medium date from the early 1880s, with the first public projection taking place in 1895, we have covered roughly 110 years of cinema production in this volume thus far. What comes next is the biggest single shift in cinema production and exhibition since the invention of the motion picture itself, a change more profound than the introduction of sound, color, CinemaScope, or any other refinements of the conventional cinematic process. Starting in the early 1990s, digital technology became a practical method of film production.

Suddenly, the cinema was in the range of everyone. Lightweight, inexpensive portable cameras with superior image quality proliferated. The digital revolution would transform the landscape in ways both large and small, helping to create mega-blockbusters, while giving even the most impoverished filmmaker the tools to pursue his or her vision. In the final chapter, we see how the Hollywood cinema developed from the 1970s through the turn of the twenty-first century, and how this new technology has changed the face of the cinema forever.

TEN

THE NEW HOLLYWOOD

Facing a new set of challenges, Hollywood continued to evolve in the 1970s. Filmmaking was becoming exponentially more expensive, a new system of ratings was in effect, and movie audiences were becoming younger as parents increasingly stayed home to watch cable television and, in the 1980s, videocassettes. As a result, spectacle began to rule at the box office and much of the experimentation of the 1960s was jettisoned in favor of formula films, though many remarkable American movies were still being made.

Martin Scorsese and Francis Ford Coppola

Martin Scorsese first emerged as a major force in American cinema with *Mean Streets* (1973). He consolidated his reputation with *Taxi Driver* (1976), which made a star out of Robert De Niro as psychotic cabbie Travis Bickle, who slowly goes insane as he cruises the streets of nighttime Manhattan. *Raging Bull* (1980) also featured De Niro in a bravura performance as heavyweight boxer Jake LaMotta. Scorsese angered many fundamentalist Christians with the revisionist storyline of *The Last Temptation of Christ* (1988), but since then his work has been strongly associated with plots involving the mafia. *Goodfellas* (1990) was one of his most accomplished films, a brutally violent mob drama; in *Gangs of New York* (2002), Scorsese set out to prove that nineteenth-century Manhattan was just as violent, if not more so, as the "mean streets" of modern-day New York. *The Departed* (2006), which won the Academy Award for Best Film of 2006 (and Scorsese's first, and long overdue Oscar as Best Director) concerns the Irish mafia infiltrating and being infiltrated by the Massachusetts police. In 2010, Scorsese created the rather traditional horror film *Shutter Island*, which nevertheless was a massive box office hit, and followed this up with the intensely personal *Hugo* (2011), an homage to the early days of cinema, shot in 3-D, and featuring a

Robert De Niro in his most famous role as psychotic New York cabbie Travis Bickle in Martin Scorsese's *Taxi Driver* (1976).

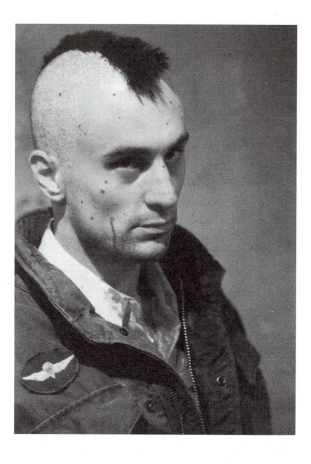

Raging Bull (1980), Martin Scorsese's brutal biography of prizefighter Jake LaMotta (Robert De Niro), was one of the few post-1970 Hollywood movies shot in black-and-white.

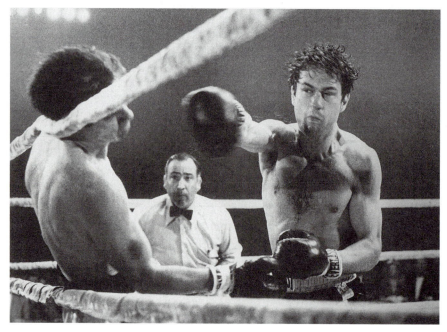

Francis Ford Coppola on the set of *The Godfather* (1972).

standout performance by Ben Kingsley as Georges Méliès. Scorsese is also an outspoken advocate for film preservation and uses much of his personal fortune to rescue classic films that are on the verge of disintegration.

Francis Ford Coppola cut his teeth working for Roger Corman, then broke into directing with the early splatter film *Dementia 13* (1963, produced by Corman). He burst into prominence with *The Godfather* (1972) and *The Godfather: Part II* (1974), followed by the Vietnam War epic *Apocalypse Now* (1979). After a string of smaller films in the 1980s he returned to epic scale with *The Godfather: Part III* (1990). Coppola's films have always been either deliberately low-key or lavishly expansive. In *The Conversation* (1974), surveillance expert Harry Caul (Gene Hackman) descends into a world of paranoia and self-doubt as the tools of his trade turn against him. By contrast, in *Apocalypse Now* Coppola works on a vast canvas that visualizes the chaos of the Vietnam War through the sheer scope and scale of the production. To finish the film, Coppola had to mortgage nearly everything he owned. The film, of course, more than justified his faith in the project and many feel it is Coppola's masterpiece.

BLOCKBUSTERS

As the economics of the industry changed, small studios became an anomaly. Films such as John Guillermin's *The Towering Inferno* (1974) packed in audiences eager for escapist entertainment in the Watergate era. Then two new faces came on the scene, with films that solidified the hold of block-busters on cinema audiences: Steven Spielberg's *Jaws* (1975) and George Lucas's *Star Wars* (1977) are both action-driven films that lack depth, but provide nonstop thrills and espouse a new, more effects-driven visual style.

Spielberg took to movies from an early age, making a plethora of Super 8 mm shorts as a child. With a short student film, *Amblin'* (1968), under his belt, he went from directing television shows such as "Marcus Welby, M.D." and "Night Gallery" to being handed the reins of a television movie, *Duel* (1971), in which a man driving on a business trip is chased by a monster truck for no apparent reason, with the frenetic action culminating in a violent conclusion. In addition to its U.S. television broadcast, the movie was released theatrically in Europe, and received significant attention from critics.

The Sugarland Express (1974) proved that Spielberg had a flair for action comedy, and then *Jaws* catapulted him in a single stroke to the top ranks of the American commercial cinema. With a mechanical shark that often broke down during shooting, Spielberg relied on music cues and sharp editing to bring the material to life, while also getting solid performances from stars Richard Dreyfuss and Robert Shaw. But it was the saturation booking marketing campaign that really set *Jaws* apart from the rest of the pack. Aggressively marketed during the summer as an "event" movie, *Jaws* swept away the competition. Its wild success led to a new style of filmmaking that echoed the Saturday morning serials of such directors as William Witney at Republic Pictures in the 1940s: the hard-driving, action-centered adventure movie. *Close Encounters of the Third Kind* (1977), a metaphysical science fiction film, followed in short order, and then came *Raiders of the Lost Ark* (1981), an action-adventure movie more indebted to the serial format than any other Spielberg film up to that time. With its breathless chases, exotic locale, cartoonish Nazis (which Spielberg later regretted), and epic sense of adventure, the film set Spielberg firmly on the path to his mature style as an action filmmaker without parallel.

E.T. The Extra Terrestrial (1982) was a more sentimental, family-oriented film, essentially a fable of tolerance designed for mass consumption. *Indiana Jones and the Temple of Doom* (1984) was a violent follow-up to *Raiders of the Lost Ark,* in what would become an ongoing series. *The Color Purple* (1985), based on Alice Walker's novel, and *Empire of the Sun* (1987) demonstrated that Spielberg was looking for something more than spectacle and kinetic excitement in his films, and both were respectable successes at the box office. *Indiana Jones and the Last Crusade* (1989) was a return to form for the action specialist, while *Always* (1989) and *Hook* (1991) fared less well

Hollywood in the 1980s: Kate Capshaw, Steven Spielberg, George Lucas, and Harrison Ford on the set of Spielberg's *Indiana Jones and the Temple of Doom* (1984).

with the public. With the dawn of digital special effects, Spielberg got in on the ground floor with *Jurassic Park* (1993), a spectacular film about a theme park with real, live, hungry dinosaurs and other prehistoric creatures that had been cloned by the park's somewhat mad impresario. The movie is more of a thrill ride than an actual narrative; once the situation is set up, it is simply a matter of who will survive until the final reel, as the theme park's numerous safeguards fail and the newly reconstituted creatures go on a rampage. Filled with eye-popping special effects and deftly directed for every last ounce of suspense and narrative drive, *Jurassic Park* was an enormous hit and has since spawned several sequels.

But even as *Jurassic Park* was breaking records, Spielberg had embarked on the most personal and challenging film of his meteoric career, *Schindler's List* (1993). The film demonstrated greater depth and maturity than any of the director's works thus far, as well as real commitment to the material. The film chronicles the struggles of the Jews of Nazi-occupied Kraców, Poland, to survive the horrors of World War II, led by the unassuming Itzhak Stern (Ben Kingsley). The Jews of the ghetto are pressed into service by Oskar Schindler (Liam Neeson), who initially sees them merely as a cheap labor force for his factory. But gradually, Schindler becomes drawn into their plight, and when the ruthless Nazi commandant Amon Goeth (Ralph Fiennes, in one of his finest performances) liquidates the ghetto, killing most of its residents in the process and shipping the survivors off to a concentration camp, Schindler bribes Goeth to let him continue his factory work inside the walls of the camp.

Stern, functioning as Schindler's accountant, adds numerous Jewish intellectuals, writers, rabbis, and other workers to the factory payroll; now, as Goeth's predations grow ever more ferocious, Schindler launches his own plan to save as many Jews as he possibly can from Hitler's Holocaust, at great personal risk to himself. Shot in newsreel black-and-white with splashes of color to highlight key visual elements, the film is a tribute to Spielberg's Jewish heritage and also a moving personal testament of faith. The film won seven Academy Awards, including Best Picture and Best Director, and Spielberg, who had heretofore often been dismissed as a mere entertainer, was now being taken seriously as a dramatic filmmaker. He followed this film with *Amistad* (1997), a drama about a mutiny on a slave ship in 1839 and the trial that followed in the United States; it was perhaps less successful, yet contains moments of great power.

As if to demonstrate that he had not lost his touch with genre entertainment, Spielberg then launched into *The Lost World: Jurassic Park* (1997), a nail-biting sequel that did not improve on the original, but still delivered a satisfactory share of thrills. *Saving Private Ryan* (1998), a World War II action drama, opened with a bravura sequence in which hundreds of soldiers storm a beachfront stronghold and sustain disastrous losses, deftly choreographed for maximum visceral and visual impact. For many observers, the film brought home the horror and sudden death of combat with more immediacy than any film before it. Spielberg has continued to direct a series of commercially successful films, including *Minority Report* (2002), a remake of *War of the Worlds* (2005), *The Adventures of Tintin* and *War Horse* (both 2011), as well as the historical spectacle *Lincoln* (2012).

The most commercially successful filmmaker of his generation (along with George Lucas), Spielberg is one of the owners of the production company DreamWorks, and produces television series, movies, and even cartoon series under his own banner of Amblin Productions. A mainstream artist, Spielberg is nevertheless a canny observer of American values and mores, and his films not only reflect, but also have helped to shape, the face of American cinema today.

George Lucas has also had considerable commercial success, but his work as a filmmaker is much more circumscribed, with only a handful of films to

his credit as a director. After graduating from the University of Southern California with a short film *THX 1138* (a k a *Electronic Labyrinth THX 1138 4EB,* 1967) in hand, Lucas created a longer, more ambitious version of *THX 1138* for theatrical release in 1971. A dystopian science fiction fantasy of a depersonalized, authoritarian future world, *THX 1138* was followed by *American Graffiti* (1973), essentially a remake of Federico Fellini's *I Vitelloni* (*The Young and the Passionate*) of 1953. As in Fellini's original, *American Graffiti* tracks a group of teenagers over the course of one night, as they kill time, dream of the future, and try to escape from the small-town lifestyle that is slowly stifling their hope of a better life. With a cast of then relatively unknown actors who would soon become stars, including Ron Howard, Richard Dreyfuss, Harrison Ford, Suzanne Somers, Cindy Williams, and Charles Martin Smith, and a running cameo by disc jockey Wolfman Jack, the film is warm, relaxed, and intimate in a way that seems at odds with Lucas's later, more distanced work.

Partly based on Lucas's own teen years as a budding hotrod driver in Modesto, California, *American Graffiti* took in more than $100 million at the box office on a $750,000 investment, making it a major hit. The film's success allowed Lucas to bankroll *Star Wars* (a k a *Star Wars: Episode IV—A New Hope,* 1977), which Lucas has spun into a long-running and hugely profitable series of films, including *Star Wars: Episode I—The Phantom Menace* (1999), *Star Wars: Episode II—Attack of the Clones* (2002), and the final (for the moment) film in the series, *Star Wars: Episode III—Revenge of the Sith* (2005). Lucas managed to retain a large chunk of the merchandising and ancillary rights to the *Star Wars* series and its characters, which have made him a very wealthy man. Lucas has also embraced, perhaps more than any other mainstream director, the full range of digital imagery technology in his films, even going so far as to reedit and reshoot sections of the first three *Star Wars* films, two of which he did not direct but controls the rights to. Thus an early movie in the series such as Irvin Kershner's *Star Wars: Episode V—The Empire Strikes Back* (1980) has been successfully re-released to theaters with up-to-date special effects added. Recently, Lucas retooled the films in the *Star Wars* series yet again, this time reprocessing them electronically into 3-D.

Hollywood Independents

Another 1970s filmmaker of note in America was John Carpenter, whose career began with the science fiction movie *Dark Star* (1974), which he began making as a student with virtually no budget at all. He then moved on to the police action drama *Assault on Precinct 13* (1976), one of the finest films of his career. As a disciple of Howard Hawks, Carpenter knew how to build an action sequence with judicious cross-cutting and detailed character development, and *Precinct 13*'s plot of a group of desperate people fighting for their lives in an abandoned, barricaded police station has clear links to such Hawks classics as *Rio Bravo* (1959) and *El Dorado* (1966). Carpenter also edited the film himself under the pseudonym John T. Chance, the character played by John Wayne in *Rio Bravo*. Made for $100,000 on a decidedly short schedule, *Precinct 13* made a major impression on festival audiences worldwide.

Carpenter followed with *Halloween* (1978), perhaps the first classic "slasher" film in a soon-to-be crowded subgenre. The movie cost roughly $325,000 and eventually brought in an astounding $50 million, leading to a long string of sequels by other directors, and allowing Carpenter, for the moment, to pursue whatever project he pleased. He directed a television movie, *Elvis*, in 1979, then the ghost story *The Fog* (1980) and the futuristic science fiction action film *Escape from New York* (1981). But the film that most dramatically shaped Carpenter's later career was *The Thing* (1982), a big-budget science fiction film that was a direct remake of the Hawks/Nyby 1951 original. Amped up with Rob Bottin's spectacular special makeup ef-

John Carpenter's *Halloween* (1978) revitalized the American horror film and led to a wave of sequels.

fects, which were mostly done on the floor during shooting rather than added in post-production, *The Thing* tells the same story as the original picture: a group of scientists and researchers trapped in Antarctica's endless winter are forcefully roused from their enforced hibernation when a large, unfriendly alien from another world crash-lands in their camp and starts killing them off one by one. To make matters worse, the Thing has the ability to change into an exact duplicate of any living organism, including any of the expedition's members.

Carpenter's version of *The Thing* is an epic exercise in fatalism; by the film's end, all the protagonists are dead except for group leader MacReady (Kurt Russell) and perpetual malcontent Childs (Keith David). One of them, it is strongly suggested, may be the Thing in human disguise, but it doesn't matter; MacReady, determined not to let the Thing get out of the camp and invade civilization, has torched the entire research station. With no power or heat, MacReady and Childs are last seen freezing to death while drinking a bottle of scotch, and the ending is left unresolved. *The Thing* came out within weeks of Spielberg's *E.T.* in June 1982, and audiences decisively rejected it, much to Carpenter's chagrin—the film was a major commercial failure. Carpenter's career never really recovered, although he continued to make films such as *Starman* (1984), *Prince of Darkness* (1987), *Village of the Damned* (1995, a remake of Wolf Rilla's 1960 original), and *Ghosts of Mars* (2001). His most recent film is the horror film *The Ward* (2010).

Robert Altman emerged as the preeminent social satirist of the period with the corrosive military satire *M*A*S*H* (1970), which became a long-running television series, and *Brewster McCloud* (1970), a bizarre fantasy about a young boy who lives in the Houston Astrodome and dreams of being able to fly. Altman's subsequent films, such as the revisionist western *McCabe & Mrs. Miller* (1971), the updated Philip Marlowe thriller *The Long Goodbye* (1973), and the "buddy" film *California Split* (1974), marked Altman as one of the most inventive and original directors of the era. With *Nashville* (1975), a sprawling essay on the country music industry, Altman moved into his signature late style, creating a multilayered narrative with numerous characters that is nothing so much as a tapestry of human experience. He also accelerated his long-standing use of overlapping dialogue (as practiced by Hawks in *His Girl Friday* and Welles in *Citizen Kane*) to create a dense, complicated soundtrack in which several conversations occur at the same time. Altman has used this strategy in such subsequent films as *The Player* (1992), one of the best movies ever made about contemporary Hollywood politics, *Short Cuts* (1993), *Ready to Wear* (*Prêt-à-Porter*, 1994), *Gosford Park* (2001), and his last film, *A Prairie Home Companion* (2006), released only months before his death that same year.

Woody Allen began his remarkably prolific career as a filmmaker, after a long stint as a stand-up comedian and writer, with the clever satire *What's Up, Tiger Lily?* (1966), a spoof of Clive Donner's sex comedy *What's New, Pussycat?* made in 1965, for which Allen wrote the script. In *What's Up, Tiger Lily?* Allen took an existing Japanese secret agent film and redubbed it into a wild parody, as the characters search for the perfect recipe for an egg-salad sandwich. The film was a surprise hit and allowed Allen to make his first real film, the comedy bank-robbery caper *Take the Money and Run* (1969). This was followed by the comedy of revolutionary South American politics, *Bananas* (1971), and *Everything You Always Wanted to Know About Sex** (**But Were Afraid to Ask*) (1972). In all these films, Allen functioned not only as director and writer (and often producer), but also the star, handcrafting vehicles that showcased his peculiar talents as a hapless everyman, perpetually clumsy, unlucky in love, and ceaselessly complaining.

Allen's work deepened considerably with the romantic comedy/drama *Annie Hall* (1977), and then took a detour into serious drama with *Interiors* (1978), a

Woody Allen and Diane Keaton in Allen's romantic comedy *Manhattan* (1979), one of the director's most successful works.

psychological character study deeply influenced by Allen's respect for Ingmar Bergman, who remains Allen's favorite director. *Manhattan* (1979) was Allen's most commercially and critically acclaimed film, a bittersweet romance set against the backdrop of New York City, while *Stardust Memories* (1980), *A Midsummer Night's Sex Comedy* (1982, an homage to Bergman's *Smiles of a Summer Night* [*Sommarnattens leende,* 1955]), and *Zelig* (1983, about the fictitious Leonard Zelig, a human chameleon played by Allen) marked a return to various forms of comedy.

Since then, Allen has racked up a truly stunning array of credits, including the brutal marital drama *Crimes and Misdemeanors* (1989), the 1930s period piece *Bullets Over Broadway* (1994), the sex comedy *Mighty Aphrodite* (1995), the acidic *Deconstructing Harry* (1997, another Bergman homage, this time to *Wild Strawberries* [*Smultronstället,* 1957]), and the jazz-themed comedy *Sweet and Lowdown* (1999), with a brilliant performance by Sean Penn as an arrogant, heartless jazz guitarist who shows up for gigs late, drunk, or not at all, and whose favorite pastime is shooting rats at the city dump. Allen went through a difficult personal period in the early 1990s, and at the turn of the millennium it seemed that such films as *The Curse of the Jade Scorpion* (2001) and *Hollywood Ending* (2002) were playing to diminishing returns, both

Divine in John Waters's "exercise in bad taste," the cult film *Pink Flamingos* (1972).

artistically and commercially. But Allen confounded his critics by moving to London to make the sharply observed *Match Point* (2005), which gave him some of his best notices in years and rejuvenated his career; he followed with the equally adroit *Scoop* in 2006. In 2011, Allen scored his greatest success in some time with his love letter to Paris in the 1920s, *Midnight in Paris,* which was both a box-office and critical hit.

John Waters emerged as a cheerfully reliable purveyor of bad taste with the "midnight movie" classic *Pink Flamingos* (1972), a low-budget 16 mm film that Waters shot, edited, and directed using a minimal crew. The film featured Divine (born Harris Glen Milstead), as Divine/Babs Martin, a 250-pound transvestite, and Mink Stole (born Nancy Stoll), as Connie Marble, in a contest to find "the world's Filthiest People." Shot in Waters's hometown of Baltimore, *Pink Flamingos* was the most ornate of Waters's early films, which include *Mondo Trasho* (1969), *Multiple Maniacs* (1970), *Female Trouble* (1974), and *Desperate Living* (1977).

With *Polyester* (1981), again starring Divine and also former 1950s teen heartthrob Tab Hunter (as Todd Tomorrow), Waters began a calculated move toward the cinematic mainstream. He still held true to his "trash" aesthetic, but worked in 35 mm and toned down, to some degree, his resolutely anarchic style of filmmaking. *Hairspray* (1988) was a pro-integration musical comedy set in 1960s Baltimore starring Ricki Lake and Divine in a dual role, while *Cry-Baby* (1990) featured Johnny Depp as teenage heartthrob and gang member Wade "Cry-Baby" Walker, leader of a gang of juvenile delinquents. *Serial Mom* (1994) is one of Waters's best late films, starring Kathleen Turner as a seemingly normal suburban mother who becomes a serial killer when the most trivial rules of social etiquette are breached, while *Pecker* (1998), Waters's most gentle satire, follows the adventures of a young photographer trying to establish himself in the art world. *Cecil B. DeMented* (2000) stars Melanie Griffith as a Hollywood "A" list star who is kidnapped by a group of cinematic renegades as an attack on conventional Hollywood cinema, while *A Dirty Shame* (2004) stars Tracey Ullman in a raucous satire on American sexual mores. All of Waters's films confront the conventional morals and social codes of contemporary American society, and while he may have mellowed, he is still ferociously dedicated to life on the margins of the American Dream.

OLIVER STONE'S ACTIVIST CINEMA

Oliver Stone emerged as the foremost provocateur of the New Hollywood; although his first two films, *Seizure* (1974) and *The Hand* (1981), were seemingly conventional horror pictures, they dealt persuasively with issues of masculinity and loss of power. In particular, Michael Caine's performance in *The Hand,* as a comic book artist who loses his drawing hand in an automobile accident and is subsequently reduced to teaching in a community college, is an affecting portrait of male desperation and impotent anger. But Stone soon moved on to more ambitious projects with the Vietnam War epic *Platoon* (1986), which draws on his own life experience as a ground soldier in the conflict. *Salvador* (1986), featuring James Woods as a battlefield photographer caught up in the intricacies of life in a perpetual war zone, critiques American involvement in foreign affairs when it serves only partisan political interests.

Stone's *Wall Street* (1987) is the definitive "go-go eighties" film, in which corrupt financier and stock manipulator Gordon Gekko (Michael Douglas, in one of his best performances) suckers young and naive Bud Fox (Charlie Sheen) into a massive swindle that brings about the ruin of both men. *Talk Radio* (1988) features a corrosive performance by Eric Bogosian (the film is adapted from Bogosian and Tad Savinar's play of the same name) as a "shock jock" who will do and say anything to stay on the air. *Born on the Fourth of July* (1989) is one of Stone's most moving films, about real-life Vietnam veteran Ron Kovic (Tom Cruise), who returns from the war paralyzed and gradually becomes an antiwar activist in a wrenching process of self-examination. *The Doors* (1991), with a cameo by Stone as a UCLA film professor, casts Val Kilmer as Jim Morrison, the lead singer of the 1960s rock group the Doors.

JFK (1991), perhaps Stone's most notorious film, was criticized by many for its sensationalism and hyperkinetic editorial style. The movie is a lengthy and detailed examination of the assassination of President John F. Kennedy in 1963, using real-life New Orleans district attorney Jim Garrison (Kevin Costner) as the central character and striving to build a convincing case that Lee Harvey Oswald could not have acted alone in JFK's murder. *Natural Born Killers* (1994) raised more eyebrows with its explicit portrayal of a charismatic serial killer and his girlfriend who go on a bloodthirsty, senseless rampage, urged on by an unscrupulous tabloid reporter who milks the killers' exploits for maximum shock value. Shot on a variety of film stocks, mixing color and black-and-white in a whirlpool of violent imagery, *Natural Born Killers* is frenzied filmmaking, a self-reflexive examination of instant celebrity and the American cult of violence. *Nixon* (1995) is a more visually sedate film, with a surprisingly convincing performance by Anthony Hopkins as the beleaguered president, and an equally deft performance by Joan Allen as Nixon's wife, Pat. Stone sees Nixon's presidency as the tragedy of a man who overreached his limitations, and who, insulated in the seat of power by a group of sycophantic cronies, gradually lost touch with the nation he was elected to serve.

Of late, Stone has turned to more traditional genre films: *U Turn* (1997) features Sean Penn as a hapless motorist whose car breaks down in a small town in Arizona where his life rapidly becomes a tourist's worst nightmare, while *Any Given Sunday* (1999) explores the macho ethics of football culture. *Alexander* (2004) is a historical epic that was not well received; Stone's *World Trade Center* (2006), depicts rescue efforts in the aftermath of the 9/11 attacks. In 2010, Stone revisited one of his biggest successes with the sequel *Wall Street: Money Never Sleeps,* which picks up Gordon Gekko after he is released from prison, but the film failed to excite much attention with critics or the public.

MOVIES AT THE MARGINS

Gus Van Sant broke into national prominence with *Drugstore Cowboy* (1989), a harrowing look at the addict lifestyle with an excellent performance by Matt Dillon as a junkie who raids drugstores for his supply of illicit narcotics. Van Sant's *To Die For* (1995) is a brutal satire of media celebrity, with Nicole Kidman as an unscrupulous reporter, while *Good Will Hunting* (1997), a more conventional film, casts Matt Damon as a working-class math prodigy who finds his gift more of a curse than anything else. *Elephant* (2003), a documentary-like drama shot in Portland, Oregon, about high school violence—inspired by the Columbine High School massacre of April

1999 in Colorado, in which a pair of students went on a violent and deadly rampage—was a more risky, personal work. Van Sant, like Stone, never shies away from difficult material; indeed, he seems drawn to it. In 2008, he directed the biopic *Milk,* centering on the life and times of Harvey Milk, the pioneering gay activist, with a standout performance by Sean Penn in the leading role, and Van Sant continues to work on new and adventurous film projects.

American cinema from the 1970s onward was marked by a curious bifurcation. On the one hand, strictly commercial blockbusters—such as Robert Wise's *Star Trek: The Motion Picture* (1979), which took the long-running television series and turned it into a theatrical franchise; Richard Donner's *Superman* (1978) and its attendant sequels; as well as Ivan Reitman's *Ghost Busters* (1984), John Badham's *Saturday Night Fever* (1977), and Joe Dante's *Gremlins* (1984)—were consciously aimed at mass audiences and usually hit their marks. On the other hand, there were much quieter films such as *My Dinner with Andre* (1981), the low-budget art-house hit by long-time director Louis Malle, which presented a two-hour dinner-table conversation between Wallace

Wallace Shawn in Louis Malle's *My Dinner with Andre* (1981), a surprise hit that consists almost entirely of a dinner conversation.

Shawn and playwright Andre Gregory, and a fascinating one at that. Independent mavericks such as John Cassavetes, the Coen brothers, Jim Jarmusch, and John Sayles also flourished during this time, making films that, for the most part, were designed primarily to please only themselves. Cassavetes was an early pioneer of "indie" films, using his earnings as an actor to finance the dramas *Shadows* (1959), *Husbands* (1970), *A Woman Under the Influence* (1974), and *Love Streams* (1984), many starring his wife, Gena Rowlands, as well as friends Peter Falk and Seymour Cassel.

The Coen brothers (Joel and Ethan) started with the hard-boiled neo-noir *Blood Simple* (1984) before moving on to the quirky cult comedy *Raising Arizona* (1987), the gangster drama *Miller's Crossing* (1990; a remake of Stuart Heisler's *The Glass Key* [1942], itself a remake of Frank Tuttle's 1935 version of the same title, both based on a Dashiell Hammett novel), and the 1930s Hollywood satire *Barton Fink* (1991). The Coens' other films include the corporate comedy *The Hudsucker Proxy* (1994), the offbeat crime drama

Fargo (1996), and the oddball comedy *The Big Lebowski* (1998), all of which became cult favorites. In 2004, the Coens directed an updated remake of Alexander Mackendrick's *The Lady Killers* (1955), which was received with little enthusiasm, but the brothers rebounded with the brutal revenge drama *No Country For Old Men* (2007), in which Javier Bardem stars as the unstoppable hit man Anton Chigurh. Bardem won an Academy Award for Best Supporting Actor for his performance in the film, and the Coens won for Best Director, Best Motion Picture, and Best Adapted Screenplay. In 2010, the Coens directed a remake of Henry Hathaway's 1969 western *True Grit.* Hathaway's film starred John Wayne in the role of Rooster Cogburn, and won Wayne the Oscar for Best Actor; in the Coens' version, Jeff Bridges took over the iconic role.

Jim Jarmusch has always marched to his own drumbeat, as he made abundantly clear with the screwball comedy *Stranger Than Paradise* (1984), produced on an extremely low budget, and the quirky mystery comedy *Mystery Train* (1989), featuring several interlocking narratives in the manner of Quentin Tarantino's later *Pulp Fiction* (1994). In 2003, he released a series of droll, often comic vignettes under the umbrella title *Coffee and Cigarettes,* which Jarmusch had been compiling over the course of several years. A minimalist in terms of visual style, Jarmusch teamed with Bill Murray in 2005 for the bittersweet *Broken Flowers,* a romantic comedy drama about a man who discovers that he has a son from a relationship many years earlier and goes on a road trip visiting previous lovers to find out who might be the mother. Gradually deepening into stark tragedy, the film is a tour de force for both director and star. His most recent film is the loosely structured, episodic film *The Limits of Control* (2009).

John Sayles began his career with the micro-budgeted *Return of the Secaucus 7* (1980), in which a group of college friends reunite at the house of one of their number to reflect on the passing of time and the evanescence of their dreams of youth, a film that seems to have served as the inspiration for Lawrence Kasdan's *The Big Chill* (1983). Sayles followed with such films as the science fiction race-relations parable *The Brother from Another Planet* (1984); the labor drama *Matewan* (1987); the intricately plotted crime drama set in Texas, *Lone Star* (1996); and the scathing satires *Sunshine State* (2002) and *Silver City* (2004), among many other projects, demonstrating a personal commitment in all his work. This continued with *Amigo* (2010), which dealt with the events of the Philippine-American War starring Chris Cooper, and was shot on location in the Philippines.

WOMEN IN THE DIRECTOR'S CHAIR

By the 1990s, women were directing films in every conceivable genre, a far cry from the 1950s when Ida Lupino was the only woman director working in Hollywood. Amy Heckerling's first movie, *Fast Times at Ridgemont High* (1982), a parody of high school comedy films, was a hit and introduced Sean Penn, Judge Reinhold, and Jennifer Jason Leigh to general audiences. Heckerling also directed the gangster comedy *Johnny Dangerously* (1984), a clever homage to 1930s gangster films, and *European Vacation* (a k a *National Lampoon's European Vacation,* 1985), but neither was successful at the box office. On her next movie, however, Heckerling was able to work with her own script, and *Look Who's Talking* (1989) became one of the biggest draws of the year, starring John Travolta, Kirstie Alley, and the voice of Bruce Willis. The movie quickly spawned a sequel, *Look Who's Talking Too* (1990), which she again wrote and directed. *Clueless* (1995), a modern-day version of Jane Austen's novel *Emma,* continued Heckerling's triumphs, but *Loser* (2000), like *Clueless* a comedy of young adult angst, was overlooked at the multiplex. Underneath the laughs, Heckerling's films have shown her ability to use comedy to expose sexism, hypocrisy, and the absurdities of the American consumer-oriented lifestyle.

Kathryn Bigelow has developed a reputation as a director of action movies. Her claustrophobic psychological thriller *The Loveless,* co-directed with Monty Montgomery, is a cerebral punk biker film starring a young Willem Dafoe. The movie was inspired by dark and gritty "B" pictures such as Joseph H. Lewis's *Gun Crazy* (a k a *Deadly Is the Female,* 1950) and Edgar G. Ulmer's *Detour* (1945). Bigelow's *Near Dark* (1987), a brilliant thriller that exposes a horror latent in rural America, is about a mysterious young woman who is actually a vampire, part of a gang of vampires who drive through the Midwest in search of victims. *Point Break* (1991), a visually stunning portrayal of power and relationships between men and women, stars Patrick Swayze as a macho surfer and part-time bank robber who buddies up to an undercover FBI agent (Keanu Reeves). The movie's success led to Bigelow's next assignment, *Strange Days* (1995), a futuristic mind-control film with a distinctly sadistic edge. *The Weight of Water* (2000) is a much more subdued film about two women living in different centuries, both trapped in destructive relationships. One is a news photographer, while the other is part of a story the photographer is researching for a book, about a nineteenth-century Norwegian immigrant who may be a murderer.

Bigelow's next movie was *K-19: The Widowmaker* (2002), a submarine action drama that was a substantial box office hit, but she really struck gold with *The Hurt Locker* (2008), a riveting, documentary-style film on the war in Iraq, which aroused a storm of controversy and admiration, and won six Academy Awards, including Best Director for Bigelow, the first time the honor was ever bestowed upon a woman. Shooting in Super 16 mm with multiple film crews simultaneously, Bigelow brought home the reality of the conflict with violent cross-cutting and hand-held intensity; the film also shut out James Cameron's escapist fantasy *Avatar* (2009) at the Oscars, a sign that perhaps more mature work was finally being recognized by the Academy's members. Ironically, Bigelow had been married to Cameron from 1989 to 1991.

Allison Anders directed *Gas Food Lodging* (1991), a low-budget film that was an immediate hit with both critics and audiences. Based on a novel by Richard Peck, the movie is a representative example of the new American cinema that revels in realism as much as romantic narrative. Anders created a film that effectively depicts not only the difficulties of single motherhood but also the pain of female adolescence in contemporary American society. Anders followed with the teen gang film *Mi Vida Loca* (*My Crazy Life*, 1994), which further consolidated her reputation as an uncompromisingly honest director. In 1995, she was the recipient of a MacArthur Foundation "genius grant."

Sofia Coppola made a splash with her first feature, *The Virgin Suicides* (1999), but won more attention for *Lost in Translation* (2003), starring Bill Murray as an over-the-hill star who travels to Japan to make a whisky commercial for some quick cash. Feeling culturally isolated from his immediate surroundings in Tokyo, physically and emotionally isolated from his wife, and temporally isolated from his earlier successes as an actor, he meets a young woman (Scarlett Johanssen) with doubts about her own life and marriage. Together they lend each other perspective about where they are in their lives. The film is deeply reminiscent of Alain Resnais's *Hiroshima, My Love* (and at one point we see the pair watching Fellini's *La Dolce vita* on television in the hotel), but it is an entirely original film and an assured and surprisingly mature work. Coppola won an Academy Award for Best Original Screenplay and was the first woman nominated for Best Director. Her next movie was a punk-rock version of the life of *Marie Antoinette* (2006), shot in period costumes but with a soundtrack featuring the Gang of Four and other punk artists; it was met with a mixed reception, due in part to its radical construction as a movie with little to do with history and much to do

Natasha Lyonne is unsure of her sexual identity in Jamie Babbit's lesbian comedy *But I'm a Cheerleader* (2000).

with Coppola's obsession with alienated and misunderstood young women.

Rose Troche's experimental lesbian feature *Go Fish* (1994) became the first breakthrough lesbian feature film. The movie is crafted as a series of deeply textured, carefully sculpted black-and-white images, and the narrative structure of the film pushes far beyond anything previously done in commercial cinema. Nancy Meyers is another highly successful director, with the hit films *The Parent Trap* (1998, a remake of David Swift's 1961 original film), *What Women Want* (2000), *Something's Gotta Give* (2003), and *The Holiday* (2006). Mary Harron created the deeply disturbing *I Shot Andy Warhol* (1996) and *American Psycho* (2000), reveling in the spectacle of sexual violence, while Jamie Babbit directed the cheerfully "pop" lesbian comedy *But I'm a Cheerleader* (1999), in which a sexually confused teenager (Natasha Lyonne) is packed off to the New Directions "reprogramming" center when her parents fear that she is gay. Nancy Savoca directed the coming of age romantic drama *Dogfight* (1991), in which folk song enthusiast Rose (Lili Taylor) and raw Marine recruit Eddie (River Phoenix) fall in love during a twenty-four-hour leave on the eve of the Vietnam War. In all of these films, the audience is given a vision of human existence remarkably different from that of male genre artists; one could argue that in the 1990s through the current era, women filmmakers have finally found a permanent home in Hollywood.

AFRICAN AMERICAN VOICES

Julie Dash's saga of African American slavery, *Daughters of the Dust* (1992), won considerable critical attention upon release. The first African American

369

Julie Dash's tale of the Gullah people living off the coast of South Carolina at the turn of the century forms the basis of her film *Daughters of the Dust* (1991), a complex meditation on race, identity, and heritage.

woman to direct a major feature film, Dash expresses a vision that is at once poetic and deeply outraged, conveying centuries of oppression and inequality in a brief but brilliantly executed period piece. Dash's characters, the Gullah, descendants of slaves who lived on islands off the coast of Georgia and South Carolina in the early 1900s, fight to hang on to their West African identity in a world they never chose to inhabit. Since that film, however, Dash has struggled to find funding for her next projects; in the twenty-first century, African-American filmmaking is still a tough business, given over for the most part to Eddie Murphy and Tyler Perry comedies or other crowd-pleasing movies; more serious films often find it hard to get financing or distribution.

Spike Lee, arguably the most important African American filmmaker the medium has produced, began his career at Morehouse College, where he made his first student film, *Last Hustle in Brooklyn* (1976). From there, he enrolled at New York University and graduated with a Master of Fine Arts degree in 1982; his thesis film, *Joe's Bed-Stuy Barbershop: We Cut Heads,* released in 1983, was screened at Lincoln Center's New Directors/New Films festival. In 1985, Lee shot his first feature film, *She's Gotta Have It* (1986), on a bare-bones budget of $160,000 in 16 mm black-and-white, with one brief color sequence. The film was an unexpected hit when released, earning more than $7 million in its initial theatrical run. Lee was on his way, creating a series of compelling interrogations of race, sexuality, and cultural politics in films such as *School Daze* (1988), *Do the Right Thing* (1989), *Mo' Better Blues* (1990), *Jungle Fever* (1991), *Malcolm X* (1992), *4 Little Girls* (1997), *He Got Game* (1998), *Bamboozled* (2000), and the atypically straightforward genre thriller *Inside Man* (2006).

Lee's visual style, a mélange of bold primary colors and strikingly dynamic camera angles, gives his work a distinctive punch. *School Daze* tackles racial tensions within the black community. *Do the Right Thing* is a simmering interrogation of racism in Brooklyn on the hottest day of summer, where tensions finally explode in a maelstrom of violence; *4 Little Girls* is a wrenching documentary about the Birmingham church bombings in 1963, with a mixture of archival footage, interviews, and stage material effortlessly intertwined. *Jungle Fever* explores drug abuse and the difficulty of interracial romance in an unforgiving white society. *He Got Game,* notable for its use of music by Aaron Copland, stars longtime Lee collaborator Denzel Washington as Jake Shuttlesworth, a prison inmate who must coerce his son into playing college basketball for Big State, the governor's alma mater, in order to be paroled for the murder of his wife years before. Jake is torn between his desire to get out of jail early and the knowledge that he is selling his son to "the man" in order to gain personal favor. Like all of Lee's films, *He Got Game* is about conscience, responsibility, and the overpowering effects of racism in American society.

Throughout his career, Lee has thrived on controversy. He has been outspoken about the inherent racism of the film industry and has gone out of his way to hire and nurture African Americans, many of whom might never have had the opportunity to work on a major Hollywood film. Lee scoffed at predictions that *Do the Right Thing* would incite riots in black neighborhoods (he was proven correct), but later found that studio chiefs were wary of funding *Malcolm X* for fear that a biopic of the controversial black leader would lead to violence. With financing for the project about to fall

Denzel Washington and Spike Lee in Lee's *Mo' Better Blues* (1990); Lee is perhaps the most influential African American director of late-twentieth-century American cinema.

371

through, Lee turned to Oprah Winfrey and Bill Cosby, among others, for funds to complete the filming. Outside assistance notwithstanding, Lee answers to no one but himself in his films, which has led some to charge him with self-indulgence. At times, his sprawling films seem to explode at the seams, layered with so many characters and plot lines that they are difficult to digest in one viewing. In 2012, Lee released *Red Hook Summer,* in which a young boy from Atlanta spends the summer with his grandfather, whom he has never seen before, in Red Hook, a section of Brooklyn.

Mario Van Peebles, son of the pioneering African American director Melvin Van Peebles, directed the crime drama *New Jack City* (1991), followed by the black western *Posse* (1993); the historical drama about the Black Panther Party, *Panther* (1995); and *Baadasssss!* (2003), an homage to his father's breakthrough film, *Sweet Sweetback's Baadasssss Song* (1971). Rusty Cundieff used the conventions of the horror film to create a work of trenchant social commentary in *Tales from the Hood* (1995), which explores issues of gang violence, racism, and drugs in the guise of a traditional genre piece, and then-nineteen-year-old Matty Rich created the searing drama *Straight Out of Brooklyn* (1991), an indictment of a social system that lets millions grow up in grinding poverty due to inequality and racism. Kasi Lemmons fought to create the nostalgic coming-of-age story *Eve's Bayou* (1997), set in the American South of the 1960s. A young girl learns about love, racism, and her cultural heritage as the adults around her try to come to terms with their

Kasi Lemmons's *Eve's Bayou* (1997), with Jurnee Smollet as ten-year-old Eve and Samuel L. Jackson as her father, Dr. Louis Batiste, is a refreshingly honest coming-of-age story.

372

complex emotional and romantic relationships. Lemmons, an actor since childhood, had to direct several short films, and obtain the help of one of the film's stars, Samuel L. Jackson, in order to raise financing for the film, which was a remarkably assured debut feature.

A more commercial filmmaker is John Singleton, whose debut film *Boyz n the Hood* (1991) attracted considerable commercial acclaim when first released, with its gritty tale of a young black man trying to get into college, when all of his friends are stuck in the "gang" lifestyle. Since that debut, Singleton's films have become steadily more audience driven, with the melodramas *Poetic Justice* (1993) and *Higher Learning* (1995), as well as the remake of *Shaft* (2000). However, the historical drama *Rosewood* (1997), about racist riots in 1920s Florida, demonstrated that Singleton still can tackle a serious subject when he chooses to do so, and he also served as the producer of the critically acclaimed movies *Hustle & Flow* (2005) and *Black Snake Moan* (2006). In 2011, Singleton directed the action thriller *Abduction*.

The current renaissance in black filmmaking comes after a period in the 1970s when African American action films dominated the landscape, such as Gordon Parks's *Shaft* (1971, remade by John Singleton in 2000), and Gordon Parks Jr.'s *Super Fly* (1972); Jack Hill's *Foxy Brown* (1974) and Arthur Marks's *Friday Foster* (1975) were career boosters for dynamic actress Pam Grier. For many emerging auteurs of the new Hollywood, these action films, along with those of other directors, were an inspirational force that offered new opportunities for genre filmmaking.

Pam Grier broke through as an African American action heroine in a string of movies in the early 1970s, such as Arthur Marks's *Friday Foster* (1975).

TWENTY-FIRST CENTURY HOLLYWOOD STYLE

Quentin Tarantino made a name for himself as a purveyor of stylish violence in *Reservoir Dogs* (1992), a brutal crime thriller, and then capped his reputation with *Pulp Fiction* (1994), one of the most complex and intelligent crime films ever made, which teeters on the edge of parody one moment, only to swing back to vicious reality the next. *Jackie Brown* (1997) is an uncharacteristically subdued crime drama starring 1970s action icon Pam Grier, while *Kill Bill: Vol. 1* (2003) and *Vol. 2* (2004) are revenge dramas that use 1970s action films, particularly Kung Fu films, as a visual reference point. In 2009, he directed *Inglourious Basterds,* a World War II action drama with his usual trademark style of over-the-top violence and long, detailed speeches by the main characters, presented in a series of bold, bravura visuals. Shot in Germany, the film was highlighted by a superb performance from the gifted Christoph Waltz, who won an Academy Award as Best Supporting Actor for his role as the obsessed Nazi Jew-hunter Col. Hans Landa. *Inglourious Basterds* also offered viewers the satisfying spectacle of seeing Adolf Hitler (Martin Wuttke) blasted to death by machine gun fire in a burning movie theater.

The equally bold Abel Ferrara created a group of dark and violent films with *King of New York* (1990) and the ultra-explicit *Bad Lieutenant* (1992), starring Harvey Keitel as a cop gone spectacularly wrong, as well as *The Addiction* (1995), *The Funeral* (1996), *The Blackout* (1997), and *'R Xmas* (2001). Shot on minimal budgets with gritty production values, Ferrara's films often feature his friend, the actor Christopher Walken. Recently, Ferrara has teamed with actor Willem

Graphic violence rose to new levels with Abel Ferrara's *Bad Lieutenant* (1992), starring Harvey Keitel as a corrupt, drug-addicted New York policeman.

Dafoe in *4:44: Last Day on Earth* (2011), an apocalyptic tale effectively filmed on a shoestring budget.

Samuel L. Jackson, John Travolta, and Harvey Keitel in Quentin Tarantino's genre-breaking crime thriller, *Pulp Fiction* (1994).

Jonathan Demme's breakthrough came with *Melvin and Howard* (1980), followed by the Talking Heads concert film *Stop Making Sense* (1984), the grisly crime drama *The Silence of the Lambs* (1991), and *Philadelphia* (1993), featuring Tom Hanks as a gay attorney afflicted with AIDS. Ron Howard, who began as a child actor on the television series "The Andy Griffith Show" and then played a teenager on "Happy Days," emerged as a competent craftsman with a string of traditional mainstream films such as *Splash* (1984), *Cocoon* (1985), *Apollo 13* (1995), the moving biographical film *A Beautiful Mind* (2001), and his adaptation of Dan Brown's best-selling novel *The Da Vinci Code* (2006). In 2008, Howard made one of his most effective films with his adaptation of the stage play *Frost/Nixon*, starring Frank Langella as Nixon.

Wes Craven is best known for horror films, such as *A Nightmare on Elm Street* (1984) and the self-reflexive *Scream* franchise (1996, 1997, 2000, and 2011), which efficiently deliver the requisite amount of gore and suspense necessary to the genre. Brian De Palma's violent thrillers include *Carrie* (1976), *Dressed to Kill* (1980), *Scarface* (1983, a remake of Howard Hawks's 1932 classic of the same name), *Body Double* (1984), and *The Black Dahlia* (2006). The perpetually *outré* David Lynch began his career with the bizarre student film *Eraserhead* (1977), and then continued with such hallucinatory films as *Blue Velvet* (1986), *Wild at Heart* (1990), and *Mulholland Drive*

David Lynch made a successful crossover from independent filmmaking with *The Elephant Man* (1980), elegantly photographed by Freddie Francis and starring John Hurt as John Merrick, whose horrible disfigurement leads to his cruel nickname.

(2001), along with the surprisingly straightforward period drama *The Elephant Man* (1980), the science fiction epic *Dune* (1984), and *The Straight Story* (1999), the touching real-life story of a man who traveled three hundred miles on his tractor-style lawnmower to see his ailing brother after a long estrangement. Lynch remains a staunch experimentalist with his more recent work, such as the dreamy, evanescent *Inland Empire* (2006).

Equally quirky, but in a more restrained fashion, is Tim Burton, whose student film *Vincent* (1982), with Vincent Price, led to the live-action *Frankenweenie* (1984) and then to *Pee-wee's Big Adventure* (1985), a colorful fantasy film with Paul Reubens in his Pee-wee Herman persona. *Beetlejuice* (1988), a mordant comedy with Michael Keaton in the title role as a rambunctious ghost, was a substantial hit on a modest budget and led to *Batman* (1989), which reinvented the classic comic book franchise with a much darker edge. *Edward Scissorhands* (1990) starred Johnny Depp (a frequent Burton collaborator) in a charming satirical comedy, and *Ed Wood* (1994) featured Depp as Edward D. Wood Jr., the famously inept filmmaker whose

Plan 9 from Outer Space (1959) is much beloved by aficionados of bad cinema. *Mars Attacks!* (1996), perhaps the only film in history to be inspired by a series of bubble-gum cards, is essentially a big-budget remake of Fred F. Sears' Cold War classic *Earth vs. the Flying Saucers* (1956). With *Charlie and the Chocolate Factory* (2005), *Corpse Bride* (2005), *Sweeney Todd: The Demon Barber of Fleet Street* (2007), *Alice in Wonderland* (2010), and *Dark Shadows* (2012), Burton retained his hold on the macabre, while giving the source material a gentle, humorous twist that makes his work all his own.

Ridley Scott came to feature filmmaking through advertising, making a splash with his third feature, *Alien* (1979), still one of the most original and inventive science fiction films ever made, and helping to revisualize the science fiction film as a futuristic noir universe. Scott's *Blade Runner* (1982) is another futuristic dystopian tale, set in Los Angeles, with hard-boiled cop Harrison Ford on the trail of a group of aberrant androids who are posing a threat to a repressive society. The film has touches of Fritz Lang's *Metropolis* (1927) in its visual style, but Scott's image of the world as an earthly hell has a genuine tactile quality that is his alone.

Scott's *Thelma & Louise* (1991) is a controversial "feminist" road movie; two women (Susan Sarandon and Geena Davis) go on the run when one of them accidentally kills a would-be rapist. Fearing that no one will believe them, the women become outlaws, much to the consternation of the various male authority figures sprinkled throughout the film. But ultimately, as the women drive their car off the edge of a canyon to avoid capture by the police, the film's message becomes muddled; why must they die in order to be free? Scott handles the material with his customary assurance, but the film is still a bone of contention for many observers. *G. I. Jane* (1997) is a feminist service drama in which Demi Moore toughens up to join a crack team of Navy SEALs despite the disapproval of her commanding officer, and *Gladiator* (2000) is a lavish historical drama of ancient Rome, with eye-popping visual effects and a solid performance from Russell Crowe in the leading role. *Black Hawk Down* (2001) documents the carnage that followed a failed U.S. military raid in Somalia. Scott's more recent films include *American Gangster* (2007), *Robin Hood* (2010), and *Prometheus* (2012), all well-designed commercial entertainments.

As digital cinema became more commonplace, the stylization of films was pushed to new extremes. Graphic novelist Frank Miller collaborated with established directors Robert Rodriguez and Quentin Tarantino to create *Sin City* (2005), a "neo-noir" film that expertly blended comic book backgrounds with live actors to create a sort of living comic strip, albeit one with exceedingly dark overtones. In 2006, Zack Snyder's *300,* based on Miller's graphic novel about the Battle of Thermopylae in 480 B.C.E., was an even more extreme example of comic book violence and nonstop action, eliminating plot and acting almost completely to create a sweeping vision of bloodlust run wild. Snyder followed this up with his film version of the graphic novel *Watchmen* (2009), which, however, failed to duplicate the success of *300.*

THE RESPONSE TO 9/11

Many Hollywood films became more overtly political in the wake of the September 11, 2001, attacks on the World Trade Center and the Pentagon, but it took Hollywood five years to come to terms with the tragedy itself. Paul Greengrass's *United 93* (2006), which preceded Oliver Stone's *World Trade Center* by four months, faithfully and painfully re-creates the events of that dark day, in which the hijacked passengers fought a group of terrorists to bring down their plane over a Pennsylvania field before it could do significant damage elsewhere. Despite the emotional subject matter, Greengrass's direction is a model of restraint, and his use of nonprofessional and unknown actors heightens the realism of the film, which emerges as an effective response to our shared need to understand the motives behind the worst terrorist attack on American soil.

Controversy seems to fuel many films in the post-9/11 era. Michael Moore's provocative documentary *Fahrenheit 9/11* (2004) gave audiences a peek into the Bush administration's preparation for the war in Iraq and it became the most profitable documentary of all time in the process. In the same year, action star Mel Gibson used his own money to fund the religious drama *The Passion of the Christ,* which also generated record returns at the box office. Actor George Clooney took on the McCarthy era with the technically ambitious *Good Night, and Good Luck* (2005), which documents the fight of veteran CBS newsman Edward R. Murrow against Senator Joseph McCarthy, a leader of the Cold War anti-Communist witch hunts. That 9/11 was still at the forefront of American consciousness was demonstrated by the continued wave of films centering on the attack, such as Stephen Daldry's *Extremely Loud and Incredibly Close* (2011), based on Jonathan Safran Foer's novel of the same name. More than a decade after the destruction of the Twin Towers, 9/11 remained the defining event of twenty-first-century America, something that could never be forgotten.

THE NEW HOLLYWOOD

The last thirty-five years of twentieth-century American cinema have given birth to a wide variety of films and filmmakers, with the line between "independent" films and studio productions often being blurred. In addition, a wave of mergers, corporate takeovers, and buyouts have shaken the industry, starting with Universal's purchase by the talent agency MCA in 1962, and then moving through Paramount's takeover by Gulf & Western Industries in 1966. The case histories of several of the major studios during this period exemplify the trend toward hyper-conglomerization, in which the studios became just cogs in a larger wheel of media organizations that controlled vast empires of television, print, and Internet outlets. It was either adapt or perish, and the major companies realized that in changing times, they had to ride the new wave of corporate takeovers.

Universal would change hands several times, sold to Japanese electronics giant Matsushita in 1990 and in 1995 to Seagrams, a Canadian liquor distributor. In a head-spinning series of subsequent negotiations, the French media company Vivendi acquired Seagrams in 2000, to become Vivendi Universal. But mounting debt proved too much, and Vivendi sold off Universal's studio and theme parks to General Electric, the parent company of NBC Broadcasting. Now known as NBC Universal, the studio functions as a production arm for the television network, in addition to making films for theatrical release. Paramount went through an equally turbulent series of corporate identities after its acquisition by Gulf & Western; in 1994 Viacom, owner of the CBS Television Network, purchased the studio outright. However, Viacom announced in 2005 that it would split into two distinct entities: one for the CBS television and radio networks and another for production of programming, which is now home to Paramount Pictures.

Warner Bros. was purchased by Kinney National Services in 1969 and began concentrating on big-budget co-production deals with major stars of the era, such as Paul Newman, John Wayne, and Clint Eastwood. In the 1980s, Kinney abandoned its other interests, which included a chain of funeral parlors and parking lots, to concentrate solely on film production, and in 1989 merged with Time, Inc., publishers of *Time* and *Sports Illustrated*. In 2000, Internet service provider America Online (AOL) took over Time Warner, and the firm was briefly known as AOL Time Warner, but when AOL's stock took a hit in the dot-com crash, the company became known simply as Time Warner. Rupert Murdoch's News Corporation now owns Twentieth Century Fox, after a series of equally Byzantine transactions.

Columbia Pictures was purchased by Coca-Cola in 1982, and announced a new slate of family pictures that would include no R- or X-rated films; the rule was quickly broken when John Badham's action drama *Blue Thunder* and John Carpenter's horror film *Christine* both appeared with an R rating in 1983. A complex series of negotiations and alliances followed, until the failure of Elaine May's multimillion-dollar comedy *Ishtar* (1987) caused Coke to spin off Columbia Pictures as a stand-alone operation. In 1989, Columbia was sold to Sony, the Japanese electronics manufacturer.

MGM, once the ruling studio in the business, went through a series of humbling takeovers that stripped it of its film library, which went to media mogul Ted Turner; Turner used the collection as the backbone for his Turner Network Television (TNT) cable and satellite channel, and later Turner Classic Movies (TCM). Turner had actually owned MGM/UA (MGM bought United Artists in 1981) for a brief time in 1985, but less than three months later, Turner sold back the MGM name and United Artists to financier Kirk Kerkorian, while the famed MGM lot itself, home to studios for nearly a century, was sold to Lorimar Television. More heartbreak followed, as the Italian financier Giancarlo Paretti purchased MGM/UA, minus the film library; eventually ownership of MGM/UA passed to the European banking firm Crédit Lyonnais because of financial problems, and then Crédit Lyonnais decided to sell MGM/UA again, once more to Kirk Kerkorian. In 2004, after a typically complex series of transactions, MGM was sold to a consortium of investors headed by Sony, Providence Equity Partners, and the Texas Pacific Group, resulting in a super conglomerate that now combined MGM, UA, and Columbia all under one corporate umbrella.

All this wheeling and dealing is partly due to the immense cost of making motion pictures in the present market, and partly to the current desire to build media conglomerates that control vast empires of broadcasting, print, music, television, and film production, with the necessary means to distribute these products through newly emerging technologies, such as the World Wide Web and cable television. "A" list stars routinely command $20 million or more per picture; two or three "A" list personalities can push the production cost of a film past the $100 million mark before a frame of film has been shot. Directors, too, command hefty salaries, running into the tens of millions of dollars per film, often in addition to "back end points," a percentage of the film's profits. The same often holds true for the stars. The studios are no longer the one-stop production centers they once were in the 1940s and 1950s; they now function basically as distribution and funding entities, providing the cash to green-light more commercial films, and aggressively seeking to promote "franchise" projects, such as the *Superman, X-Men,* and *Batman* films, which seem assured of making continual profits. Studios today in Hollywood are really umbrellas for a variety of smaller production companies, where actors, directors, producers, and writers compete to get their projects funded and distributed to theaters. The system of a stock group of actors, directors, and technicians belonging to any one studio is a thing of the past; today, everyone is a free agent.

The Internet emerged as a viable tool for the promotion and even the production of films with Daniel Myrick and Eduardo Sánchez's *The Blair Witch Project* (1999), a micro-budgeted movie that cost $35,000 and ultimately grossed more than $240 million at the box office. David R. Ellis's campy action thriller *Snakes on a Plane* (2006) was extensively hyped using the Internet, and some of the dialogue for the film was suggested by e-mail correspondence to the film's producers. Oren Peli's low-budget "mockumentary" *Paranormal Activity* (2007) was shot for a pittance, but cleaned up at the box office and spawned several sequels by virtue of a clever Web-based ad campaign. Web downloads of feature films on a legal basis began in early 2006, and DVDs almost immediately began to slip into the background as streaming video took off, available on sites from Hulu to Amazon to Netflix, as well as numerous other content providers. Today, DVDs are almost an artifact of an earlier era, as streaming video—on your iPad, cell phone, television, or computer—becomes the new norm for home viewing.

Today, a film typically gets most of its revenue not from its initial theatrical run, but rather through foreign theatrical playoff, cable television, pay-per-view (also known as "on demand"), and streaming video, which now comprise most of the profit stream for Hollywood films. With the cost of exhibition rising daily, streaming downloads look increasingly attractive, as consumers become more comfortable with digital technology and on-line purchasing. Disney, for example, was one of the first to license many of its shorts and cartoons for download through Apple's iTunes; in short order, the rest of Hollywood followed suit, so that streaming has now become the main home video market.

THE DIGITAL DOMAIN

Against this backdrop of hyper-conglomerization, Hollywood also had to compete with another new fundamental technological shift: the advent of digital photography. Briefly put, for the first hundred years of the cinema, all images had been generated on film, edited on film, and reproduced on film for final exhibition. Suddenly, all that changed. In the late 1980s, the Avid editing system was introduced, which allowed editors to do away with film altogether and edit movies on a computer with remarkable ease, moving scenes and shots with the flick of a finger rather than the long and laborious process of making physical edits entailed by a standard Moviola editing machine.

In 1997, film editor Walter Murch received the Academy Award for editing on Anthony Minghella's *The English Patient* (1996), the first Oscar-winning film to be cut entirely on digital equipment. But advances in film editing technology did not stop there; in 2003, Murch edited Minghella's *Cold Mountain* (2003) on a standard PowerMac G4 computer, using Apple's Final Cut Pro software—costing less than $1,000—to create the finished film. Only seven years earlier, it had taken a powerful Avid machine to edit the complex images and soundtracks of a feature film; now, a standard home computer has the power to do the same thing.

This flexibility extended to the production process as well. Digital cinematography can be defined as the process of capturing images on digital video rather than film. Indeed, many of these new digital movies could never have been created on film. Andy and Larry (now Lana) Wachowski's *The Matrix* (1999) kicked off a series of computer special effects movies, such as *The Matrix Reloaded* and *The Matrix Revolutions* (both 2003), which used extensive digital imagery to depict the adventure of Neo (Keanu Reeves) as he battles the subterranean forces that seem to control the universe. With extensive use of "green screen" technology, in which backgrounds and details within each shot are inserted after principal photography through the use of digital imagery, the Wachowskis created a world at once fantastic and yet tangibly real, in which objects and people seamlessly morphed from one incarnation to the next.

George Lucas famously declared in 1999 that he would never shoot traditional film again, because the results with digital video were far superior. Ten years later, it's clear that digital cinema has won the day. In the early days of the twenty-first century, most movies were still shot on 35 mm color negative film, but as the quality of the digital image increased, the days of film became numbered. In the last few years, 35 mm film has all but vanished, and as of 2012, the major Hollywood studios issued an ultimatum to movie theaters around the country: adapt to digital or die. The movie companies no longer see the point in making 35 mm prints of anything; the cost of handling, shipping, and insurance has become prohibitive. This is perhaps the most profound shift that the cinema has ever undergone; the complete absence of film from the production process.

For most of the directors considered in the earlier chapters of this volume, the use of film was a given throughout the entire production and exhibition process; this changed only slightly when television came along, and old movies began popping up there on a regular basis. Today's directors can be called the "digital generation," because they shoot, edit, and distribute their work on video. Bryan Singer's *Superman Returns*, Mel Gibson's *Apocalypto*, Robert Altman's *A Prairie Home Companion*, Michael Mann's *Miami Vice*, David Fincher's *Zodiac*, and Frank Coraci's *Click* (all released in 2006) were shot entirely in digital video; conversion to 35 mm film was done simply to allow existing theater facilities to screen the film. Fincher, in particular, embraces digital filmmaking and shot the Mark Zuckerberg/Facebook biopic *The Social Network* (2010) entirely in digital format, shooting numerous takes of each scene, and erasing unusable material during shooting.

Keanu Reeves in Andy and Larry Wachowski's science fiction allegory, *The Matrix* (1999).

Movies—one can't really call them films anymore—are now routinely shot on digital video, with the image recorded on a hard drive; the image is edited digitally into the final product, and then delivered as a DCP (Digital Cinema Package), a series of digital video files stored on a hard drive, to be shown in a theater using a digital projector. Thirty-five millimeter equipment is becoming obsolete as all around the world traditional projection booths are being rapidly torn down and replaced with digital technology, and by 2015, 35 mm will be almost completely gone. There's no doubt that, at its best, the image quality is superb; digital cinema offers a high-resolution image that is scratch-free, bright, and easy to manipulate in post-production. Additional pluses for production and distribution companies are the considerable cost savings; a 35 mm print of a film might cost roughly

$1,500, multiplied by three thousand prints or so for an international release, but a Digital Cinema Package can be either sent to the theater for a fraction of the cost, or downloaded at the theater from a satellite at no physical expense, allowing a movie to open worldwide in thousands of locations simultaneously.

However, there is a downside to the embrace of this new technology: the preservation of the image. When movies were shot on film, a studio could simply make a fine-grain master negative and stick it into a cold storage vault, where it would last for close to one hundred years under optimal conditions, and could be readily pulled out of the library and copied as the need arose. Digital films—films that are nothing but electronic code—require much more intensive preservation and cost roughly $20,000 per year to store on servers, which must be constantly upgraded as new platforms emerge. By contrast, a 35 mm fine-grain negative costs about $1,000 a year to store, and is, in many ways, much more stable. Around the world, archivists and historians are already raising the alarm; as we move into an all-digital future, how will we preserve the past? If every 35 mm film in existence now has to be archived electronically—a daunting task—as 35 mm film, along with 35 mm cameras and projectors, cease to be manufactured, how much will it cost? What will be lost? What will be saved? Will we lose a large portion of cinema history forever?

Along with the conversion to digital technology comes the increased reliance on digital imagery for special effects, the most obvious use of the technology, and also the one most fraught with signs of viewer fatigue. While early experiments in computer-generated special effects can be traced to Michael Crichton's *Westworld* (1973) and its sequel, Richard T. Heffron's *Futureworld* (1976), the technology remained in a fairly primitive state through Steven Lisberger's *Tron* (1982) and Nick Castle's *The Last Starfighter* (1984), until James Cameron incorporated brief sections of digital "water" effects (via CGI imaging) in *The Abyss* (1989), stunning audiences with the fluidity of the technique. Cameron's *Terminator 2: Judgment Day* (1991) used CGI extensively, and the wall-to-wall special effects created a violent yet believable universe of spectacular, nonstop action that suddenly made the industry aware of the potential of the new technology.

Cameron's *Titanic* (1997), a lavish spectacle about the sinking of the famous ocean liner which won a record-tying eleven Academy Awards, cost nearly $200 million, but made close to $2 *billion* by 2012, at which point Cameron revamped the film for a theatrical re-release in 3-D, raking in additional revenues. *Titanic* remains a triumph of digital filmmaking. The ship

Arnold Schwarzenegger in James Cameron's *Terminator 2: Judgment Day* (1991), the visually stunning sequel to Cameron's 1984 original.

used in the film never left the harbor but was used as a model for all the impressive special effect set pieces that mark the film's 194-minute running time. Digital-effects cinema arguably reached its zenith with Cameron's futuristic fantasy film *Avatar* (2009). For many viewers, *Avatar* represented the apotheosis of CGI (computer-generated imagery) technology; Cameron's vision of the future, presented in striking 3-D, used green screen technology to the fullest possible extent, and offered viewers a fully realized dream world of vivid intensity. The film was also a smash box-office hit, making more than $760 million worldwide. Clearly Cameron's vision had moved far beyond the precincts of Roger Corman's Venice, California, studio, where he started in the late 1970s. His work as a digital filmmaker is both breathtaking and visually enthralling.

Steven Spielberg employed the technology in 1993 to present lifelike cloned dinosaurs in *Jurassic Park,* and Robert Zemeckis used CGI to remove actor Gary Sinise's legs to show him as an amputee war veteran in the film *Forrest Gump* (1994). The movie also featured extensive use of archival footage digitally manipulated to make the title character (Tom Hanks) appear to interact with various historical figures, such as President John F. Kennedy. In 1995, CGI invaded the domain of traditional animation with John Lasseter's *Toy Story,* the first fully computer-generated cartoon film, created by the Pixar Company and released through Walt

Disney Productions. The film was a resounding success and ink-and-print animation has now almost been retired entirely from the screen.

The final step, it would seem, is to create lifelike human characters for use within a film. While this is already done with extras in crowd shots, who are simply digitally copied and then mapped in as needed for large-scale scenes, the first full-scale attempt to create believable human characters for a film, Hironobu Sakaguchi and Motonori Sakakibara's *Final Fantasy: The Spirits Within* (2001), demonstrated that the technology still had a long way to go before becoming interchangeably convincing with the real world. It may be that such "replacement of the real" will never be accepted by audiences. While CGI can enhance a performance, by creating scenes and situations that formerly only matte photography and miniature work (as in the 1933 *King Kong*) could do, creating the human connections that audiences have with Johnny Depp, Nicole Kidman, or other human actors would seem hard to replace or relinquish. Nevertheless, in Peter Jackson's *Lord of the Rings* trilogy (2001–03), the character of Gollum was created entirely by CGI technology and took "his" place as a leading figure in the story; in Paul Verhoeven's *Starship Troopers* (1997), visual-effects supervisor Phil Tippett's monstrous arachnids were also created entirely by CGI technology, yet seemed to have as much important substance as any of the human protagonists in the movie. In Gore Verbinski's *Pirates of the Caribbean: Dead Man's Chest* (2006), this final shift may already have taken place. Although actor Bill Nighy performed the role of Davy Jones for the camera with a motion capture suit on, in orderto give animators a reference point in their creation of his final on-screen character, nothing whatsoever of Nighy's visual image remains in the final film; the entire performance is a digital construct.

TWENTY-FIRST CENTURY HOLLYWOOD AUTEURS

The rise of digital cinema also allowed smaller, independent filmmakers to create personal visions with a minimum of backing, and even in big-budget films, the judicious use of digital imaging allowed directors, actors, and writers to work quickly and efficiently to create films that resonated with critics and audiences alike. One of the most commercially and critically successful big-budget movies in recent memory is Christopher Nolan's *The Dark Knight* (2008), the second in Nolan's trilogy of Batman films, with a stunning performance by the late Heath Ledger as the Joker. Ledger had mesmerized audiences with his anguished portrayal of the bisexual cowboy Ennis Del Mar in Ang Lee's *Brokeback Mountain* (2005); in his last role as the

Heath Ledger as the Joker in Christopher Nolan's *The Dark Knight* (2008).

Joker, Ledger demonstrated that had he lived, he might well have become the twenty-first century James Dean, so great were his gifts as an actor. He died tragically young, at the age of twenty-eight, but given more time, who knows what he might have accomplished?

Christopher Nolan, born in London in 1970, has become one of the cinema's most accomplished auteurs, with such films as *Following* (1998), his first feature, shot on 16 mm film on weekends; *Memento* (2000), a brain-teasing film centering on the effects of short-term memory loss; *The Prestige* (2006), about dueling magicians in the early days of the twentieth century; and *Inception* (2010), a mind-blowing film that uses digital imaging to create effects that are both inventive and utterly seductive. Interestingly, Nolan prefers, for the moment, to shoot on 35 mm film, as does Steven Spielberg; what will they do when the technology to do so is no longer available?

Other directors who have emerged of late include J. C. Chandor, whose debut feature *Margin Call* (2011) documents the 2008 financial meltdown in excruciating detail, with superb performances by Kevin Spacey, Zachary Quinto, Jeremy Irons, Demi Moore, and Paul Bettany. Shot in a few weeks in the offices of a defunct brokerage firm for $2.8 million using digital cameras, the film is a small-scale vision of the financial apocalypse, which continues to reverberate to the present day. Bennett Miller began his career with the documentary *The Cruise* (1998), an all-digital look at very eccentric New

Director J. C. Chandor and Kevin Spacey
on the set of *Margin Call* (2011).

York tour bus guide; he then graduated to feature films with *Capote* (2005), starring Philip Seymour Hoffman as the writer Truman Capote, tracking him through the writing of his groundbreaking nonfiction novel *In Cold Blood.* Hoffman won an Academy Award for Best Actor for the film, and Miller went on to direct the equally uncompromising *Moneyball* in 2011. Courtney Hunt directed the bleak rural drama *Frozen River* (2008) on a budget of less than $1 million; star Melissa Leo was nominated for Best Actress, and Hunt for Best Screenplay, at the 2009 Oscars.

Gary Ross, whose small-scale film *Pleasantville* (1998) was a modest hit, broke through commercially with *The Hunger Games* (2012), based on the novel by Suzanne Collins, which depicts a future dystopia in which the world is divided into the very rich and the very poor. Each year, lots are drawn to see which of the young men and women of the outlying districts—the very poor—will be forced to compete in a gladiatorial spectacle once a year, which can have only one winner. Everyone else has to die. Though the film has more than a few echoes of Kinji Fukasaku's Japanese film *Battle Royale* (2000), *The Hunger Games* is rousing entertainment, and offers in its heroine Katniss Everdeen (Jennifer Lawrence), a twenty-first century role model for young women: an entirely self-reliant protagonist who can take care of herself in the clinches. These are just some of the young men and

388

women who are making today's movies; we can only speculate as to what they may offer us tomorrow.

As movies become all digital, what new works will be created, from the moment of image capture to the projection of the final image on the screen? Other than effects-driven extravaganzas, the same films that have always moved audiences will continue to be the most popular with worldwide viewers: films that have strong narratives and tell compelling stories, with characters audiences can relate to. We have moved in this book through thousands of films and hundreds of filmmakers, all of them intent on bringing their personal visions to the screen, no matter what the genre or production cost. The methodology and mechanics of the motion picture have been under constant revision since the first frames of film were shot by Louis Aimé Augustin Le Prince in 1888; how could it have been otherwise? But the images and visions discussed in this text will now inform an entirely new generation of auteurs, using digital technology from start to finish, as the cinema becomes ever more popular, and moves smoothly into the second decade of the twenty-first century, exploding onto laptops, iPads, cell phones, through streaming video, in theaters, and in the now somewhat antiquated medium of television. The movies will always exist. It will be fascinating to see what happens next.

Jennifer Lawrence as Katniss Everdeen in Gary Ross's *The Hunger Games* (2011).

GLOSSARY OF FILM TERMS

auteur theory: A critical theory, developed first in France in the 1940s, which holds that the director can be the primary creator of a film. However, the star, the production designer, the producer, or even the special effects supervisor (to name just a few possibilities) can also be the driving force behind the production.

back projection: Projection of film onto a transparent screen, which serves as a background while the action is being shot. Most frequently used in car scenes in which the passing street is back-projected. This has been replaced in current technology by blue-screen or green-screen imaging, in which performers act in front of a green or blue background and only the images of their bodies are used; backgrounds and other visual materials are added later.

blimp: A sound-deadening housing designed for movie cameras to ensure that they are quiet during filming and that the motor can't be heard on the set.

camera operator: The person who actually operates the camera on the set, under the instructions of the *director* and the *director of photography.*

cinéma vérité: A style of filmmaking in which the camera simply documents the action in front of it, without interfering with the actors or participants, as in a documentary. There is no narration. Also known as direct cinema in England.

CGI: Computer Generated Images, used today in films to depict crowd scenes, huge buildings, giant monsters, and other special effects that would be too costly or impossible to do otherwise.

close-up: A shot that takes in the actor from the neck upward, or an object from a similarly close position.

crane: A piece of apparatus that can lift the camera vertically in the air.

depth of field: Depth of composition of a shot, e.g. where there are several planes, a foreground, a middle ground, and a background.

depth of focus: A technical adjustment that ensures that a shot with depth of field remains in focus in all its planes. The technique of depth of focus was popularized by cinematographer Gregg Toland in *Citizen Kane* (1941), but it was used as far back as the early silent films of Alice Guy and D. W. Griffith.

digital production: Shooting a movie entirely on digital video, post-producing it entirely using video editing methods (such as the Avid editing system), and then projecting the final image onto the screen with a high intensity projector. Completely eliminates traditional 35 mm film. The final three *Star Wars* films pioneered this technology; increasingly, many major and independent films also use this method of production.

director: The person who is responsible for staging the action in a film, directing the actors, supervising the director of photography, and making sure that the performances and visuals of the film are effective.

director of photography: The person who is responsible for the look of a film, supervising camera placement, lighting, and camera movement.

dissolve: A gradual transition from one shot into another, so that at a certain point both images overlap and are visible simultaneously. Often used to suggest the passage of time.

editing: Splicing together a series of *shots* to create a scene in a film.

establishing shot: A shot, usually at the beginning of a sequence, that establishes the location of the action or the time of day.

executive producer: The person who arranges the financing for a film, and/or packages the stars, screenwriter, and other key elements of a film.

fade in: A device used at the beginning of a sequence, where the image gradually lightens from complete darkness.

fade out: Used at the end of a sequence, where the image gradually darkens to complete blackness.

film gauge: The width of the motion picture film used in the camera. The standard gauges are 35 mm (for theatrical features), 16 mm (for documentary and student films), and 8 mm (home movies). Only 35 mm is still used regularly today; digital video has replaced, for the most part, 16 mm and 8 mm film.

film noir: A style of filmmaking, popular in the United States after World War II, which used harsh shadows, *flashbacks*, and *voiceovers*, and typically presented a downbeat, fatalistic view of society.

film rip: The film breaking or shredding in the projection gate during the screening of a film, or in the camera during the photography of a film.

fast motion: A camera device whereby the movement of the action is speeded up, generally used for comic effects.

flashback: Occurs when the film's forward narrative is interrupted by an event from the past, usually introduced by a character reminiscing about past events.

Foley: Sound effects added in post-production to enhance the visuals, such as gunshots, footsteps, or explosions.

freeze: An optical effect whereby one image is held for a time and the action seems to become a still photograph.

gaffer: The head electrician on a movie set.

genre film: A film that follows a predictable plot pattern, such as a horror film, a western, or a musical.

grip: A person on a film set who lays down dolly tracks, sets up lights, and generally does the hard physical work.

high angle shot: A shot from above that points down on the action.

insert: An inserted shot, usually a close-up, used to reveal something in greater detail.

intercut shots: A series of *shots* that are alternated to create suspense, usually of two different events happening at the same time; for instance, a plane about to crash into the ground while horrified spectators in *close-up* look on.

irising: Gradual opening up or closing down of the image from or to a small point of light, often used in silent film.

jump cuts: An abrupt cut from one scene to the next, or within a scene, to compress time and make the film move more quickly, e.g., Godard's New Wave classic *Breathless*.

long shot: Shot taken from some distance (usually not less than fifty yards from the action).

low angle shot: Shot taken from below and pointing up at the action.

mask: A device for covering part of the screen with blackness, frequently used to create the effect of looking through binoculars or a keyhole.

master shot: A wide shot in a film, usually of a group of people, performing a scene in its entirety. This is usually shot first, and then individual *close-ups* of the actors are photographed to cut into the scene during *editing*.

medium shot: A shot from five to fifteen yards, e.g., one that includes a small group of people in its entirety.

montage: The structure of editing within a film.

MTV editing: Named after the MTV video channel, a style of editing popularized in the 1980s that relies on rapid editing, jump cuts, speeded up motion, and multiple camera angles for dazzling effect, e.g., Oliver Stone's *Natural Born Killers*.

off-screen: Action or dialogue that occurs outside the area viewed by the camera

overexposed: Describes a shot in which more than a usual amount of light has been allowed to reach the film, thus producing a blinding, glaring effect.

overlap: Dialogue in which two or more characters speak simultaneously.

pan (or *panoramic shot*): A horizontal and circular movement of the camera on its pivot.

post-production: The editing, musical scoring, and final completion of a film after shooting. Today, this routinely involves digital post-production to get rid of mike booms or scratches, to change facial expressions, "sweeten" visual backgrounds, or enhance exterior/interior locations.

post-synchronize (a k a *ADR* [*Automatic Dialogue Replacement*] or *post synching*): To make a recording of the sound track for a film (especially of the dialogue) in a sound studio (as opposed to during the shooting of the film), with the actors speaking their lines in accompaniment to the projected film.

producer: The person who supervises the production of the film, arranges the financing, hires the cast, director, and crew, and is responsible for keeping the film on schedule.

reverse motion: A trick effect that reverses the movements of the characters and objects.

runner (a k a *go-fer* or *gopher*): Person on the film set who runs errands, assists the other technicians, and does general chores.

rushes: The result of a day's shooting when the film comes back from the laboratories after development and has not yet been edited. Rushes are usually screened for the director each day during the shooting of a film. Also called "dailies."

shock cuts: The abrupt replacement of one image by another, usually for dramatic effect.

shooting script: The final script used by the director, technicians, and actors, with the complete breakdown of the scenario into separate shots.

shot: The smallest unit in the grammar of film; one angle of a specific person or object within the film, before editing.

soft focus: The effect obtained by gauze in front of the lens of the camera, which creates a hazy, romantic effect, used often in films of the 1930s.

stock shot (a k a *stock footage*): Shot taken from a film library that has been photographed for another film, but which is spliced into a new film to save money or present a historical event (e.g., scenes of Pearl Harbor or 9/11).

studio system: In Hollywood from the 1920s to the late 1950s, the system by which each film studio had a roster of actors, directors, composers, cameraman, costume designers, and the like on regular salary, under contract, to create their films on an assembly-line basis.

telephoto lens: A lens that magnifies like a telescope, bringing the object closer to the viewer without moving the camera.

tilt up, or down: when the camera tilts up toward the action, usually to exaggerate the authority or menace of a character; or tilts down, to indicate superiority, omniscience, or power-lessness.

track in, track back: A movement of the camera on a dolly (a tracking or traveling shot), to-ward or away from an object or character.

underexposed: The opposite of overexposed, thus producing a dim, indistinct image.

voiceover: Narration or dialogue presented on the sound track of a film to explain the film's action, plot, or characters.

wide-angle lens: A lens with a wide range of field, which exaggerates depth and perspective.

wipe: A device whereby a line moves across the screen, replacing one image and introducing another, e.g., in the *Star Wars* films.

zoom: A lens of variable focal length. It can, by gradually magnifying or reducing the image, give the effect of moving closer to or farther away from an object.

BIBLIOGRAPHY

DIRECTORS

Akerman, Chantal

Foster, Gwendolyn Audrey. *Identity and Memory: The Films of Chantal Akerman*. Carbondale: Southern Illinois University Press, 2003.

Margulies, Ivone. *Nothing Happens: Chantal Akerman's Hyperrealist Everyday*. Durham, N.C.: Duke University Press, 1996.

Allen, Woody

Blake, Richards A. *Street Smart: The New York of Lumet, Allen, Scorsese, and Lee*. Lexington: University Press of Kentucky, 2005.

Desser, David, and Lester D. Friedman. *American Jewish Filmmakers*. Urbana: University of Illinois Press, 2004.

Lax, Eric. *Woody Allen: A Biography*. New York: Da Capo Press, 2000.

Almodóvar, Pedro

D'Lugo, Marvin. *Pedro Almodóvar*. Urbana: University of Illinois Press, 2006.

Altman, Robert

Sterritt, David. *Robert Altman: Interviews*. Jackson: University Press of Mississippi, 2000.

Thompson, David. *Altman on Altman*. London: Faber & Faber, 2006.

Antonioni, Michelangelo

Brunette, Peter. *The Films of Michelangelo Antonioni*. Cambridge: Cambridge University Press, 1988.

Arzner, Dorothy

Mayne, Judith. *Directed by Dorothy Arzner*. Bloomington: Indiana University Press, 1994.

Bergman, Ingmar

Bergman, Ingmar. *Bergman on Bergman*. Trans. Paul Britten Austin. London: Secker & Warburg, 1973.

Kalin, Jesse. *The Films of Ingmar Bergman*. Cambridge: Cambridge University Press, 2003.

Michaels, Lloyd, ed. *Ingmar Bergman's Persona*. Cambridge: Cambridge University Press, 2000.

Bertolucci, Bernardo

Kline, Thomas J. *Bertolucci's Dream Loom: A Psychoanalytic Study of Cinema*. Amherst: University of Massachusetts Press, 1987.

Blaché, Alice Guy

Blaché, Alice Guy. *The Memoirs of Alice Guy Blaché*. Trans. Roberta and Simone Blaché. Ed. Anthony Slide. Metuchen, N.J.: Scarecrow, 1986.

McMahan, Alison. *Alice Guy Blaché: Lost Visionary of the Cinema*. New York: Continuum, 2002.

Boetticher, Budd

Boetticher, Budd. *When in Disgrace*. Santa Barbara, Calif.: Neville, 1989.

Bresson, Robert

Bresson, Robert. *Notes on Cinematography*. New York: Urizen Books, 1977.

Reader, Keith. *Robert Bresson*. Manchester: Manchester University Press, 2000.

Buñuel, Luis

Acevedo-Muñoz, Ernesto R. *Buñuel and Mexico: The Crisis of National Cinema*. Berkeley: University of California Press, 2003.

Baxter, John. *Buñuel*. London: Fourth Estate, 1994.

Buñuel, Luis. *An Unspeakable Betrayal: Selected Writings of Luis Buñuel*. Trans. Garrett White. Berkeley: University of California Press, 2000.

De La Colina, José, and Tomás Pérez Turrent. *Objects of Desire: Conversations with Luis Buñuel*. Trans. and ed. Paul Lenti. New York: Marsilio, 1992.

Capra, Frank

Capra, Frank. *The Name Above the Title: An Autobiography*. New York: Da Capo Press, 1997.

McBride, Joseph. *Frank Capra: The Catastrophe of Success*. New York: Simon & Schuster, 1992.

Smoodin, Eric Loren. *Regarding Frank Capra: Audience, Celebrity, and American Film Studies, 1930–1960*. Durham, N.C.: Duke University Press, 2004.

Carpenter, John

Boulenger, Gilles. *John Carpenter: The Prince of Darkness*. Los Angeles: Silman-St. James, 2001.

Chahine, Youssef

Fawal, Ibrahim. *Youssef Chahine*. BFI World Directors Series. London: British Film Institute, 2001.

Chaplin, Charles

Lynn, Kenneth Schuyler. *Charlie Chaplin and His Times*. New York: Simon & Schuster, 1997.

McDonald, Gerald D., Michael Conway, and Mark Ricci. *The Films of Charlie Chaplin*. New York: Citadel, 1965.

Cocteau, Jean

Anderson, Alexandra, and Carol Saltus. *Jean Cocteau and the French Scene*. New York: Abbeville, 1984.

Cocteau, Jean. *The Art of Cinema*. Trans. Robin Buss. London: Marion Boyars, 1994.

————. *Beauty and the Beast: Diary of a Film.* Trans. Ronald Duncan. New York: Dover, 1972.

Cocteau, Jean, and André Fraigneau. *Cocteau on the Film.* New York: Dover, 1972.

Steegmuller, Francis. *Cocteau.* Boston: Little, Brown, 1970.

Coen, Joel and Ethan

Palmer, Burton R. *Joel and Ethan Coen.* Urbana: University of Illinois Press, 2004.

Coppola, Francis Ford

Browne, Nick. *Francis Ford Coppola's Godfather Trilogy.* Cambridge: Cambridge University Press, 2000.

Lewis, Jon. *Whom God Wishes to Destroy: Francis Coppola and the New Hollywood.* Durham, N.C.: Duke University Press, 1995.

Philips, Gene D., and Rodney Hill, eds. *Francis Ford Coppola: Interviews.* Jackson: University Press of Mississippi, 2004.

Corman, Roger

Will, David, and Paul Willemen, eds. *Roger Corman: The Millennic Vision.* Edinburgh: Edinburgh Film Festival, 1970.

Cromwell, John

Denton, Clive, and Kingsley Canham. *The Hollywood Professionals: King Vidor, John Cromwell, Mervyn LeRoy.* London: Tantivy Press, 1976

Cukor, George

Levy, Emanuel. George Cukor: *Master of Elegance.* New York: William Morrow, 1994.

Denis, Clair

Beugnet, Martine. *Claire Denis.* Manchester: Manchester University Press, 2004.

Mayne, Judith. *Claire Denis.* Urbana: University of Illinois Press, 2005.

Deren, Maya

Nichols, Bill, ed. *Maya Deren and the American Avant-Garde.* Berkeley: University of California Press, 2001.

Dreyer, Carl Theodor

Skoller, Donald, ed. *Dreyer in Double Reflection.* New York: Dutton, 1973.

Duras, Marguerite

Gunther, Renate. *Marguerite Duras.* Manchester: Manchester University Press, 2002.

Dwan, Allan

Bogdanovich, Peter. *Allan Dwan: The Last Pioneer.* New York: Praeger, 1971.

Eisenstein, Sergei

Bordwell, David. *The Cinema of Eisenstein.* Cambridge: Harvard University Press, 1993.

Eisenstein, Sergei. *Notes on a Film Director.* London: Lawrence & Wishart, 1959.

Goodwin, James. *Eisenstein, Cinema, and History.* Urbana: University of Illinois Press, 1993.

Karetnikova, Inga, Sergei Eisenstein, and Leon Steinmetz. *Mexico According to Eisenstein.* Albuquerque: University of New Mexico Press, 1991.

Fassbinder, Rainer Werner

Braad Thomsen, Christian. *Fassbinder: The Life and Work of a Provocative Genius.* Minneapolis: University of Minnesota Press, 2004.

Hayman, Ronald. *Fassbinder: Film Maker.* London: Weidenfeld & Nicolson, 1984.

Thomsen, Christian Brad. *Fassbinder.* London: Faber & Faber, 1999.

Ford, John

Eyman, Scott. *Print the Legend: The Life and Times of John Ford.* New York: Simon & Schuster, 1999.

Gallagher, Tag. *John Ford: The Man and His Films.* Berkeley: University of California Press, 1986.

Place, J. A. *The Western Films of John Ford.* Secaucus, N.J.: Citadel Press, 1974.

Franju, Georges

Ince, Kate. *Georges Franju.* Manchester: Manchester University Press, 2005.

Frankenheimer, John

Champlin, Charles. *John Frankenheimer: A Conversation.* Burbank, Calif.: Riverwood Press, 1995.

Pratley, Gerald. *The Cinema of John Frankenheimer.* New York: A. S. Barnes, 1969.

Fuller, Samuel

Fuller, Samuel. *A Third Face: My Tale of Writing, Fighting, and Filmmaking.* New York: Knopf, 2002.

Hardy, Phil. *Samuel Fuller.* New York: Praeger, 1970.

Will, David, and Peter Wollen, eds. *Samuel Fuller.* Edinburgh: Edinburgh Film Festival, 1969.

Godard, Jean-Luc

Dixon, Wheeler Winston. *The Films of Jean-Luc Godard.* Albany: SUNY Press, 1997.

Godard, Jean-Luc. *Godard on Godard.* New York: Viking Press, 1972.

Locke, Maryel, and Charles Warren, eds. *Jean-Luc Godard's Hail Mary: Women and the Sacred in Film.* Carbondale: Southern Illinois University Press, 1993.

MacCabe, Colin. *Godard: A Portrait of the Artist at Seventy.* New York: Faber & Faber, 2003.

Roud, Richard. *Godard.* 2nd ed. Bloomington: Indiana University Press, 1970.

Sterritt, David, ed. *Jean-Luc Godard: Interviews.* Jackson: University Press of Mississippi, 1998.

———. *The Films of Jean-Luc Godard: Seeing the Invisible.* Cambridge: Cambridge University Press, 1999.

Goulding, Edmund

Kennedy, Matthew. *Edmund Goulding's Dark Victory.* Madison: University of Wisconsin Press, 2004.

Griffith, D. W.

Lang, Robert, ed. *The Birth of a Nation: D. W. Griffith, Director.* New Brunswick, N.J.: Rutgers University Press, 1994.

Schickel, Richard. *D. W. Griffith: An American Life.* New York: Simon & Schuster, 1984.

Hawks, Howard

Hillier, Jim, and Peter Wollen, eds. *Howard Hawks, American Artist.* London: British Film Institute, 1996.

McCarthy, Todd. *Howard Hawks: The Grey Fox of Hollywood*. New York: Grove Press, 1997.

Hitchcock, Alfred
Anobile, Richard J., with Harry Chester. *Psycho*. New York: Avon, 1974.
Freedman, Jonathan, and Richard Millington, eds. *Hitchcock's America*. New York: Oxford University Press, 1999.
McGilligan, Patrick. *Alfred Hitchcock: A Life in Darkness and Light*. New York: Regan Books, 2003.
Spoto, Donald. *The Dark Side of Genius: The Life of Alfred Hitchcock*. Boston: Little, Brown, 1983.
Sterritt, David. *The Films of Alfred Hitchcock*. Cambridge: Cambridge University Press, 1993.
Truffaut, François. *Hitchcock*. Rev. ed. Helen G. Scott. New York: Simon & Schuster, 1985.

Jarman, Derek
Jarman, Derek. *Smiling in Slow Motion: The Journals of Derek Jarman*. Ed. Keith Collins. London: Vintage, 2001.
Parkes, James Cary, Matt Cook et al. *Derek Jarman: A Portrait*. London: Thames and Hudson, 1996.

Kar-wai, Wong
Brunette, Peter. *Wong Kar-wai*. Urbana: University of Illinois Press, 2005.

Keaton, Buster
Knopf, Robert. *The Theater and Cinema of Buster Keaton*. Princeton, N.J.: Princeton University Press, 1999.
McPherson, Edward. *Buster Keaton: Tempest in a Flat Hat*. New York: Newmarket Press,
Robinson, David. *Buster Keaton*. Bloomington: Indiana University Press, 1969.

Kiarostami, Abbas
Saeed-Vafa, Mehrnaz, and Jonathan Rosenbaum. *Abbas Kiarostami*. Urbana: University of Illinois Press, 2003.

Kurosawa, Akira
Prince, Stephen. *The Warrior's Camera: The Cinema of Akira Kurosawa*. Princeton, N.J.: Princeton University Press, 1999.
Richie, Donald. *The Films of Akira Kurosawa*. 3rd ed. Berkeley: University of California Press, 1999.
Richie, Donald, and Joan Mellen. *The Films of Akira Kurosawa*. Berkeley: University of California Press, 1984.

Kurys, Diane
Tarr, Carrie. *Diane Kurys*. Manchester: Manchester University Press, 1999.

Lang, Fritz
Bogdanovich, Peter. *Fritz Lang in America*. New York: Praeger, 1967.
Jensen, Paul M. *The Cinema of Fritz Lang*. London: A. S. Barnes, 1969.
McGilligan, Patrick. *Fritz Lang: The Nature of the Beast*. New York: St. Martin's, 1997.

Lee, Spike
Donalson, Melvin Burke. *Black Directors in Hollywood*. Austin: University of Texas Press, 2003.

Fuchs, Cynthia, ed. *Spike Lee: Interviews.* Jackson: University Press of Mississippi, 2002.

Lee, Spike. *Spike Lee's Gotta Have It: Inside Guerrilla Filmmaking.* New York: Simon & Schuster, 1987.

Lee, Spike, and Terry McMillan. *Five for Five: The Films of Spike Lee.* New York: Workman, 1991.

Leone, Sergio

Frayling, Christopher. *Sergio Leone: Something to Do with Death.* London: Faber & Faber, 2000.

LeRoy, Mervyn

Denton, Clive, and Kingsley Canham. *The Hollywood Professionals: King Vidor, John Cromwell, Mervyn LeRoy.* London: Tantivy Press, 1976.

Lloyd, Harold

Lloyd, Annette D'Agostino. *The Harold Lloyd Encyclopedia.* Jefferson, N.C.: McFarland, 2003.

Vance, Jeffrey, and Suzanne Lloyd. *Harold Lloyd: Master Comedian.* New York: Harry N. Abrams, 2002.

Loach, Ken

Leigh, Jacob. *The Cinema of Ken Loach: Art in the Service of the People.* New York: Wallflower, 2002.

Losey, Joseph

Caute, David. *Joseph Losey: A Revenge on Life.* New York: Oxford University Press, 1994.

Ciment, Michel. *Conversations with Losey.* London: Methuen, 1985.

Leahy, James. *The Cinema of Joseph Losey.* New York: A. S. Barnes, 1967.

Milne, Tom. *Losey on Losey.* Garden City, N.Y.: Doubleday, 1968.

Lubitsch, Ernest

Eyman, Scott. *Ernst Lubitsch: Laughter in Paradise.* New York: Simon & Schuster, 1993.

Paul, William. *Ernst Lubitsch's American Comedy.* New York: Columbia University Press, 1983.

Lupino, Ida

Donati, William. *Ida Lupino: A Biography.* Lexington: University Press of Kentucky, 1996.

Kuhn, Annette, ed. *Queen of the B's: Ida Lupino Behind the Camera.* Westport, Conn.: Praeger, 1995.

Stewart, Lucy Ann Liggett. *Ida Lupino as a Film Director, 1949–1953: An Auteur Approach.* New York: Arno, 1980.

Malle, Louis

Frey, Hugo. *Louis Malle.* Manchester: Manchester University Press, 2004.

Mamoulian, Rouben

Milne, Tom. *Mamoulian.* Bloomington: Indiana University Press, 1970.

Marker, Chris

Alter, Nora M. *Chris Marker.* Urbana: University of Illinois Press, 2006.

Mizoguchi, Kenji
Kirihara, Donald. *Patterns of Time: Mizoguchi and the 1930s.* Madison: University of Wisconsin Press, 1992.
Le Fanu, Mark. *Mizoguchi and Japan.* London: British Film Institute, 2005.

Oshima, Nagisa
Turim, Maureen. *The Films of Oshima Nagisa: Images of a Japanese Iconoclast.* Berkeley: University of California Press, 1998.

Ozu, Yasujiro
Bordwell, David. *Ozu and the Poetics of Cinema.* London: British Film Institute, 1988.
Richie, Donald. *Ozu.* Berkeley: University of California Press, 1974.

Pasolini, Pier Paolo
Pasolini, Pier Paolo. *A Violent Life.* London: Cape, 1968.

Peckinpah, Sam
Prince, Stephen, ed. *Sam Peckinpah's The Wild Bunch.* Cambridge: Cambridge University Press, 1999.
Seydor, Paul. *Peckinpah: The Western Films.* Urbana: University of Illinois Press, 1980.

Polanski, Roman
Polanski, Roman. *Roman by Polanski.* New York: Ballantine Books, 1985.

Powell, Michael, and Emeric Pressburger
Christie, Ian. *Arrows of Desire: The Films of Michael Powell and Emeric Pressburger.* London: Faber & Faber, 1994.

Preminger, Otto
Pratley, Gerald. *The Cinema of Otto Preminger.* New York: A. S. Barnes, 1971.

Ray, Satyajit
Robinson, Andrew. *Satyajit Ray: The Inner Eye.* Berkeley: University of California Press, 1992.

Renoir, Jean
Bergan, Ronald. *Jean Renoir: Projections of Paradise.* Woodstock, N.Y.: Overlook Press, 1992.
Faulkner, Christopher. *The Social Cinema of Jean Renoir.* Princeton, N.J.: Princeton University Press, 1986.
Renoir, Jean. *Renoir on Renoir: Interviews, Essays and Remarks.* Trans. Carol Volk. Cambridge: Cambridge University Press, 1989.

Richardson, Tony
Richardson, Tony. *Long Distance Runner: A Memoir.* London: Faber & Faber, 1993.

Rossellini, Roberto
Brunette, Peter. *Roberto Rossellini.* New York: Oxford University Press, 1987.
Gallagher, Tag. *The Adventures of Roberto Rossellini.* New York: Da Capo Press, 1998.
Guarner, José Luis. *Roberto Rossellini.* Trans. Elisabeth Cameron. New York: Praeger, 1970.

Scorsese, Martin
Friedman, Lawrence S. *The Cinema of Martin Scorsese*. New York: Continuum, 1998.
Thompson, David, and Ian Christie, eds. *Scorsese on Scorsese*. Rev. ed. London: Faber & Faber, 2004.

Sennett, Mack
Louvish, Simon. Keystone: *The Life and Clowns of Mack Sennett*. New York: Faber & Faber, 2004.

Spielberg, Steven
Friedman, Lester. *Citizen Spielberg*. Urbana: University of Illinois Press, 2006.
McBride, Joseph. *Steven Spielberg: A Biography*. New York: Simon & Schuster, 1997.
Perry, George C. *Steven Spielberg*. New York: Thunder's Mouth Press, 1998.

Straub, Jean-Marie
Roud, Richard. *Straub*. New York: Viking, 1972.

Suzuki, Seijun
Field, Simon, and Tony Rayns, eds. *Branded to Thrill: The Delirious Cinema of Suzuki Seijun*. London: Institute of Contemporary Arts, 1994.

Tourneur, Jacques
Fujiwara, Chris. *The Cinema of Nightfall: Jacques Tourneur*. Baltimore: Johns Hopkins University Press, 2000.

Truffaut, François
Ingram, Robert, and Paul Duncan, eds. *François Truffaut: The Complete Films*. London: Taschen, 2004.
Truffaut, François. *Correspondence 1945–1984*. Trans. Gilbert Adair. Eds. Gilles Jacob and Claude de Givray. New York: Noonday/ Farrar, Straus and Giroux, 1990.

Varda, Agnès
Smith, Alison. *Agnès Varda*. Manchester: Manchester University Press, 1998.

Vidor, King
Denton, Clive, and Kingsley Canham. *The Hollywood Professionals: King Vidor, John Cromwell, Mervyn LeRoy*. London: Tantivy Press, 1976.

Vigo, Jean
Gomes, Salles. *Jean Vigo*. London: Secker & Warburg, 1972.
Temple, Michael. *Jean Vigo*. Manchester: Manchester University Press, 2005.

Visconti, Luchino
Nowell-Smith, Geoffrey. *Visconti*. New York: Doubleday, 1968.

Von Stroheim, Erich
Kozarski, Richard. *Von: The Life and Films of Erich von Stroheim*. New York: Limelight Editions, 2004.

Von Trier, Lars
Björkman, Stig, ed. *Trier on Von Trier*. London: Faber & Faber, 2004.

Wajda, Andrzej
Wajda, Andrzej. *Double Vision: My Life in Film*. London: Faber & Faber, 1989.

Warhol, Andy
Bourdon, David. *Warhol*. New York: Abrams, 1989.
Doyle, Jennifer, Jonathan Flatley, and José Esteban Muñoz, eds. *Pop Out: Queer Warhol*. Durham, N.C.: Duke University Press, 1996.
Wolf, Reva. *Andy Warhol, Poetry and Gossip in the 1960s*. Chicago: University of Chicago Press, 1997.

Welles, Orson
McBride, Joseph. *Orson Welles*. New York: Da Capo Press, 1996.
———. *What Ever Happened to Orson Welles? A Portrait of an Independent Life*. Lexington: University Press of Kentucky, 2006.
Truffaut, François. *Orson Welles: A Critical View*. New York: Acrobat Books, 1992.

Whale, James
Curtis, James. *James Whale: A New World of Gods and Monsters*. Boston: Faber & Faber, 1998.

Wilder, Billy
Chandler, Charlotte. *Nobody's Perfect: Billy Wilder, a Personal Biography*. New York: Simon & Schuster, 2002.
Crowe, Cameron. *Conversations with Wilder*. New York: Alfred A. Knopf, 1999.
Dick, Bernard F. *Billy Wilder*. New York: Da Capo Press, 1996.
Staggs, Sam. *Close-up on Sunset Boulevard: Billy Wilder, Norma Desmond, and the Dark Hollywood Dream*. New York: St. Martin's Press, 2002.

Woo, John
Elder, Robert K., ed. *John Woo: Interviews*. Jackson: University Press of Mississippi, 2005.

Yimou, Zhang
Gateward, Frances, ed. *Zhang Yimou: Interviews*. Jackson: University Press of Mississippi, 2001.

Zinnemann, Fred
Nolletti, Arthur Jr., ed. *The Films of Fred Zinnemann: Critical Perspectives*. Albany: State University of New York Press, 1999.

GENERAL HISTORY

Abel, Richard, ed. *Encyclopedia of Early Cinema*. Abingdon; New York: Routledge, 2005.
Balio, Tino. *Grand Design: Hollywood as a Modern Business Enterprise, 1930–1939*. New York: Scribner, 1993.
Barnouw, Erik. *Documentary: History of the Non-Fiction Film*. Oxford: Oxford University Press, 1993.
Bergman, Andrew. *We're in the Money: Depression America and Its Films*. New York, Harper & Row, 1971.

Bogdanovich, Peter. *Who the Devil Made It?* New York: Knopf, 1997.

Cherchi Usai, Paolo. *Silent Cinema: An Introduction.* London: British Film Institute, 1999.

Cook, David. *A History of Narrative Film, 1889–1979.* New York: Norton, 1980.

Cousins, Mark. *The Story of Film.* New York: Thunder's Mouth Press, 2004.

Crafton, Donald. *The Talkies: American Cinema's Transition to Sound, 1926–1931.* New York: Scribner, 1997.

Cripps, Thomas. *Hollywood's High Noon: Moviemaking and Society Before Television.* Baltimore: Johns Hopkins University Press, 1997.

Dick, Bernard F. *City of Dreams: The Making and Remaking of Universal Pictures.* Lexington: University Press of Kentucky, 1997.

Ellis, Jack C., and Virginia Wright Wexman. *A History of Film.* 5th ed. Boston: Allyn and Bacon, 2002.

Ellwood, David, ed. *The Movies as History: Visions of the Twentieth Century.* Stroud: Sutton, 2000.

Eyman, Scott. *The Speed of Sound: Hollywood and the Talkie Revolution, 1926–1930.* New York: Simon & Schuster, 1997.

Foster, Gwendolyn Audrey. *Women Film Directors: An International Bio-Critical Dictionary.* Westport, Conn.: Greenwood, 1995.

Galt, Rosalind. *The New European Cinema.* New York: Columbia University Press, 2006.

Katz, Ephraim. *The Film Encyclopedia.* 5th ed. Rev. Fred Klein and Ronald Dean Nolan. New York: Collins, 2005.

Kelly, Richard. *The Name of This Book Is Dogme 95.* London: Faber & Faber, 2000.

Kindem, Gorham A. *The International Movie Industry.* Carbondale: Southern Illinois University Press, 2000.

Monaco, James. *The Encyclopedia of Film.* New York: Perigee, 1991.

Musser, Charles. *Edison Motion Pictures, 1890–1900: An Annotated Filmography.* Washington, D.C.: Smithsonian Institution Press, 1997.

Nowell-Smith, Geoffrey. *The Oxford History of World Cinema.* Oxford: Oxford University Press, 1996.

O'Brien, Geoffrey. *The Phantom Empire.* New York: Norton, 1993.

Parkinson, David. *History of Film.* New York: Thames and Hudson, 1995.

Rawlence, Christopher. *The Missing Reel.* New York: Atheneum, 1990.

Sadoul, Georges. *The Dictionary of Films.* Berkeley: University of California Press, 1992.

Sklar, Robert. *Film: An International History of the Medium.* 2nd ed. New York: Prentice-Hall and Harry N. Abrams, 2002.

Unterberger, Amy L., ed. *The St. James Women Filmmakers Encyclopedia: Women on the Other Side of the Camera.* Detroit: Visible Ink, 1999.

Willis, Holly. *New Digital Cinema: Reinventing the Moving Image.* London: Wallflower, 2005.

Genre

Action

Gallagher, Mark. *Action Figures: Men, Action Films, and Contemporary Adventure Narratives.* New York: Palgrave Macmillan, 2006.

Schneider, Steven J. *New Hollywood Violence.* Manchester: Manchester University Press, 2004.

Tasker, Yvonne. *Spectacular Bodies: Gender, Genre and the Action Cinema.* London: Routledge, 1993.

African American

Bobo, Jacqueline, ed. *Black Women Film and Video Artists.* New York: Routledge, 1998.

Bogle, Donald. *Blacks in American Films and Television: An Encyclopedia.* New York: Garland, 1988.

———. *Toms, Coons, Mulattoes, Mammies, and Blacks: An Interpretive History of Blacks in American Film.* 3rd ed. New York: Continuum, 1994.

Bowser, Pearl, Jane M. Gaines, and Charles Musser, eds. *Oscar Micheaux and His Circle: African-American Filmmaking and Race Cinema of the Silent Era.* Bloomington: Indiana University Press, 2001.

Cripps, Thomas. *Black Film as Genre.* Bloomington: Indiana University Press, 1979.

———. *Slow Fade to Black: The Negro in American Film 1900–1942.* London: Oxford University Press, 1977.

Davis, Natalie Z. *Slaves on Screen: Film and Historical Vision.* Cambridge, Mass.: Harvard University Press, 2000.

Gabbard, Krin. *Jammin' at the Margins: Jazz and the American Cinema.* Chicago: University of Chicago Press, 1996.

Gaines, Jane M. *Fire and Desire: Mixed-Race Movies in the Silent Era.* Chicago: University of Chicago Press, 2001.

Jones, G. William. *Black Cinema Treasures: Lost and Found.* Denton: University of North Texas Press, 1991.

Reid, Mark. *Black Lenses, Black Voices: African American Film Now.* Lanham, M.D.: Rowman & Littlefield, 2005.

Stewart, Jacqueline Najuma. *Migrating to the Movies: Cinema and Black Urban Modernity.* Berkeley: University of California Press, 2005.

Animation

Adamson, Joe. *Tex Avery: King of Cartoons.* New York: Popular Library, 1975.

Gabler, Neal. *Walt Disney: The Triumph of the American Imagination.* New York: Knopf, 2006.

Goldmark, Daniel. *Tunes for Toons: Music and the Hollywood Cartoon.* Berkeley: University of California Press, 2005.

Lenburg, Jeff. *The Great Cartoon Directors.* New York: Da Capo, 1993.

Kanfer, Stefan. *Serious Business: The Art and Commerce of Animation in America from Betty Boop to Toy Story.* New York: Da Capo Press, 2000.

Klein, Norman M. *Seven Minutes: The Life and Death of the American Animated Cartoon.* New York: Verso, 1993.

Comedy

Dale, Alan. *Comedy Is a Man in Trouble: Slapstick in American Movies.* Minnesota: University of Minnesota Press, 2000.

Winokur, Mark. *American Laughter: Immigrants, Ethnicity, and 1930s Hollywood Film Comedy.* New York: St. Martin's Press, 1996.

Experimental

Brakhage, Stan. *Film at Wit's End: Eight Avant Garde Filmmakers.* Kingston, N.Y.: McPherson, 1989.

Curtis, David. *Experimental Cinema: A Fifty-Year Evolution.* New York: Universe, 1971.

Dixon, Wheeler Winston. *The Exploding Eye: A Re-Visionary History of 1960s American Experimental Cinema.* Albany: State University of New York Press, 1997.

Dixon, Wheeler Winston, and Gwendolyn Audrey Foster, eds. *Experimental Cinema: The Film Reader.* London: Routledge, 2002.

Mekas, Jonas. *Movie Journal: The Rise of a New American Cinema, 1959–1971*. New York: Macmillan, 1972.

Petrolle, Jean, and Virginia Wright Wexman, eds. *Women and Experimental Filmmaking*. Urbana: University of Illinois Press, 2005.

Sargeant, Jack. *Naked Lens*. London: Creation, 1997.

Sitney, P. Adams. *Visionary Film: The American Avant-Garde, 1943–2000*. Oxford: Oxford University Press, 2002.

Youngblood, Gene. *Expanded Cinema*. New York: Dutton, 1970.

Film Noir

Abbott, Megan E. *The Street Was Mine: White Masculinity in Hardboiled Fiction and Film Noir*. New York: Palgrave Macmillan, 2002.

Christopher, Nicholas. *Somewhere in the Night: Film Noir and the American City*. New York: Free Press, 1997.

Kaplan, E. Ann. *Women in Film Noir*. London: British Film Institute, 1998.

Naremore, James. *More Than Night: Film Noir in Its Contexts*. Berkeley: University of California Press, 1998.

Silver, Alain, Elisabeth Ward, and James Ursini, eds. *Film Noir: An Encyclopedic Reference to the American Style*. Woodstock: Overlook Press, 1992.

Wager, Jans B. *Dames in the Driver's Seat: Rereading Film Noir*. Austin: University of Texas Press, 2005.

German Expressionist

Eisner, Lotte. *The Haunted Screen: Expressionism in the German Cinema and the Influence of Max Reinhardt*. Berkeley: University of California Press, 1974.

Elsaesser, Thomas. *Weimar Cinema and After: Germany's Historical Imaginary*. New York: Routledge, 2000.

Kracauer, Seigfried. *From Caligari to Hitler: A Psychological History of the German Film*. Revised and expanded edition. Princeton, N.J.: Princeton University Press, 2004.

Horror

Brottman, Mikita. *Offensive Films*. Nashville: Vanderbilt University Press, 2005.

Butler, Ivan. *The Horror Film*. New York: Barnes, 1967.

Clover, Carol J. *Men, Women, and Chain Saws: Gender in the Modern Horror Film*. Princeton, N.J.: Princeton University Press, 1992.

Grant, Barry Keith. *The Dread of Difference: Gender and the Horror Film*. Austin: University of Texas Press, 1996.

Pinedo, Isabel C. *Recreational Terror: Women and the Pleasures of Horror Film Viewing*. Albany: State University of New York Press, 1997.

Pirie, David. *A Heritage of Horror: The English Gothic Cinema 1946–1972*. New York: Equinox, 1974.

Siegel, Joel E. *Val Lewton: The Reality of Terror*. New York: Viking, 1974.

Latina/Latino

Bender, Stephen W. *Greasers and Gringos: Latinos, Law, and the American Imagination*. New York: New York University Press, 2005.

Berg, Charles Ramírez. *Latino Images in Film: Stereotypes, Subversion, and Resistance*. Austin: University of Texas Press, 2002.

Rodríguez, Clara E. *Heroes, Lovers, and Others: The Story of Latinos in Hollywood.* Washington, D.C.: Smithsonian Institution Press, 2004.

Musicals
Bergan, Ronald. *Glamorous Musicals.* London: Octopus, 1984.

Feuer, Jane. *The Hollywood Musical.* New York: Palgrave Macmillan, 1992.

Sennett, Ted. *Hollywood Musicals.* New York: Abrams, 1981.

Springer, John. *All Talking! All Singing! All Dancing!: A Pictorial History of the Movie Musical.* New York: The Citadel Press, 1966.

Thomas, Lawrence B. *The MGM Years.* New York: Columbia House, 1972.

Thomas, Tony, and Jim Terry (with Busby Berkeley). *The Busby Berkeley Book.* New York: A & W Visual Library, 1973.

Neorealism
Bondanella, Peter E. *Italian Cinema: From Neorealism to the Present.* New York: Ungar, 1983.

Marcus, Millicent. *Italian Film in the Light of Neorealism.* Princeton, N.J.: Princeton University Press, 1986.

Rocchio, Vincent F. *Cinema of Anxiety: A Psychoanalysis of Italian Neo-realism.* Austin: University of Texas Press, 1999.

New Wave
Douchet, Jean. *French New Wave.* Trans. Robert Bonnono. New York: Distributed Art Publishers, 1999.

Hillier, Jim. *Cahiers du Cinéma: 1960–1968: New Wave, New Cinema, Reevaluating Hollywood.* Cambridge, Mass.: Harvard University Press, 1986.

Kline, Thomas J. *Screening the Text: Intertextuality in New Wave French Cinema.* Baltimore: Johns Hopkins University Press, 1992.

Neupert, Richard J. *A History of the French New Wave Cinema.* Madison: University of Wisconsin Press, 2002.

Russell, Catherine. *Narrative Mortality: Death, Closure, and New Wave Cinemas.* Minneapolis: University of Minnesota Press, 1995.

Political
Combs, James E. *American Political Movies: An Annotated Filmography of Feature Films.* New York: Garland, 1990.

Wood, Robin. *Hollywood from Vietnam to Reagan—and Beyond.* New York: Columbia University Press, 2003.

Queer
Barrios, Richard. *Screened Out: Playing Gay in Hollywood from Edison to Stonewall.* New York: Routledge, 2003.

Dyer, Richard. *Now You See It: Studies on Lesbian and Gay Film.* London: Routledge, 1990.

Ehrenstein, David. *Open Secret: Gay Hollywood 1928–2000.* 2nd ed. New York: Perennial, 2000.

Gever, Martha, John Greyson, and Pratibha Parmar, eds. *Queer Looks: Perspectives on Lesbian and Gay Film and Video.* New York: Routledge, 1993.

Russo, Vito. *The Celluloid Closet: Homosexuality in the Movies.* Rev. ed. New York: Harper & Row, 1987.

Romantic Comedy

Harvey, James. *Romantic Comedy in Hollywood: From Lubitsch to Sturges*. New York: Da Capo, 1998.

Rubinfeld, Mark D. *Bound to Bond: Gender, Genre, and the Hollywood Romantic Comedy*. Westport, Conn.: Praeger, 2001.

Science Fiction

Hardy, Phil, ed. *Science Fiction*. New York: Morrow, 1984.

Hefley, Robert M., with Howard Zimmerman. *Robots*. New York: Starlog Press, 1979.

Lucanio, Patrick. *Them or Us: Archetypal Interpretations of Fifties Alien Invasion Films*. Bloomington: Indiana University Press, 1987.

Nicholls, Peter, ed. *The Science Fiction Encyclopedia*. Garden City, N.Y.: Dolphin Books/Doubleday, 1979.

Rose, Mark. *Alien Encounters: The Anatomy of Science Fiction*. Cambridge, Mass.: Harvard University Press, 1981.

Sobchack, Vivian. *Screening Space: The American Science Fiction Film*. 2nd ed. New Brunswick, N.J.: Rutgers University Press, 2001.

Spectacle

King, Geoff. *Spectacular Narratives: Contemporary Hollywood and Frontier Mythology*. London: I. B. Tauris, 2001.

Teen Films

Betrock, Alan. *The I Was a Teenage Juvenile Delinquent Rock 'n' Roll Horror Beach Party Movie Book: A Complete Guide to the Teen Exploitation Film*. New York: St. Martin's Press, 1986.

Doherty, Thomas. *Teenagers and Teenpics: The Juvenilization of American Movies in the 1950s*. Philadelphia: Temple University Press, 2002.

Lewis, Jon. *The Road to Romance and Ruin: Teen Films and Youth Culture*. New York: Routledge, 1992.

War

Eberwein, Robert, ed. *The War Film*. New Brunswick, N.J.: Rutgers University Press, 2005.

DeBauche, Leslie Midkiff. *Reel Patriotism: The Movies and World War I*. Madison: University of Wisconsin Press, 1997.

Doherty, Thomas. *Projections of War: Hollywood, American Culture and World War II*. New York: Columbia University Press, 1993.

Isenberg, Michael T. *War on Film: The American Cinema and World War I, 1914–1941*. Rutherford, N.J.: Fairleigh Dickinson University Press, 1981.

Koppes, Clayton R., and Gregory D. Black. *Hollywood Goes to War: How Politics and Propaganda Shaped World War II Movies*. New York: Free Press, 1987.

Lant, Antonia. *Blackout: Reinventing Women for Wartime Britain Cinema*. Princeton, N.J.: Princeton University Press, 1991.

Schindler, Colin. *Hollywood Goes to War*. London: Routledge, 1979.

Westerns

Bingham, Dennis. *Acting Male: Masculinities in the Films of James Stewart, Jack Nicholson, and Clint Eastwood*. New Brunswick, N.J.: Rutgers University Press, 1994.

Buscombe, Edward. *The BFI Companion to the Western*. New York: Atheneum, 1988.

Cawelti, John G. *The Six-Gun Mystique*. Bowling Green, Ohio: Bowling Green University Press, 1971.

Davis, Robert Murray. *Playing Cowboys: Low Culture and High Art in the Western*. Norman: University of Oklahoma Press, 1992.

Frayling, Christopher. *Spaghetti Westerns: Cowboys and Europeans from Karl May to Sergio Leone*. London: Routledge, 1981.

Kitses, Jim. *Horizons West: Directing the Western from John Ford to Clint Eastwood*. London: British Film Institute, 2004.

Mitchell, Lee Clark. *Westerns: Making the Man in Fiction and Film*. Chicago: University of Chicago Press, 1996.

Tompkins, Jane. *West of Everything: The Inner Life of Westerns*. New York: Oxford University Press, 1992.

Wright, Will. *Six Guns and Society: A Structural Study of the Western*. Berkeley: University of California Press, 1975.

Women

Acker, Ally. *Reel Women: Pioneers of the Cinema 1896 to the Present*. New York: Continuum, 1991.

Basinger, Jeanine. *A Woman's View: How Hollywood Spoke to Women, 1930–1960*. New York: Knopf, 1993.

Bean, Jennifer M., and Diane Negra, eds. *A Feminist Reader in Early Cinema*. Durham, N.C.: Duke University Press, 2002.

Beauchamp, Cari. *Without Lying Down: Frances Marion and the Powerful Women of Early Hollywood*. New York: Scribner, 1997.

Flitterman-Lewis, Sandy. *To Desire Differently: Feminism and the French Cinema*. Urbana: University of Illinois Press, 1990.

Heck-Rabi, Louise. *Women Filmmakers: A Critical Reception*. Metuchen, N.J.: Scarecrow, 1984.

Kaplan, E. Ann. *Looking for the Other: Feminism, Film, and the Imperial Gaze*. New York: Routledge, 1997.

LaSalle, Mick. *Complicated Women: Sex and Power in Pre-Code Hollywood*. New York: St. Martin's/Griffin, 2000.

Mahar, Karen Ward. *Women Filmmakers in Early Hollywood*. Baltimore: Johns Hopkins University Press, 2006.

Mayne, Judith. *The Woman at the Keyhole: Feminism and Women's Cinema*. Bloomington: Indiana University Press, 1990.

Mulvey, Laura. *Visual and Other Pleasures*. Bloomington: Indiana University Press, 1989.

Petro, Patrice. *Aftershocks of the New: Feminism and Film History*. New Brunswick, N.J.: Rutgers University Press, 2002.

Quart, Barbara Koenig. *Women Directors: The Emergence of a New Cinema*. New York: Praeger, 1988.

Slide, Anthony. *The Silent Feminists: America's First Women Directors*. Lanham, Md.: Scarecrow Press, 1996.

REGIONAL AND NATIONAL CINEMAS

Africa

Armes, Roy. *Postcolonial Images: Studies in North African Film*. Bloomington: Indiana University Press, 2005.

———. *Third World Film Making and the West*. Berkeley: University of California Press, 1992.

Armes, Roy, and Lizbeth Malkmus, eds. *Arab and African Film Making*. London: Zed Books, 1991.

Balseiro, Isabel, and Ntongela Masilela, eds. *To Change Reels: Film and Culture in South Africa*. Detroit: Wayne State University Press, 2003.

Burns, James. *Flickering Shadows: Cinema and Identity in Colonial Zimbabwe*. Athens: Ohio University Press, 2002.

Cameron, Kenneth M. *Africa on Film: Beyond Black and White*. New York: Continuum, 1994.

Davis, Peter. *In Darkest Hollywood: Exploring the Jungles of Cinema's South Africa*. Athens: Ohio University Press, 1996.

Diawara, Manthia. *African Cinema: Politics and Culture*. Bloomington: Indiana University Press, 1992.

Foster, Gwendolyn Audrey. *Women Filmmakers of the African and Asian Diaspora: Decolonizing the Gaze, Locating Subjectivity*. Carbondale: Southern Illinois University Press, 1997.

Leaman, Oliver, ed. *Companion Encyclopedia of Middle Eastern and North African Film*. London: Routledge, 2001.

Mayer, Ruth. *Artificial Africas: Colonial Images in the Times of Globalization*. Hanover, N.H.: University Press of New England, 2002.

Pfaff, Françoise. *Focus on African Films*. Bloomington: Indiana University Press, 2004.

Russell, Sharon A. *Guide to African Cinema*. Westport, Conn.: Greenwood, 1998.

Tomaselli, Kenya G. *The Cinema of Apartheid: Race and Class in South African Film*. London: Routledge, 1989.

Udeman, Adrienne. *The History of the South African Film Industry, 1940–1971*. Johannesburg: University of the Witwatersrand, 1972.

Ukadike, N. Frank. *Black African Cinema*. Berkeley: University of California Press, 1993.

———. *Questioning African Cinema: Conversations with Filmmakers*. Minneapolis: University of Minnesota Press, 2002.

Arab

Shafik, Viola. *Arab Cinema: History and Cultural Identity*. Cairo: American University in Cairo Press, 1998.

Asia

Berry, Michael. *Speaking in Images: Interviews with Contemporary Chinese Filmmakers*. New York: Columbia University Press, 2005.

Ciecko, Anne. *Contemporary Asian Cinema: Popular Culture in a Global Frame*. New York: Berg, 2006.

Dissanayke, Wimal, ed. *Colonials and Nationalism in Asian Cinema*. Bloomington: Indiana University Press, 1994.

Server, Lee. *Asian Pop Cinema: Bombay to Tokyo*. San Francisco: Chronicle Books, 1995.

Australia

McFarlane, Brian. *Australian Cinema, 1979–1985*. London: Secker & Warburg, 1987.

Rayner, Jonathan. *Contemporary Australian Cinema: An Introduction*. Manchester: Manchester University Press, 2000.

Brazil

Johnson, Randal and Robert Stam, eds. *Brazilian Cinema*. New York: Columbia University Press, 1995.

Canada

Evans, Gary. *In the National Interest: A Chronicle of the National Film Board of Canada from 1949 to 1989*. Buffalo: University of Toronto Press, 1991.

Gittings, Christopher E. *Canadian National Cinema: Ideology, Difference, and Representation*. New York: Routledge, 2002.

Malnyk, George. *One Hundred Years of Canadian Cinema*. Toronto: University of Toronto Press, 2004.

China

Berry, Chris, ed. *Perspectives on Chinese Cinema*. London: British Film Institute, 1991.

Chi, Shugin. *Women Through the Lens: Gender and Nation in a Century of Chinese Cinema*. Honolulu: University of Hawaii Press, 2003.

Hu, Jubin. *Chinese National Cinema before 1949*. Seattle: University of Washington Press, 2003.

Yang, Jeff. *Once Upon a Time in China: A Guide to Hong Kong, Taiwanese, and Mainland Chinese Cinema*. New York: Atria, 2003.

Czechoslovakia

Hames, Peter. *The Czechoslovak New Wave*. New York: Wallflower, 2005.

Skvorechy, Josef. *All the Bright Young Men and Women: A Personal History of the Czech Cinema*. Toronto: Martin Press, 1971.

Whyte, Alistair. *New Cinema in Eastern Europe*. London: Studio Vista, 1971.

France

Armes, Roy. *French Cinema*. New York: Oxford University Press, 1985.

Bazin, André. *Bazin at Work: Major Essays and Reviews from the Forties and Fifties*. Trans. Alain Piette and Bert Cardullo. Ed. Bert Cardullo. New York: Routledge, 1977.

Lanzoni, Rémi Fournier. *French Cinema from Its Beginnings to the Present*. New York: Continuum, 2002.

Williams, Alan. *Republic of Images: A History of French Filmmaking*. Cambridge, Mass.: Harvard University Press, 1992.

Germany

Bergfelder, Tim, Erica Carter, and Deniz Göktürk. *The German Cinema Book*. London: British Film Institute, 2002.

Guerin, Francis. *A Culture of Light: Cinema and Technology in 1920s Germany*. Minneapolis: University of Minnesota Press, 2005.

Hake, Sabine. *Popular Cinema of the Third Reich*. Austin: University of Texas Press, 2001.

Kaes, Anton. *From Hitler to Heimat: The Return of History as Film*. Cambridge, Mass.: Harvard University Press, 1989.

Koepnick, Lutz P. *The Dark Mirror: German Cinema between Hitler and Hollywood*. Berkeley: University of California Press, 2002.

Kreimeier, Klaus. *The UFA Story: A History of Germany's Greatest Film Company 1918–1945*. Trans. Robert and Rita Kimber. New York: Hill and Wang, 1996.

Murray, Bruce. *Film and the German Left in the Weimar Republic: From Calgari to Kuhle Wampe*. Austin: University of Texas Press, 1990.

Great Britain

Aldgate, Anthony, and Jeffrey Richards. *Britain Can Take It: The British Cinema in the Second World War.* New York: Basil Blackwell, 1986.

Armes, Roy. *A Critical History of the British Cinema.* New York: Oxford University Press, 1978.

Ashby, Justine, and Andrew Higson. *British Cinema, Past and Present.* New York: Routledge, 2000.

Barnes, John. *The Beginnings of the Cinema in England.* New York: Barnes & Noble, 1976.

Barr, Charles. *All Our Yesterdays: 90 Years of British Cinema.* London: British Film Institute, 1986.

Curran, James, and Vincent Porter. *British Cinema History.* Totowa, N.J.: Barnes & Noble, 1983.

Friedman, Lester D. *Fires Were Started: British Cinema and Thatcherism.* Minneapolis: University of Minnesota Press, 1992.

Gillett, Philip. *The British Working Class in Postwar Film.* Manchester: Manchester University Press, 2003.

Hill, John. *Sex, Class, and Realism: British Cinema 1956–1963.* London: British Film Institute, 1986.

Landy, Marcia. *British Genres: Cinema and Society 1930–1960.* Princeton, N.J.: Princeton University Press, 1991.

Lant, Antonia. *Blackout: Reinventing Women for Wartime British Cinema.* Princeton, N.J.: Princeton University Press, 2001.

Hong Kong

Bordwell, David. *Planet Hong Kong: Popular Cinema and the Art of Entertainment.* Cambridge, Mass.: Harvard University Press, 2000.

Fu, Poshek, and David Desser. *The Cinema of Hong Kong: History, Arts, Identity.* New York: Cambridge University Press, 2000.

Yau, Ching-Mei Esther. *At Full Speed: Hong Kong Cinema in a Borderless World.* Minneapolis: University of Minnesota Press, 2001.

India

Rajadhyaksha, Ashish, and Paul Willemen. *Encyclopedia of Indian Cinema.* London: British Film Institute, 1995.

Iran

Dabashi, Hamid. *Close Up: Iranian Cinema, Past, Present, and Future.* London: Verso Books, 2001.

Ireland

Hill, John, and Kevin Rockett. *Film History and Nation Cinema.* Dublin: Four Courts Press, 2005.

MacKillop, James. *Contemporary Irish Cinema: From the Quiet Man to Dancing at Lughnasa.* Syracuse, N.Y.: Syracuse University Press, 1999.

McIlroy, Brian. *Shooting to Kill: Filmmaking and the "Troubles" in Northern Ireland.* Wiltshire: Flicks Books, 1998.

O'Brien, Harvey. *The Real Ireland: The Evolution of Ireland in Documentary Film.* New York: Manchester University Press, 2004.

Israel

Kronish, Amy, and Costel Safirman. *Israeli Film: A Reference Guide*. Westport, Conn.: Greenwood, 2003.

Italy

Bertellini, Giorgio. *The Cinema of Italy*. New York: Wallflower, 2004.

Bondanella, Peter. *The Cinema of Federico Fellini*. Princeton, N.J.: Princeton University Press, 1992.

Dalle Vacche, Angela. *The Body in the Mirror: Shapes of History in Italian Cinema*. Princeton, N.J.: Princeton University Press, 1992.

Landy, Marcia. *Fascism in Film: The Italian Commercial Cinema, 1931–1943*. Princeton, N.J.: Princeton University Press, 1986.

———. *Italian Film*. Cambridge: Cambridge University Press, 2000.

Marcus, Millicent J. *After Fellini: National Cinema in the Postmodern Age*. Baltimore: Johns Hopkins University Press, 2002.

Japan

Bock, Audie. *Japanese Film Directors*. London: Kodansha Europe, 1995.

Bowyer, Justin. *The Cinema of Japan and Korea*. New York: Wallflower, 2004.

Burch, Noël. *To the Distant Observer: Form and Meaning in Japanese Cinema*. London: Scholar Press, 1979.

Desjardins, Chris. *Outlaw Masters of Japanese Film*. London: I. B. Tauris, 2005.

Desser, David. *Eros Plus Massacre: An Introduction to the Japanese New Wave Cinema*. Bloomington: Indiana University Press, 1988.

Ehrlich, Linda C., and David Desser, eds. *Cinematic Landscapes: Observations on the Visual Arts and Cinema of China and Japan*. Austin: University of Texas Press, 1994.

McDonald, Keiko I. *Cinema East: A Critical Study of Major Japanese Films*. Rutherford, N.J.: Fairleigh Dickinson University Press, 1983.

Richie, Donald. *The Japanese Movie*. New York: Kodansha International, 1982.

Korea

Bowyer, Justin. *The Cinema of Japan and Korea*. New York: Wallflower, 2004.

Kim, Kyung Hyun. *The Remasculinization of Korean Cinema*. Durham, N.C.: Duke University Press, 2004.

McHugh, Kathleen, and Nancy Abelmann, eds. *South Korean Golden Age Melodrama: Gender, Genre, and National Cinema*. Detroit: Wayne State University Press, 2005.

Min, Eungjun, Jinsook Joo, and Han Ju Kwak. *Korean Film: History, Resistance, and Democratic Imagination*. Westport, Conn.: Praeger, 2003.

Shin, Chi-Yun, and Julian Stringer, eds. *New Korean Cinema*. New York: New York University Press, 2005.

Latin America

Hart, Stephen M. *A Companion to Latin American Film*. Rochester, N.Y.: Tamesis, 2004.

King, John. *Magical Reels: A History of Cinema in Latin America*. London: Verso Books, 1990.

Martin, Michael T. *New Latin American Cinema*. Detroit: Wayne State University Press, 1997.

Noriega, Chon. *Visible Nations: Latin American Cinema and Video*. Minneapolis: University of Minnesota Press, 2000.

Shaw, Deborah. *Contemporary Cinema of Latin America: The Key Films*. New York: Continuum, 2003.

Mexico

Berg, Charles R. *Cinema of Solitude: A Critical Study of Mexican Film, 1967–1983*. Austin: University of Texas Press, 1992.

Foster, David W. *Mexico City in Contemporary Mexican Cinema*. Austin: University of Texas Press, 2002.

Mora, Carl J. *Mexican Cinema: Reflections of a Society, 1896–1980*. Berkeley: University of California Press, 1989.

Paranagua, Paulo Antonio, ed. *Mexican Cinema*. London: British Film Institute, 1996.

Rashkin, Elissa. *Women Filmmakers in Mexico: The Country of Which We Dream*. Austin: University of Texas Press, 2001.

Schaefer, Claudia. *Bored to Distraction: Cinema of Excess in End-of-the-Century Mexico and Spain*. Albany: State University of New York Press, 2003.

Russia/USSR

Attwood, Lynne, ed. *Red Women on the Silver Screen*. London: Pandora, 1993.

Goulding, Daniel J. *Post New Wave Cinema in the Soviet Union and Eastern Europe*. Bloomington: Indiana University Press, 1989.

Youngblood, Denise J. *The Magic Mirror: Moviemaking in Russia, 1908–1918*. Madison: University of Wisconsin Press, 1999.

Spain

Kinder, Marsha. *Blood Cinema: The Reconstruction of National Cinema in Spain*. Berkeley: University of California Press, 1993.

Marsh, Steven. *Popular Spanish Film Under Franco: Comedy and the Weakening of the State*. New York: Palgrave Macmillan, 2006.

United States of America

Barson, Michael, and Steven Heller. *Red Scared! The Commie Menace in Propaganda and Popular Culture*. San Francisco: Chronicle Books, 2001.

Black, Gregory D. *Hollywood Censored: Morality Codes, Catholics, and the Movies*. New York: Cambridge University Press, 1994.

Bodnar, John E. *Blue-Collar Hollywood: Liberalism, Democracy, and Working People in American Film*. Baltimore: Johns Hopkins University Press, 2003.

Bordwell, David, Janet Staiger, and Kristin Thompson. *The Classical Hollywood Cinema: Film Style and Modes of Production to 1960*. New York: Columbia University Press, 1985.

Doherty, Thomas. *Pre-Code Hollywood: Sex, Immorality, and Insurrection in American Cinema 1930–1934*. New York: Columbia University Press, 1999.

Hoberman, J. *The Dream Life: Movies, Media, and the Mythology of the Sixties*. New York: New Press, 2003.

Horowitz, Josh. *The Mind of the Modern Moviemaker: 20 Conversations with the New Generation of Filmmakers*. New York: Plume, 2006.

James, David E. *Allegories of Cinema: American Film in the Sixties*. Princeton, N.J.: Princeton University Press, 1989.

Kashner, Sam, and Jennifer McNair. *The Bad and the Beautiful: Hollywood in the Fifties*. New York: Norton, 2002.

Kendall, Elizabeth. *Runaway Bride: Hollywood's Romantic Comedies of the 1930s*. New York: Knopf, 1990.

Leff, Leonard J., and Jerold L. Simmons. *The Dame in the Kimono: Hollywood, Censorship, and the Production Code from the 1920s to the 1960s*. London: Weidenfeld & Nicolson, 1990.

Mast, Gerald, ed. *The Movies in Our Midst: Documents in the Cultural History of Film in America*. Chicago: University of Chicago Press, 1981.

McCarthy, Todd, and Charles Flynn, eds. *Kings of the Bs: Working Within the Hollywood System*. New York: Dutton, 1975.

Musser, Charles. *The Emergence of Cinema: The American Screen to 1907*. Berkeley: University of California Press, 1994.

Schaefer, Eric. *"Bold! Daring! Shocking! True!": A History of Exploitation Films 1919–1939*. Durham, N.C.: Duke University Press, 1999.

Schneider, Steven Jay. *New Hollywood Violence*. Manchester: Manchester University Press, 2004.

INDEX